THE MAN WHO PUSHED
AMERICA TO WAR

THE MAN WHO PUSHED
AMERICA TO WAR

The Extraordinary Life, Adventures, and Obsessions of AHMAD CHALABI

ARAM ROSTON

NATION
BOOKS

NEW YORK

Copyright © 2008 by Aram Roston

Published by
Nation Books, a Member of the Perseus Books Group
116 East 16th Street, 8th Floor
New York, NY 10003

Nation Books is a co-publishing venture of the Nation Institute and the Perseus Books Group.

Books published by Nation Books are available at special discounts for bulk purchases in the
United States by corporations, institutions, and other organizations. For more information,
please contact the Special Markets Department at the Perseus Books Group, 2300 Chestnut
Street, Suite 200, Philadelphia, PA 19103, or call (800) 255–1514, or e-mail
special.markets@perseusbooks.com.

www.nationbooks.org

Designed by Jeff Williams

Library of Congress Cataloging-in-Publication Data
Roston, Aram.
    The man who pushed America to war : the extraordinary life, adventures and obsessions of
Ahmad Chalabi / Aram Roston. — 1st ed.
        p. cm.
    Includes bibliographical references and index.
    ISBN 978-1-56858-353-2 (alk. paper)
    1. Chalabi, Ahmad, 1944- 2. Shiites—Iraq—Biography. 3. Statesmen—Iraq—Biography.
4. Iraq—Politics and government—1991-2003. 5. Iraq War, 2003- I. Title.

DS79.66.C45R67 2008
956.7044092—dc22
[B]
                                                                                    2007041983

10 9 8 7 6 5 4 3 2 1

Contents

Prologue

ON THE AFTERNOON of Thursday, April 28, 2005, Ahmad Chalabi smiled as he stepped from one group of journalists to the next in the Baghdad Convention Center. They eagerly surrounded him with cameras and microphones. The space was modern and well lit and even air-conditioned, built under Saddam Hussein when he had ruled Iraq and now protected by U.S. soldiers who guarded the Green Zone. Silent bodyguards, like unobtrusive servants, shadowed Chalabi as he walked with dignity to the next clutch of fascinated reporters.

It was an important day for him. Two events touched him and his family: one political and one financial. The first development was the reason journalists had gathered to chat with him: the triumphant creation of a new government for Iraq, which had been scourged by violence and disorder since the U.S. invasion two years earlier. Chalabi was confirmed that day as the deputy prime minister and acting oil minister of a transitional Iraqi government. This would be a temporary government, by design, but even so, it was the first time in his life that Chalabi, now sixty, was confirmed as a member of any government at all. Exhilarated he may have been, and he held his head high that day, but he did not even refer to his own central role in all this, nor did he boast that this whole new Iraq was a product, in part, of his own making. Cajoling and shaming his American friends and enemies, Chalabi had managed to harness the power of the United States to his own mission: the unseating of a dictator, Saddam Hussein, and the installation of a sovereign new Iraqi government.

The second event that touched Chalabi on April 28 involved money; it concerned his family business and attracted far less attention from the world. That very day, the official Trade Bank of Iraq signed a deal with a London company that, in fact, Chalabi and his relatives had founded years earlier. The Trade Bank, actually run and owned by this new government of Iraq, was created as if from the air after Saddam's fall. The Trade Bank was headed by Chalabi's grandnephew, Hussein al-Uzri, a forty-three-year-old man with a hearty smile. After the U.S. invasion, Chalabi had worked hard to place his younger relative in the position, pressuring his friends among the U.S. occupation authorities. It was a job of immense influence: staggering amounts of money were funneled through the fingers of the younger man.

The Trade Bank's deal, a "strategic agreement," was awarded to Card Tech, Ltd., owned and run by the Chalabi family for more than a decade. Ahmad Chalabi himself, the new deputy prime minister, had an ownership interest in a Card Tech affiliate in his own name. The company did a niche business specializing in helping banks around the world deal with their customers' credit and automatic banking cards. In a final knot, Card Tech, too, like the Trade Bank of Iraq, was run by one of Chalabi's relatives, a nephew named Jaffar Agha-Jaffar. Agha-Jaffar had the distinction of having worked for his uncle Ahmad more than fifteen years earlier at a Jordanian bank that was engulfed by scandal and allegations of fraud.

So that spring day when Ahmad Chalabi received his coveted government appointment in the new Iraq was also the day that one of his nephews in the Iraqi government awarded a contract to a family company. Everything came together on this day in a symphony of political and business success for Chalabi. He had weathered many shifts in his fortunes to arrive at this moment. What he had always sought, and at this moment appeared to have achieved, as he moved through the convention center shaking hands and giving interviews, was a glorious return to the Baghdad of his youth, when the Chalabis had been prosperous merchants, comfortably ensconced in the ruling class of pre-revolutionary Iraq, before the dark era of Saddam.

During his media interviews that day, Chalabi made no mention of Card Tech or the Trade Bank of Iraq, nor was he asked about them. It was not the news of the day. Instead, he basked in his new official role. "This government represents the Iraqi people," he told interviewers, describing the Shiite-led government dominated by members of the Islamist Dawa Party.

Asked about the role of the United States, he cocked his head a bit toward his interviewer, raised his eyebrows, and said, "President Bush was very happy with the Iraqi elections." He went on: this government, he said, would get American support. "The United States is a strategic ally, we believe, of Iraq, and we will work with them on this basis."[1]

His inner circle called him The Doctor, because of his PhD in mathematics. Some of his operatives called him Our Big Brother. The Central Intelligence Agency called him by a code name—which intelligence sources reveal as PULSAR ONE. Whatever you call him, Ahmad Abdul Hadi Chalabi, a shrewd Iraqi Arab from a family of Shiite bankers, literally changed the world. The United States, which he referred to so respectfully as a "strategic ally" that day of his triumph, had sponsored him, flown him and his people to Iraq, even toppled Saddam Hussein for him, as he would boast. The Iraq War has many critics and some fierce defenders, but many insiders on both sides of the debate agree on this: without Chalabi there would have been no war.

He is a man of large appetites, with a flair for theatrics, and a brilliant and untiring mind. He had a single-minded hatred of the sadistic Saddam Hussein, a loyalty to his own Shiite heritage, and an inexplicable certitude in his own entitlement. Chalabi's medium is people, and as an Iraqi exile his grazing area was America; his genius was his ability to make loyal friends among adventurous spirits. He epitomized "charismatic leadership." Over dinners, lunches, and coffee, he spoke in grand and colorful language about the human right to freedom, about the delightful world to come in the Middle East, about the great things that could be done. As he talked, Chalabi was physically transformed. What strangers saw as a smug smirk curled on his fleshy lips disappeared, and was replaced by a wise yet merry smile. Whereas once he had a stiff back and clumsy walk, now he appeared to have a regal and noble bearing.

Some of his closest advisers were Democrats. Some were liberals. Some were pro-Israel; others were anti-Zionists. It didn't really matter once they met him. But in the end it was notoriously the recruitment of the American neoconservatives and the hawkish wing of the Republican Party that got him what he needed. They satisfied his needs, and he theirs.

He touched America in three ways. His first success could be called ideological: he was able to affirm for a generation of thinkers the urgent need to overthrow Saddam. Toppling Saddam, and ending his aggression and his feared weapons of mass destruction, became the keystone of transforming the Middle East. Chalabi was not the sole source of this vision, but he was the chief intellectual facilitator for a now well-known cadre of hard-liners whose influence was extraordinary in the early part of the new millennium. They included Richard Perle, Paul Wolfowitz, I. Lewis "Scooter" Libby, John Hannah, Michael Ledeen, and Danielle Pletka. They dined with him and met him and conversed, and through well-placed op-eds and clever talking points and sound bites, their ideas bled into the mainstream.

Second, Chalabi fed intelligence and sources to journalists and the U.S. intelligence services. This was, for him, the easiest task. Much of the world already believed Saddam had WMDs. And Saddam was indeed a sadistic tyrant. Chalabi's contribution was to give the allegations flesh and muscle and specificity. The tidbits he provided were often quickly discredited by intelligence officers, but they had tremendous impact on public opinion. His use of the press helped prepare the political battleground for war. The *New York Times*, CBS News's *60 Minutes*, PBS's *Frontline*, and *Vanity Fair* became his chosen outlets. The splash from his stories was immense. Saddam, the intelligence services knew, had no ties to the attacks of 9/11, but as Chalabi's friend Fouad Ajami wrote once to explain the war, "These distinctions did not matter; the connection had been made in American opinion."

Third, Chalabi had political impact that was virtually unheard of for a foreigner. He used his personal magnetism, lobbying skills, and tactical abilities to merge U.S. policy with his own ambitions. The U.S. Congress passed a law written largely to achieve his vision and to boost the fortunes of his political vehicle, the Iraqi National Congress. He had a battery of supporters on Capitol Hill. U.S. senators like Trent Lott, John McCain, Sam Brownback, Joe Lieberman, and Bob Kerrey became his champions. But even more important, he knew how to manipulate the key aides who work anonymously in the back rooms to make Capitol Hill run. He courted key Republicans like Trent Lott's Randy Scheunemann and House international affairs staffer Steve Rademaker, as well as Senate Democratic aides like Chris Straub and Peter Galbraith.

As a younger man, Chalabi had presided over the wholesale collapse of his family's business empire, a worldwide venture riddled with fraud insider dealing and disastrous investments. But he was able to bounce back after locating a rich vein of financing from the U.S. government. American taxpayers generously funded him and his Iraqi National Congress during his fifteen-year campaign against Saddam. Although he was not an American, and in fact distrusted the United States, he moved from one federal agency to another with the easy grace of a hummingbird drifting from flower to flower. First he was funded by the Central Intelligence Agency, then by the State Department, and finally by the Defense Department. When he called the United States a "strategic ally," maybe it was a taunt as much as it was reality.

═══

So who was he really? A corrupt businessman or a somewhat deluded visionary? A brilliant con man or perhaps, as some still see him, a persecuted genius? Was he an agent of the Islamic Republic of Iran, or of America, or solely of his own ambition? Or was he all these things? Ahmad Chalabi has refused to cooperate with this book in any way. But many of his friends and family were extremely helpful, usually requesting anonymity. Some revere him, some despise him, and some fear him. Most are in awe at the tangled plots he weaves around him.

He has left no substantial written record of his political philosophy or his life, but he has over time—in some speeches and opinion articles and through the voices of his admirers—exposed his ambitions, disappointments, and triumphs. And just as important, around the world, in courthouses and company files in Washington, Switzerland, London, Jordan, Lebanon, Hong Kong, and the offshore tax haven of the Cayman Islands, he and some family members left a trail littered with bankruptcies, allegations of fraud, and and devastated victims. This narrative follows that trail and chronicles the improbable adventures of Ahmad Chalabi.

PART I

1

Golden Age

1944–1958

"We liberated Iraq."

—Ahmad Chalabi's campaign slogan in Iraq, 2005

"**WE HAVE UNDERTAKEN** to liberate the beloved homeland," announced the voice on the radio through the static one early morning in Baghdad in 1958.[1] The calendar showed it was July 14, Bastille Day, the anniversary of the start of the French Revolution. Iraqis had slept on their rooftops to avoid the summer heat, and now, all over the city, people began to stumble out into the street.

The radio crackled on, repeating a lengthy message. "We have undertaken to liberate the beloved homeland from the corrupt crew that imperialism installed. Power shall be entrusted to a government emanating from you and inspired by you."

In the palace, the Crown Prince, the power behind the throne, got out of bed and turned on the radio to hear the news of his downfall, and then rushed out to surrender.[2] The story goes that when the royals gathered in the courtyard, an Iraqi army captain slaughtered them, riddling their bodies with machine-gun fire in one long-sustained burst.

It was still the early hours of the morning when members of the wealthy Chalabi family, at their homes in the Baghdad neighborhood of Adhamiya, learned of the coup. Three majestic adjacent homes all belonged to the Chalabis, a close-knit clan. The Chalabis gathered hurriedly to consult on what to do in this new and sudden crisis. The children had slept on the roofs too, under the Baghdad sky, and now they watched the adults as they debated in fright. Children can sometimes sense these things, and the children there had a foreboding that this day was different, that it symbolized an ending of things as they had known them. The grown-ups quickly reached their decision, and then they acted.

Young Ahmad Chalabi, thirteen years old, black-haired and serious, was herded with his mother and the others into a convoy of big American sedans to flee their mansion. Ahmad left behind the basketball hoop he had helped to set up. He left behind the ping-pong table, which slid behind a specially constructed wall. Abandoned as well, just for a time that day, were the pet parrots in the massive cage—almost as big as an aviary—squawking away in the excitement. The brightly colored birds were just one of the delightful and distinctive things in their stately home that the Chalabis were leaving behind.

The family split up. Some of the men, joined by the foreign minister of the country, Fadhil al-Jamali, and by Chalabi's much older brother Rushdie Chalabi, fled from town to hide. The rest, including Ahmad and his mother and several siblings and nephews and cousins, drove to Khadimiya, back then just a suburb just north of Baghdad. Khadimiya, a Shiite stronghold, had been the Chalabi family's main base going back for generations. In fact, Medina Abdul Hadi was an adjacent enclave named for Ahmad's father. Luckily, on this day Ahmad's father, Abdul Hadi Chalabi, was out of town; he was in Tehran when the revolution began.

But according to family lore, the Chalabis did not even venture into their compound in Khadimiya, called Seef, which had been a splendid place to play and hunt and celebrate in a well-tended orchard—a wonderland where Iraq's royalty and elite held their parties and festivities. No, the family didn't even go there; instead they crowded into the home of an ally in Khadimiya. They needed somewhere to hide from the soldiers and mobs. While the rest of Iraq was celebrating the bloody revolution, the Chalabis were targets, clustered in their host's estate for shelter.

At one point, according to the story the family tells of those old days, the soldiers came bursting into their hiding place, led by a high-ranking officer, demanding to know where Abdul Hadi, the patriarch, and Rushdie, the older brother, were. Over the years Ahmad Chalabi himself has told how the soldiers swept in, a platoon armed with heavy machine guns. "Like a movie" is the phrase he uses, and he tells people it surprised him at the time, even as a thirteen-year-old, that he felt no fear. As the story goes, the soldiers held a gun to his mother, and Chalabi, not even old enough to shave, volunteered as a hostage instead. Even his mother used to tell the story, laughing about it. In his version Chalabi volunteered to accompany the soldiers searching their property. Here is how one writer described it: "In the 115-degree heat of the Mesopotamian summer, the Chalabi brothers sat squashed between two soldiers, the officer slowly driving around the farm while his men performed their search."[3] In the end, the soldiers failed to find the men they were looking for until a bit later.

It was not an especially violent episode compared with the bloody life experience of many Iraqis at that time. It was downright tame compared with the gore that filled the streets. But it left an impression on Ahmad, who would dream for decades of returning to reclaim his homeland from the regime and its successors, who took it away from him. The moment must have been heavily symbolic for him: his space was invaded, his homes were no longer shelters, and the shell of privilege and entitlement he had known was shattered.

One of Chalabi's relatives, a boy his age, Mahdi al-Bassam, had stayed overnight in Adhamiya with his cousins and uncle. But Mahdi lived elsewhere in Baghdad himself. He had watched the Chalabi clan gather to consult on where to go when the revolution broke out that morning. But instead of joining Ahmad and the rest of the family on their convoy to Khadimiya, young Mahdi, who was the son of one of Ahmad's older sisters, walked back to his home on the Tigris, trudging through the carnage of Baghdad's streets, alone. Ignored, just a boy on the street, young Mahdi passed the rioters in the heart of town. He walked on and on, past soldiers hunting the old regime. The coup leaders, led by the mustached Gen. Abdul Karim Qasim of the Free

Officers, treated the body of the young king they killed with respect, but they gave the corpse of the king's uncle, Crown Prince Abdul-Ilah, to the crowd, like tossing fish guts to a flock of seagulls. The body of the hated Abdul-Ilah, despised for his subservience to the West, was paraded like a trophy through the street. It was hung up for all to see. A butcher, according to some Iraqis, was called to hack up the royal corpse properly, as if the old government itself was being dismembered by the new order.

———

With the entire royal family dead, there was still one man at large who had come to symbolize the old hated Iraq: Nuri as-Said, Iraq's seventy-year-old premier and the grand old man of Arab politics. He was a patron of the Chalabis, a friend of the British, and an ally of the Americans. He had helped to build the country himself decades ago and had survived innumerable coups. The wealthy and powerful depended on him, but everyone else loathed and feared him.

In the confusion of that bloody morning of July 14, as-Said had escaped. The premier fled his house in his blue pajamas as soon as he sensed danger, grabbing the pair of revolvers he always kept near him, just like a gunman in an old American Western. He also apparently managed to get hold of a handful of cash, and then he scrambled along the banks of the Tigris to escape. First, dressed in his pajamas and toting his revolvers, he tried getting into a small ferry. The plan was that the boatman would row him past the flock of ducks and geese and swans he kept, to cross the river to safety. But the premier quickly abandoned the idea for some reason. Instead of crossing the river, the old man snuck into the house of his loyal neighbor Dr. Bassam, whose wife happened to be Ahmad Chalabi's older sister, Thamina. These were the parents of young Mahdi al-Bassam.

T.E. Lawrence—Lawrence of Arabia—wrote that Nuri as-Said was a "calm" man under fire. But that wasn't the case on July 14, 1958. As-Said was a shadow of the warrior he had once been, and in fact he was just a pale resemblance of the autocratic ruler he had been the day before. When Ahmad's nephew Mahdi got home from his long walk from the Chalabi home in Adhamiya, as-Said was there, still in the pajamas he had escaped in, shaking in fright and talking to Mahdi's parents. First he would go to Khadimiya, the old man swore, and then to Iran, using the old Shiite pilgrimage route, and then he would return leading a military force of allies.

So the Bassams, politely sheltering the old man but eager to get him out of their home as soon as possible, also tried to help as-Said escape. Thamina helped dress him up as a woman, borrowing a thick black abaya from her children's old nanny. They put the abaya over as-Said's pajamas so it concealed everything but his eyes, and he looked just like an old Arab woman. To smuggle the premier past the hunters, they helped the old man step into the trunk of their big American sedan and slammed it shut on him.

Before they could even drive out of the gates, they heard banging from inside the car's trunk. They rushed to open it; Nuri as-Said was gasping. He was claustrophobic, he said: it didn't matter if the crowds were looking to kill him; he could not abide the heat and horror of that airless and black space.

So they helped him climb out of the trunk and let him sit in the backseat. A driver and one of the Bassam family drove him out through the streets of Khadimiya to a relative's house. No one outside the car realized that the shrouded figure in the back, the old Arab woman in the black abaya, was the premier, the most wanted man in the new Iraq.

By the next day, July 15, while the Chalabis were still holed up in Khadimiya, still crowded at their friend's home, the new government declared a bounty on Nuri as-Said's head. 10,000 dinars ($28,000) would go to the man who found him, came the official word, as Iraqis eagerly listened to the radio for news. That was a staggering reward in those muddy days of obscene poverty.

Rioters took to the streets looking for him. People who survived those days of revolution say just riding in a car was terrifying, as seething crowds hunted the rich and powerful. "You couldn't see the streets for people," says Tamara Daghistani, just a girl back in those days. She was the daughter of a loyalist and proud general who refused to participate in the coup and would face charges. She would become, when she grew older, a lifelong friend and supporter of Ahmad Chalabi. She rode in a car during the revolution and described how the interior was darkened by the mobs all around searching for their targets. "You couldn't see the sky. All you could see were these faces, on the window, just to see if we were sort of 'killable.' Are we the ones that they want to lynch and drag though the streets? All their faces were just stuck on the windows." Men in long flowing dishdashas, carrying ropes and swords and weapons, milled through the streets.

So on July 15, in Khadimiya that second day after the end of the monarchy, a car inched its way through the crowds, not far from where the Chalabis were staying. In the back were the figures of two elderly women, covered in the full traditional black abayas. One of the two shrouded figures was the crowd's target. It was Nuri as-Said, still clutching a revolver underneath the woman's garb. Underneath the unfamiliar abaya, the old premier would have been breathing hard, his sparse white hair matted with sweat. The other person in the backseat of the car was Mrs. Bibiya Istrabadi, a secular and educated Shiite woman who was trying to protect her precious cargo. It was as if there was a little ad hoc underground railroad, trying to save the grand old man of Iraqi politics. Again, the furious throngs missed their target.

While the Chalabi family waited and hid, Ahmad Chalabi, the boy, saw Mrs. Istrabadi arrive and discuss things with his mother. The two women fretted over what to do with old Nuri as-Said, the hunted man. Perhaps if he could survive he could restore what had been. Chalabi family history has it that Jawad Chalabi, Ahmad's thirty-year-old brother, also discussed Nuri as-Said with the two women. And then, it seems, the premier made a deal with Jawad. Jawad, who was already a businessman with his hands in lots of affairs, evidently offered the family's help to the scared old man dressed in a woman's robe. But Baghdad and Khadimiya were too dangerous for even the Chalabis to help. As one member of the family explains it, "Jawad said, 'You get him out [of Khadimiya] and I will take charge after that.'" If as-Said could get out of Baghdad, into the countryside, where the Chalabi family owned so much land, the family would help smuggle him out of the country.

But the Chalabis' efforts, and Nuri as-Said's disguise, failed to save him. As he was walking along the street in his abaya, the premier tripped and stumbled, and a boy spotted the pajamas underneath.

Some say he was betrayed by a resident of a house he visited for help. A squad of soldiers came for him. Surrounded, Nuri as-Said pulled out a revolver and shot himself so he could not be taken alive, so the story goes. Mrs. Istrabadi, too, was gunned down right there on the street, dying with the old man she tried to save. What is certain is that the mob later took its fury out on the premier's body. Vehicles drove slowly over the old man's corpse again and again, mashing the body into the dust and blood. His fingers were held up like trophies by the mob. One account has it that at the end Nuri as-Said's remains resembled *bastourma*, preserved, spiced meat. Another account says it was even worse: an Iraqi who remembers the events of the day says that "his body was pulverized. There was nothing left."

That day, July 15, 1958, the day that Prime Minister Nuri as-Said was hunted down and killed in the garb of an old woman and pulverized, was the end of the old Iraq that Ahmad Chalabi knew as a young boy. And the Chalabis had not helped the old man at all. "I think he felt that his family was somehow responsible," said one journalist who interviewed Ahmad Chalabi forty years later.

———

Born October 30, 1944, toward the end of World War II, when the British still quietly pulled the strings in Iraq, Ahmad Chalabi was his parents' ninth and final child. He was born nine years after his next oldest brother, Hazem, and their mother, Bibi, used to joke occasionally that Ahmad was a "mistake," an "accident." Yet she doted on her youngest son. And since some of his older brothers were old enough to be his father, it was as if he had a half-dozen parents tending to him.

The Chalabis were a leading Shiite merchant family, entwined with the monarchist government of Iraq. Before the monarchy they had allied themselves with the British occupiers and before that with their Turkish overlords. In the context of the Middle East, they had converted to Shiism relatively recently. Family members say that Ahmad's great-great-grandfather was a Sunni who adopted the Shiite faith. Perhaps the zeal of the convert impressed itself on his offspring, because they became pillars of the Iraqi Shiite community.

Iraqi historian Hanna Batatu describes Chalabi's great-grandfather as an extremely brutal and powerful man, with his own "special prison at his disposal" and a "bodyguard of armed slaves" that he used to impose his will on the Shiite community of Khadimiya. "When he died the people of Khadhimiyyah heaved a sigh of relief," Batatu wrote, citing Jawad Chalabi, Chalabi's elder brother, as the source.[4]

Chalabi's father, Abdul Hadi, shed the oppressive reputation of his forebear. He functioned as a financier of the Iraqi monarchy, but also of the Shiite clerical leadership in Najaf. Family members say he gave a percentage of his wealth to the Shiite religious leaders, as was expected of those in his position. As for rulers of Iraq, in 1938 Abdul Hadi "got in the good graces of the regent-to-be, 'Abd-ul-Illah, by coming to his assistance with loans." The prince, a gambler, "in due course made him a minister of public works and eventually the vice president of the Senate."[5]

Indeed, a year after young Ahmad Chalabi was born, Prince Abdul-Illah brought Abdul Hadi with his entourage to the United States on a state visit. They stayed at the Waldorf-Astoria in New York before going to Washington, D.C., where the prince overnighted at the White House.

The Chalabi family was part of the old Baghdad business elite: the word "Chalabi"—of Turkish origin—originally was an honorific applied to high-ranking merchants. As Batatu summed it up, "Translating economic power into political influence, and political influence into economic power, the Chalabis climbed from one level of wealth to another, and on the eve of the 1958 revolution surpassed other business families."

Pampered and happy, Ahmad Chalabi was a studious boy. And in the play room of his father's big house, he played ping-pong with Jasseem, the son of a police official who helped to protect the place. He and Jasseem—boys of a different class entirely—played against each other, rhythmically tapping the ball back across the fragile table.

Chalabi would later evoke the pleasant times in Iraq that preceded those atrocities of 1958. From his childhood perspective, waist-high to the wealthy, well-educated men around him, this Iraq was an eclectic, tolerant place, where Shiites, Sunnis, Christians, Jews, and even Yazidis worked together. Chalabi kept a photograph for decades that he would show to his friends. "It was the board of his father's company," as one man recalled, "and it was a Turcoman, a Jew, an Assyrian, a couple Shiite, a couple of Sunni. It was like a cross-section of Iraqi Society, and his big thing was, *this* is how Iraq was. This is how we were, this is how we will be again!"

It was, in one account by a Chalabi supporter, a "golden age." He wrote that "Iraq had a constitution, elections, a reasonably free press, a market economy, expanding public schools, a rising middle class."[6] Another writer described it this way: "Iraq in the 1950s was multi-racial and increasingly prosperous."[7] That Iraq was a place to which anyone would want to return.

And indeed, for the rich, the Iraq of the day was a dreamland. The Iraqis mimicked the British nobility. Iraq even had the only foxhunting between Rome and Peshawar, diplomats would quip.[8] But that Iraq existed for only a privileged few. The real Iraq of the day was nothing like it. Even the young Ahmad Chalabi must have caught a glimpse, or a smell at least, of the poverty of that other Iraq. The year before the coup of 1958, he has said, he had traveled to London. Like any boy, he must have looked out the car window on his drive to the Baghdad airport to see the surroundings: "clusters of medieval mud huts, holes for windows, a rusty piece of sheet iron for a door." That was the way the *Washington Post* described it at the time.[9] One historian writes, "Throughout the 1950s massive slums spread around Baghdad, with the hovel inhabitants periodically swamped by muddy overflows from the Tigris." "The infant mortality [rate] is 250 per thousand. A woman has a 50:50 chance of raising a child to the age of ten. There are no social services of any kind. . . . On the adjacent dumps dogs with rabies dig in the sewage and the slum-dwellers pack it for resale as garden manure."[10]

Today, in the wake of the U.S. invasion of 2003, Iraq is often called a central front in the war against international terrorism. But the Iraq of the 1950s was considered a central front in the war against international communism. Prime Minister Nuri as-Said had endeared himself to the Americans and the British as an anti-Communist leader. They in turn funded his military, armed it, and trained it. Just days before the revolution of 1958, in fact, the United States delivered six F-86 fighters, some of the most advanced jet fighters of the period, to Baghdad.[11]

Nuri as-Said was brutal in his treatment of the Iraqi Communist Party, which had a strong base throughout the country, not just among the ruling Sunni class and the Kurds but especially among marginalized Shiites. The U.S. Ambassador, Waldemar J. Gallman, considered as-Said a valuable ally against the Communist threat. "He was unshakably convinced that the Soviet Union and communism were constant threats to the Middle East," Gallman wrote in a memoir called *Iraq Under General Nuri.* "He had the colleges and secondary schools closed indefinitely. Martial law was strictly applied, including military censorship of the press. Parliament was suspended."[12]

Nuri as-Said crushed but did not silence the opposition. The day after Ahmad Chalabi's eleventh birthday in 1955, the holy Shiite city of Najaf to the south erupted in riots against the government. "Down with the criminal Nuri as-Said," said placards waved by demonstrators. As religious as it was, Najaf was a Communist hotbed too, and a haven for Arab nationalists, who often found common cause with the Communists in their protests. So as-Said, the ruler of the country, actually enlisted Ahmad's father, the wealthy Shiite merchant, on a particularly sensitive mission, to drive down the dusty highway to Najaf and convince the ayatollahs to use their religious authority against the Communists. It was a clever gambit, but in the end the protestors defied their turbaned ayatollahs and continued their resistance.[13]

Another aspect of the real Iraq of the childhood that Chalabi would rarely mention as an adult is its treatment of its Jewish community. Before 1950, Jews made up as much as 30 percent of Baghdad's population. But in 1951, after the creation of Israel, they had been pushed out under as-Said through the 1950 "Denaturalization Law." Where their property wasn't confiscated, they were forced to sell at rock-bottom prices, a boon for Shiite merchants.

By 1958, the fury in Iraq previously suppressed so effectively by the premier and the royal family was hard to ignore. It was not the Communist Party, nor the Baath Party, but the Arab nationalist movement, spearheaded by Egypt's President, Gamal Abdel Nasser, that really swept the Middle East. Said tried to keep it out of Iraq, as if he were stamping out a fire. But young men throughout the region huddled around radios listening to broadcasts, read tracts covertly, and gathered to hear the militant message of Arab pride. Even some of Chalabi's relatives, wealthy as they might have been, marched with the Nasserite demonstrators as a prank, when they could. Young Ahmad, though, never did.

———

The turmoil of that hot July in 1958, that revolution, had an extraordinary impact on Ahmad Chalabi. Nearly fifty years later, an elegant but slightly overweight Chalabi would say theatrically of the revolution: "The bastards set us back 700 years!" But it was unclear which bastards he meant: the Communists, the Baathists, or the Arab Nationalists, or maybe all of them.

"If you are trying to find 'Rosebud,' look for the 1958 revolution," a relative of Chalabi's advised in an interview. "He's not an idealist. But he had certain things that motivated him: The 1958 revolution that disempowered our family." The 1958 revolution took it all away for the Chalabi family. So the only thing the Chalabis could have hoped for was a U.S. intervention. The United States had the might and the motive to invade Iraq and topple the new dictator, Gen. Abdul Karim Qasim. Historians think it came close. President Dwight D. Eisenhower was notified of the crisis at 7:30 Eastern Standard Time, and by 8:15 a.m. he had an intelligence briefing from Secretary of State John Foster Dulles. They were well aware of the threat from Arab nationalism and from Nasser's attraction in the region, but they decided to send military forces to Lebanon, not Iraq. The Lebanese president, a Christian, had been pleading for U.S. peacekeepers for months. So the White House took preliminary action to stem the tide of Arab nationalism, ordering in two Marine battalions from the Sixth Fleet. The heavily armed Marines landed on a tourist beach in Beirut. They trudged past the sunbathers toward the airport, and then pursued their mission: to shore up the Lebanese president and fend off any Nasserite revolution there. If the Marines had landed earlier, Iraq's coup leaders told diplomats, they would never have dared to depose the royals.[14]

"There seems no doubt that the U.S. and Britain would have invaded Iraq in 1958," one historian wrote, "if there had been any reasonable hope of restoring the monarchy. But no one could [be] found in Iraq to collaborate with. Everyone was for the revolution."[15] Everyone, that is, except the Chalabis and their allies. And in fact even one branch of the Chalabi family ardently supported the revolution as well. The Chalabi family itself was split, for some were not as wealthy as the others. "One branch of the Chalabi family were Communists," an Iraqi who lived through the revolution recalled. "The Communists were using the revolution to settle scores."

Three days after the coup in Iraq, the Americans made their decision after much deliberation. They would do nothing. Eisenhower met with Dulles and British Foreign Secretary Selwyn Lloyd. "West to Keep Out of Iraq Unless Oil Is Threatened," read the headline of the *New York Times* on July 18, 1958. "Intervention," the article read, "will not be extended to Iraq as long as the revolutionary government in Iraq respects western oil interests."[16]

Many years later, the gray-haired Ahmad Chalabi rested on his couch in London and talked of America to a reporter. There was no mention of the revolution of 1958, but he said something that may be relevant: "America betrays its friends," he said. "It sets them up and betrays them. I'd rather be America's enemy."[17]

━━━

The regime, under Gen. Abdul Karim Qasim, was quick to erase any remnants of the influence of Abdul Hadi Chalabi, young Ahmad's father. It renamed Medina Abdul Hadi, a neighborhood near the old family estate, Medina Hurriya—Freedom City.

Even so, the Chalabis figured out how to adjust their sails in this new wind, and some of the family stayed in Iraq. Members of the family say they arranged to work with General Qasim's brother. One family member says they put him on the payroll of their milling company. According to another family member, Qasim's brother collected a 50 percent fee for helping get the family assets out of the country.

In a short time the world would right itself: the Chalabis settled down in a massive new flat in Britain with servants and all the luxuries they knew. But first, young Ahmad Chalabi's eyes were opened. His father, who had been in Iran during the coup, flew to London. There for a time the mogul rented a small one-bedroom apartment in Dolphin Square, according to those close to him, and waited for the dust to settle. Ahmad went to his father's small flat and watched him cook a batch of rice, for the first time without servants.[18]

2

Chalabi in America

1962–1968

"Fascists of the left."

—Ahmad Chalabi, explaining what he thought
of the people who took over Iraq

A TWENTY-YEAR-OLD Ahmad Chalabi and a handful of other students from the Massachusetts Institute of Technology's renowned mathematics department huddled around the blackboard, brainstorming in their professor's office. They called one another by their last names, each holding a piece of chalk and scribbling on the blackboard. Professor Warren Ambrose liked to hold these informal sessions for some of his best students during office hours. Ambrose even brought his teenage son, Adam, whom Chalabi would entertain with jokes.[19] Ambrose, a tall, cultured New Englander, was Chalabi's intellectual mentor during his college days in 1960s America, when theoretical algebra was the young Chalabi's passion. Ambrose was a brilliant mathematician who dabbled in leftist activism and whose politics paralleled those of Noam Chomsky, the noted MIT linguist and political theorist.

In his first year at MIT, Chalabi lived in the East Parallel dormitory on campus, according to Whitfield Diffie, one of his classmates, who lived at the nearby West Parallel dormitory. Diffie, another brilliant young mathematics major, who would go on to become a leading cryptographer, has one distinct memory of Ahmad Chalabi at MIT. "I remember walking with him, and he must have picked up his mail or something. It had a check in it." Diffie said he thought Chalabi had a cheery and humorous reaction to discovering the check. "He said, 'Unexpected funds! They must be spent!'"

———

Chalabi's ties to Professor Warren Ambrose are interesting because of Ambrose's reputation. Ambrose was a hero to some Latin American intellectuals for the way he tried to bring attention to right-wing dictatorships. "Ambrose was about defying power. Ambrose was about not accepting the status quo for the sake of it," said one of his students, the mathematician Graciella Chichilnisky, who is Argentine-American. Chichilnisky didn't meet Chalabi until after his graduation in 1965, but she recalls how fond Ambrose was of him. Chalabi, she said, "always had this dual character: on the one hand he wanted to be a responsible serious intellectual; on the other hand, he was a playboy who came from a very rich family." Still, she remembers Chalabi arguing even back then about the need to modernize the Middle East.

Ambrose was so taken by Chalabi that, Chichilnisky says, he tried to set her up with him on a date. Ambrose "always tried to get me to his house and to get me interested in him. . . . I found him interesting, but I found an edge to him I didn't like." She says he had a strange and yet offensive charisma.

Ambrose exposed Chalabi to more than just mathematics and ill-fated dates. In addition to his interest in social activism, Warren Ambrose was also a connoisseur of food and wine, and he loved jazz. Ambrose was such an avid follower of jazz trumpet legend Charlie "Bird" Parker that he would follow Parker the way Deadheads would later follow the Grateful Dead around the country, up and down the East Coast, his son recalls. And Chichilnisky says Ambrose used to take his students with him touring jazz clubs. "Ambrose *loved* jazz, and he used to play the sax. I think he and Chalabi spent a lot of time in the middle of Boston, Beacon Hill, and some of these fancy jazz places listening to jazz. That was one of the things they had together."

After graduation, Chalabi was accepted to the University of Chicago's elite mathematics PhD program but not to the one at MIT. In 1966, he went on the hajj—the sacred pilgrimage—to Mecca with his father. They both became "Hajis," an honorific applied to men who have made the journey. "His father was Haji Chalabi, and he was little Haji Chalabi," joked an old Iraqi associate in an interview, and once he returned to the United States, he focused on getting through the mathematics program as fast as he could, according to his colleagues.

Amid the activism and social turmoil of the 1960s, Chalabi seemed aloof. "Ahmad was always very dubious about mass politics and the politics of mass liberation," according to an Arab MIT student who was close to him. "He always thought that what mattered was power. And power does not grow through street demonstrations; it grows through military power and the ability to influence decision makers."

Perhaps part of the reason for Chalabi's detachment was that, even during his undergraduate years, his focus was not politics in the United States or even other Arab nations but Iraq, the country he had left as a child. While other Arabs of the period were inflamed by the Six-Day War of 1967, Chalabi had little interest in the dispute with Israel. He focused on Iraq's internal politics. His preoccupation was not so much ideological, a colleague said, but personal. He talked about Iraq occasionally while at university. "He said his country had been taken over by 'fascists of the left,'" recalled a professor. "He used that expression. It was an odd idea to me at the time."

At the time, the University of Chicago was going through conflict. It was a center of conservative thought, but at the same time it was saturated with the ideas of the left—and the leftists were sometimes getting their heads cracked. A case in point was the 1968 Democratic National Convention. But for Chalabi, the legendary protests and the notorious police crackdown at the Chicago convention would have been overshadowed by something much more interesting to him— developments in Iraq. While Chalabi dabbled in politics and math at American universities, Saddam Hussein was bringing fear and terror to politics and society in Iraq.

In fact, Saddam's involvement in Iraqi politics had started even earlier, while Chalabi was attending Seaford College, an English boarding school. As Saddam was surviving on the fringes of Iraqi power struggles, Chalabi was initiated into the arcana of English "public" school life, on 400 acres of bucolic rolling English countryside in Petworth, West Sussex. In October 1959 Saddam Hussein, then just a Baath party thug, had taken part in a failed assassination attempt against Gen. Abdul Karim Qasim, who was angering people with his refusal to make common cause with Nasser and the wider Arab cause. Qasim survived to preside over the crackling mess of Iraqi power. So-called "Pan-Arab" nationalists battled for the ideology of Nasser, while Baath Party zealots pushed an organizational agenda of Arab identity liberated from Islam. The Baathists, just like the Communists, drew their recruits not just from Sunni youth but from the vast pool of disenfranchised and impoverished Shiites looking for inspiration as they turned away from their clerics. Qasim tried to build up Iraqi pride, first alienating the Baathists and then the Communists. What is key is this: while most of the Chalabi family had built a life outside Iraq and continued to repatriate their wealth out of the country, the Iraqis who remained jostled in this newly violent place.

In the winter of 1963, just as Ahmad Chalabi was a sophomore at MIT's campus along the Charles River, back in Iraq the Baath Party launched a coup against the government of Qasim, arresting and executing the revolutionary leader. Later, as the Baath Party ruled in a kind of coalition government with pan-Arabists, from 1965 to 1968, Saddam, according to most authorities, built up the enforcement arm of the Baath Party, Jihaz Haneen (or Jihaz Hunein, as some call it). Even among the repressive regimes of the Middle East, the Jihaz Haneen was unparalleled in its ruthlessness and effectiveness. After a bloodless Baath Party coup in 1968, Saddam personally, at gunpoint, rousted his party's top rival in Iraq's intelligence service. It was his first step in taking over the country.

Plenty of Iraqis believed that the United States had a role in the coup. There is evidence that Chalabi looked at it this way as well: through the prism of American involvement. He believed the 1968 coup was "the second stage of CIA-Baath cooperation," as cited by his interviewer Said Aburish.[20] Chalabi believed, or at least would claim, that the coup was engineered by the CIA, acting on behalf of U.S. oil and sulfur-mining interests. In reality the agency did not engineer the coup but did support it. But for Chalabi, the suspicions about the CIA and American meddling may have put him on the same intellectual route as those protesters demonstrating against American meddling in Southeast Asia.

As indeterminate as Chalabi's politics really were in America, his fellow students could tell he both knew and loved mathematics. It was a language they could all share. He had an original mind that could come up with neat solutions to long-standing problems. "He did an excellent thesis," recalled one adviser. "He solved a problem which had been proposed about ten years earlier. It wasn't an outstanding problem in the field, but it was certainly something that the senior faculty members and a few others had tried and hadn't done." His work had no practical application whatsoever, but experts who have read it say it was a pleasing and orderly form of algebra, involving insightful solutions.

Discussing his university days in America, Chalabi has claimed he worked on a revolutionary type of unbreakable secret code. It's one of the quiet legends about the man—giving him a certain mystique as a master of both secrecy and puzzles. The code had to do with large prime numbers, he has explained. And there *was* such a revolution in cryptography around that time. His friends and supporters took for granted that the accomplishment he boasted of was indeed his. The claim first arose publicly in an article in *Vanity Fair* in 2002: "In Chicago, he also began to work on using computers to encrypt messages with codes based on huge prime numbers. 'I was warned off by the authorities. They told me not to pursue it, because what I was doing was at the cutting edge of work at the National Security Agency.'"[21] Using secret codes based on large prime numbers was a breakthrough discovery in the 1970s. The codes were virtually unbreakable, a failsafe way to communicate. It is usually referred to as "public key code" and sometimes as "RSA code," for the initials of Rivest, Shamir, and Adleman, who first applied it in a practical setting. It became a common method of encryption, from the popular Pretty Good Privacy (PGP) system to national security codes and even for financial transactions. Chalabi's sudden public move to claim that he worked on this so many years later took the mathematics community by surprise. It "just doesn't seem very likely," said Professor Marty Isaac, an algebraist who had helped Chalabi on his PhD thesis. "The NSA doesn't go around telling people to stop doing things!"

The strangest thing about Chalabi's claim is that his old classmate Whitfield Diffie was actually the one behind the breakthrough. Indeed, Diffie is quite famous for it. He co-wrote the seminal paper on "codes based on huge prime numbers" in 1976, with a mathematician named Martin Hellman. It was titled "New Directions in Cryptography."

Diffie was simply baffled when he learned that Chalabi, almost forty years after they had last seen each other, was apparently claiming credit. Diffie, who now oversees computer security issues for computer giant Sun Microsystems, was intrigued enough when the Chalabi claim came out in 2002 that he tried to reach out to his old classmate.

"I looked for him at the time," he said. If Chalabi really had done work on the code, "his not having contacted me once I became very public as having worked on that subject would have been surprising." It is inconceivable that Chalabi would not have recognized his old classmate's name. Diffie doesn't believe Chalabi. "I don't give the claim a lot of credence."

3

Beirut

1971–1977

"It's a pity he did not stay in mathematics. It's really a pity."

—Professor Azmi Hanna, former chair of the mathematics
department at the American University of Beirut

THEY DROVE ALONG THE CORNICHE, the cliffs to their right dropping off to the Mediterranean. It was a spring day in the peaceful Beirut of 1971, and twenty-six-year-old Ahmad Chalabi sat in the passenger seat of the beat-up old car, listening to Professor Azmi Hanna. Ahmad was a young man, and he was applying for his first job, so he sat relaxed and polite during the first drive. It is a beautiful route, the road that curves steeply uphill past the Beirut landmark of Pigeon Rock.

Hanna was a Christian Palestinian professor of mathematics at the American University of Beirut. He was in charge of hiring an assistant professor and was impressed by the young man. Thirty-five years later, he still remembers that pleasant drive.

Chalabi's application had stood out as soon as Hanna received it. Some of the best algebraists in the United States had weighed in: Irving Kaplansky, George Glauberman, Warren Ambrose. But Chalabi also had included recommendations from heavyweights in political and academic life. One letter of recommendation even came from

Charles Malek, one of the drafters of the UN's declaration of human rights twenty years earlier. All that political clout seemed like overkill—the professors sniffed at what looked like crude political bigfooting. "It almost worked against him," Hanna said. But in the end they decided to test him out.

For that test, the faculty invited Chalabi to give a colloquium, and he had simply stunned them with his presentation. It was based on his PhD thesis, and explored Jacobson Radicals, as Hanna recalls, a theoretical concept in advanced algebra. To any layperson who had stepped in the room in the Daniel Bliss Building, the whole thing would have been incomprehensible, and the mess up on the blackboard would have looked like some strange and alien language: the young mustached Chalabi happily lecturing about obscure theoretical concepts like "semi simplicity," "submodules," and "nilpotence."

After it was over, Professor Hanna offered the young man a ride home, and Chalabi accepted. That is how he ended up in Hanna's old automobile, driving along the Beirut Corniche.

Hanna reached into his pocket and peeled off $50. He was a bit apologetic to the young scholar. Usually, he told Ahmad, mathematicians were honored with $100. But the well was running dry at the mathematics department. "He took the money," Professor Hanna recalls, "and he thanked me. And I was happy that I helped a striving person looking for a job. Fifty dollars was quite an amount of money at that time. You could have ten dinners, ten good dinners at very good restaurants!"

The next day Hanna heard about Ahmad's wealth, from an Iraqi colleague, as they talked on campus. "Are you crazy?" said the colleague. "Don't you know a limousine was waiting for Ahmad Chalabi, with a chauffeur? And you take him in your lousy car!"

Chalabi was hired for the next school year, and thus his short academic career began. The life of the intellect suited him, it seemed back then, better than the mercantile trade of his family. The American University of Beirut 1971 yearbook has a picture of him on the mathematics faculty page. He is in a sweater, sitting back with his head cocked, eyeing the camera. He has longish hair and wears a mustache that is something like Pancho Villa's, long and droopy but not as bushy. Above the array of faculty photographs, the professors had selected as a quote the famous line credited to the English statesman Benjamin Disraeli: "There are three types of lies. Lies, damn lies, and statistics."

==========

Beirut floated in a rare and gentle peace. And the American University of Beirut, up on the hill overlooking the Mediterranean, was a haven even there. Chalabi would walk along the huge oval, past fan palms, where students gathered on benches and on the lawn, flirting or talking politics. The gardens of the campus are threaded with walking paths, and cats sleekly skulk around as if they own the place.

Chalabi's office was at the mathematics department at Daniel Bliss Hall. He ordered new furniture for his first-floor office and paid for it himself, Hanna remembers. It wasn't gaudy or expensive enough to upset his colleagues, but it was good enough to remind them he had money. Other than his office, Bliss Hall was a disheveled wreck, with paint peeling off the walls, broken furniture, and books and papers piles around. Rats infested the upper floors of the building like little djinns.

Chalabi knew all along that "ultimately, he would have to get into the family banking business," as one friend explains. Abdul Hadi may have indulged his young son, but it was inconceivable that he could do this forever. The family ran the Middle East Banking Company, with interests in England, Abu Dhabi, Sudan, Cairo, and elsewhere. The family calls the network The Group. Chiefly Chalabi's brother Jawad ran it, but the Chalabi family corporation was not so much a strict vertical structure as a cloudlike, informal one, without edges and run by consensus. The employees tended to be happy and were treated well, and at the beginning, at least, it seems that the bank was content to operate in a stable, conservative way.

Ahmad Chalabi's venture into academia was not a first for the family; the second oldest brother of the family, Hassan, was a law professor. Hassan was considered brilliant beyond all the others in the family. He was also blind, because of a childhood infection, and required a secretary to help with daily chores. But just because Hassan was in academia did not mean the young prodigy Ahmad could remain there as well. "His father was pressuring him to leave academic life and get into business," Professor Hanna recalls. "And Ahmad resisted! For this I began to admire him more and more. A person who so rich accepts a job as an assistant professor! Maybe at that time, he was paid maximum $7,000 a year."

In Lebanon, the Chalabi clan solidified its ties to the Shiites through a series of marriages. One of the Chalabi brothers married into the wealthy Beydoun banking family; another had married another wealthy Shiite bride; and Ahmad married the daughter of the nearly seventy-year-old Adil Osseiran, a stalwart Shiite chieftain. Osseiran was a legend, a hero of Lebanese independence who had once been thrown in jail by the French colonialists. Osseiran, a landowner as well as a politician, had a strong political base among the repressed and impoverished Shiites of southern Lebanon.

When Ahmad Chalabi married Osseiran's daughter, presiding over the ceremony was the mystical leader of the Shiite community, Iman Musa Sadr. Sadr was not a mere cleric but a political leader. He had refined the doctrine of Shiite political life, pushing for the sect to establish a stronger presence in Lebanon's government and internationally. Sadr's family was a key element in Shiite cultural life in both Lebanon and Iraq. And he was a key connection for the Chalabi family, spiritually, politically, and later financially as well.

His legacy would be made permanent because of his sudden disappearance. He vanished while on a trip to Libya to visit the young Muammar Qaddafi. In time, that turned him into something of a cult figure, as impoverished Shiites waited for Musa Sadr to return as the legendary twelfth imam, the Mahdi whose reappearance would signify the end of the world. Chalabi's friend Fouad Ajami wrote a book about him years later called *The Vanishing Iman*, for which he relied somewhat on Chalabi's information. (Years later, Musa Sadr's relative Muqtada al-Sadr in Iraq, born after Musa's death, called his militia the Mahdi Army.)

═════

As for Ahmad Chalabi, although he was living the secluded and tranquil life of a professor at Bliss Hall, he kept dipping his toes in chaos.

"He was smuggling guns to the Kurds," exclaimed a longtime friend of his with admiration. Chalabi managed to get himself in the rind of one of the notorious covert operations of the 1970s. It was 1974, the height of an effort by Mullah Mustafa Barzani, the old revered head of the Kurdish Barzani clan, to win autonomy from Saddam Hussein in northern Iraq. Barzani got weapons and supplies from the Iranian government and its feared secret service, the SAVAK.

Iran wasn't alone in backing Barzani's rebellion: the old Kurd, in his tribal headdress, was getting money and weapons from the United States and Israel at the same time. All the players might have been doing the same thing, but they had different motivations and wanted different outcomes: Barzani wanted autonomy from Saddam; the United States wanted to destabilize Saddam but wanted to make sure Barzani didn't get autonomy; and the Shah of Iran was involved mainly to keep pressure on Saddam because of a long-running border dispute.

Ahmad Chalabi, coming on thirty years old, wanted to be in the thick of it. He did what he could, encouraging journalists to cover the fray. A young journalist named Peter Jennings, then a bright and handsome reporter trying to understand the Middle East for ABC News, wanted to cover the conflict. Jennings's soundman and researcher at the time was Charles Glass, who would later become a correspondent for the network. Glass recalled how Ahmad Chalabi arranged for Jennings to contact Barzani's forces. Jennings and Glass and cameraman Vince Gaito flew to Iran on their way toward Kurdistan. At the last minute the Iranians pulled the plug on their coverage—forbidding them from crossing into Kurdistan. The journalists guessed that the Shah probably had a change of heart: it would be bad press if a famous American journalist got killed in a bombardment during his covert operation.

Ahmad Chalabi was more successful with *Guardian* reporter David Hirst, who has been the chief Middle East correspondent for the British *Guardian* for thirty years. He met Chalabi in 1975 and was immediately impressed by him. The two men formed a friendship that would last for decades. Chalabi made a plea, arguing that if the Kurds of the north and the Shiites of the south banded together, they could overthrow the young dictator Saddam Hussein.

Chalabi, even as a young mathematician, seemed to have developed a knack for understated blandishments. Or perhaps he simply liked to compliment people who deserved it. "He was always very flattering to me," Hirst recalled. "He always used to say, 'Oh, David, you are the only journalist who really knows what's going on!'"

The little war in Kurdistan ended in 1975, when Barzani was betrayed by virtually all the powers involved. The Shah of Iran dropped his support for Barzani's rebellion as soon as Saddam reached an agreement over their petty border dispute. The Israelis and the Americans quickly followed suit. The CIA barely even waved good-bye, abandoning the Kurds after pouring $16 million into their cause. Saddam's forces swept north to punish the abandoned Kurds. Back in Washington, Henry Kissinger came up with a terse justification: "Covert action is not missionary work," he said. He was understating the facts: the Kurds were massacred when Saddam finally went in. Like he would with many incidents to come, Chalabi blamed this debacle on America and the CIA.

Just then, Chalabi's obsession with Iraq and Kurdistan had to be put aside. In 1975 war fractured Lebanon. It was just the first wave of a long war that few saw coming. That first bit of chaos, really, had nothing to do with the Chalabis: phalangist Christians clashed with Palestinians, who were regarded as pesky intruders in Lebanon by the Shiites, who had Chalabi's sympathies.

The war, indirectly, caused Chalabi to experience a moment of true academic freedom before he walked away from his mathematics career forever. What happened was this: in 1976 the Board of Trustees of the American University of Beirut regretfully ordered the school shut until peace returned to Beirut. The place could not operate in conflict.

The professors protested en masse, according to Professor Hanna. As he describes the protest, it seems like academia at its best: intellectuals in solidarity against violence. Imagine it: Ahmad Chalabi and his friends in the mathematics department, joined in the auditorium with the assembled intellectuals of the campus. Whether they were agricultural experts or theoretical physicists or literary experts, they all came. And there in the ad hoc meeting of professors, Chalabi for the first time saw true democracy in play. War wouldn't close down their schools. Ordered to abandon their students, the professors were defiant. "We refused," said Professor Hanna. Hanna recalls how the meeting filled him with immense pride. "We all took a unanimous vote to keep open the university against the decision of the board of trustees, and to teach for free." He paused and then repeated it. "To teach for free."

The professors defied the trustees and kept their university open on their own steam. "We taught for free for three months," Hanna said. He smiled: "Honesty compels me to say that AUB later paid us." With four other professors, Chalabi and Hanna now ran a skeletal math department.

The war changed everything for Chalabi personally. Professor Hanna and Chalabi family members say that Chalabi's brothers and father, who had been based in Lebanon, fled to England, leaving their banking empire in the youngest son's hands. Living at the family home, he would dash to work nearby at the Beydoun building, doing the best he could. Then he'd rush back to the school, his driver speeding along the Corniche and up the hill to AUB's main entrance, where a handful of graduate students waited for him in their classroom. It was a challenge that he was undertaking, and it was a workload that would fatigue anyone.

As it turned out, it was perhaps too much for him. Professor Hanna was feeling the pressure. In the end, all he had—with no money coming in, a handful of students, and a mathematics department to run— was pride at doing things right. "I noticed that Ahmad Chalabi was coming late to his classes, and then I found out that he was taking care of the MEBCO bank," Hanna said.

Hanna called Chalabi to his office for a rare rebuke. "Ahmad, it doesn't work that way!" Hanna recalled saying, "coming late or missing classes. Although we are working for no pay, but still, we aren't here to do it that way!" Hanna told Chalabi that he had to come to his classes on time and teach. Or if he wanted to, he could go off and take a leave of absence. No one would think the worse of him. Hanna says he didn't intend to offend Chalabi. "I did not mean to make him angry. He was really busy with MEBCO bank, and I thought I would relieve him, to let him take leave without pay."

Chalabi stood up without a word and left the office. "Maybe he felt insulted," said Hanna, of the man he had mentored and befriended. Hanna sometimes wonders if he should have been more delicate, as he wonders what must have gone through Chalabi's head. "'Azmi Hanna comes and tells me to apply for leave or come on time to classes!' But I did not mean it that way. I meant only to help him! But maybe I was abrupt in the way I did it, you see!"

The next day, early, Chalabi had made his decision. He didn't take the leave of absence. Instead he submitted a curt letter of resignation, dropping it on Professor Hanna's desk at Bliss Hall. He never even told Professor Hanna to his face.

"This ended his career as a mathematician," Hanna said, with almost a pained expression on his normally cheery face. Hanna believes that the Lebanese civil war cemented Chalabi's destiny as a banker. "It seems the war convinced him to be in the family business, in the banking business. So he left."

Chalabi's legacy in mathematics was a minor one: he never liked to write or publish. He published a total of three algebra papers, all based on his PhD in "group rings." Two were in rather obscure journals in Trieste and Hong Kong, and the third was in the well-regarded *Annals of Mathematics*.

Still, to those who know him, it was clearly what he loved and where he belonged.

Professor Hanna shook his head. "It's really a pity. He should have stayed in mathematics."

4

Petra Bank

1977

AHMAD CHALABI SHED HIS CAREER as a mathematician at the age of thirty-two and plunged into his family's trade as if that had always been his plan. There was a bit of tension in the clan, although it was bickering rather than a family feud. Family members recall that Ahmad, the youngest of the brothers, was in competition with his nephew Ali Allawi. Each wanted to run the new family venture being launched in Jordan. Unnerved by the war in Lebanon, the Chalabi family had been probing for new terrain, and they needed to bring new blood into their expansive but brittle banking group. The Kingdom of Jordan, with a bubbling economy, seemed like a good choice politically, financially, and geographically. The Hashemite king was of the same bloodline as the old pre-1958 regime of Iraq, where the Chalabis were known as staunch monarchists. Also, Crown Prince Hassan stumbled across some of the Chalabi brothers in London and gushed at the idea of their bank.

So Ahmad Chalabi's brother Jawad paid a visit to the chairman of the Jordanian Central Bank in Amman to get his blessing for a bank license. The chairman, Jordanian economist Mohammed Said Nabulsi, recalled the visit. Jawad was a real fixer in the family, just like Ahmad, who could make loyal friends quickly, practically as fast as it takes to drink a cup of tea. "He's a smooth talker," one family member explains." The chairman of the Central Bank agreed to push for the Chalabis. But who would run it: Ahmad or his nephew? Both were brilliant and highly educated and wanted a chance to play at the big table. Their elders decided on a compromise: they would run the bank together. But the Chalabi family soon learned that two objects couldn't occupy the same space. Before long, through some familial elbowing, Ahmad took sole command of what would be called Petra Bank.

———

Ahmad Chalabi built and controlled Petra Bank, but his ownership interest was minuscule, less than 1 percent of the shares, with only about 25,000 dinars, equal to about $75,000 at the time. Banks, like most businesses, are started with capital investments, and Petra Bank's entire initial capital investment was quite small—just 3 million dinars, or about $9 million. The Chalabi family, through businesses and as individuals, put in a little less than 20 percent of that, or about $1.4 million. Most of the other substantial owners of the shares were rich Palestinians, like Sabih Masri, who owned about 5 percent of the shares.[22] (Masri was heavily involved in financing for the Palestine Liberation Organization, or PLO.) Some were rich Christian Palestinians, like Farah Tamari, and some apparently were from Gulf states, like Hamdan Nhayan of the United Arab Emirates, and the Wazzam family of Kuwait.[23] Even though Chalabi only invested 25,000 Jordanian dinars personally, as the head of the bank he would single-handedly and without challenge control assets of hundreds of millions of dinars and exercise remarkable control over the economy of Jordan.

———

Ahmad Chalabi liked to show off the new computers he bought. They were big gray noisy things in those days, of course, and computers were still a novelty in the Middle East, with intimidating DOS programming. For the mathematician in Chalabi, it was a love affair. One day he showed them off to David Hirst, who was visiting from Beirut. He took Hirst down to the basement, Hirst recalled, and announced that with all that computing power, he'd be able to attract more and more depositors, by offering better interest rates.

Petra Bank seemed sensational—the banking version of a Broadway hit. The bank was a phenomenal success. It had $40 million in assets in 1978 and $400 million in 1982, a tenfold increase. The growth charts show a remarkable rise, almost vertical, it seemed.[24]

Chalabi quickly became one of the most interesting men in Amman, sought out by businessmen, investors, academics, and reporters. He basked in the attention, sparkling in conversation and still an avid reader. He was an expert on everything, with a genuine interest and knowledge on subjects as diverse as music, philosophy, art, and fine furniture.

He had unusual habits: he liked to play with knives, for example. In meetings or interviews in his office, he would open and close folding knives from his collection, show them off, even throw them into the wall. He liked knives with rare and expensive handles and knives where the blades flicked out. He played with them the way many Arab men play with beads. "It was childish," said a friend, "but pleasantly childish."

Chalabi also charmed Americans, who were drawn to him as his power increased in Amman. The elegant Judith Kipper, of the American Enterprise Institute (then moderately conservative but not as far to the doctrinaire right as it would later become), found him brilliant. "He was an Iraqi patriot," she said. She introduced him to other influential Americans, like Peter Galbraith, then an aide on the Senate Foreign Relations Committee. He cultivated journalists, with varying degrees of success. John Kifner at the *New York Times* met him and was unimpressed. Kifner, the paper's Amman correspondent, had a colleague in the Cairo bureau—a young, ambitious reporter named Judith Miller. At ABC News, Chalabi befriended investigative producer Christopher Isham. And one day he even was interviewed by a young reporter for the conservative *Insight Magazine* who was working on a piece on a Palestinian issue. Her name was Danielle Pletka, and in later years, she would go on to work in the Senate Foreign Relations Committee and the American Enterprise Institute. An interesting point came as well one day when, according to intelligence officials, an undercover CIA officer posing as a diplomat met him, considered trying to recruit him, thought it through, and then dropped the idea.

To add to his legend, Chalabi built an unusual mansion for himself, in one of the best neighborhoods of Amman, just within walking distance of Abdoun Circle and not far from the residence of the British ambassador. His home was both majestic and somewhat spooky. By one account he found the design in a book on ancient Persian temples. The place is almost fortresslike, with large bastions leading to a pointed arch, like a temple. Inside, the rooms are laid around a small courtyard decorated by Greek sculpture.

A distinctive feature of his home were the wind towers, mimicking those in traditional Iranian buildings, to catch the breeze outside and funnel it through the massive home. When you stare up at them from inside, they look like skylights, divided by a crosslike structure, but they manage to suck wind through the home in an ancient form of air-conditioning, and Chalabi was immensely proud of it.

The main salon had the somber cool echo of a chamber in an ancient castle. It was intimidating and big enough to hold a basketball court. It stretched sixty feet long and twenty feet tall, the size of a small auditorium, lit by elaborate chandeliers. He decorated this cavernous and chilling space with Chinese tapestry, Italian furniture, and even a Koranic inscription made by a Jordanian princess.

It must have been an unusual place for his children to grow up. Chalabi had two girls and two boys. His oldest son was afflicted by a mental disability. He was, as all those close to the family describe it, mentally handicapped, requiring extra attention and care. For Chalabi, with the massive pride in his own extraordinary intellect, it was a devastating blow, according to his friends. But he never acted ashamed, they said, and he still loved his son. Still, he took great pride in his older daughter, Tamara, who was brilliant and quite beautiful. "She is his intellectual heir," his friend Fouad Ajami, a cheerleader of Chalabi's, would say.[25]

———

At Petra Bank, there were some early signs of an aggressive, unusual banking style, banking officials and economists say. "He was not a banker," says a relative who knew him then. "He was a relationship person." Chalabi also insisted on doing much of the banking in coded communications. And he seemed to run everything himself, delegating very little, if anything.

Growth is a good trait in banking, experts say, but runaway growth is something else and can even be a sign of problems. Even some members of the Chalabi family were raising their eyebrows. Mohammed Said Nabulsi, chairman of the Central Bank, approached Ahmad Chalabi's brother Jawad and asked him to make sure that things were in hand.

One Chalabi associate involved in Petra Bank put it this way: "You could determine that some things were not kosher. The point is that Ahmad was an extremely smart man who grew to play a role in the Jordanian economy that was bigger than his capital base would have. His business expanded, and he was doing things that were more than banking—merchant banking. He was doing a lot more than his capital base would warrant. He was an aggressive banker."

To understand Petra Bank, though, it's fair to look at it as just one piece of a complex web of banks and corporations run by the Chalabi family at the time. The Chalabis, since leaving Iraq, had founded a banking and trading network. Imagine it as a vast set of prairie dog tunnels, where all you see are the holes but not how the tunnels connect underground. In this case it was as if that network of tunnels was spread across oceans and borders, from Hong Kong to the Cayman Islands. Aside from Jordan and Lebanon, one place it surfaced was at 100 Rue de Rhone, the Fifth Avenue of Geneva, Switzerland, where the family bank MEBCO occupied one floor and a company called Socofi the next.

The nest surfaced again in Washington, D.C., at 1801 K Street, smack in the middle of the lobbying corridor in a modern building, where Petra International, a subsidiary of Petra Bank, did business. It showed itself in London, where SCF traded in commodities and foreign currency. And it surfaced even in Africa, where Ahmad and Jawad had set up the National Bank of the Sudan in Khartoum.

The thing is, Ahmad Chalabi and his brothers were doing an awful lot of business with one another, using their depositors' money. These transactions became quite clear in later years, in various audits. They occurred largely out of sight, underground, in the warren below, so to speak.

======

One of the men who saw a lot of Ahmad Chalabi in Jordan was his friend the historian Kamal Salibi, who trusted and even loved him for more than twenty years. Salibi is a treasured if controversial intellectual for many people in the region, and a well-known figure to many experts on the Middle East. Salibi trusted the Chalabis enough to deposit his savings with them. He was not a rich man, but he had made some profits from his books.

Salibi's friendship with Ahmad went all the way back to Ahmad's university days. It had started one night far from the Middle East, over dinner in Cambridge, Massachusetts, back in 1967. Chalabi was on one of his frequent visits from Chicago, for MIT and Boston were more his academic home. He and Salibi and their host were just a few Arabic intellectuals watching the political ferment of America around them and eating some home-cooked Arabic food. The two men, brilliant conversationalists with a wealth of knowledge between them, hit it off. Like so many others, Salibi was enchanted by Chalabi's brilliance. He was "bafflingly perceptive," Salibi found. Chalabi at the time, just briefly, wore a scraggly beard, which he shaved off soon, to Salibi's relief.

Salibi and Chalabi had rekindled their friendship in Lebanon, where Salibi also taught at the American University of Beirut. Sometimes Chalabi accompanied him on historical expeditions. "It was great fun, you know," Salibi remembered.

One day, in Lebanon, Salibi was talking about his bank, and Ahmad Chalabi said, "Why don't you bank with us? We'll be your bankers!" Soon, Salibi had opened an account in the MEBCO Bank. He would come to regret it.

5

Iran and Shiism

1978–1988

IN HIS OFFICE IN AMMAN, Chalabi strode to the desk and unrolled one of the large military maps he had obtained from the British War Office. He devoured every tidbit of news and every battlefield development as the Iran–Iraq War roiled the muddy ground of southern Iraq. He spread the map out on his desk and showed where the latest fighting was.

In September 1980 Saddam Hussein had invaded the newly empowered Shiite nation of Iran. It was an act of strategic idiocy by Saddam, which triggered the eight-year war against the Khomeini regime. The United States favored Saddam in this crucial conflict, viewing him as at least a bulwark against the hard-line Shiite fundamentalism of Iran, which had ousted the U.S.-friendly Shah just a year before and declared its intention of spreading its "Islamic revolution" far and wide. Iran, of course, made no secret of its animosity toward America, which it called The Great Satan. Most Arab states, including Jordan, also supported Saddam in the conflict, not just because of the Sunni–Shiite split but also because it was a fight between Arabs and outsiders, the Persian forces of Iran.

Chalabi, on the other hand, was openly rooting for Iran, under Ayatollah Khomeini, to win the war. David Hirst recalls visiting Chalabi's office frequently and standing with him, bent over the maps. "He derived great satisfaction from the signs of the Iraqi army collapsing," recalled Hirst. "He wanted the Iranians to win, he wanted them to bring down the regime." Salibi noticed this as well, and was perplexed by it.

It is worth asking whether it was Chalabi's loyalty to the Iranians or his hatred of Saddam Hussein that prompted his emotional immersion in the Iran–Iraq War. Or was it a bit of both? Clearly, his hatred of Saddam was consistent. But there was also a marked tilt toward Iran, according to those who have known him since childhood. In later years, as he grew older, some people came to believe Ahmad Chalabi was an agent of influence for Iran. But at the time he was running Petra, it is fair to say this was not the case. He was not active enough for that. He was a fan, not a player. The Iranian Revolution, according to the Arabs who know Chalabi best, had a remarkable impact on him. The year after Petra opened for business, events in Iran inflamed the Middle East with the sudden explosion of Shiite fundamentalist power. When the Shah was ousted, Ayatollah Khomeini stepped into authority, undercutting the frequent Shiite claims that their clerics stayed out of politics. The revolution seemed to pose a direct threat to U.S. interests, and the brutality against American diplomatic hostages after an embassy takeover showed the new Iranian regime was willing to shatter rules of international law. These new radical Shiite revolutionaries wanted revenge on America for all the wrongdoing of the deposed Shah.

For the Chalabi family, it was a confusing development. The father, Abdul Hadi, had been in the Shah's Iran during the 1958 revolution in Iraq and had been sheltered there in the first months of his exile. Ahmad Chalabi and his blind brother, Hassan, had worked through the Shah's forces with the Kurds in an attempted uprising against Saddam. They had decent relations with the old government, according to people close to the family. Still, when the Shiite revolution hit Iran, the students took over the American Embassy, and Ayatollah Khomeini rose suddenly to the stature of a world-renowned figure, for the Chalabis there was a sense of empowerment.

As an old friend put it, "For Chalabi, Iran is the place where power and Shiism have come together in the form of the Islamic Revolution. He is very loyal to Iran. He was loyal to the Shah, but when the Iranian

Revolution took place he switched allegiance." David Hirst, Chalabi's friend at the *Guardian*, noticed the same thing after the Islamic revolution in Iran: "He was very, very excited about Shiite self-assertion."

———

While Chalabi in Jordan was rooting for Iran during the war, the Chalabi family in Lebanon was also growing closer to the Shiite leadership, as Shiite activism grew to a boil. The Chalabis found a niche as the bankers for the growing Shiite political party in Beirut—the Amal militia—which at the time was considered a terrorist group by the United States. In fact, the first member of the Chalabi family to get public attention in the West did so because of his involvement with one of the most significant terrorist incidents of the 1980s: the hijacking of TWA Flight 847.

The Amal, fostered by Syria and Iran, had organized and inspired the Shiites of Lebanon as the fighting between the various groups continued. The Amal thrived as a military force and a political movement and also, in American eyes, as a terrorist group. Nabi Berri, a charismatic and manipulative leader, worked his way into the leadership of the Amal. Born in Sierra Leone, a hub of Lebanese expatriate traders and bankers, Berri is widely considered the most financially successful of the distinctly Lebanese variant of sophisticated warlords/statesmen/finaglers.

In June 1985, as TWA Flight 847 departed Athens for the short flight to Rome, it was hijacked by two grenade-wielding members of an Amal splinter group, who forced it to land in Lebanon. The hijackers, part of a sect dedicated to the vanished Musa Sadr, forced the pilot to fly between Beirut and Algiers twice. They beat and then murdered one American passenger, a navy diver, and dumped his body like trash on the runway, where it lay for two hours.

And then the hijackers, with the help of Amal and the Hezbollah, a rival group coming to power at the time, held the thirty-nine passengers as hostages.

Nabi Berri, whose English was poor even though his family lived in Michigan at the time, turned to the Chalabis for assistance, according to sources in the family. He selected Jaafar Jalabi—young, U.S. educated—to be his spokesman in dealing with the Americans and the press. Jalabi, the son of the friendly Jawad, was only twenty-eight but was already working for MEBCO. (He spells his name in English with a "J" instead of a "Ch.")

Like his uncle, Jalabi was engaging and always seemed forthright, blunt, and honest. He wore a Rolex and was in no way the model of a terrorist. He appeared in U.S. news outlets, gave good quotes, and appeared to put a face of reasonableness on the terrorist position. It was not necessarily a healthy place to be for a young man who was not a true believer, but it appears he did his best. In any case, in two weeks, the hostages were released, with Nabi Berri as the apparent fixer.

Shortly after his successful representation of Berri, Jaafar Jalabi got a job in government as a bank regulator: he was appointed to Lebanon's Banking Control Commission. The Chalabis now not only ran the Shiite Bank MEBCO with hundreds of millions of dollars on deposit but also had a representative on the board overseeing all the banks in Lebanon. That board decided which banks, if any, to take over. And years later, as the Chalabi businesses hit the skids, that would be an important position to have.

And Nabi Berri, according to a source very familiar with MEBCO, took the proceeds of lucrative oil dealings he conducted at a Shiite port—more than $20 million—and parked them in the Chalabi family's bank.[26]

In June 1987, Ahmad Chalabi rushed to Lebanon. Hezbollah had kidnapped his brother-in-law Ali Osseiran along with noted author and ABC correspondent Charles Glass. Chalabi apparently wanted to control the situation, with a kind of "I'm here, now we can start" attitude. He would later tell friends that he walked immediately into the Iranian Embassy in Beirut and offered cash. He was willing to pay, but he wanted the men released. As he related this story to American and Iraqi associates, he apparently took great pride in his negotiating skills. Sources say he rushed to see Sheikh Fadlallah as well, the leader of Hezbollah. Fadlallah, in person a merry and philosophical man, also banked with MEBCO, according to a source close to the family.

But in the end Chalabi certainly had less impact than he thought. Ali Osseiran was the son of a Lebanese national hero, who was then the defense minister. The outrage among Shiites was fierce. Ali was not the target anyway: the American Charles Glass was. So within a week the gregarious Ali had been released.

Although Chalabi would later claim credit, in reality the defense minister of Lebanon, the justice minister, and all the political parties had pushed for Osseiran's release. Charles Glass was kept for two more months, handcuffed to a radiator, until he finally escaped.

6

Business with Saddam

1980–1989

FROM HIS PERCH AS A BANKER in Amman, Ahmad Chalabi did try to convince the West to drop its support for Saddam Hussein, and on this issue his voice was one of the few that was heard in the United States. He had collected a number of influential American friends by this point—Judith Kipper, Peter Galbraith of the Senate Foreign Relations Committee, as well as Jim Hoagland of the *Washington Post*—and they were all receptive to his simple, powerful message: Iran was less of a threat than Iraq. Chalabi, Galbraith says, even got his first taste of lobbying in Washington, D.C., when he was brought to the American Capitol during the push for the Prevention of Terrorism Act of 1988. That legislation was supposed to slap Saddam for the gassing of the Kurds, but it was effectively blocked by the Reagan White House.

In spite of his anti-Saddam feelings, as a businessman in Jordan, Chalabi faced some tough and complex choices: Iraq was, after all, Jordan's biggest trading partner. To what degree did he and Petra engage with Iraq? He certainly provided loans to businessmen doing deals in Iraq. But he apparently was looking to expand his operations in Iraq. An American friend of Chalabi's, Glenn Golonka, says he was sent to Baghdad on behalf of Petra Bank. Fiercely loyal to Ahmad

Chalabi, he speaks of "The Doctor" with reverence. In 1988, Golonka says, as a young employee of Petra, he flew to Iraq. Apparently, the Chalabis believed sending an American as their emissary would be safe. "Ahmad sent me to Baghdad in 1988–89 on a fact-finding mission to start setting up correspondent banking relationships in Iraq, specifically for doing trade in Iraq."[27]

Golonka says his business cards referred to him as the marketing officer for Petra Bank. He stayed for three or four nights at the Al Rashid Hotel. This was before the first Gulf War, and the place was in its heyday as the pride of Baghdad.

"We were right on the cutting edge of doing some incredible things," Golonka said. "We had set up an unlimited funding credit facility with EXIM bank to, you know, set up exports to Iraq and everything." EXIM is shorthand for the United States Export Import Bank, a U.S. federal agency that helps U.S. companies by financing exports. Governments guarantee purchases under the program, so this would have meant Petra would deal directly with the Iraqi government of Saddam Hussein.

"Jawad Chalabi was really instrumental in introducing me to people," Golonka recalled. Iraq's entire trade apparatus was government-owned, and each state enterprise apparently handled business through its own bank. "And we had sent bank test-key information in order to start our banking relationships and everything."

So as much as Ahmad Chalabi hated Saddam Hussein, he was also ready to do business with his government in the days before the first Gulf War.

7

The Collapse of the Chalabi Empire

1989–1990

> "Different members of the Chalabi family are at the head of,
> or control, the firms most indebted to Socofi."
>
> —Liquidation Report of Socofi, 1990

ON MARCH 9, 1989, old Abdul Hadi Chalabi, Ahmad's father, passed away in London; his body was loaded onto a Royal Jordanian jet, which lifted off to Syria for burial in a Shiite cemetery. The death of the old man—and the flight of his remains to the Middle East—was a kind of marker for the family, for it heralded the beginning of a spiral of collapse, as if he was the only thing holding their businesses together.

Just a month and a half after his death, in the morning hours of April 27, 1989, a group of somberly dressed accountants and lawyers stepped into the foyer of 100 Rue de Rhone in Geneva, where the Chalabi family businesses in Switzerland were headquartered. The lawyers and accountants were polite but firm. For all their businesslike appearance and formality, however, they were the financial equivalent of the Grim Reaper, implacable and stolid, sent by the venerable Swiss Federal Banking Commission. The commission notified MEBCO that its banking license had been revoked. "This is the way it is done," said one of the Swiss lawyers who went in that day. "We had to go in and tell them, 'Your bank has been closed. We are the liquidators.'"

Perhaps it was a good thing for the old man that he died when he did, because MEBCO Geneva, run by Hazem Chalabi, was just the first to fall in the long and painful collapse of the Chalabi enterprises worldwide. Petra Bank, in Amman, would be taken over in August, and after that Socofi in Geneva went down, and still later MEBCO in Beirut, all caught in a whirlpool that sucked away the life savings of a large number of investors. What's more, criminal investigations would hound the Chalabis in Switzerland, Lebanon, and Jordan.[28]

In later years, Ahmad Chalabi blamed the governments of Iraq and Jordan for the collapse of his Petra Bank. It was a frame-up, he convinced his followers, including powerful members of the U.S. political establishment. According to Chalabi, he was the victim of a massive, politically motivated conspiracy to destroy his successful operation. The real story is far more complex and disturbing, involving mysterious business deals, fraud, embezzlement, an executive's love affair gone wrong, and secretive companies located in offshore tax havens like the Cayman Islands.

To chronicle the collapse of Petra Bank and its sister banks, it's best to start with a look at the circle of people the Chalabis were doing business with. The must unusual of the Chalabis' business associates was an American named Wayne Drizin. Back in the 1980s, when he met the Chalabis, he was operating in Lugano, Switzerland. Drizin would travel the world first-class,.accompanied, sources say, by a small lap dog. He carried on business through a company called Welfin SA, and he would later boast, in securities filings, that he "orchestrated the sale of Welfin S.A. to [a] Swiss-based multi-national banking group indirectly wholly owned by the Chalabi Family including Mr. Ahmed Chalabi." Drizin seems like a mismatch as a Chalabi business partner.

He first surfaces in public record in the summer of 1980 in connection with the legalized prostitution industry in Nevada. He and a well-known madam announced they were about to purchase the famous Mustang Ranch brothel in Nevada. The brothel, a large pink structure, was home to sixty or seventy prostitutes, and was owned by the notorious Joe Conforte, an alleged mob associate. The deal attracted attention across the country, from Los Angeles to New York. Drizin said he had financing from London for the transaction, and he wasn't shy about publicity about his grandiose plans for the infamous brothel. Drizin said he planned to buy the facility, hire an additional seventy prostitutes, and build an airstrip so that the "johns" could fly in to the place to attend to their desires.[29] It would become a massive enterprise, if the publicity was to be believed.

But the deal fell through. Still, Drizin quickly pushed to open another brothel, clearly enthralled by the business. County commissioners balked at granting him a license, and he lambasted them. "They seem to be more interested in stopping competitive brothels than helping the county,"[30] he told a reporter, in a unique take on the need for competition in the prostitution industry.

Drizin would later blame a series of legal troubles on various government conspiracies against him. He was charged with a felony for bouncing a check in Broward County in 1982, and that same year, records show, the Florida Bar Association disbarred him.[31] He had bounced a check for $75,000 to one person, a check for $125,000 to another, and then a check for $18,000 to yet a third. Years later, he would face serious trouble with the law: a federal jury in Arizona found him guilty of wire fraud in 2003.[32]

Drizin brought the Chalabis into ventures that suggest they had a penchant for high-risk schemes rather than conservative banking. One was a 300-foot ship called the *Nissilios*, supposedly being built at the shipbuilding port in Piraeus, Greece. It was to be an ultraluxurious cruise liner, more elaborate than anything ever built, a concept that fed off the conspicuous consumption of the Reagan years. It would boast massive staterooms designed for the extremely rich, who would shell out $7,000 a week for them. Like so many other shipping schemes, it turned out that it was like pouring money into a hole in the water.

In one quite mysterious deal that would lead to lawsuits around the world, Drizin raised almost $15 million for the ship in borrowed funds. He did it in cahoots with Chalabi, through a fairly convoluted financing mechanism. Chalabi's Petra Bank put a stamp on some documents, guaranteeing the lender that if Drizin didn't pay the money back, Petra Bank would. The concept is not much different from a parent's guarantee of a student's college loan.

Ahmad Chalabi would later say he intended to make good on the notes. But the problem is, the money never went to the ship at all. It seems to have disappeared somewhere along the way, if that is possible. Drizin would later claim in a deposition that Chalabi's Petra Bank actually stole the money from him. "Petra Bank took the balance of the proceeds and actually misappropriated them."[33] A judge presiding over one case corroborated that in fact the loan payments never did find their way to Drizin. And in any case, no one ever paid back the company that lent Drizin the $15 million, until much later, when the Chalabi operations came unhinged.

The family's investments with Drizin, much of which they blame on an employee of theirs, helped suck the Chalabis into a whirlpool of financial trouble. Drizin would have a major impact on the Chalabi family fortunes, investigators say. Chalabi has rarely mentioned this disbarred lawyer, convicted felon, and onetime aspiring pimp. Still, as Drizin said in a deposition related to one of his collapsed deals, "I had a substantial relationship with the principal owner of Petra Bank, Amman, PIBC, Socofi SA, MEBCO Bank, etc. It was one particular family that held all of this and they used all of these banks as their personal company, cash drawer, you know, their personal business."[34]

As colorful as Drizin was, he was no match as a big spender for the most lavish of Ahmad Chalabi's business associates, a Jordanian businessman named Taj Hajjar. Like the Chalabis themselves, Hajjar operated through a complex set of corporate fronts, and allegedly had as many as forty corporations, in Luxembourg, Liberia, Switzerland, and Panama. Also like the Chalabis, he had a passion for large, ambitious investments. He had a mansion in Sussex, England, and a horse farm where he kept some fine Arabians. His creditors claim he lived large and spent 340,000 British pounds, more than $600,000, on jewelry over the course of two years.[35]

In 1985 court records indicate the British police raided his office, investigating involvement in illegal arms traffic to places like Libya.[36] He was never charged. He had other ventures going too: nuclear power plants in China, food and various other items in Iraq, and oil and gas in the United States. It was in the mid-1980s that he became entwined with the Chalabi businesses. He owed millions to various banks but persuaded Chalabi to work with him. "The guy is an operator. He was acting bigger than he warranted," said one associate of Chalabi. "And Ahmad started funding him."

Chalabi put $5 million in a shrimp farm in Malaysia run by Hajjar. In another case, the family went into business with him to help him collect debts and evade creditors. They even bought real estate from him to settle bank debts.

Yet another businessman the Chalabis dealt with in a small way was Spyridon Aspiotis, a Greek citizen who lived in Geneva. Aspiotis got involved in several financing deals with the Chalabis and worked with Wayne Drizin on raising funds in the scheme to retrofit the giant *Nissilios*, as well as a deal involving yet another ship (an oil tanker, in this case).

Aspiotis was later charged criminally in Switzerland in connection with the Chalabi case. But he would gain true notoriety only several years later, in the 1990s, when he was convicted of trying to bilk the U.S. government out of three-quarters of a billion dollars through loan guarantees from an obscure U.S. bureaucracy, the U.S. Federal Maritime Administration.[37] Like Ahmad Chalabi, Aspiotis eventually had shifted his operations to Washington, D.C. Aspiotis's attempted crime against U.S. taxpayers was of staggering dimensions, but ultimately it was unsuccessful.

Back in the 1980s Ahmad Chalabi did a lot of business with a friend of his in Washington, a contractor named Huda Farouki. Farouki had a busy social life in Washington, which helped his company, American Export Group, as it leaped from contract to contract. Farouki's wife was a socialite, friendly with Princess Haifa of Saudi Arabia, and Farouki ended up with some major Saudi contracts. One of Farouki's companies was called Hai Finance.

In April 1987, Farouki's business went bankrupt and pursued a Chapter 11 reorganization, but even while it was bankrupt, Petra International in Washington continued to lend the firm millions of dollars and granted millions in unsecured letters of credit.[38] It was part of Chalabi's high-risk banking style: lending his depositors' money to a firm in bankruptcy run by an individual he knew.

━━━━━

But as high-risk as Chalabi's deals were, it was the Swiss takeover of MEBCO in April 1989 that finally shed light on it all. Ahmad Chalabi's name was nowhere to be found near MEBCO in Geneva on 100 Rue de Rhone. The Swiss bank's board was headed by his brother Hazem Chalabi, who was nine years older. Contrary to Swiss regulation, authorities found, Hazem was acting as both a board member and an executive. Yet investigators and family members say Hazem relied heavily on the advice and business recommendations of his younger brother Ahmad.

According to several former employees of the company, MEBCO in Geneva specialized in providing banking services to the vast Lebanese population in West Africa: the diamond dealers, traders, oilmen, and fixers of Sierra Leone, Liberia, and the Ivory Coast. The Lebanese diaspora consisted of brilliant merchants who needed a safe and discreet place to bank. In 1986 Swiss regulators wrote a warning letter about the way the bank was operated. Swiss banks have a reputation for soundness and low risk, but there were major troubles here. The Chalabi family had too much control, the Swiss said, and the bank lent out funds without adequately reviewing the risks. The Chalabis missed a deadline to get the bank in order. By the time the bank liquidators stepped into MEBCO in Switzerland, few of the employees were surprised that the operation was getting shut down.[39]

With MEBCO's collapse in Geneva, the genie was out of the bottle. The world could now see how the Chalabi businesses were run.

The Chalabi family's Swiss-based company, Socofi—a huge unregulated investment firm in Geneva, located directly above MEBCO at their offices at the Rue de Rhone—was the mother ship of the Chalabi fortune. Founded in 1966, it never even got a Swiss banking license. Instead, it simply took in depositors' money with no regulation, making depositors sign "fiduciary agreements." Plenty of wealthy Arabs, especially Iraqis, put their money into Socofi over the years. Since it wasn't a bank, it seemed to offer the stability of Switzerland without the intrusive hand of the Swiss banking authorities.

Although Ahmad Chalabi wasn't in the official management of So- cofi, just as in the case of MEBCO, he was certainly one of the owners, through a complex web of holding companies based in the corporate tax havens of Luxembourg and the Cayman Islands. The brothers' Luxembourg firm was Rafidain Holdings, and the holding company in the Cayman Islands was simply called Socofi.

When Lebanese historian Kamal Salibi put his money in Socofi, he was told it was a "fiduciary company." He wasn't quite sure what that meant, but he trusted Ahmad Chalabi and his family and signed the "fiduciary agreement." Even members of Chalabi's own family had money in Socofi: the Allawis and the Bassams had invested in the hope of building up their nest eggs. Sharif Ali bin al-Hussein, the closest thing to royalty that remained among the Iraqi diaspora, put his money into it. "Socofi was not a bank," explained a Swiss investigator who worked on the case, "but it worked like a bank." The problem was, there was no protection for the Chalabis' investors.

═══

The end of Socofi would be comical if it had not caused so much suf- fering to its depositors. Its demise was precipitated, the story goes, by the disastrous love affair of the company's general manager, whose shenanigans soon went out of control. Socofi was lending its money to the other enterprises run by the Chalabi family, but this practice, it seems, was exposed only when the general manager, Paul Mouawad, was himself uncovered as an embezzler. In his fifties, balding, with a prominent nose, Mouawad chain-smoked Peter Stuyvesant cigarettes in his office in Geneva. He was the last man, everyone says, who would have been suspected in a massive embezzlement scheme. In the late 1980s the Chalabis stumbled across some evidence that Mouawad had been stealing.

Glenn Golonka, the young American who worked with the Chal- abis, was once again in the thick of it. He says he and Salem Chalabi, the son of Jawad, started hunting for Mouawad's loot. "It was a very, very awkward situation," he said. "Me and Salem, we went into his house, and we took these paintings out of his bathtub and statues out from under the piano."

Sources close to the case confirm Golonka's account. Mouawad had been using Socofi's money to buy art. "There was Chagall," Golonka explained. "There were Monets and Manets, and there was one in particular. The most outrageous thing he had done was, he had used the bank's money to purchase $5.5 million worth of jade. . . . He basically had a warehouse that was full of jade!" The discovery of the jade warehouse came by accident; the Chalabis stumbled across it when looking over some accounts. Inside there were jade chess sets, jade carvings, even, by one account, a jade table. This was indeed a bizarre find for the Chalabi family, which somehow had to figure out a way to dump it all back on the market.

Paul Mouawad's defenders, speaking on condition of anonymity, say he had fallen in love and taken a mistress, and after he tasted what it was like to live beyond his means, had gotten out of control. He allegedly bought his mistress lavish presents, like a vacation villa and a Cartier watch. But what the Mouawad incident did as well was expose a series of massive problems at Socofi.

Mouawad, according to lawyers in the case on both sides, did not want to go down alone. He admitted his crimes, they say, in front of a magistrate named Christine Sordet, and then pointed at the Chalabis. The whole thing was corrupt, he said, and he was just the low thief in the pile.

One of the cadre of Swiss lawyers involved in cleaning up the mess explained it this way: "Mouawad was aware that the Chalabis took money from the company for their own business, and he did the same." He laughed at the absurdity of it. "He went before the judge, and he explained what happened. He accused the Chalabis in front of the judge." Another lawyer in Switzerland who was close to Mouawad confirms the report of his testimony against the Chalabis. (Mouawad was convicted later, and he passed away in 1997.)

By the time Swiss authorities finally stepped in to force Socofi into liquidation in late 1989, they found a wreck. Most of the money invested in Socofi by hundreds of people like Kamal Salibi had been lent out to businesses owned by the Chalabis. A Swiss attorney who worked on the case was perplexed by the whole thing, and he explains it simply and slowly, as if teaching a lesson in fraud. "They take the money from Socofi, money from clients, and they put this money in the Chalabi family businesses," he said, "and all these companies did not pay back their loans."

A liquidation report about Socofi confirms this in more technical language: "Its principle debtors were members of the Chalabi family or businesses owned and operated by members of the Chalabi family."[40] Ahmad Chalabi, from his base in Jordan, personally owed 84,000 Swiss francs to the company, while the various Chalabi enterprises owed a total of 74 million Swiss francs. The amount of money involved was enormous for the period: a loss of 140 million Swiss francs, reportedly, or more than $110 million. It's like what would happen at Citibank if it lent its deposits to the private businesses of its chairman and his family, who never repaid them. No one would bank there.

In their defense, one member of the Chalabi family said they structured the loans that way initially for tax reasons: instead of taking profits as dividends, he said, accountants recommended lending out the profits to the family.

"The Chalabis—it is a very strange family," one Swiss investigator said, emphasizing the word "strange."

8

The Fall of Ahmad Chalabi

1989

"I left Jordan legally and through the airport on holiday."
—Ahmad Chalabi, 1989

ON AUGUST 7, 1989, in the dark of night, Ahmad Chalabi fled Amman, Jordan. He took few possessions with him, a sign either that he thought he would return soon or that the urgency of his departure left him no time to pack. He drove north, which would take him through the hills on the outskirts of the city and then toward the Syrian border. The wrath of Jordan would follow him as he left because Petra Bank, more than any other Chalabi family enterprise, left the most damage in its wake.

Back in the winter and spring of that year, Ahmad Chalabi, at his office in Wadi Saqri, had done his best to weather the storm after his father died. The problem was this: just as the Chalabi family businesses were coming apart at the seams, and the web of insider dealings was about to become exposed, the façade of health in the Jordanian economy was also shattered. Dubbed the Gucci Kingdom for its lavish and stylish ways, the place was in turmoil: hunger, food riots, bank runs, and inflation. For months the Central Bank authorities were trying to prevent the collapse of the local currency, taking a variety of restrictive monetary steps. The Jordanian government put the brakes on spending, skidding the economy into tough times as it sought to curtail waste. It was an awful mixture just when Ahmad Chalabi needed liquidity the most.

It was nothing exceptional in the scheme of things: the loose practices of the Reagan years were coming to an end, and economies seemed to be collapsing everywhere. Savings and loans were going bust in the United States. U.S. Attorney Rudy Giuliani indicted the king of Wall Street, Michael Milken.

In the spring of 1989, the king of Jordan brought Mohammed Said Nabulsi back into the Central Bank to try to rein in the economic havoc of the country. The diminutive economist, who had actually helped get Petra its banking license in the first place in 1978, had chaired the Central Bank from 1972 to 1985 and then worked for the United Nations in Iraq.

Once Nabulsi returned to Jordan, his first job was to prop up its crumbling currency. The dinar was under attack, and he needed to go to war to defend it or the nation's paper money would be worthless. Ahmad Chalabi mistrusted Nabulsi and viewed him as his nemesis.

First, Nabulsi dropped the artificial price of the dinar and let it float a bit. Then, the Central Bank's currency reserves were completely depleted, so he ordered all banks to help him. They were commanded to deposit, with interest, a share of their foreign funds into the Central Bank. He had that authority according to the laws of the country. So in May 1989, the Central Bank of Jordan ordered all banks to deposit 35 percent of their foreign currency in the bank.[41] This fact is undisputed.

It was Chalabi's response—or lack thereof—that ended up exposing the extent of Petra Bank's problems, according to Nabulsi, who says Petra Bank was the only bank to deposit nothing in the Central Bank. "What happened is that all banks did it, except Petra," he explains. Chalabi's supporters say that Nabulsi had always had a bitter relationship with Ahmad Chalabi, and that the new cabinet in Jordan was less friendly to him than the last. Nabulsi says he was perplexed and disturbed. Personal dislikes aside, Nabulsi says, he called Chalabi up and Chalabi tried to allay his concerns over the phone. "He said, 'We are working on it!'" recalled Nabulsi.

Who can say what Ahmad Chalabi was thinking at this point? For some men of wealth and status, the idea that everything can come unglued is like getting suffocated, almost intolerable. There seems to be no way out. The collapse, the possibility of poverty—they are all horrors. But worst of all is the fear of possible shame and exposure, the sense that one may look ridiculous and petty. Did Ahmad Chalabi feel these things? It's possible. But perhaps he was immune to the psychological pressures of impending bank failure. Perhaps he did not realize just how tenuous his economic situation was. Possibly he believed he had done nothing wrong.

In fact, at that time there were no public allegations of criminal misdoings by Chalabi. There may have been questions, but there were no specific allegations until several months later. On the contrary, back then, everyone assumed it was all just an accounting issue. No one knew about the various interlaced loans between the Chalabi banks.

Whatever Chalabi was thinking, Nabulsi admits that by this time he was getting concerned. The second-largest bank in Amman was not responding to his command as governor of the Central Bank. "I started to doubt the whole situation. Why is he not giving the Central Bank *anything?*" Nabulsi wondered. So he summoned Ahmad Chalabi to his office at the Central Bank. The two men faced each other across his desk awkwardly. Nabulsi said Chalabi, as usual, was playing with a pocketknife as if it were a set of worry beads. And then, he says, Chalabi gave him an unusual explanation. "He claimed that all the foreign currency he was supposed to have had been redeposited in certain companies or banks." Nabulsi was upset. "I said, 'Look, Ahmad, this is not legal! You should be able to give me immediately something of your deposits.'"

———

A lawyer for Chalabi admits that Chalabi resisted depositing funds in the Central Bank as ordered, but he cannot explain why. Certainly Petra Bank had engaged in some public relations stunts to prove it had foreign currency. It once stacked U.S. currency in its lobby, for example, to show that it had reserves on hand. But it would not obey the Central Bank; Nabulsi alleged that the real reason soon became clear:

the Petra Bank books were a fraud. He says it became clear once he sent in a team to check. They told him they found no major overseas foreign currency deposits, as Chalabi had claimed there were. Then, Nabulsi sought an audience with King Hussein of Jordan. He wanted to take drastic measures to secure the bank. King Hussein, in his deep, quiet, smoker's voice, a calm voice, said, "Go ahead and do what you need to do." The king told him he wanted to be kept informed at every step of the way.

Arguing that Petra's books were a sham and that the huge bank's collapse would be a massive crisis, Nabulsi and the prime minister petitioned a powerful group, called the Economic Security Committee, for authority to step in under martial law. They went in with security forces, according to bank employees, in a heavy-handed move nothing like the low-key sophistication of the Swiss, who had more experience in bank regulation.

That morning a visitor to Chalabi's mansion found Chalabi eating breakfast in the cavernous dining room. Chalabi had woken up late when the Jordanian government came to alert him, at his mansion, to their actions. He was laughing dramatically to himself. "They have handed me to my worst enemy," he proclaimed, referring to the Central Bank's Nabulsi.

Jordan appointed a management team to oversee the bank. The six-man team included Chalabi because, without him, Nabulsi felt, they might never know what had happened to the bank. But less than a week later, giving notice to no one, even his closest friends, Ahmad Chalabi fled into the night and made the 100-mile drive to Damascus. It came as a sudden shock to his loyal friends in Amman. They were confused and beside themselves. His cook was sobbing pitifully in the kitchen.

But the nation of Jordan was in an outcry and a fury. This sort of thing, the chairman of a bank absconding in the middle of the night, was a major scandal. One of Chalabi's loyalists at Petra was grabbed and imprisoned when he tried to leave the country. Others were arrested.

Chalabi quickly began calling journalists, although he refused to say where he was. His first story was that he had not fled at all: it was just a vacation, he protested, a misunderstanding. "I left Jordan legally and through the airport on Tuesday for holidays," he told a reporter for Reuters. "I was never informed about a travel ban and I plan to return to Amman."[42] He told the same thing to the *Jordan Times*. It was just an unfortunate mix-up, and he would return soon and straighten everything up.

Soon he changed his story—saying what he would say for the rest of his life: that he believed the government of Jordan would have handed him over to a team from Iraq. A three-man team of Iraqis, he said, linked to Saddam Hussein's Mukhabarat, was in Amman when he fled. He feared for his life, he claimed, and believed he would be handed over to Saddam Hussein, tortured, and then killed.

For their part, the Jordanians maintain that the idea of handing Chalabi over to Saddam's forces at the time was absurd. They had not taken him into custody, after all, and they had left him on the management committee of the bank. They needed him to help sort through the tatters of Petra Bank. Moreover, they say, if Saddam Hussein had wanted to assassinate Ahmad Chalabi, he would have done it without their help. It would have been easy.

How Chalabi got out of Jordan is still a mystery, although the best explanation is that he drove himself. One rumor in Jordan among those who know him is that he borrowed the car of one of the younger, minor princes, a nephew of the king, perhaps, to help him across the border. Another colorful story was that he was spirited out of the country in the trunk of Crown Prince Hassan's car—Hassan, an intellectual, was always partial to the brilliant Chalabi. But that's been largely discounted. Some suspected Tamara Daghistani, but others say she was in shock when she learned he'd left. She won't discuss it, but sources close to her say that she was so fiercely loyal to Chalabi that she had helped get some of his personal belongings out of the country to keep them from the hands of the banking officials. The Jordanian government was furious. The Mukhabarat quickly snatched her up for interrogation and took her to their vast and ominous headquarters up near the eighth circle overlooking the city of Amman.

Just two months after the takeover of the bank, still in hiding, Chalabi threatened to sue Jordanian officials in federal court in Washington, D.C. He faxed a copy of a lawsuit to the *Jordan Times* in Amman so they could write it up, and the copy is still in the paper's library. The suit, which was never actually filed, alleged that Nabulsi and other Jordanians had conspired to force a run on his bank and then manipulated the Jordanian political system to take it over.

Chalabi's friend Jim Hoagland at the *Washington Post* picked up this thread, without directly quoting Chalabi. It was one of the few stories about the scandal in the Western press. Hoagland's column in September 1989 hinted that the Jordanian government had railroaded Chalabi. The piece was titled "Hussein Needs All His Survivor Skills Now," referring to King Hussein of Jordan. He wrote that "the Petra affair seems to have heavy political overtones involving the king's surprising new friendship with the Baathists in Baghdad." The implicit allegation was that the king of Jordan might have shut down Petra to appease the government of Iraq, which had Chalabi in its sights. This was exactly the line put forward by Chalabi himself. But no one has provided any compelling reason to believe it has a basis in fact.

Chalabi's public relations counteroffensive was fierce and noisy, but in Jordan it was meaningless. Likewise, in other countries it did nothing to shore up the remaining family businesses. And he never returned. Ever. He simply never went back to Jordan to face the court or claim what he thought was his.

A devastating blow to Chalabi may have come when he learned that his exotic mansion had been sold from under him. Auditors in Jordan claimed that he'd built his home with a loan of $1.2 million from the bank (800,000 Jordanian dinars) and then registered the somber, castle-like home in the name of his young son instead of in his own name.[43]

According to Central Bank chairman Nabulsi, when the bank tried to sell off the home, the bidders all got threatening letters from Chalabi, warning them not to bid on it. The eventual buyer, who got a low insider price—practically a steal for the prime real estate—was the leader of a vast Jordanian tribe, a powerful man named Sultan Odwan. Chalabi's supporters, for their part, say Odwan is related to Nabulsi's family by marriage and that the deal was intrinsically corrupt.

In an interview inside the home, Odwan explained that he got a threatening note from Chalabi warning him of consequences to him and his family if he bought the place. So Odwan claims he settled things in the brutal old tribal way. He could not find Chalabi himself to retaliate in kind, he says, so he tracked down some of Chalabi's family members in London and issued a threat of his own against them. The threats, he warned them, had better stop. He said they did stop after that, and he went ahead and bought the house for a fraction of what it was worth.

By early 1990, the scope of Petra Bank's crisis was becoming clear. Some of the first devastating news came from a January 15, 1990, audit the Jordanians commissioned to examine the bank's balance sheet on the day before it had been taken over—a financial snapshot in time. The auditors from Arthur Andersen found the Petra Bank books were a massive compilation of lies or mistakes.

They found enormous losses: 40 percent of the bank's outstanding loans, about 126 million dinars ($176 million), were not being paid back, they said. The euphemism they used was "non performing." Instead of 104 million dinars ($140 million) in cash on hand, as its books claimed, Petra had only 8.6 million dinars (about $12 million).[44]

The auditors said the bank was undercapitalized for its size. While there were 30 million dinars in capital at the bank, or $42 million, the auditors said that was short to the tune of about 157 million dinars, or $220 million.

Another interesting thing the audit found was very similar to what the auditors would find at Socofi: a vast web of insider deals. Forty-four million dinars had been lent to what was dryly called "related parties," meaning borrowers connected to the Petra management. Meanwhile, there was a morass of deposits crossing over between Petra, Socofi, and MEBCO. The Arthur Andersen beancounters figured that might put Petra another $130 million in the red.

═══

As the accountants continued to dig, they found new and strange issues at Petra. Some of what they uncovered was in Washington, D.C., where "the Bank paid the rent of a house that the Chalabi family owned in George Town [sic], Washington in the amount of JD 75000 annually."[45] That is to say that Petra Bank was renting one Chalabi-owned home for more than $100,000 a year.

Another unusual deal they found in the United States involved more real estate, a beautiful place called the Peace and Plenty Farm: "Petra Bank/Washington . . . paid the rent of a ranch in Washington for raising horses. The ranch was most probably owned by the Chalabis and its annual rent was U.S. $102,000."[46] What that referred to was something quite plush. For years, the Chalabi family had made use of a horse plantation set in the rolling green hills of Loundoun County, Virginia, just an hour from downtown Washington. The $1.3 million compound boasted a 6,000 square-foot manor house and a stable. Ahmad Chalabi had hosted senate aides like Peter Galbraith at the Peace and Plenty Farm, and apparently members of the Chalabi clan used it for relaxation. It was only after the bank was taken over that it became clear the Chalabis were allegedly charging Petra for their own vacation spot.

The response by Ahmad Chalabi's defenders has been conflicted. Reading between the lines in certain correspondence, it becomes clear that they may have believed the Georgetown house was for couriers to stay in, this way saving money on hotels. A source close to the case says the family argued that the Virginia plantation, set in the middle of horse country, had a business justification as well—it was a storage facility for documents.

Eventually, the Jordanians launched what are known as liquidation proceedings. They sold off the bank piece by piece, decimating its assets. It was a merciless and quite unpleasant liquidation, and there seems to be no doubt that there was possible insider dealing by those involved. It would be similar to a series of rigged foreclosures in the United States. Investments, like a Chalabi family–owned Safeway store, were sold at bargain prices to insiders with connections to Jordanian officials.

Ahmad Chalabi has always insisted that his bank was healthy when it was taken over. His lawyers claim the Arthur Anderson report was a "fraudulent audit report," based on false numbers supplied by Nabulsi, who engineered the collapse of the entire establishment. But they have never confronted one of the central allegations: the interconnected loans and business between Petra, Socofi, and MEBCO.

The fact is that even Chalabi's family members knew Petra was having problems. Some insist that while Petra was fundamentally run in a dangerous way, it was not a criminal problem. "Ahmad can be accused of mismanagement of Petra Bank, he can be accused of negligent mismanagement of Petra Bank, but he is not a crook," said one relative of his. "The problem with Ahmad is that people around him often are."

Some of the more reasoned of Chalabi's defenders say although his bank was badly run and undercapitalized, the Jordanian government response was too heavy-handed. The institution could have been saved, they argued. It could have been shored up or rescued, and that would have done far less damage to Jordan's economy. The cure, they argue, was worse than the disease.

It is unclear if Ahmad Chalabi ever saw it this way. Like so many rich bank officials whose operations go under, he claimed he was undercut by a conspiracy of regulators. It's a common defense. Consider Charles Keating, whose giant S&L, Lincoln Savings, cost the U.S. government $3 billion when it was taken over, in the same era as the Petra debacle. Keating, like Chalabi, said that Lincoln Savings was fundamentally healthy, and that he was the victim of vindictive and aggressive bank regulators. "I didn't do anything wrong," Keating told a reporter. "Didn't do anything wrong at all. . . . The people that did something wrong are in government."[47]

———

Chalabi's old friend Kamal Salibi, the deep-voiced and revered historian, tells a revealing and tragic personal anecdote about the mess. Salibi had invested what he says was $200,000 with the Chalabis, first putting it in their MEBCO Bank in Beirut and finally in the Chalabis' Socofi operation in Switzerland. Salibi had been a loyal friend to Ahmad Chalabi. In Jordan he had stood up for Chalabi, offering him companionship and moral support when the Jordanian regulators moved in on the bank. He had believed in Chalabi's innocence, and did not then doubt him.

While Petra Bank unwound, Salibi never even asked Chalabi about his own money. He saw him in Jordan the night before his unexpected disappearance, but he says he never felt it was the right time. He didn't want to burden his old friend. "I thought it was wrong that I would add to his problems by asking about my money, so I didn't," he said.

But back in Beirut, in the subsequent months the historian trod around the town, trying to find Ahmad Chalabi without success. Chalabi's building seemed lived in, but no one was coming to the door. He even tried to drop off some Chalabi family memorabilia he had brought back from Amman. One day Salibi finally did track down Jawad Chalabi, Ahmad's older brother and a key member of the Chalabi banking group, to ask about his life savings. By now Jawad, like everyone in the family, was looking over his shoulder and trying to figure a way out of this massive mess the family had dug itself into in the cycle of insider dealing and strange transactions. Jawad tried to console Salibi, though.

Salibi, relaying the conversation, talked slowly because this was an important event in his life: "We owe you a lot money," Jawad told him, "and we are going to pay it back to you." Then Jawad took him to show him the family plans. That's the first Salibi heard about a variety of the Chalabi schemes: one idea was a factory that would make building materials out of garbage. The company was called Catrel. Another Chalabi scheme he then heard about for the first time was the *Nissilios* ship in Greece—the cruise liner for the extremely wealthy.

Salibi suddenly had an awful moment of recognition, he says, as if a curtain had risen. At first, as he listened to Jawad Chalabi, he was almost angered hearing the strange business proposals Jawad was discussing; they sounded so risky and unconventional. But until he heard them, he had actually thought he would recover his money, despite the collapses of MEBCO and Petra. And then he realized that his money was gone. "I came home and said, 'Well, that was my money. Now I have to live without it.'"

Shortly after that confrontation, Salibi says, Ahmad Chalabi, who had indeed arrived in Beirut months after fleeing Jordan, came to see him in his Beirut apartment. Salibi lives in a building just off Bliss Street, adjacent to the American University of Beirut.

Chalabi stood there in the lobby, and Salibi invited him upstairs. There, the two men chatted politely but awkwardly. Salibi never once mentioned his life savings. "I didn't raise the question at all with him. And the worst thing is, he didn't raise it!" With both men exchanging gossip and pleasantries, neither mentioned the reason Ahmad Chalabi was there: the fact that Chalabi's family was not returning Salibi's money. Salibi didn't want to press Chalabi when he was a guest. He thought it was incumbent on Chalabi to bring it up. "As far as I'm concerned," Salibi said, slowly, explaining why he didn't demand his money, "my honor as a host is more important than money!"

———

Beirut was becoming hairy for the Chalabi family in 1990. There is a photograph from the period of a crowd gathered round a figure in effigy hung from a fake scaffold, with the words "Al-Chalabi" pinned to its chest. What happened is that MEBCO in Beirut, the family's oldest operation, was the last bank to fall in the Chalabi family group. It tried to resist, but it was like the last domino, and all the weight of the rest finally pushed it over. It kept its doors open as long as it could, but with the family's operations in Switzerland wiped out, and with Petra dissolved in Jordan, MEBCO in Beirut couldn't be salvaged either.

Sources close to MEBCO and the Amal militia say one of the big depositors there was Nabi Berri, Amal's leader. As the source tells it, Amal had millions in MEBCO, much of it from a particular oil deal. Over a period of time, the source says, the Amal Party removed its money, safely, leaving the bank vulnerable to a run. The Chalabis' bank was known, after all, as Amal's bank. Berri seems to have escaped unscathed financially. The source says Berri even approached the Chalabis, including Ahmad, with an offer to take control of the bank. It never happened. Financial doom moved quicker than Berri could. The depositors, hardworking, poor Shiite families who kept their life savings in what they thought was the Shiite bank, made a run on the bank and found its doors locked. It was no quiet thing, no dignified financial liquidity crunch: it was a messy embarrassment for the family and a major scandal in Lebanon.[48]

MEBCO's collapse brought ominous violence to the streets. On December 14, 1990, protesters were gathering right in the center of the government area, according to *An Nahar*, Lebanon's best-known daily newspaper. There was the stench of black smoke from burning rubber tires on Hamra Street, a wide thoroughfare that is one of the most well known in town. The Banking Control Commission, where Jaafar Jalabi worked while his family ran MEBCO, is on the second floor of the Central Bank of Lebanon there. The protesters gathered that cold December day were trying to bring some attention to the financial doom brought down on them by the Chalabi-owned bank. They demanded the return of their savings.

They also called for the death of the MEBCO bank management—the Chalabis. It was at that protest that demonstrators in front of the Central Bank hung a figure labeled "Al-Chalabi" in effigy, although it is not clear which Chalabi is intended. A photograph of the demonstration was published later in the Lebanese daily *Al Akhbar*.

By that time Ahmad Chalabi had already fled to London. At the age of forty-five, he found himself in exile for the second time in his life. There is no way to get inside his head, but there is ample evidence that he appeared to believe the story that he would so compellingly present to the receptive audiences he found in the West: that he was the victim of persecution, the target of an elaborate conspiracy, which could almost always be traced back to his original nemesis, Saddam Hussein in Iraq.

PART II

9

Desert Storm

1990–1991

"Wallowing in his narcissism, victory to him
means only one thing: his own political survival."

—Ahmad Chalabi writing about Saddam Hussein,
Washington Post, March 12, 1991

CHALABI CYCLED DOWN KNIGHTSBRIDGE toward his office. A portly middle-aged Arab peddling down the drab British streets in winter, he wore a bright red rain jacket and matching rain pants, almost the color of the double-decker buses on the street, to protect him from London's sudden rainstorms and wind gusts. Some associates didn't know what to make of his new affinity for riding around town; most assumed he was trying to prove he could not afford a limousine, to stave off the Iraqis who had lost their savings in the banking debacle. After fleeing Jordan in a cloud of scandal, Chalabi, rather remarkably, was able to remake himself quickly in London. While he found himself humbled by his reduced circumstances, his hatred of Saddam Hussein animated him, giving his life passion and single-minded purpose.

Cycling was actually a convenient way to get from his flat to his new office, which was just across the street from the Knightsbridge Cavalry barracks in one of the most elite neighborhoods in London, a few blocks from the landmark Harrods department store. Despite the expensive address, Chalabi's office upstairs at 199 Knightsbridge was not the lavish space he used to have at Petra Bank. It was efficient and well protected, but one visitor described it as "shabby." It was in a business called Card Tech, a somewhat secretive family operation started just before the collapse of Petra Bank. Security was tight. To gain entry, Chalabi and other visitors had to punch in a code on the cipher locks on the doors. Back then, before there was an automatic teller machine on every corner, Card Tech was one of the companies pioneering the sensitive network of security in ATM and credit cards. Card Tech's niche was software enabling even small banks to detect fraud and perform credit card validation through servers. Members of the Chalabi family, fighting allegations of fraud in three countries, were now running what was in essence an antifraud credit card corporation. Chalabi himself had provided much of the funding through Petra Bank, those involved say. "He financed it," said one relative. And indeed, auditors believed some Petra Bank profits had been used to help Card Tech. Chalabi owned one-fifth of one part of the company, records indicate, holding 200 of 1,000 shares of Card Tech Research in his name.[1] A related firm named Card Tech Ltd. does not directly bear his name but is owned by family members and a holding company.

But though he dabbled in business and worked out of the Card Tech office, he spent the bulk of his energy on politics. A newcomer to serious organizing against Saddam Hussein, he quickly bonded with Shiite opposition leaders like activist Laith Kubba, and firmed up his links to Shiite clerics like Muhammad Bahr al-Ulum. It was a frustrating time at first, because Washington and London ignored Iraqi opposition activists as if they were street beggars. While the West offered both tacit and material support to Saddam, the opposition was shunned as a sort of untouchable and irrelevant caste by the State Department. So Saddam's invasion of Kuwait in August 1990 was almost like a gift to Ahmad Chalabi. His enemy of so many years, the enemy of Iran and the Shiite community, had suddenly, in one quick and disastrous move, become the enemy of the United States.

The U.S. reaction to Saddam's aggression, when it came, was stolid in defense of its Kuwaiti allies: Defense Secretary Dick Cheney personally persuaded Saudi Arabia's ailing King Fadh to allow U.S. divisions to land on its desert sands. Operation Desert Shield ground on, bringing hundreds of thousands of troops from the United States, England, and France—a true coalition force—into the Kingdom to prepare for battle.

War was just as inevitable as U.S. victory, and Ahmad Chalabi saw the opportunities. From his base in London, Chalabi became the perfect source for journalists: debonair, with an interesting back story, always good for a quote. The grand old lady of the *New York Times* editorial page back then was columnist Flora Lewis. She wrote the first sentence ever in the *Times* about Ahmad Chalabi, calling him

> an international banker who fled Jordan for London after learning that King Hussein was prepared to turn him over to the Iraqi police. He points out that until the gulf war began, Saddam Hussein had Iraqis convinced that there was no alternative to his rule, since he was backed by the West as well as most other Arabs. "There was never any sign, never any message, that he was seen as a pariah," Mr. Chalabi said. "He is not a Hitler. He is a Frankenstein's monster created by others."[2]

In later years the *New York Times* would have a complex relationship with Chalabi; he contributed to one of its greatest journalistic humiliations. But in 1991 he was just a newcomer, a refreshing new voice, beginning to sound the same themes he'd hammer home for the coming decade. In February 1991, in the *Wall Street Journal*, Chalabi penned an opinion piece titled "A Democratic Future for Iraq."* Saddam could and should be toppled by the United States, he argued. He pushed the United States to finish the job it had begun with Desert Storm. "Democracy is possible in Iraq," he wrote. "The united opposition can effectively claim legitimacy through its promise of free elections and a constitution." He used the words "democracy" and "democratic" nineteen times in the short opinion piece, ending with

---

*Years later, Chalabi would indicate that Albert Wohlstetter, a powerful influence on conservative strategists, had helped him place this article in the *Journal*. Wohlstetter, who taught at the University of Chicago, was a mentor for Defense Department officials in the Reagan and Bush administrations, including Richard Perle and Paul Wolfowitz. When Wohlstetter passed away in 1997, Chalabi wrote the family a condolence note from London, indicating that he had met Wohlstetter once or twice and owed him a debt for helping get an article published in the *Wall Street Journal*.

the proclamation that "'Stability' in Iraq has not in the past brought peace to the region. Democracy just might."[3]

As a piece of analysis or even rhetoric, it wasn't especially original, but it was his first public statement to American readers. Given the influence he would have in the years to come, it is worth considering what he meant. Was he committed to democracy or was he just using the word? The idea of democracy in Iraq was more revolutionary than it might sound.* But there is no evidence in Chalabi's background that he cared about "democracy" as a form of government or method of choosing leaders any more than he cared about monarchy. What is clear is that he disliked Saddam Hussein, and he had hit upon a concept—democratic reform—that served neatly as a powerful critique of Saddam's rule and a rallying cry for the opposition. There is no hint at all that at this point that he saw himself as anything more than an organizer, an advocate. There are no claims, here, to the seat of power in Iraq.

Chalabi worked with Iraqi opposition groups who founded the Joint Action Committee, which called on the West to allow them to battle Saddam and wanted to declare a provisional government to step in when Saddam was toppled. It was a disparate grouping of Kurds, Shiite clerics, and even a few Baathists opposed to Saddam and others.

As an opposition leader, Chalabi had no constituency on a grassroots level but had contacts in rarified circles of power and a savvy grasp of Western media and politics. He became a coordinator of a grand-sounding group called the International Committee for a Free Iraq, through which he signed up dignitaries from around the world. It provides one of the first insights into his burgeoning mastery in assembling coalitions. Patrons included Peter Galbraith's boss, Democratic Senator Claiborne Pell, head of the Foreign Relations Committee, as well as Senator John McCain, freshly battered by his role as a member of the Keating Five (the group of senators who supported Charles Keating, head of Lincoln Savings and Loan, which had destroyed so

---

*Dilip Hiro, author of several books on the Iran–Iraq War and regional politics, at the time spelled out the problem: "The opposition is so divided and so disparate that I can't see them getting their act together. The best way of ensuring stability is to keep Iraq in one piece, chastened but run by one strong personality."

many investors). Ann Clwyd, a left-wing English Parliamentarian who would form a tight bond with Chalabi, was also on board. So was Bernard Lewis, the Princeton professor whose devastating critiques of Islamic culture became so important to influential American thinkers. Albert Wohlstetter was on the list, as was the Reagan-era military strategist Richard Perle. The goal of the International Committee for a Free Iraq was at first to ensure that, once the United States tossed Saddam's troops from Kuwait, as it surely would, America's military forces would go on to pursue Saddam and "liberate" Iraq.[4]

They were bitterly disappointed. The ground war in Kuwait lasted 100 hours and left Saddam's forces humiliated. In February 1991 President Bush and Defense Secretary Dick Cheney decided to leave Saddam in power after ousting him from Kuwait. Cheney himself negotiated a secret Status of Forces Agreement with Kuwait that would keep soldiers on the emirate's sand as a bulwark against Saddam. Kuwait would have to pay the United States for its continued defense against its neighbor.

Bush Sr.'s decision to leave Saddam in place came as cynical news to human rights activists, aggrieved Shiites and Kurds, and of course Chalabi and his allies too. Bush would famously explain his decision in a book with his National Security Adviser, Brent Scowcroft: "We would have been forced to occupy Baghdad and, in effect, rule Iraq. The coalition would instantly have collapsed, the Arabs deserting it in anger and other allies pulling out as well." The insights were extraordinary, seen in later light. "Had we gone the invasion route, the U.S. could conceivably still be an occupying power in a bitterly hostile land. It would have been a dramatically different—and perhaps barren—outcome."

But while he slammed the brakes on a U.S. ground invasion of Iraq and all that would entail, President Bush wanted a revolt or coup to finish off Saddam. On February 15, even before the short ground war, Bush issued what seemed like a call on Iraqis in their own country to revolt against Saddam. "There's another way for the bloodshed to stop, and this is for the Iraqi military and the Iraqi people to take matters into their own hands and force Saddam Hussein, the dictator, to step aside."

The Shiites and the Kurds apparently took that message as a call to arms. But when the southern Shiites did "take matters into their own hands," they were crushed like insects by Saddam's forces, and the United States let it happen. On March 12, 1991, Chalabi managed to place an op-ed in the *Washington Post*, where his friend Jim Hoagland was a columnist. It was called "Democracy for Iraq." Chalabi railed against the hypocrisy of the U.S. government, which was allowing Saddam not just to stay in power but to slaughter Shiite insurgents. "De facto," he wrote, "the United States, covered by the fig leaf of non-interference in Iraqi affairs, is waiting for Saddam to butcher the insurgents in the hope that he can be overthrown later by a suitable officer." (That "fig leaf" zinger drew attention. Even Noam Chomsky, the leftist analyst who coincidentally was friendly with Chalabi's intellectual mentor, Warren Ambrose, once quoted it in a paper.)

Chalabi's bitter accusations were not unique or even consequential in the deluge of condemnation. Saddam's crushing of the rebellion— gruesome and gory mass murder—continued in Iraq as the United States just watched. Saddam used Soviet-made helicopters to gun down rebels gathering in the southern deserts and in the streets. Politicians on both sides of the aisle pressured the Republican administration: "I think the U.S. should support the U.N. to take a more active role in preventing Saddam Hussein's army from slaughtering the people of Iraq," said Republican Senator Alfonse D'Amato.[5] "I don't think it's right for us to stand by and do nothing," said then-Senator Al Gore, Democrat of Tennessee, "while the Kurds and others who oppose Saddam Hussein are being slaughtered."[6]

In April, President Bush finally announced support for the Kurds and for safe zones in northern Iraq. The Kurds came under the wing of U.S. military protection, which had been denied the Shiites during their slaughter.

A CIA officer who worked for the Near East Division at the time says that's when the agency was tasked with coming up with a plan for Saddam Hussein's overthrow. The CIA was to do what America's generals had not. The order came from the White House. Under pressure from the media and Congress but unwilling to send U.S. forces into Iraq again, in the spring of 1991 President George H.W. Bush signed a "finding," a massive document in a thick binder, authorizing covert operations against Saddam. From the start the CIA was nervous. Just as it was signed, the agency assigned Frank Anderson to be chief of the Near East Division. "I don't like it!" he scrawled over the document when he looked it over at a classified conference with other CIA brass.

"You don't have to like it," he was told. The Central Intelligence Agency was serious about this operation, preparing to spend money. The budget was a hefty $38 million.

10

Recruitment

1991

IN THE SPRING OF 1991, an unsolicited phone call changed Ahmad Chalabi's life. The call came to his private line in the expansive London apartment he had inherited from his parents after he fled Jordan. It was elegant, and a sharp contrast from his office at Card Tech. The Chalabi residence overlooks the well-tended eighteenth-century Mount Street Gardens, which comes into verdant bloom at that time of year. The voice at the other end of the line was an American who introduced himself politely, with a crisp and confident New England accent. "I'm with the U.S. government," the caller said. The voice belonged to Whitley Bruner, the officer at the Central Intelligence Agency who was then dealing with Iraqi exile affairs. He sometimes used the alias Bill Ryder when he dealt with exiles. Bruner had worked in operations in the Mideast for more than two decades, including a stint in Baghdad before Iraq invaded Kuwait.

Why didn't Bruner come over to Chalabi's flat, Chalabi suggested. It was right near the embassy, and they could meet in person. So on May 11, 1991, a date Chalabi would remember for a decade, Whitley Bruner strolled out of the U.S. Embassy on Grosvenor Square, a hideous five-story fortresslike structure set amid the quaint Mayfair architecture and cobblestone, to meet with him. The five-minute walk to Ahmad Chalabi's flat from the U.S. Embassy became a well-trod path for the CIA, at least for a few years. Bruner walked past the Audley Pub, past Purdey's Gun and Rifle. Just past the Counter Spy Shop—which sold surreptitious bugging devices to amateur spies—Bruner would have made a left to cut through the Mount Street Gardens: the quickest way to Chalabi's elegant terra cotta brick apartment complex.

When he arrived at Chalabi's flat, Bruner had the impression that Chalabi was wary. Chalabi seemed "guarded, cautious"—a gracious but somewhat careful host. Bruner told Chalabi the plan, a grand vision for an Iraqi opposition to put pressure on Saddam Hussein. Chalabi was not to be the leader of a new Iraqi opposition group; rather, he was supposed to be like an office manager. He would handle the administration, the organizing, the nuts and bolts of anti-Saddam advocacy and behind-the-scenes strategizing. "What we needed was a manager," Bruner explained. "We needed somebody who could do PR, somebody who could handle the contacts, to do the cajoling and kind of run the thing." Bruner says he is not sure if he specified at that time who the Americans wanted as the leader of this brave new group of Iraqis, but the plan was to choose Muhammad Bahr al-Ulum, a Shiite cleric; Hassan Naqib, a Sunni living in Syria; and Masoud Barzani, the Kurdish leader. Chalabi, in that first meeting, acted intrigued but noncommittal.

Chalabi's reserve during that meeting with Bruner was uncharacteristic. Perhaps he so despised the CIA that he hesitated to work with the agency. After all, he considered it in part responsible for the Baath Party's rise in Iraq.[7] He believed it had helped Saddam during the war against Iran, funneling money and intelligence to the Iraqi dictator.

Or maybe Chalabi was just surprised that the CIA was reaching out to him and uncertain of its motives. In January, as the widely distributed newspaper *An Nahar* in Lebanon described, a Beirut judge had issued an arrest warrant for Jawad Chalabi, Ahmad's brother.[8] The investigation into the disastrous collapse of MEBCO in Lebanon and Switzerland was well under way. Jawad was hardly the only one who had to worry about an arrest warrant. That year, the government of Jordan requested Interpol's help in detaining Ahmad Chalabi himself; Interpol seemingly shadowed him wherever he went. Luckily, most countries didn't always honor such warrants, especially requests like Jordan's, which had been issued under martial law. Certainly Britain had no interest in extraditing him to Jordan on the Petra Bank case. Britain was a bit of a haven. Still, a warrant was more than an embarrassment for him. Technically, it meant he was a fugitive. And it would have made travel difficult. Visas were harder to obtain, and at that point he was still traveling on a Lebanese passport, not a British one.

Meanwhile, lawsuits were stacking up around the world. In Hong Kong, Switzerland, New York, Vienna, Greece, Jordan, Lebanon, Washington, and London, the lawyers crawled all over the carcass of the Chalabi banking empire.

Whatever the reason for his apparent initial reserve at the meeting with Whitley Bruner, Ahmad Chalabi invited the CIA officer to lunch, as Bruner recalls, either that day or the next. The two ate at an Italian place nearby, and Chalabi now seemed more at ease. He complimented Bruner on his expertise in the Middle East. Chalabi, when he eats, usually tucks his napkin into his collar to protect his shirt and is, all in all, an entertaining companion. The two men sealed the deal: Ahmad Chalabi and the CIA would work together. As Bruner remembers it, Chalabi insisted on settling the tab for lunch.

Shortly after that, according to former CIA officers familiar with Langley's files, Ahmad Chalabi received a visit from his new American friends at his office at Card Tech in Knightsbridge. Whitley Bruner's approach to Chalabi had just been the pickup line, but the real dance between Chalabi and the CIA would start with this guest to his somewhat shabby office. For this would be the first time Chalabi would taste the financial generosity of the U.S. government. Would the United States put its money where its mouth was?

Chalabi's visitor, according to people familiar with the CIA files, was Linda Flohr, a forty-four-year-old CIA officer, a veteran of the Counter Terrorism Center, the Panama invasion, and other covert operations. Considered attractive, she dressed conservatively, almost prim in her appearance. She was considered one of the best facilitators at the CIA, able to work her way through the agency's legendary piles of paperwork and forms with ease. When covert bosses wanted to file for "presidential findings" to get approval to run a classified operation, they often went to her first to get a sense of how to apply. If she had worked at a nonprofit, she would have been the one helping people figure out how to apply for grants. At the CIA, her specialty was "political action."

That first financial meeting involving Flohr and Chalabi sounds almost like a bargaining session. Those familiar with the CIA's files on the matter say that Chalabi was cordial while Flohr was cautious. In the end, the meeting came down to money, and the two sat politely negotiating, as if over a rug or house redecoration. The CIA was offering $50,000 as a test run to have him show what he could get done in Iraq. The issue wasn't price, though; it was accountability: Ahmad Chalabi said he would sign no receipts for his work on behalf of the CIA. On this he would not waiver. Nothing stays secret in America, he argued at one point. Arabs, he claimed at another point, did not sign receipts. No doubt he did not want his signature on file in some CIA vault deep underground in Langley, Virginia. Clearly Chalabi wanted the money, and clearly the CIA wanted to pay him. In the end, they settled their differences. People familiar with the CIA's files say that money would be wired to an account. Chalabi's bank would send confirmation that the payment was received. In this way, the CIA could satisfy its accounting requirements, and Chalabi would not have put anything to paper. As someone once wrote, once two people have decided to go to bed together, it doesn't much matter what they say over dinner.

The $50,000 was a test run, really. For a man who had dealt with hundreds of millions, it was a spoonful. But it came at a time when he was needy, and it was the first time that he tasted U.S. funds. It seems to have made a deep impression on him. The story of Chalabi's life, for well over a decade following that meeting, is largely the story of his relentless and almost obsessive pursuit of U.S. taxpayer funding.

Although Chalabi became an agent of influence for the CIA, he never entirely worked in their service. "Agent" is a technical term for the CIA, and it usually requires a polygraph. A real CIA agent is someone the CIA completely controls, and with Ahmad Chalabi that never happened, as the agency began to realize much too late. Back then, from Chalabi's standpoint, the money was just part of it: the CIA also helped him out by fixing his "Interpol problem." The first time CIA officials wanted to bring their fresh new find to Washington, D.C., they realized they would have a problem. The Jordanian government had petitioned Interpol to put a "red notice" out for Chalabi. It was a strange irony that Ahmad Chalabi, at the beginning of his relationship with the U.S. government, was having visa problems.

At the State Department under then-Secretary James Baker III, there was a dry and competent diplomat named David Mack, who oversaw Near Eastern Affairs. "One of my CIA contacts," he said, "told me that there was a guy who wanted to come to Washington and meet with me, but he was having some troubles getting a visa." The problem, Mack recalled, was that, since Chalabi had a Lebanese passport, not a British one, he wouldn't be approved for a visa with the Interpol warrant over his head, even if the United States had no intention of actually helping Jordan take him into custody.

Mack said he called over to the Justice Department for advice and then arranged a waiver for Chalabi. The CIA, meanwhile, worked on another track, negotiating the issue with Interpol and Jordan on his behalf. "We worked out a compromise," said one case officer who was involved, "so the warrant was suspended."

Chalabi was escorted into the massive State Department building in Foggy Bottom, a maze where colored marks on the walls were used to help guide visitors through the endless hallways. When Mack met him, "he came in with an agency handler—proper tradecraft was used—but I met with him alone, and then they asked me for his assessment, which was very positive. I thought he was the kind of person we could deal with."

It was an important stamp of approval, because whatever the covert operatives were doing at Langley, Mack was to be the overt face of the liaison with the Iraqi opposition. "I was coordinating with the CIA, but I never let on to Ahmad that I knew he was on salary to the CIA," he said.

Bureaucratic envy meant that other parts of the U.S. government wanted to dip their spoons in the soup, Mack recalled. One man who seemed intrigued at the Pentagon was the civilian head of the defense policy, an academic named Paul Wolfowitz. "Wolfowitz wanted to meet with these guys, but he didn't," Mack said. "I was the only person who was meeting with Iraqi oppositions groups." Mack is confident of this, but that does not mean he is entirely correct, because even back then Wolfowitz was certainly close to various friends of Ahmad Chalabi.

And the CIA Iraqi Operations Group did make sure to give a briefing to Wolfowitz. He was extremely receptive to the plans, back in 1991, according to someone who was there. But he was warned by the CIA that this was just to pressure Saddam. He was told specifically, according to the source, that if the plans ever called for actually removing Saddam Hussein, the U.S. government would have to provide military support, not just covert operations.

And Ahmad Chalabi, commuting between London and Washington, lay in wait. He was polite and helpful to the Americans. "He became the 'indispensable man,'" the CIA's Bruner said. But at the State Department, Mack, the diplomat, said the seeds of jealousy were sown in Ahmad when he was enlisted as an administrator rather than as the overt face of the opposition: "His job was to get these people to Washington and get them settled in their hotels and into their cars. One might surmise that he resented that a lot. He bided his time until he could improve his position as an Iraqi national leader."

11

Going After Jordan

1992

"He likes money. He has a lot of expenses,
both political and personal."

—Ahmad Chalabi, 1991,
discussing King Hussein of Jordan

PETRA BANK RESIDUE clung to Chalabi like a fungus even after he fled Jordan, and he took every chance he could to attack the Kingdom of Jordan. Just days before he got that propitious call from Whitley Bruner, he'd had the satisfaction of writing out a rare affidavit that would help stick it to the Jordanians who had taken over his bank, and to the depositors as well. It concerned an issue that would not go away: a lawsuit involving the *Nissilios*, that ship in Piraeus, Greece, which the Chalabis had tried to finance as a luxury cruiser in an ambitious deal gone bad.

By 1991 the ship was not at sea but at the center of a whirlpool of lawsuits in Greece, Vienna, and New York, as investors tried to recover money sucked away. In the 1989 deal Chalabi had helped Drizin raise $15 million, much of it from well-known financial institutions, by guaranteeing his loans. Drizin, the alleged American con man who had brought the Chalabi family into several high-risk business deals, claimed in turn that Chalabi and Petra Bank had "misappropriated" the money that was borrowed and had since disappeared, and never even let him have it.[9]

As a U.S. federal judge wrote about the case, "Petra Bank began to suffer large losses, apparently due to misconduct on the part of some of its officers. The Jordanian government eventually put the bank into receivership. . . . By January 1990 it had refused payment of the six notes involved in this case, which set off a chain reaction of lawsuits."

The loans reeked of fraud. And once the Jordanian government took over the bank, it did not view it as its responsibility to pay Wayne Drizin's loans, even if they were guaranteed, for whatever reason, by Chalabi. Jordan argued in court that it was not bound by Chalabi's loan guarantee and that the U.S. courts were the wrong place for the dispute anyway. If someone wanted to enforce the guarantee that Chalabi had made for Drizin, they could pursue it in Jordan, the lawyers argued.

That's where Chalabi struck back. He now had nothing whatsoever at stake, but he took the time away from his efforts on behalf of the Iraqi opposition to cause a loss to his old bank. Petra Bank, now managed by Jordan, owed the money on behalf of Drizin, he said: "I am fully familiar with the facts" involved in the Drizin transaction, he wrote in his affidavit. "But for the acts of certain parties in Jordan—which in my mind were illegal and without foundation," Petra Bank would have paid off the guarantee. He did not explain in the affidavit who Wayne Drizin was or that the Chalabi family had even once sought to have him criminally charged. Nor did Chalabi elaborate on what had become of the disastrous *Nissilios* project or where the borrowed money eventually ended up. He signed the affidavit on May 3, 1991.[10]

The lawyer who handled the case and got him to sign the affidavit was Michael Sullivan, who was taken aback when he saw in later years that Chalabi was becoming an Iraqi opposition leader. "My limited frame of reference with him was not a frame of reference that suggested statesmanship," Sullivan recalled. "He was someone involved in a significant commercial dispute that had with that commercial dispute allegations of fraud."

Later in 1991 Ahmad Chalabi struck out at the King of Jordan again, virtually slapping him to shame with the long reach of U.S. television journalists from America's biggest TV network, CBS. The story on *60 Minutes* accused King Hussein of sanctions-busting and allowing Saddam Hussein to smuggle goods into his country. Lowell Bergman, the legendary newsman portrayed later by Al Pacino in the 1999 movie *The Insider*, produced the piece. The correspondent was Steve Kroft.

"Ahmad Chalabi is a leader of the Iraqi resistance movement. Until two years ago he owned and operated the second-largest bank in Jordan," Kroft narrated, as cameras fixed on Chalabi. "Today he is a fugitive accused by the Jordanians of bank fraud and embezzling tens of millions of dollars." Chalabi, the chief on-camera source for the story, calmly leveled devastating allegations against the king and his followers.

"They are helping Iraq import all contraband goods through Jordan," he said. The camera holds tight on Chalabi's face as he talks. Occasionally a mysterious and polite half-smile barely appears, but mostly his expression is one of intense gravitas. His black hair had just a few wisps of gray.

The video shows Chalabi in the London streets in a windbreaker. He had gained a bit of weight and walked stiffly, but he did not, at that time, have that regal, straight-backed posture that would be so distinctive later on, when his ambitions to become the next leader of Iraq were well known.

King Hussein of Jordan, whose ties to the United States were famously close, had indeed made the devastating decision to embrace Saddam Hussein during the first Gulf War. He would pay the price as well. The story by *60 Minutes* was an honest effort to examine the Iraqi smuggling, but it also gave Chalabi the chance to throw in a few digs at King Hussein, with some choice sound bites. "The king always needed the money. He likes money." Then a little Mona Lisa–like smile played on Chalabi's face as he spoke. "He has a lot of expenses, both political and personal."

———

Sometimes Ahmad Chalabi would tug on his red rain jacket and pedal his bicycle over to the London office of Kroll Associates, a highly regarded private investigative firm, which hired the best snoopers in the

world. Kroll's offices, based in Leconfield House in Mayfair—the former headquarters of MI-5, Britain's domestic intelligence service—
were full of mystique back then. One of Chalabi's contributions to the
battle against Saddam was becoming a willing and unpaid source for
Kroll, which had been hired by the government of Kuwait to sort
through Saddam's ill-gotten gains—in Switzerland, France, and elsewhere. Former Kroll investigator Ambrose Carey, a master at tracking
down complex financial networks, recalled fondly that Chalabi was
"quite helpful, definitely." Carey found Chalabi entertaining and eager.
"The material provided by Chalabi was very accurate and on-the-
ball," he said.

Later on, though, Chalabi's relationship with Kroll went for a spin.
Like the Pink Panther turning around and suddenly tracking Inspector Clouseau, the tables were turned on Chalabi through a sheer quirk
of fate. Chalabi became the hunted. Ambrose Carey recalled he found
himself in a quandary when Kroll Associates was hired by creditors of
Petra Bank to track down Chalabi's assets and see what could be recovered. It was a confusing turn: Chalabi was Carey's source on one
investigation but was now supposed to be his target on another one.
"He was never a client, so technically there was no conflict of interest,"
he said, "but it was unusual. I now recall I remember thinking, 'This is
a bit odd. I can't be involved.'" So Carey recused himself from Kroll's
investigation into Chalabi's assets as they tried to unravel corporate
connections in the early 1990s, without success. Kroll apparently was
far more successful at tracking down Saddam's wealth than pinpoint-
ing any assets of Ahmad Chalabi.

━━━

To anyone burrowing through the Chalabi family records in England, Lebanon, Jordan, the United States, Hong Kong, and Switzerland looking for assets, one thing becomes quite clear: the threads
often lead to the Cayman Islands. It is an offshore haven with an unparalleled passion for secrecy. "I chased it to Switzerland, Hong
Kong, Lebanon, and I lost the trail in the Cayman Islands," said one
investigator who tried to track down the Chalabi assets to try to recover funds for his clients. "There is not a trace of it, and no one will
help you."

The Chalabis liked to incorporate in the anonymity of the Caribbean. Consider Socofi Holding, for example. There was also Levantine Holdings, owned by all the brothers, which started in Luxembourg but moved to the Cayman Islands, according to a deposition by Jawad's daughter.[11] The list goes on: HATH Finance Co., or Strategy Investment, started in 1980, and also involving Ahmad, Jawad, and other brothers, according the judicial decision from Jordan.[12] One of the holding companies involved in interests in Card Tech—Card Technology Ltd.—is incorporated there too.

One starts to see a pattern. At least five companies in the Cayman Islands have surfaced, and the secrecy of the islands means one may never know how many more there are. The problem is that it is impenetrable. These companies are all just post office boxes in that tourist and tax haven, and even the best investigators in the world can never crack open their secrets.

Indeed, it is an odd thought that the treasures of the Chalabi family, if they exist, may not be anywhere near the Middle East and nowhere near the gory chaos of Baghdad but instead near the calm blue waters, the reefs, the tranquillity of the Caribbean.

12

The Founding of the Iraqi National Congress: Audit by Burglary and Little Coffins

1991–1992

"I picked the name myself!"

—Ahmad Chalabi

WHEN THINGS WITH THE CIA started picking up in earnest in 1992, Chalabi whispered to no one in his circle where money for his operations came from. The gravy train would have stopped if he let the secret out. Instead, he said it was from a group of wealthy Iraqi businessmen who were trying to shore up the opposition to Saddam Hussein. That's what he told the intellectuals who joined his cause, the clerics, and the Kurds. The story about the anonymous donors was a weak cover. Chalabi might as well have claimed that he had won it in the lottery, because no sensible Iraqis could believe that any wealthy compatriots would shell substantial funds out to Chalabi after the collapse of Petra, MEBCO, and Socofi. With the warrant on Chalabi's head, most wealthy Iraqis would have put their money elsewhere.

So no one believed it. One early participant said he guessed it was American funding. "The verbiage of it," he said, "was that Ahmad was getting money from these wealthy Iraqi contributors." He called it "wishful thinking," since he said he had tried to raise funds from wealthy Iraqis himself and knew it was impossible. Young Nabeel Musawi, a sincere and competent young Iraqi whose father had been killed by Saddam Hussein, would go on to work with Chalabi for more than a decade. He was curious, too, about the source of the funding but figured he wouldn't question it.

Real Chalabi loyalists didn't care where the money came from. Tamara Daghistani, who was functioning as Chalabi's assistant at the time after fleeing Jordan as she was interrogated for allegedly assisting in his escape, figured there was no point in rocking the boat. "No one really knew," said Daghistani, who was closer than anyone to it. "You don't say it. And you don't think it."

But there were some grumblings, sources say, among the idealists in the group. They wanted answers. Sources say one man, longtime activist Laith Kubba, sometimes badgered Chalabi to learn where the money came from. If this was a democratic group, he insisted, they had to be open about their finances. Who were these shadowy donors, he wanted to know. Where were they? Why was it all so secret? Eventually, according to some veterans of the times, Kubba would quit over the secret source of funding. But at first it really didn't seem to matter.

═════

When did Ahmad Chalabi come to believe it was his destiny, one day, to rule Iraq? Was it during this early period, when his past as a banker lay shattered? Certainly the CIA, as it funded him, told him that was not part of the future. Whitley Bruner said the CIA insisted on that over and over: "A lot of people took the time to say to him, 'Ahmad, we are not backing you to be the next president of Iraq.' He knew!" But journalists who interviewed him back then, and intellectuals who met him, began to detect something unusual in his manner, a shift, a change. "He acted as if he were entitled to it," explained one journalist who saw him during this period. In his apartment in London, Chalabi pulled out a book tracing his family lineage and showed it to strangers, as if to underline and anchor his position in some as-yet-unknown Iraq to come.

═════

As the group built up its little opposition, Chalabi had a way of making each one of his Iraqi associates feel like they were at the center of it all. At the beginning some of the Iraqis worked out of a two-bedroom flat that they made into a headquarters, though they sometimes gathered with Chalabi at his Card Tech office. Like other émigré groups, maybe they were naïve, but at least they were idealistic and brave. While those Iraqis in London worked out of passion and sincerity, they were unaware that they were also pawns in an operation set in motion by people they didn't even know. But to the Iraqis who were most active, there was a feeling that somehow they'd been liberated from their fears of Saddam Hussein. "We threw caution to the wind," one said. They were battling "The Republic of Fear," as Kanan Makiya, one of them, had dubbed Saddam's Iraq.

And except for Ahmad Chalabi, they also didn't know, at first, that they were all being carefully tended by a specialist in these matters, an American company hired by the CIA. The American firm had made its first foray into London with some quick work by discreet London lawyers who incorporated a company called TRG UK. About a third of the shares were in the name of someone called John Walter Rendon, in Washington, D.C., while another third were owned by John Walter Rendon Sr. in New Jersey. And yet another third were held by Rendon's wife. "Political consultancy" was the business of the group, which reported about $1 million of business in 1992.

TRG in London was a subsidiary of the Rendon Group, based in Washington. The Rendon Group was no ordinary political consultant. It was a CIA contractor specializing in propaganda and public relations, and it was a central part of the CIA's operation to build up the appearance of a unified Iraqi opposition.

Back at Langley, where the bills were being paid and the real decisions were made, the CIA auditors made a stink about how much Rendon was spending. At one point, the head of the agency's Near East Division walked right into a pitched battle between the Iraq Working Group and the auditors, who complained they didn't have enough access to Rendon's books. He worked out a compromise, sources say, with Rendon: they called it "audit by burglary"—sneaking an accounting team into the office late at night when no one was there. John Rendon and his top aides, according to those involved, had a habit of flying first-class back and forth to London, and the bills were running high. When Rendon rented a set of suites at Le Crillon Hotel, the landmark property in Paris, some people at the CIA raised questions, according to a former officer in the CIA's Iraq Working Group. They were beginning to think they were being taken for a ride. The Rendon Group was insistent, however: they needed to put on a good front.

One of the early hires by Rendon was a young Pakistani British media expert, ambitious and sociable, named Zaab Sethna. He had helped Rendon run a successful PR blitz for the Kuwaiti government after Saddam's invasion of Kuwait, and so he made the shift to the CIA account with ease. A suave and intelligent man connected to London's social elite, Sethna made sure everyone knew he was a Zoroastrian, a Parsi. The ancient faith, originally from Iran, emphasizes the belief in a deity and in good and evil; the harpoon crew of Captain Ahab in *Moby-Dick* was made up of Zoroastrian Parsis and were Ahab's most dedicated followers in his pursuit of the White Whale. Sethna would become a key aide to Ahmad Chalabi over the years in his battle against Saddam, even after splitting from Rendon.

Another hire by Rendon was Francis J. Brooke, a lanky, sandy-haired American with no experience in Iraq or anywhere else internationally. A political junkie, he had been a minor Democratic Party operative in Georgia and a lobbyist for the beer industry. Just thirty years old, he shipped off to London for Rendon at a salary of $19,000 per month including expenses, according to his boasts, and quickly clashed with the head of the office, Jean Sklarz. He claimed to be a deeply religious Christian.

According to one account Brooke told to friends, he became close to Ahmad Chalabi after a propaganda stunt in London. It was staged outside the Iraqi Embassy in London on Saddam Hussein's birthday, April 28, in 1992. "Demonstrators" that rainy day tried to deliver 17,000 miniature black coffins to the Iraqi Embassy in London, each coffin said to symbolize one of Saddam's victims.[13] For public consumption, the "protest" was said to be arranged by something called the Campaign for a Free Iraq. It was, though, paid for by the Rendon Group, collecting its money from U.S. taxpayers through the CIA. One Iraqi who was there says Ahmad Chalabi's daughter Tamara Chalabi was in attendance, although Chalabi himself didn't go. A "Sara Gelabi" gave a quote to reporters, and the Iraqi says this was Hazem Chalabi's daughter. British police gently prevented the theatrical demonstrators from actually piling the coffins in front of the embassy, but the point was made.

That the American government would have sponsored such a propaganda effort right on London's streets is surprising even to veteran CIA officials. Still, as Brooke has told the story, the coffin caper greatly impressed Chalabi, who warmed to him. Brooke and Chalabi bonded in soul and purpose.

As for the name Iraqi National Congress, Ahmad Chalabi himself has insisted that he, not the CIA, invented it, in John Rendon's presence: "I picked the name myself. Rendon was there when I did it!"[14] Clearly it appears to be a play on the more famous African National Congress, which fought apartheid so successfully in the 1980s, as well as the Indian National Congress, which forced the British from India. Research indicates that the words Iraqi National Congress first appeared in the press in April 1992, in connection with a sensational wire service report that two of Saddam Hussein's opponents in the army were diagnosed with thallium poisoning and were being treated at a London hospital.[15]

The real breakthrough for Rendon and Chalabi came in 1992, sources say, when the CIA bosses back at Langley were getting grumpy about the results of what the group had been spending. Agency operators told Rendon and Chalabi they wanted something concrete done, more than just tiny coffins and shows. They wanted to see the Iraqi opposition united, as they had been discussing from the beginning.

So Chalabi and the Rendon Group decided to convene a gathering of all Iraqi opposition leaders brave enough to come and denounce Saddam. It would be held on neutral ground, in Vienna, Austria. Anyone who fought Saddam and wanted to come would be able to attend, all expenses paid. "I don't think it's unfair," recalled one CIA officer, "to say the Vienna conference was really the result of our pressure on them."

From the beginning, Ahmad Chalabi controlled the cash for the Vienna conference, and he controlled the agenda. He assigned Tamara Daghistani to help out. She'd find out how much the travel agent needed, and Chalabi would write out the checks. "I had an airline booking agency that we used," Daghistani said, "and every single ticket was through this airline and through myself. I was billing Dr. Chalabi himself. I just gave the bills to Dr. Chalabi. And he would give me the money."

In June, when the conference finally took place, it was like a long-awaited wedding, and Ahmad Chalabi watched it all unfold. He seemed unusually quiet, witnesses said. He played the role of the subdued host, and everyone was quite aware that he had funded it. It was his party, one could say, so he didn't need to do the entertaining. "Chalabi didn't say anything," one Kurd who saw the meeting recalled. "He evaluated everyone. Found out who was who. Who was useful. Who was useless."

Chalabi had always been the most political of his brothers, with the exception of Hassan. And here, Hassan got a chance to shine. Hassan, the brilliant blind professor, was one of the few family members who had not been tainted by the scandal that brought the banking empire down and tarnished the Chalabi name.

Hassan lectured the assembly, drawing on the authority of his law background. He told them they could install a representative, elected organization in Kurdistan, protected by the West. This was directly in contradiction with the U.S. government's stated intentions, but he said it anyway. One can only wonder if Chalabi confided in his blind brother that this gathering itself was part of an American operation.[16]

———

Within a few months, in the fall of 1992, Ahmad Chalabi was already pushing for another, wider conference. This time, the chosen site was in Kurdish-held Iraq, now under the protection of U.S. warplanes. Northern Iraq was autonomous and off-limits for Saddam Hussein, but it was still Iraqi territory. It would be a symbolic challenge to Saddam, a sign of his impotence. It was also the territory of Mustafa Barzani, the Kurdish leader Chalabi had met back in the 1960s and whose father he had once known. Barzani tried to help Chalabi out, Kurds say, and gave him an aide, a well-educated youngster. The kid spoke English and Arabic, which Chalabi spoke, as well as Kurdish and Farsi, which Chalabi did not.

Chalabi quickly invested vast authority in the young man. His name was Aras Habib Kareem, and he would later claim that he managed to get together 400 cars for the convention at a moment's notice. He was a Shiite Kurd who had by various accounts spent a significant amount of time in Iran and had close ties to that country.

He would in time become one of Chalabi's chief operatives, one of his only longtime Iraqi aides. He would, in a way, become Chalabi's enforcer, his head of operations, his chief of intelligence and security and money. "He was completely loyal to Chalabi," recalled one Iraqi who worked with them in those early days. "And Chalabi taught him." Chalabi would be the brains, the voice, and the inspiration; Habib was the muscle, nerve, and sinew. It was a partnership that came to be crucial.

Once again, for the Kurdish conference, Chalabi handed his old loyalist Tamara Daghistani the mission, and she pushed ahead like a bulldog. The hotel in Salahaddin was ratty, the toilets a vision of hell. She bought sheets at the local bazaar, trying to purchase all the fresh supplies that she could. "Aras used to give me bags, trash bags full of money," she says. "And this whole bag would be worth less than a hundred dollars. He'd give me a garbage bag full of money and I'd go down and do my shopping—my shopping being a mop and bucket . . . toilet cleaners. And I was literally sitting there scrubbing. I got a whole band of people, and we had sponges and everything, and we were just sponging and scrubbing and cleaning walls. I was just trying to finish in time." By October, when they finally held the conference in Kurdistan, Chalabi's team had made the location presentable. This time they felt they had achieved legitimacy. They were also achieving something different.

Chalabi now had the nucleus of a team that would last him a long time, a diverse group of young men, all extraordinarily loyal to him, all clever and determined with their uniting purpose: Aras Habib Kareem, Nabeel Musawi, Francis Brooke, and Zaab Sethna. They would be the mainstay of his inner circle as he plotted his future: a Kurdish Shiite, an Arab Shiite, an American Christian, and a Zoroastrian—an eclectic but effective crew. For Chalabi was moving away from the more modest and pragmatic vision of the CIA. In fact, fundamental to this new mission of Chalabi's was this proclamation announced in his Kurdistan conference: "The INC endeavors to become the nucleus of an actual provisional government that will extend its authority over parts of the territory of Iraq and seek to expand it to cover all the territory of Iraq and to overthrow Saddam Hussein and his regime."

That was well beyond what the CIA had planned for. The CIA was about to lose control of Chalabi. Mack, at the State Department, said that the dynamic had shifted: "Instead of him being dependent on the CIA, the CIA became dependent on him."

13

IBC Communications: The Funding

1992

"His business lines are completely insulated.
But depending on what he's doing with the
U.S. government, his assets swell incrementally."

—An ex-CIA official discussing
Chalabi corporate interests in the early 1990s

CHALABI'S FAMILY IS INSISTENT that Card Tech, the family business where he held an office, never received any of the CIA funding that was sloshing in during the 1990s. But if Card Tech had no funding from the CIA, another corporation Chalabi founded apparently did. It was called IBC Communications, as in Iraqi Broadcasting Company. IBC is of vital importance in understanding the Iraqi National Congress because the INC was all about money to fund an Iraqi opposition. The problem was that the INC did not actually exist as an incorporated entity anywhere back then, or ever. It could not write checks, rent property, hire people, or own bank accounts. The CIA needed a way to get Chalabi his $4 million per year. And so, according to various sources, Chalabi's IBC Communications was founded in January 1992 as a for-profit company.

Corporate records in England show that IBC was owned fifty-fifty by Chalabi and a relative of his. A director was Ali Sarraf, who had worked for Chalabi in Petra Bank and had spent time in Jordanian custody after Chalabi fled the country. In London, using IBC Communications, Chalabi gradually built himself a radio station for the Iraqi National Congress. He owned it, and he controlled it. Renting spaces over in Acton on Barlby Road, the station could feed through Europe and then on into Kurdistan. And the best part, sources say, was that it was funded directly by the CIA as well. It was not lavish, but it was state of the art—with a sound booth and facilities for callers. It would become known as Radio Hurria—Radio Freedom. It was supposed to pipe anti-Saddam broadcasts into Iraq, feeding propaganda that might not bring the regime down but would at least embarrass it.

But IBC Communications was far more than this; it was, sources say, the legal front through which the Central Intelligence Agency poured money into Chalabi's operations. A CIA official who worked in the Iraqi Operations Group confirms this, cautioning, however, that not all the funding went through IBC. Nabeel Musawi, the young man who would later become Chalabi's close aide and confidant, also confirms it. A descendant of a family with strong Shiite roots, Musawi has a dashing air about him, and so one journalist dubbed him Nabeel Flynn, as in Errol Flynn.

"IBC Communications is the key," explained Musawi in a recent interview, recalling the early days of the INC. "All the money went through the IBC Communications. The INC could not register as a political party and collect covert funding, so the London end was all IBC Communications." It is not possible to confirm this with the IBC's public records, because the company reports assets of about 115,000 pounds in 1994, but not its actual revenue. Yet there is no reason to doubt Musawi, who was in the inner circle of the INC, or to doubt the CIA officials who were involved.

And if they are right, this financing gimmick means IBC was basically laundering the CIA's funding of the Iraqi National Congress, concealing the agency's involvement. IBC was for all intents and purposes the front company. And so not only did Ahmad Chalabi control the Iraqi National Congress; he controlled the avenue through which it received the CIA funding. He was indeed indispensable, because if some upstart rivals in the Iraqi opposition tried to remove him from the INC, they would not be able to touch IBC Communications.

14

Conviction

1992

ON APRIL 9, 1992, a panel of military judges in Jordan issued a 223-page judgment that weighed two and a half pounds and transformed Ahmad Chalabi from a simple fugitive to a convicted fugitive. As may be expected in the Middle East, the document begins with the simple words, "In the Name of God, Most Merciful, Most Compassionate." Then, in lint-dry language, the document devolves into descriptions of knots of financial fraud that the judges did their best to untangle. The court had been convened under Jordan's martial law after the bank's collapse.

Seventy-two financial deals at the heart of Petra Bank's operations stretched like routes on a *National Geographic* world map, whizzing through Poland, Sudan, the Cayman Islands, London, Washington, and Geneva. Two dozen witnesses had testified over a period of months at hearings that had started that year. While nineteen defendants in the case showed up for the trial and the hearings, Ahmad Chalabi and eighteen others never returned to face the charges. Chalabi and his family didn't even send a lawyer to argue about the court's jurisdiction.

The judges wrote of a web of banks "connected in one way or another with the Al-Chalabi family, serving his interests and those of his family." And the court noted Chalabi's extraordinary way with people. "The accused no. 1," the judges wrote, "has been assisted by his pervading influence, sharpness, immense influence and dominating personality." The judges found that Chalabi's personality "led his subordinates at the bank . . . to believe that he is a symbol of probity and integrity, dedicating his life for the interest of the bank. It never occurred to them, even remotely, that he is committing any wrongdoing."[17]

For investigators, much of Petra's operations were impenetrable secrets. Chalabi issued many of his orders verbally and kept the paper trail to a minimum. He used secret codes to run his bank: "a special system for telegraphic codes and PINS." (His followers say that he did this to protect Iraqi depositors fearful of discovery.)

Much of the case against Chalabi involved inside deals for his family members. He was accused of embezzlement because various Chalabi family enterprises were enriched at the expense of depositors at Petra Bank. In one such example, the Chalabi brothers allegedly siphoned money out of Petra and into other family businesses through a company called Abhara. The way it worked was not complex: Petra Bank allegedly backed loans to Abhara from other Chalabi family concerns in an incestuous game of financial musical chairs. In one case, the Chalabi's Swiss bank lent $10 million to Abhara, on December 30, 1987. Then Petra Bank guaranteed the loan. When the loans didn't get paid back, Ahmad Chalabi's depositors took the hit.[18]

Another company the Chalabis controlled was called Al Rimal, run by Chalabi's brother Hazem, according to the records, who also ran the MEBCO branch in Geneva. Again, according to the judgment, at the end of 1987, Hazem's bank in Geneva lent $10 million to Al Rimal, insured by a guarantee that Chalabi signed personally. Once again, that meant that losses would be carried by the depositors at Petra Bank, not Hazem Chalabi or MEBCO in Geneva or the Chalabi family.[19]

There is a repetitious nature to these insider dealings that make them appear almost routine for the Chalabi operations: rather garish. In a July 1988 incident Chalabi brothers at MEBCO in Geneva and Beirut asked Ahmad to guarantee $2,440,000 out of a $3 million loan. Again, there was a default, leaving Petra Bank on the hook for $2 million and leaving Chalabi family businesses as the beneficiaries.[20]

The judges also found that the sense of common identity among the Chalabi family banks was so strong that Ahmad Chalabi and his brothers barely distinguished one's assets and obligations from another's. They said that after the Chalabis' Swiss-based MEBCO Bank was taken over by Swiss authorities, Ahmad Chalabi used the assets of Petra Bank to reimburse the MEBCO clients who complained. "Out of his desire to preserve his family's reputation and integrity, the accused no. 1 agreed to pay these clients the value of their deposits out of Petra Bank's own money," the judges wrote.[21]

Another recurring allegation in the judgment in Jordan is that Chalabi cooked the Petra Bank books, virtually pulling numbers out of thin air. The prosecution alleged that the juggling act totaled $71 million, where some accounts "were unfounded, non-existent and had no record." It was all done for the purpose of "lowering overall losses and beautifying its end of year balance sheets in order to show the Bank was generating abundant profits." One defendant—the manager of the financial department—told the court that Chalabi would walk into her office and simply dictate to her the amounts of interest she should put down in a certain balance sheet.[22]

There are several instances of simple, outright embezzlement listed in the charges—where funds are misappropriated clumsily. Chalabi transferred $216,000 to the family bank in Switzerland in one case, and paid $4.7 million out of the bank's account in Washington in another.[23] In one case, the judges say, Chalabi took $3 million "through tampering with the computer system." But in the absence of real evidence and witnesses, it is hard to say what this all meant.

Some of the charges reflect somewhat exotic efforts to make money. For example: Chalabi had helped set up the Sudanese National Bank in Khartoum. Investigators alleged that, instead of passing the management profits to benefit his depositors, he transferred the earnings over to his family's Socofi company, just before it was to collapse. The judges do not explain why these profits might have belonged to Petra rather than to the Chalabis personally, and since the Chalabis boycotted the trial, their response to this finding, as to others, is unknown.

Also connected to Sudan was an ambitious scheme to buy Sudan's debt. Chalabi allegedly bought $20 million in Sudanese debt at just pennies on the dollar. Then he lost a third of Petra Bank's investment. He also bought Polish debt on the secondary market. The average bank executive would probably be called a bad businessman for a scheme like that, rather than a criminal, except that, according to the charges, Jordan's Central Bank had specifically banned banks from trading in high-risk third world debt.[24]

Other specific allegations in the judgment against Chalabi dealt with a variety of charismatic characters—flamboyant and persuasive businessmen who, like the Chalabis, have left a trail of lawsuits behind. Wayne Drizin's operations arise, although he is not mentioned by name. Taj Hajjar's financial dealings with Chalabi are in the mix as well, although he is not mentioned by name either. One man who was referred to specifically was the notorious Roger Tamraz. Tamraz, years later, earned the limelight when he tried to buy influence in the Clinton White House for a massive oil venture in the Caucuses and showed up on Al Gore's fund-raising call sheets. But back during his ventures with the Chalabis, he had already driven his first bank into liquidation. In the Petra case, the judges said his dealings with Chalabi amounted to about $7.5 million, in exchanges of deposits, shortly before Tamraz's bank went belly up. By one account Chalabi met Tamraz during the 1980s when the two were both attending peace talks between warring Lebanese factions in Geneva. Chalabi escorted Adil Osseiran, his father-in-law.

Some embezzlement charges seem somewhat unusual, and even petty. When Ahmad Chalabi's father died in March 1989, the judges found that Petra Bank, rather than Ahmad Chalabi personally, paid the cost of shipping the body to Syria from London, at the price of $35,000. That's a tawdry, cheap effort on Chalabi's part, if it is true. Once again, Chalabi offered no explanation; the incident took place while Petra was stuck in a cash crush, and the Chalabis would have been forced to dig deep.

And in some charges by prosecutors there was even a note of hysteria: charging Chalabi with trying to "control and dominate the Kingdom's currency exchange sector"—through various offshore companies he controlled, like SCF in London and Strategic Investments, of the Cayman Islands. To their credit, the judges did not accept those charges.

At the end of the day, the judges convicted Chalabi of embezzlement, complicity in embezzlement, accessory to embezzlement, breach of trust, and complicity in breach of trust. They sentenced Chalabi to "hard labor for a period of 22 years and a fine in the value of the amounts he had embezzled." The judges tallied up his embezzlement at $27,366,151, plus a variety of other thefts in other currencies. The total was $30 million.

The court acquitted most of the defendants but convicted most members of the Chalabi family. Jaafar Agha Jaafar, who worked with Chalabi at Petra and was by this time over at Card Tech, the new family concern, was convicted of a minor charge and sentenced to two years.

There is something lacking in the court's judgment throughout: a defense argument. It may be that Chalabi has some rational explanation for his family dealings. And it was after all a military court rather than a civilian one, convened while Jordan was under martial law. Military courts are traditionally treated with more skepticism than civilian courts.

But the ponderings of the judges seem to be balanced nevertheless. In some cases, where the three judges found the prosecution's case lacking, they throw the allegations out. For example, in the tenth charge—which involved lending to a company without enough collateral—the judges wrote that "the said facts do not constitute a crime of either embezzlement or breach of trust," dismissing a charge against Chalabi. The fact that they did dismiss charges on their own, and that not everyone was convicted, hints that it was not simple barrelhead justice. Moreover, Chalabi's claim that he could not return to face the charges because he would be handed to Saddam Hussein doesn't make sense, in light of what was going on in 1992. By that year, Chalabi had American support and was on the CIA payroll. King Hussein of Jordan was a close ally of the United States. Functionally King Hussein was practically on the CIA payroll too. The odds of Ahmad Chalabi being summarily handed over to Iraq in April 1992 if he agreed to face the charges were zero. It would not have happened.

There was not a word of reporting on the conviction in American newspapers, even the ones that routinely quoted him. The *New York Times*, the *Washington Post*, and even the financially oriented *Wall*

Street Journal, which had run Chalabi's op-ed pieces about Iraq, simply ignored it.

And so, on April 10, now a convicted felon, Ahmad Chalabi moved forward with his new effort: battling Saddam Hussein with the CIA's patronage.

15

Guerrilla Warrior

1993–1995

"What are they gonna say about him? What are they gonna say? That he was a wise man? That he was a kind man? That he had plans? That he had wisdom? Bullshit, man!"

—*Apocalypse Now*, photographer (Dennis Hopper)

ONE DAY, DRIVING ON the winding mountain road to Sulamaniya in the early 1990s, Mohamad al-Zobaidy turned thoughtfully to Ahmad Chalabi and asked a question. Zobaidy, a young member of a vast Iraqi tribe that included both Sunnis and Shiites, had joined the INC in 1992, impassioned against Saddam Hussein by the murder of his relatives. Did Chalabi think courage was inherited, Zobaidy asked in the car. Or is it something you develop yourself? Chalabi, dressed in Patagonia-brand fleece from America, thought it through and answered. It was both, he said. You have to inherit it from birth, but you also have to work to achieve bravery. If there was one thing that helped Ahmad Chalabi in Kurdistan, it was his evident pluck and nonchalance in the face of fire.

Clad in his American-made outerwear, Chalabi looked like a chubby camper, but he had heart and he had game. He was short and stumpy and wide-chested. And worst of all, he was unarmed, while the young Kurdish soldiers were well proportioned and dashing in their pantaloons and bandoliers. But several witnesses say they saw him walk right up the hill where a battle was in progress and shout— incomprehensibly in Arabic—to try to separate the fighters. He was waving a white flag, as if he was some sort of referee to war.

Talk of Chalabi's bravery, and the Kurds nod and raise their eyebrows. It would be one of two things, in the end, they respected about him, no matter what else Chalabi did or would do in the future. The second thing the Kurds respected about him was the American money he brought.

Chalabi had transformed himself again. He was no longer the mathematics professor in Lebanon, dressed in a casual sweater. He was no longer the Jordanian banker in a Saville Row suit or the budding political operator living a cosmopolitan life in Britain. He was something new again: after the 1992 INC conference in Salahaddin, he moved part-time to Kurdistan in 1993 to set up his INC operations there—still funded by the secret stream of CIA money. At that point the CIA agenda and Chalabi's agenda, according to American officials, were still in alignment. The reason for the move to Kurdistan was to operate an actual Iraqi opposition group right on Iraqi soil but out of reach of Saddam Hussein.

At that point, the INC was an umbrella group, bringing together disparate Iraqi opponents of Saddam Hussein. True, some of the earliest organizers had drifted away because of Chalabi's secrecy and control over funding. But the INC did exist as a kind of gathering place for quarreling groups. The Islamists, the Communists, and the Kurds all fought with one another, and Chalabi provided the tissue that connected them.

Chalabi ventured to Kurdistan to try to give his exile group some roots on the ground. And he seems to have reveled in his adventures in the mountains there. Some say it was the most fulfilled he had been since he was a college professor in Lebanon. David Hirst, the *Guardian* reporter, covered Chalabi's operations up in the north: "In Kurdistan," recalled Hirst, "he lived in an ordinary apartment, but he furnished it with local material in an interesting way. The furniture was the sort of thing you wouldn't find in any Kurdish house. He found some local craftsmen and told them to do it this way, this kind of wood. It is fairly typical of him that he would do that." A photograph of the place shows an elevated dining floor with rustic but elegant chairs.

His taste for good food never left him, either. One report written later says that, hankering for risotto from his base in Kurdistan, he sent a peshmerga fighter to "scour the countryside" until he could purchase "arborio rice" from an Iranian merchant. "Chalabi retired to his kitchen and happily stirred up a batch of gooey risotto."[25]

The CIA financed the Kurdish end of the operation in cash; IBC Communications bank accounts weren't much use in the mountains, as a former CIA officer explains the operation. IBC Communications was also established in Irbil, but the cash was delivered in various ways. Sometimes, a source says, CIA case officers lugged it in themselves. Early on, though, they sometimes used a different route: Chalabi and some aides drove toward the Kurdish border with Turkey to get ready. A CIA courier had flown to Ankara from Washington, D.C., under diplomatic cover with carry-on luggage—diplomatic pouch—stuffed with about $300,000 in cash. Then the courier flew to Diyarbakir, and then Turkish security forces escorted him on the mountain road as he headed to the northern Iraqi border. There, at the border, Ahmad Chalabi and his team made the pickup.[26] The cash was the foundation of his power in the mountains. But his efforts in Kurdistan meant that the CIA largely lost control of the $4 million a year it was giving him. Yet the CIA kept funding him, as one officer said, "just to be doing something."

The Central Intelligence Agency gave the local players colorful cryptonyms. Masoud Barzani's Kurdish Democratic Party was EWOK, like the furry alien species of friendly hunter-gatherers in *Return of the Jedi*. Iraq as a country was given a simple digraph code: DB. So in CIA cable traffic, Barzani, a short man whose feet barely touch the floor when he sits, was DB EWOK 1. But while ewoks in *Star Wars* are cute and cuddly, a lot of throats have been cut, gristle and all, in Masoud Barzani's region.

Jalal Talabani's Patriotic Union of Kurdistan (PUK), which was at war with Barzani, was given the code name YETI, as in the abominable snowman, which resembles Chewbacca, the Wookie character in *Star Wars* who plays Han Solo's sidekick. "Mam," or Uncle Jalal, was a big man in every way. He ate big meals, smoked big cigars, talked big plans, and his laugh was huge. In the arcane cable traffic between Kurdistan and Langley, Talabani was DB YETI 1. He was the counterweight to Barzani in Kurdistan, and was an impassioned enemy of Saddam Hussein.

As for Ahmad Chalabi's Iraqi National Congress, its radio cryptonym was PULSAR. Thus, DB PULSAR ONE was the designation for Ahmad Chalabi in classified cable traffic. PULSAR, consistent with the sci-fi theme, may have been selected because it is a type of dying star, or a weapon. Or, to speculate, it may have been based on a Marvel Comics character of the same name, who is made up of pure energy.[27]

Chalabi got a tremendous lift from a letter written to him personally by Al Gore, the new vice president, in August 1993. "I assure you that we will not turn our backs on the Kurds or the other Iraqi communities subjected to the repression of Saddam Hussein's regime," wrote Gore over his signature. It was an extraordinary testament to the way the CIA's original plan for Ahmad Chalabi had sprouted into something far bigger: a man on the agency's payroll, expected to be a mere facilitator, was now in direct communication with the White House.

Whatever the courts and the lawsuits said, Chalabi's legitimacy was now inscribed on White House stationery. It is not every man who is the recipient of a personal assurance from the vice president. Chalabi cherished the letter addressed to him from Gore at the White House like a pendant proving his worth, like a diploma. Gore had given him the stamp of approval. (Interestingly, Gore would not be the last U.S. vice president to meet with Chalabi; his Republican successor, eight years later, was even more supportive.) Chalabi would cite that letter from Gore and he would let others read it, and he would try to keep Gore to his word.

━━━━━━

In 1994, after Chalabi established his presence in Kurdistan, the fighting between Barzani and Talabani surged and finally exploded. What they fought over was beyond most Americans' comprehension: influence, money, smuggling routes. The Kurdish leaders made millions off the embargo-busting. Barzani was a bit more rural; he seemed like a village chieftain, dressing in a more traditional manner, an old warrior harkening back to the old ways, while Talabani had a more modern outlook. He seemed to be a forward thinker to the CIA officers who met him. The CIA was cynical: "You can rent a Kurd, but you can't buy one," one CIA officer joked unkindly, accusing the Kurds of siding where the money was. Of course it is easy to accuse someone of being treacherous once you betray them, as the CIA had done within memory to the Kurds.* To his credit, Ahmad Chalabi gamely tried to act as an arbitrator between the two Kurds. Tolerated because of his apparent influence with the Americans, he was able to negotiate between the two warlords.

Within the CIA, support for Chalabi was waning, however. Indeed, some officers despised him from the beginning. But others, just a few, became loyalists. Primary among them was the CIA officer Warren Marik, a gruff-voiced Chicago native. Marik was a twenty-year veteran of the agency who was immediately enchanted by Chalabi when they met at dinner in 1993 in a London restaurant with Linda Flohr and another case officer.

Marik was a great admirer of the spy novels of the British writer John le Carré. This, somehow, helped forge a bond between him and Chalabi. Marik dropped a reference to the author's books, and Chalabi opened up to him. "He said he loved them," Marik said. But Marik was skeptical: "May be true, may not be true," he thought to himself. Marik tested him out. "I ask a couple of loaded questions. Of course he gives me the novel back chapter and verse." Chalabi had passed Marik's little test with ease. Marik admired Chalabi's adaptive personality from

---

*And in any case, the CIA probably wasn't aware that the phrase about renting versus buying was not only plagiarized but perverted in the process. It was old Nuri as-Said, the long-dead premier of Iraq and ally of the Chalabis, who had first coined the saying. But the wily old politician, who had come to a bad end, had been referring not to Kurds at all: "You cannot buy an Arab," was what Nuri really quipped, "but you can rent one."

the first and in fact even saw him resembling a character from le Carré's fiction. "He has a self-image of what he is, and that's the way he plays the role. At that time it was émigré warrior." It was, certainly, the role he played for Marik, and it won Marik's admiration.

Politically, it was a complex time. The newly elected Clinton administration, beset by international chaos in Somalia, Rwanda, and the Balkans, was reluctant to turn up the heat in Iraq with the leftover operation it had inherited from George Bush. "They were handed a can of worms by the Republicans, and they really don't want a lot to do with it," said Marik, recalling the sentiment of the period. For a time, Marik became one of the agency's team leaders on the Chalabi case.

Although the CIA wanted Chalabi simply to stick to his assignment and keep the Iraqi opposition organized, Chalabi was more ambitious. He was pitching his overarching plan for Iraq: inciting insurgencies in the north and south, in three major cities, to choke out Saddam Hussein in Baghdad. The "Three Cities Plan" was a variant of a strategy he would push through the 1990s with zeal. The assumption behind his strategy was that, once he launched an uprising, Iraqi army units would defect en masse, joining his rebel forces. Leaving them behind to keep order, he would march forward, in a "rolling revolution." The Iraqi army would not fight but would simply shift its allegiance, unit by unit. Iraq, he said, was like a junkyard full of gasoline cans, and all one needed to do was throw in a match to get the fire started. The Iraqi army would come over to Chalabi's side, and they would take Iraq, city by city, circling Saddam in a tightening chokehold until he was left only in Baghdad.

The nature of the Chalabi "plan" is important to understand, because over the years Chalabi convinced key American players—including senators, congressmen, journalists, and analysts—that it could work. Yet Chalabi's plan was out of the question for the United States. "Morally," said one CIA supervisor familiar with the scheme, "it was a non-starter. In the view of the U.S. government, it would have been irresponsible to try to trigger popular insurrections because many thousands of people would have been slaughtered."

The real question, for those who know Chalabi, is whether he ever really believed that his scheme to launch an insurgency in Iraq would work, or whether he just wanted to lead the Americans into war. CIA officers who knew him best, even those who like him, think he knew the plan was preposterous from the beginning. His goal, they say, was always simply to rush America to war. The plan was just a means to that end. One of the former officers who knew Chalabi throughout said there is simply no doubt: "an invasion is what he always wanted." This officer, who likes Chalabi, believes that he was smart enough to know that any "rolling revolution" would have eventually meant U.S. military action. "Really," the officer disclosed recently at an interview in a Washington, D.C., bar, "it was all cover for a U.S. invasion."

———

The INC operated out of the Al Sadeer hotel, said one former INC member, and also out of an old schoolhouse. They diligently printed newsletters and ran refugee operations, and Chalabi's IBC Communications radio station piped out some programming.

It wasn't just propaganda that the INC was engaged with back then. They were involved in a mean and dirty spy game, and they were becoming important enough for Saddam's intelligence services to target. The Mukhabarat went after them, flicking away at these CIA-funded pests. There is no doubt Chalabi and his men were getting under Saddam's skin. They were not a strategic threat to Saddam's regime, and the CIA had never thought they would be. But they were a nuisance and an embarrassment because, after all, Kurdistan was Iraqi sovereign territory.

In one case, according to the insider Mohamad al-Zobaidy, two Iraqi agents, representatives of Saddam's intelligence service, died while being brutally questioned in INC custody. They had been, in turn, accused of carrying out a lethal attack against the INC, and the Kurds were allowing the INC to conduct the investigation. The low-level spy war continued. In one case, several INC men were poisoned with thallium, an ingredient in rat poison and a painful way to die. Safa al-Batat, an INC official involved in distributing their pamphlets, suddenly fell sick after drinking a Pepsi someone had given him. A doctor diagnosed him with thallium poisoning, and in an effort accompanied by worldwide media attention, Ahmad Chalabi had him flown to London for treatment.

But by now the INC had spread so far from its original mission that it was unrecognizable. Most distinctively proving this were the men in military uniforms, mostly Shiites, drilling along in high-stepping for-mations, and Kurds lent to Chalabi by the PUK. The Iraqi National Congress—DB PULSAR—built up its own tiny military wing: a force of about 1,000, according to former members. That meant Chalabi had his own army, his own militia. But it was not a "fighting force." "It was a Potemkin village," said Bob Baer, the CIA officer who was deputy chief of the Iraqi Operations Group. He said no one in the CIA trained the forces or took them seriously. Still, the Kurdish warlords allowed the little force to drill and train to the extent it did. American covert funds were undoubtedly used for the force, yet no one in the CIA had planned for the little army, budgeted for it, or trained it. There is no evidence that a single American ever approved spending a single U.S. dollar on Chalabi's army. It was unauthorized, unap-proved. And no one pulled the unwanted weeds out either, to halt this strange growth. Chalabi's INC was supposed to be handling propa-ganda, to unify the opposition, but instead it developed its own iden-tity—a CIA creation come alive.

═══

And still, Petra Bank's lawyers were close behind Chalabi, nipping at his heels with litigation even as he was playing mountain guerrilla leader in the fresh Kurdistan air. The Chalabi brothers' offshore com-pany Levantine Holdings was sued for the money invested in a million-dollar mansion in a luxurious neighborhood in Washington, D.C., in 1989. Back then, Chalabi had arranged to buy the elegant landmark from one of Petra Bank's creditors, the wealthy merchant Taj Hajjar, in an inside deal to settle Hajjar's debt to the bank. But when Chalabi paid for it, the lawsuit claimed, he used $640,000 that wasn't really his: the money was never even in his bank account but was instead in Petra Bank's own accounts. On its face it was fairly egregious, using the bank's money to buy a piece of property in a side deal with a bank debtor.

So in the summer of 1994, Chalabi turned his attention away from running his Iraqi National Congress operations in Kurdistan for a mo-ment and filed an affidavit in U.S. federal court responding to the charges. In the absence of any defense case to the various embezzle-ment charges, the old and crumbling declaration is worth examining.[28]

Chalabi acknowledged that the money he used was never actually in his name, but he claimed it belonged to the Chalabi family anyway. He claimed that his right to the funds hinged on a "family loyalist" from Iraq. The man, known to him as "Haji Badri," had "placed a sub-stantial amount of cash in trust" in Petra Bank. (Haji is an honorific for those who have made the hajj, the sacred pilgrimage to Mecca. Chalabi himself is a Haji.) Chalabi's explanation meant that the money he had spent may have appeared to belong to Petra Bank but actually belonged to Haji Badri. In his story, since Haji Badri was a proxy for the Chalabis, there was no problem.

This convoluted explanation was never subjected to rigorous de-bate, and Chalabi was never cross-examined, because in the end, the case became bogged down and a judge dismissed it. Levantine Hold-ings had by then relocated from Luxembourg to the Cayman Islands.[29]

———

In the summer of 1994, just as Chalabi was tangling in court in Wash-ington over that $640,000, he was still passionately peddling his war plan around Washington power circles, like a writer hustling his script. It was then that he met the CIA's Bob Baer, the adventurous and enthusiastic "paramilitary" officer newly assigned to the Iraq mission. As Baer remembers it, they met with John Rendon, the PR specialist, over at the Key Bridge Marriott hotel, and Chalabi enthusiastically re-peated the ideas he had already sold to Marik.

In 1995, Baer headed to northern Iraq with his team. He found Chalabi itching to launch some sort of operation. He told Baer that the Kurds were going to become embroiled in a new round of fighting against each other, a bad thing for the United States, which was pour-ing money into the north of Iraq. But Chalabi could stop it, he said. He could preempt the civil war by getting them both to attack Saddam Hussein, he promised. "The clock is running out," Chalabi argued to Baer. "What will Washington do if I organize an uprising?" he asked. He claimed he could get the Shiite religious parties to stir up trouble in the south while the Kurds attacked Saddam's army from the north. "Within twenty-four hours, Chalabi predicted, the army would revolt and join the uprising," recalled Baer.[30] Baer agreed to ask Washington if headquarters would go ahead with such a plan, and sent in repeated cables outlining the idea.

Chalabi told a dramatically different version of the story, as Andrew and Patrick Cockburn describe in their 1999 biography of Saddam Hussein: in Chalabi's version, he was not to blame for the idea. It was the CIA officer, "Bob," who came up with it all: "Bob said, 'Let's do the plan from the north and the south.'"[31] This particular scenario makes little if any sense, and Bob Baer certainly denies it.

One thing that everyone agrees on is that by happy coincidence an Iraqi general who had defected to the north, Wafiq al-Samarrai, argued he could launch a coup at the same time. Baer, eager to get things moving, continued cabling home fast for directions. What happened next has become lore inside the hallways of Langley. Baer sent cable after cable to the CIA, but they sent him nothing in response and left him dangling. Langley ignored him. "It was criminal negligence," said one top officer. "They needed adult supervision." The CIA would never have approved the plan. But the Near East Asia Division chief, who despised Chalabi, didn't even bother responding. According to authors Andrew and Patrick Cockburn, "in the best of all possible outcomes for Chalabi, an Iraqi counterattack in the North would in turn prompt U.S. military intervention."[32] This, indeed, would have been the result that Chalabi's associates believed he planned for almost since the beginning: stampeding the U.S. into war. The United States, even with President Clinton carefully at the reins, would have to react with force if Saddam Hussein went to war against these U.S. allies, against Chalabi and the Kurds. The American military, even if unwilling, would have to come to the glorious rescue, and the inertia would be ended. That, at least, was one interpretation.

The flames were turned down before the water boiled. In early March, just days before the planned incursion, an angry response arrived in the Kurdish mountains from the highest level, on Pennsylvania Avenue in Washington. National Security Adviser Tony Lake sent a coded but crystal-clear warning to Chalabi and the Kurds that they would get no U.S. support. "A) The action you have planned for this weekend has been totally compromised and B) We believe there is a high risk of failure. Any decision to proceed will be entirely on your own."[33]

Baer read it to Ahmad Chalabi, who "collapsed on the sofa." The United States would not back his play after all. "Does this mean we have to stop everything?" Chalabi, apparently wrecked by the news, said softly to Baer. Then Chalabi's swagger returned. "Fuck Lake!" he declared.[34] Theatrical he may have been, but he said he planned to move forward with "the plan" anyway. It seemed, as March 4 approached, that Ahmad Chalabi might have his day of glory. For the first time, he was sending men off to war. The mathematician, the banker, the statesman would now become a warrior.

But as it turned out, that glory was yet to elude him. The INC was rousted by one of the Kurdish leaders: Barzani. Still, Jalal Talabani of the PUK held firm. A man of passion and gusto, he sent his peshmerga down to the border, without Chalabi's aid. They fought, Baer says, but in the end the Iraqi army did not, as predicted, rise up and revolt. Instead it petered out, Chalabi's dream gone. Baer is skeptical that it would have worked no matter what. But the fact was, he says, that there was a betrayal—the CIA had ignored the very man it had hired.

━━━

Questions have always lingered about Chalabi's relations with Iranian intelligence while he was on the CIA payroll in the 1990s. Certainly he had dealings with both Iran's intelligence service and the Revolutionary Guards' Quds Force, which is charged with spreading Iran's Islamic Revolution. "It was a fact of life as far as we were concerned," said Nabeel Musawi. Still, Musawi says, "In the early part of the 1990s, our relations were pretty tense with these guys. I remember numerous occasions when we had serious clashes with them, and they would close the border for a few weeks, they would not let us enter. They would try to make our lives difficult."

Musawi confesses that the INC was probably penetrated by Iranian intelligence. "They probably had agents within the rank and file." Indeed, Musawi tells a story of derring-do that is downright bizarre: he says the INC sent a team to the south of Iraq, to the marshlands, by transiting through Iran without getting Iranian intelligence approval.

The team, he says, carried CIA communications equipment, and its mission was somehow to obtain information from southern Iraq. Instead, he says, "the Iranians killed the INC people." The Iranians were making it clear that unauthorized missions through Iran would not be tolerated. (In any case, Musawi says, one of the surviving INC team members went to Basra and was killed by Iraqi intelligence, which captured the CIA's equipment.)

Back in the early days, the CIA, some officers say, may have shut its eyes to Chalabi's Iran connection. Whitley Bruner, the CIA veteran who first recruited Chalabi, said the agency was frustrated that Chalabi seemed to be holding out on them about what he was doing in Iran. He wouldn't answer questions. "He was very evasive about talking about the simplest things about Iran. He could have given us a lot more." Bruner says much of the blame may lie with the CIA itself for not looking deeper into Chalabi's Iranian connection back then. "There was a complex set of relationships that we did not explore early on." In subsequent years, Chalabi's ties to Iranian intelligence would get even closer.

In 1995 Bob Baer saw how even when Ahmad Chalabi was on the CIA payroll, he played to the Iranians. Baer maintains that Chalabi forged a letter on U.S. National Security Council stationery, purportedly showing that Baer, under the name Robert Pope, had been dispatched to kill Saddam and asking Chalabi to give Pope "all assistance requested for his mission." Baer said Chalabi, after forging the letter, left it on his desk openly so that guests of his, some Iranian intelligence agents, could get a good look.

For his own ends, Chalabi was misleading Iranian intelligence into thinking the United States had sent a hit man against Saddam. Chalabi has denied fabricating such a message. But if Baer's story is true, and federal investigators took it seriously, it had been a complex ploy, a bold chess move. Chalabi's gambit was discovered, and it ended up ensnaring himself and Baer in a minor scandal. Baer faced a criminal investigation back in the United States for the forged message by Chalabi.

Once again, Chalabi blamed Baer for the whole thing. "Bob came to me and said, 'I have a message for the Iranians from the White House: "The United States would not object to Iran joining in the fight against Saddam Hussein."'" So in Chalabi's version of the story he didn't want to tell the Iranians anything like that. It wasn't his idea at all, he claimed. "I said, 'I can't do that,'" he told the Cockburns. "But Bob insisted."[35]

Whoever's fault it was, the CIA sent a message to Chalabi—PULSAR ONE—after this Iranian mess and the aborted "uprising" of 1995. "To eliminate any possible ambiguity," the cable read, "the U.S. government has not sought through you or any other channel to pass a message to the government of Iran on this matter."[36]

Soon after, Chalabi began to face a lot more scrutiny from his paymasters at the Central Intelligence Agency.

16

Victory in Hong Kong

1995

"In reaching his conclusion, the judge accepted the evidence of Dr. Chalabi."

—High Court of Hong Kong, Court of Appeals, January 20, 1995

FOR ALL OF HIS BUREAUCRATIC wins and losses in Washington and Kurdistan in 1994, Chalabi rang in one of his most important victories far from either place. It was a triumph of his persuasive style, proof of his eloquence and ability to sway an audience. The setting was a witness stand in a courtroom in Hong Kong, in the big court complex off bustling Queensway Road. A judge in black robes and a white wig presided. This was a victory in business, not Iraq, and the amount at stake was invigorating for the Chalabis. Sources say it was $19 million.

This case concerned the mess left behind by the flamboyant Taj Hajjar, the Jordanian businessman and arms dealer who had been so close to Ahmad Chalabi for a time. Hajjar, who dealt all over the world, arranged the sale of power-generating equipment to the Chinese government in the 1980s. One document indicates it was a nuclear power plant.

Legal records show Hajjar was on the skids and was trying to stay ahead of his other creditors, like a gambler avoiding his bookie. So

Chalabi had helped him out. Chalabi and Hajjar structured the Chinese payments so they went "irrevocably" through Petra Bank. The total amount due, according to a number of documents, was $19 million. The Chalabis had an interest in it all, apparently becoming Hajjar's partners rather than just his creditors. Their investment in the Hajjar operation came through one of the family's offshore companies in the Cayman Islands, HATH Finance Co. HATH, in turn, is listed as one of the owners of a Hong Kong firm called UTG Investments (Far East) Limited, which was the vehicle through which Hajjar arranged the business with the Chinese government.

Once Petra Bank and the Chalabi businesses collapsed, Petra's new managers, representing the depositors and the government of Jordan, wanted to salvage what they could from the bank's ruins. But after Chalabi was ousted from the bank, the Chalabi family decided they would try to recover the money through HATH Finance. And they convinced a judge that the money belonged to their company, not Petra Bank.

The crux of the matter was the meaning of the word "irrevocable"—whether Petra's "irrevocable" rights could be revoked. When Chalabi got on the stand, it clinched the case. The judge believed him and revoked the irrevocable. Petra lost and the Chalabis won. It revived the Chalabi family tremendously, and it came at a fortuitous moment for Chalabi: he was about to lose the funding of the CIA.

17

Tossed Out in the Cold

1996

"I'll fucking run you over."

—A CIA officer to Ahmad Chalabi, 1996

ONE NIGHT IN OCTOBER 1995, Ahmad Chalabi looked pale and upset. "He was visibly shaking," said Rick Francona, an air force officer assigned to one of the CIA teams in northern Iraq. It was the first time Francona met Chalabi. Chalabi claimed that the head of the Iranian Revolutionary Guard Council had just given him a warning, and it seems Chalabi's reputed courage had sapped away. Francona recalls that Chalabi said, "I feel threatened."

Francona never did learn who it was or how the Iranian thugs had threatened Chalabi, and in any case Chalabi quickly recovered his wits that evening, and was his normal self: an extraordinary dinner host and conversationalist. He entertained the Americans with stories about Kurds and Shiites, who was in favor and who was out. But this time his audience, including Francona and most of the intelligence officers, didn't fall under the magnetic spell of his personality.

The reason was simple: the CIA team had begun a long-due inspection of what Chalabi was actually doing with the millions of dollars in U.S. taxpayer funds. For example, he was supposed to pipe radio and

TV propaganda broadcasts into Iraq. "We were giving them money, but it just wasn't getting done," Francona says. "The radio station looked like duct tape and bailing wire. The antennas were terrible—unsatisfactory. It wasn't new, but we looked at it and said that it is unsatisfactory. We wondered where the money all went."

The INC claimed it could broadcast all the way to Baghdad. Experts say that with an FM signal it would have been extremely difficult, but using an amplitude modulation (AM) signal, bounced against the ionosphere, it should have been possible. Francona says the broadcast couldn't actually get to Baghdad because of the facility's weak antennas and low power. If it had reached Baghdad, Francona says, it wouldn't have done much good anyway, because most of the broadcasting was in Kurdish rather than Arabic.

Another officer who went on the inspection said the agency's money was being wasted. "I mean, physically there was a place, but there was no staff. Nothing on the radio. Nothing. Some old guy putting a tape in a radio for a few hours. Some bullshit stuff."

Chalabi was also supposed to be putting out newspapers, so the intelligence officer conducted a surprise site visit to the publishing facility. "There was no time for him to stage anything. I found one or two people scratching their ass doing nothing." He said the conversation proceeded thus: "'Well who are you?' 'I work here! Doing newspapers. We haven't produced a paper in ten months. We haven't been paid!'"

The officer confronted Chalabi in his office. "He just got mad that we went there. He was furious when we did that." Chalabi said he wasn't worried. A new case officer would come along.

———

Around this time the CIA began focusing its resources on an old rival of Chalabi's, Ayad Allawi, who was operating from a base in Jordan. Chalabi and Allawi seemed to compete with blasts of press releases claiming one defector or another had joined their group. There had long been a fundamental philosophical difference between the two men as well as a political one: Allawi was a Baathist, although he hated Saddam Hussein, and could recruit among former Baathists, while Chalabi insisted the Baath Party should have no future. And although both men wanted Saddam Hussein overthrown, Allawi believed it had to be a coup, while Chalabi held on to his dream of a national revolution.

It was Allawi, this time, who won over his American audience. The CIA code name for Allawi's group was PANTHER. Allawi— PANTHER ONE—was a great favorite of the agency. In 1996 the agency plotted a coup with PANTHER. It was an unmitigated disaster, a textbook case in what can go wrong in a covert direct action. It was betrayed in Baghdad: Iraqi agents even grabbed the CIA's communications gear, undetected. And in June, Iraqi security forces arrested 120 plotters, destroying the hopes of the CIA.

The leader of the coup was a former general named Muhammad Shawani who was working with Americans. Shawani's three sons were central to the plot, acting inside Iraq. After the attempted coup, the phone in Amman rang with a call from Baghdad: Saddam's agents. Rick Francona happened to be there with Shawani. The Iraqis, he says, put one of Shawani's captured sons on the line, in a cruel and final cut, to tell their father they'd been taken into custody and were about to be executed, unless he would himself travel to Baghdad.

Chalabi and his group later claimed the debacle vindicated their own strategy of an "uprising," rather than a coup, and would trumpet the defeat of their rivals in the efforts against Saddam. They would ridicule and undercut Shawani for a decade. Chalabi has even claimed he warned the CIA that the operation had been infiltrated before it happened. Indeed, in March 1996, three months before his rival's coup effort against Saddam, Chalabi was granted a final meeting with then-CIA Director John Deutch and the Near East Division chief. He has claimed he warned them, as they sat in silence, that the coup plot was fatally penetrated. Why he would have done so, if he really knew it, is not clear at all, though. The CIA's Near East Division chief later remembered no such warning at all, and there were no records indicating that Chalabi had warned them of anything, except to argue that nothing would work without his help and that he was the exile leader whom the CIA should work with, not Allawi.

The INC's own calamity came a few months later. Chalabi was in London at the time. Always famously warring with each other, Masoud Barzani and Jalal Talabani had finally reached a dead-serious confrontation. Traditionally the two had shared Irbil as a kind of joint capital, but by now Barzani's power had ebbed and Talabani's forces held the city. Barzani complained that Talabani had used the Iranians to bolster his forces. But still, the two warlords bartered, negotiated, made motions as if interested in peace. So on the very day of negotiations in London to bind the two men to a truce, Barzani dealt a master stroke to his old rival Talabani. He invited Saddam in to help him clear out the city of Irbil. Saddam obliged with an armored column residents could hear from miles away. Talabani's forces evacuated. The CIA team even fled, and some in Langley say they didn't notify headquarters at all as they took to their heels. But the Iraqi National Congress people were still at their headquarters. "The INC was an infiltrated organization with double agents," explained a Kurd who was there. The double agents apparently helped the Iraqi forces round up the INC, and more than 100 were executed. Most escaped, including Aras Habib Kareem, who made his way to safety and the Turkish border. Some hid for a few days in Irbil and then trekked up, toward Zakho on the border, terrified and convinced they had been betrayed by the United States.

Amid a publicity campaign by Chalabi and his supporters, the United States arranged a massive airlift for INC officials and other workers who had worked with the American NGOs. Thousands of Iraqis and Kurds were airlifted to Guam, and most were eventually allowed to live in the United States.

Chalabi's meager office in Kurdistan was gone, and everything was shutting down. His heyday was over. For four years he had played Talabani and Barzani against each other, and played his U.S. supporters against his Iranian ones. "He tried to manipulate everybody," said one Kurd who watched him during this period. "And that's where he went wrong—he tried to manipulate his friends. I'd love to see if he plays these games with his own family." Neither Barzani nor Talabani wanted him back, and both considered his group "extinct."[37] He was an outcast.

Worst of all, the CIA cut him off. PULSAR ONE was a thing of the past. It was a total and complete break—cold turkey. The new policy was to permit no contact with him at all, to cut him off and stitch up the wound. He was blacklisted in the agency, bad news, an untouchable. The agency had started the Iraqi National Congress, and they thought they could finish it. A CIA officer handling Iraqi operations at the time put it this way:

> The INC blurred. It was created to do two things in the beginning: gather the opposition and have a media face. That's what the plan was. And then it morphed into intelligence collection and then paramilitary activities, and then maybe some sabotage, throw that in there too. It just morphed and morphed and morphed. We cocked this up. The agency really made a mess of this whole INC stuff.

One incident in 1996 captured the bitterness. A hard-eyed CIA officer on the Iraq case, an explosives expert with years of paramilitary experience, cornered Chalabi on the street in elegant Mayfair, behind his house in the exquisite garden there, and yelled at him, as sources tell it. Years of frustration and anger had built up, and irritation at arrogant lies told in Kurdistan. "If I see you on the streets here in London and get the chance, I'll fucking run you over," he told Chalabi. Chalabi looked at him silently.

PART III

18

Rising Again: Ahmad Chalabi's Allies

1997

"Everyone has loyalties somewhere."
—Alec Guinness as Smiley in BBC's *Tinker, Tailor, Soldier, Spy*

ONE NIGHT IN FEBRUARY 1997 in Washington, the cold rain came down ferociously. At Twenty-first and R, near Dupont Circle, the townhouses are quaint and expensive, and in the night rain the sheen of the wet streets and the halo of the decorative gas lights are as dramatic as a movie set. There Ahmad Chalabi went to meet Warren Marik, whose circumstances had changed but who remained his devotee.

The depth of Marik's attachment to Chalabi is hard for those who don't know Chalabi to fathom. Some CIA officials were suspicious of Marik. Some believed he had become too close to an agent he was supposed to be running.

For two years at Langley, Marik had been kept off the "DB," or Iraq, desk, and left to push paperwork. Marik was barred by agency rules from talking to Chalabi. Still, Marik was so concerned about Chalabi's fortunes that he gathered what information he could about him, putting his ear to the rails when he could. He says he called Rend Rahim Franke, a Chalabi supporter who organized and lobbied for him in Washington, to hear the latest tidbits.

Marik finally resigned from the CIA in 1997, a year after the agency so ruthlessly cut Chalabi off. One of the first things he did was reach out to Chalabi. "I'm out!" he recalls telling the Iraqi on the phone. "Let's get together." That is what brought him out into the rain that February night in Dupont Circle. On the slick sidewalks, Chalabi, now fifty-two years old, embraced Marik. The men were soaked, as Marik tells it, so they stepped under the canopy in front of Nora's Restaurant, for shelter from the winter storm. It was a long way from the mountains of Kurdistan. Then they ran together, in the pouring rain, to the entrance to Marik's apartment. Inside they dried off, and Marik cracked open a couple of cans of soda.

Marik was depressed but started feeling better. "Everything's collapsed!" he recalled. "We were wet and cold. We had a Coke and talked about how terrible things were. It was February of '97. Nothing's going right. You know, nobody's got any money."

Nevertheless, Ahmad Chalabi was brimming with enthusiasm. As Marik put it, "He's the Energizer Bunny!" Chalabi was welcoming, flattering, enthusiastic, and exhilarated, as always. The difficulties themselves were bracing and invigorating, like walking against a strong wind. Marik says that, more than ever, Chalabi seemed like the old Soviet general in a le Carré novel, a leader trying to coax his followers along. Just as Marik had been, to a degree, abandoned by the CIA, so had Ahmad Chalabi. "Where's Vladi?" called out Marik, evoking the BBC TV series *Smiley's People*. "Where's Vladi?" Marik was never disturbed by what others saw as arrogance on Chalabi's part. "It's not arrogance exactly. It's being right!" Marik explains.

In Washington in those days President Clinton was entering his second term, while across the National Mall the Republican Congress and Senate were gearing up to investigate his campaign finances and his dalliance with Monica Lewinsky. It was a confusing time for everyone. If Ahmad Chalabi played his cards right, it would also be an opportunity. It was a time to rebuild alliances and make new ones, avenge himself against Saddam, redeem himself—and perhaps a time to strike back at the CIA.

There would be three components to his new efforts: the first was a propaganda front, a public relations campaign that involved enlisting his friends in the media; the second was a military or intelligence effort, to create a viable purpose for himself; and third was a political effort on Capitol Hill to bring key members of Congress to his side.

For Chalabi and his followers, Marik, once he left the agency, turned out to be more useful as a PR representative than as a covert operative. Operationally, Marik wasn't much use after he left the agency. Some old spies are like that: once they are out of the game, they don't want to go back in. So Marik's role in support of Chalabi would be to function as the CIA "whistleblower"—to testify to Chalabi's betrayal and the ineptness of the agency. Marik's brusque manner would underscore his credibility in the public relations battles to come.

======

One Chalabi loyalist who had become vital to his new revival campaign was Francis Brooke, the sandy-haired American political junkie from Virginia who had first started with Chalabi at the beginning of the INC with the Rendon Group in 1991. Like Chalabi, Brooke often bragged of a certain entitled heritage. "From my point of view, my life begins many hundreds of years before I was born," he has said.[1] But perhaps over the years he spent with Chalabi, he came to mimic Chalabi's claims to privilege unconsciously. Like any good public relations manager he came to believe strongly in the campaign he was paid to pitch. Brooke, a tall, somewhat stooped man with spectacles, became convinced of the nobility of Chalabi's cause in Iraq, and his zealotry was heightened by what he said were his strong religious beliefs. He claims that he saw Saddam Hussein as a demonic force: "the human satan." In 1994, Brooke had left the Rendon Group, and for two years he tried to make it back in Georgia, where he had been a Democratic political operative. But still, his thoughts returned to Chalabi.

In 1996, when Masoud Barzani invited Saddam Hussein to best Jalal Talabani, and ended the existence of the INC, Brooke felt his cause had been betrayed. "I was sick for a week," he said, "just throwing up."[2] He felt compelled to join the cause again, immersing himself in Chalabi's efforts. He moved into the Chalabi townhouse in Georgetown, which was owned through a Cayman Islands corporation, and lived there rent-free. It seems to have been a fulfilling time for him and Chalabi. The two men often lived there together, "as bachelors," Brooke described it. Later, Brooke moved his wife and children in as well.[3] He quickly became Chalabi's unregistered lobbyist; although sometimes he said he viewed himself as Chalabi's "campaign manager," he also would say, "I consider myself his *consigliere*." What is true is that the two men went to the mattresses on their new hardscrabble effort to regain relevance.

Chalabi would later confide to friends that Brooke's dedication to him was so thorough and complete that Brooke had sold his own home in the South so he could focus on the cause. With this sort of passion, Chalabi could do no less than to house him.

While Chalabi remade his old inner circle, he also forged new alliances. In December 1996, he had walked through the doors of Morton's Steakhouse in the heart of Georgetown to meet Linda Flohr, the former CIA case officer who had first offered him funds as a test five years earlier. Flohr, who was out of the service, made the introduction. The man Chalabi was meeting, sources say, was the legendary spymaster Duane "Dewey" Clarridge. Sixty-six years old, Clarridge had been a cold warrior all his life, and predictably, at the end of the cold war, his career seemed to fall apart. Clarridge had practically invented the Nicaragua Contra operation, a centerpiece of the old Reagan Doctrine of training and arming indigenous armies to fight against regimes. He was Old Agency, from a time of derring-do long past. He was a character, a stylish dresser who eschewed the conservative style of some of his peers who tried to disappear as gray men. Clarridge was a colorful character completely. In London he was a member of the Oriental Club in the West End.

Clarridge also knew Iraq and terrorism from his days at the CIA, where he had been the first director of the agency's Counterterrorism Center and had helped engineer the capture of terrorist hijacker Fawaz Yunis of the Amal militia. That's the same militia for which Ahmad Chalabi's nephew Jaafar Jalabi had once been a spokesman. Espionage can be a small world, where paths intersect in strange ways. In fact, well before Bob Baer had worked with Chalabi he had worked for Clarridge planning operations in Beirut. Clarridge even had experience in Iraq. He had flown there once to pressure Saddam, well before the Gulf War, to hand over a Palestinian terrorist: the notorious Abu Abbas, a portly Palestinian, responsible for the *Achille Lauro* hijacking, where Leon Klinghoffer, a wheelchair-bound American tourist, was murdered.

But in November 1991 the bad news hit him: Clarridge had been indicted on seven counts of perjury by an independent counsel investigating the Iran-Contra scandal. After thirteen months with his back against the wall, on Christmas Eve, in 1992, he received a pardon from President George Herbert Walker Bush, who was about to leave office.

From then on, Clarridge floundered. He got a few consultancy jobs but generally was shunned by his old friends at the agency. His notoriety itself worked against him. So he was a receptive listener when he finally met the exuberant Ahmad Chalabi at Morton's Steakhouse. "Dewey needed a cause," a friend said, "and Dewey found his cause."

Chalabi can be an extraordinary dining companion by all accounts. He will tuck his napkin into his collar to protect his shirt, and dig into his food, but he will be just as pleasant at high-end restaurants as he is at a dimly lit burger joint. As a Muslim he does not drink, but when he eats with non-Muslims he does not object if they drink whatever they like. If he gets a burger and the cook accidentally puts bacon on it, Chalabi doesn't make a scene: he discreetly plucks the bacon off and puts it aside quietly.

Chalabi and the old spy hit it off immediately, according to sources familiar with their relationship. The two became friends, with shared objectives. Chalabi flew to San Diego to Clarridge's home. Clarridge flew to London to visit Chalabi's home on South Street, in Mayfair. Outside the Oriental Club, Chalabi introduced Clarridge to Aras Habib Kareem, and these two men, who both had a bit of panache, became close as well.

As usual, Chalabi needed money. Sources say one of Clarridge's first efforts for Chalabi was to try to raise it for him. Clarridge had long-standing ties to the Taiwanese government, and the idea was apparently that Taiwan would single-handedly replace the CIA's funding. In return for this substantial investment, Taiwan could expect to benefit from oil deals in Kurdistan and favorable treatment in the event the Saddam government fell. It was an intriguing plan, although oil for cash was hardly a new concept. "They wanted oil interests in exchange for funding. Serious funding," explained Nabeel Musawi. It would have been a bold play by Taiwan, risking millions to try to topple Saddam in exchange for oil deals once Chalabi took over. Oil later in exchange for money now.

And perhaps there was, theoretically, some symmetry to the scheme. Taiwan was, in essence, a political anomaly—it was independent of Communist China and yet claimed by it. It was both recognized and ignored. It had been founded as the Kuomintang government, which was independent of the mainland. If Taiwan could be referred to as "free China," as it sometimes was, then a small enclave in Kurdistan, perhaps, could be the provisional government of a "free Iraq," run by Ahmad Chalabi and ready to destabilize.

But the Taiwan operation flopped, in the end. It was a grand idea but it was a disappointment. The Taiwanese government never ponied up any money at all. The INC believed its enemies at the State Department interfered.

Still, Dewey Clarridge proved to be a valuable friend and ally to Ahmad Chalabi, and he did him one significant favor by introducing him to a man who gave a tremendous boost to Chalabi's new lobbying campaign: the recently retired U.S. Army Gen. Wayne Downing. Once again, it was over dinner that they met, this time in the elegant dining room of the historic Hay Adams Hotel, a quiet space where the tables are set far apart from each other and the service is formal.

Chalabi's efforts were injected with credibility of a whole new order when he earned the approval of Downing, a man's man and a soldier's soldier. His father had died in combat in World War II, and he himself was a military legend. Although he was army through and through, no one would call him regimented. During the invasion of Panama, he led the team to induce Manuel Noriega's surrender, and during the Gulf War, he was in charge of a Scud-hunting team.

Downing said in an interview that as he dined with Chalabi he was impressed. Back then Chalabi struck him as an "Iraqi patriot," tolerant, honest, and sincere. Many years later, Downing revised that impression.

But in 1997, Downing and Clarridge began working on a plan tailored specifically for Ahmad Chalabi. They titled it an "Alternative Strategy for Iraq." In essence it was a variant of Chalabi's old plan for Iraq—a rolling insurgency. But this plan, instead of relying on an enclave in the north, envisioned a Shiite enclave in the south. The square-jawed General Downing had spent a quarter-century in special operations, and he had an unconventional warrior's imaginative response to problems. Downing's plan was intended to be flexible, organic, and high-intensity. The Downing Plan called for a paramilitary force to be "assembled, equipped and trained." It would be the "Liberation Army" for a "provisional government." In a detailed paper, Downing explained how "in the first 30 days of this program, a core of 300 to 500 Iraqi expatriates with military experience will be assembled in a secure training facility in the region."

The timetable was quite detailed, and one can almost feel the urgency in it: within three months, up to 3,000 more men would be assembled, while "uniforms, weapons, ammunition and equipment will be procured and assembled at the base."

These rebels would have an elite commando squad as well. "Two special units will be formed and trained: a 200-man Commando Company trained for raids, ambush and strike operations; and a 150 man/25 vehicle anti tank company armed with medium and long range anti tank missiles." In essence, the plan envisioned a tank-hunting team that would deploy out in the desert to take out Saddam Hussein's T-72s and other armor.

The U.S. government would then declare "Armor exclusion zones south and west of the Euphrates river" to give the little army some room to maneuver in southern Iraq. The "armor exclusion" meant that if Saddam launched a massed tank assault to the south, U.S. air assets, perhaps A10 tank killers or such, would splatter them. And if the tanks were dispersed and not massed in formation, the INC's elite tank-hunting teams could find them with their mobile antitank missiles.

As usual, the plan came down to funding. Indeed, "Funding" was the title for one slide in General Downing's PowerPoint presentation for senators and congressmen. That slide says: "Organization/setup/ equipment/training/political & media activities: $100–200 million in first six months; Operation of Opposition and Liberation activities for 12 months: $100–200 million." So at anywhere between $200 million and $400 million for the first year, the plan would not be cheap, but it sounded realistic and quickly became the platform of the revived Ahmad Chalabi of the late 1990s. The plan existed in part as the dream of a number of aging American cold warriors, a resurrection of the Reagan Doctrine of training indigenous fighters. Similar if not identical strategies, it could be argued, had worked, time and again, in Afghanistan against the Soviets, for example, or against the Sandinistas in Nicaragua. Chalabi here would be the Iraqi version of the Contra's Adolfo Calero or UNITA's Jonas Savimbi. The plan had an added benefit. It offered something specific to fund, not just Ahmad Chalabi but a liberation army. In Hollywood terms, the Downing Plan was a movie script, not just a treatment.

The retired General Downing would forge a relationship that lasted years with Chalabi, although much later on it collapsed. The general, a tolerant man, found Francis Brooke, Chalabi's American sidekick, disconcerting. "He's a strange dude," Downing said. "There were a couple of times I wanted to wring his neck, just shooting his mouth off about things he knew nothing about." Downing used to warn Chalabi that Brooke was a problem. "The thing I used to tell Chalabi was that Francis is a loose cannon and he better keep him under control. Because I told him I thought he did more harm than he did good."

But General Downing's advice was politely ignored. Brooke, the beer-drinking American, stayed on as a key member of the Chalabi inner circle.

While this was going on, Chalabi was persona non grata in Kurdistan. Barzani had called in Saddam Hussein, had allowed the slaughter of INC functionaries. As for Jalal Talabani, without American support, an alliance with Chalabi offered nothing. He was a liability. The Kurds had tolerated Chalabi because he brought American goodwill and cash, and now he could offer none of it.

Meanwhile, many Iraqi followers had been alienated by his closest aides. "His fatal problem," said one opposition member close to the Shiite groups, "was his inner circle." In interviews several Shiites, Sunnis, and Kurds said they felt that Chalabi had been in some way misled by the Shiite Kurd Aras Habib Kareem, whom they considered an inexperienced thug. And they were puzzled by the influence over Chalabi wielded by the non-Iraqi young men, Francis Brooke, and the British Pakistani Zaab Sethna.

So as Chalabi recruited more and more American allies in Washington, he lost his Iraqis. Ghanem Jawad, an official at an Iraqi religious foundation based in London who had worked with Chalabi since 1990, says he met with him in London to plead that he restructure the Iraqi National Congress. Chalabi, fresh from his travels to Washington, refused.

There are some hints at a bit of financial urgency—and cleverness too—at this point by those who remained in the INC. The INC had built a radio studio with CIA funds, on Barlby Road in Acton, in north London. The INC's financial alter ego in London was Chalabi's IBC Communications, the legal owner of the studio. Put another way, it was in reality a radio station owned by Chalabi but paid for with U.S. taxpayer funds, through the CIA. Without CIA funding the radio station had gone off-air, as the Chalabi newspaper, *Al Mu'tamar*, had ceased publication.

So Chalabi's people tried to turn this asset—the radio studio paid for by the American taxpayers—into a profit. There was an effort to rent out the studio, according to Saad al-Fagih, a London-based Saudi dissident, one of the few Saudis to overtly oppose the royal family of Saudi Arabia and publicly call for its overthrow. From his apartment in London, Fagih operates a small Web site and a radio station. The Saudi government claims he is an ally of Osama bin Laden, but this is true only in the sense that both men oppose the Saudi royals.

In 1997 the Saudi dissident was approached by an Iraqi National Congress official. The INC man was trying to rent out the Barlby Road radio studio, which he revealed used to be funded by the Central Intelligence Agency. "He told me that they were paid a lot of money by the CIA," Fagih said in an interview, "and all the service was paid for by the CIA. It was quite expensive. I think they wanted something like sixty thousand a year. Sixty thousand pounds, which means in the range of $110,000 a year. It wasn't a full radio station. It was just one studio. It was just one mixer and one sound booth."

It would have been a clever deal indeed if it had gone through: for a previously CIA-funded exile group to rent its facility to a separate exile group interested in overthrowing a U.S. ally. But Fagih decided against renting the space. It was just too costly, he says.

And the effort backfired badly on Chalabi's Iraqi National Congress. The Saudis were furious that the INC would even think about dealing with a Saudi dissident. The Saudi Arabian ambassador called in Nabeel Musawi, Chalabi's young loyalist, to the embassy, and laid the guilt on thick. How could the INC have even contemplated such a move? The dabbling with the Saudi opposition cost Chalabi yet another friend. "The Saudis never forgave us," Musawi said.

═══════

In June 1997 Chalabi launched his first salvo against the CIA in an ABC News documentary hosted by anchor Peter Jennings. The narrative put forward by the Chalabi movement took hold: that the CIA had betrayed him by looking for a "silver bullet" coup rather than his "uprising" plan. It was the first time the U.S. public was told in full about the CIA operations in the north of Iraq. Jennings, who had met Chalabi back in the 1970s in Beirut, unveiled the secret background, explaining Rendon Group's tens of millions and the INC's $4 million a year from the CIA.[4] On camera, Chalabi argued again that Saddam Hussein was "coup-proof." He explained the crux of his own plan, where Iraqi forces would join him in an uprising. "We always thought of ourselves not as an army to fight the Iraqi army. We thought of ourselves as a catalyst to attract Iraqi army units to join us, to defect to us, in order to sap Saddam Hussein's power and bring him down." Once again, how this "catalyst" effect was supposed to work is not explained at a detailed level; evidently Chalabi thought that just existing, projecting a presence, would lure these Iraqi military units from their side to his.

He charged, in the broadcast, that the CIA had betrayed him. The CIA, he said, had initially committed to help him with his plan. This was his chance to relay his version of the whole episode with Bob Baer, which had ended so badly. But in this account, the CIA and the Clinton administration finally betrayed the INC in 1995 by pulling away support at the last minute. "We proceeded to actually engage Saddam Hussein in battle," Chalabi told Jennings on camera with pride. He was probably referring to actions of the PUK, under Jalal Talabani, since Chalabi hadn't been near the fighting. Since Chalabi called the INC an "umbrella group," he was able to take credit for anything his constituent groups did, and technically Talabani had been under the "umbrella." Warren Marik, the former CIA officer who was another Chalabi loyalist, vouched for the operation. "For what it was, I thought it was a very effective operation," he said. To viewers, it sounded like Marik had been involved, although that was not the case.

Then, in counterpoint, ABC News explained how the CIA-funded coup against Saddam collapsed in 1996, thoroughly infiltrated by the Iraqis, who butchered the plotters. And finally the report outlined Saddam's incursion into northern Iraq. "Ahmed Allawi," an INC member, went on camera too. Ahmed Allawi is an alias of Aras Habib Kareem. He told ABC he assumed that the Americans would fight off the Iraqis. "Everybody was waiting for the American fighters. It was 6:00, 7:00, 8:00, they will come at 9:00. We are waiting for the Americans. We are waiting for their promise. And there was no answer." It was in this telling a clear betrayal and abandonment by the CIA.

It was the first wave in Chalabi's efforts to wash the past and redeem himself once more.

19

Wooing the Neocons

1997–1998

"Ahmad came, and all of a sudden, we had an angel!"

—Mey Wurmser, Hudson Institute and co-founder of MEMRI

ONE APPARENT SOURCE OF FRUSTRATION for Ahmad Chalabi was that the Mossad, Israel's intelligence service, distrusted him and refused to work with him. Without the Mossad, he could never gain the trust of the Israeli government. The Israelis had dealt with Chalabi's family in Lebanon, but that was in the old days, and that had nothing to do with Iraq. They were resolute, throughout the '90s, in refusing to help in his Iraqi endeavors. Still, he never stopped trying.

Ironically, despite the Mossad's distaste for him, he had great success in working closely with American supporters of Israel, eventually persuading them that he offered new insights into the Middle East. Ideologically, he had an extraordinary impact. His ideas were to affect people in ways no one could ever have predicted. Chalabi had known Richard Perle since 1985, and he had known Paul Wolfowitz for years as well. He had met Bernard Lewis in 1991, and was his friend and adviser. A British expatriate, Lewis was the Princeton academic who became the guru of Middle East studies, cited constantly by experts on the right. Neoconservatives readily acknowledge Chalabi's role in their strategic thinking. "Meeting him helped our intellectual juices to flow," recalled Meyrav Wurmser, the wife of David Wurmser, a Naval Intelligence reservist who would go on to write a book touting Chalabi's ideas. The Wurmsers lived in the Washington suburbs and were members of a close-knit group concerned about Israel's security and Clinton's foreign policy. Many of their names would become familiar later. They included Richard Perle, Michael Ledeen, Harold Rhode, Paul Wolfowitz, and Douglas Feith, among others.

"Ahmad Chalabi is a hundred times smarter than all of them," said Bob Baer, the former CIA officer who handled Chalabi in Iraq.

Meyrav Wurmser is a petite woman with a pleasant laugh, and she laughs often. Back when she met Chalabi, she says, she and her fellows were not very popular. "We were outcasts!" she says. They were indeed outcasts, because they were so far to the right, so hawkish on matters related to Israel. Wurmser says she and her group were even too far right for the American Israeli Public Affairs Committee (AIPAC), the most powerful pro-Israel lobby in America. "AIPAC hated us, I think," she says. "They were polite, but it was clear that there was tension in the air. We were the crazy uncle at the wedding." She laughs again. "We had an Israeli ambassador who turned against us, Ambassador Itamar Rabinowich, who basically was threatening each and every one of us that his career . . . would be hurt if he doesn't shut up."

"Look," she says, "my expertise is Palestinians, and, you know, for years I've dealt with, you know, bad Palestinian leadership." She claims she's had a lot of experience. "I've met some of them and got to know some of them. Always the little genie comes out: they are anti-Semites or they want the 'right of return' and destruction of Israel. They might act nice, but always the bad stuff comes out later."

Into this group, introduced with good credentials, stepped Ahmad Chalabi, climbing back from his calamities in Kurdistan. "He was looking for allies," recalled Wurmser thoughtfully, leaning back in her office chair at the Hudson Institute, an influential conservative think tank that produces policy papers on domestic and foreign policy issues. "He was looking for allies in Washington." Wurmser was wary when her husband mentioned Ahmad Chalabi. David Wurmser had been impressed by him after meeting him through U.S. Defense Department analyst Harold Rhode.

"I said, 'Yeah, what is it that I don't see about him? When will it come out of the bag that he's an anti-Semite or something bad?'" So when she finally met him, Mey Wurmser says she gave him the third degree, on her particular issue. "I was asking tough questions, like, attitude towards Israel: 'Are you willing to visit Israel?' Like, 'How do you feel about the Palestinians, the Palestinian question?'"

She says Chalabi passed her test, easily. "Everything he answered like he should have." Palestinians, he told her, "have rights, but they should not come at the expense of Israel. In his view Israel played an important role in the Arab world."

And in fact there is no strong evidence that Chalabi was misrepresenting his views when he wooed the neoconservatives. He was not an anti-Semite, and was no supporter of Palestinians. Shiites in Lebanon and the PLO had a combative attitude toward each other—and much of the Lebanese war reflected that. Not only that, but Chalabi would often argue that the persecution suffered by the Jews was something the Shiites could relate to. He would point to the fact that, before 1951, a large percentage of Baghdad had been Jewish. His nanny had been Jewish, he told Meyrav. He said he'd actually gone to Israel just to visit her. Indeed, his father had done business with Jewish businessmen.

Ahmad Chalabi also flattered Meyrav Wurmser. She is the cofounder of a think tank called MEMRI, which assembles and translates the most outrageous broadcasts of Saudi clerics, Iranian mullahs, and various radicals in the Middle East. It provides, in many ways, a valuable service—highlighting the strong incidents of intolerance and anti-Semitism and radicalism in the Arab world. On the negative, solely reading MEMRI could give subscribers a distorted impression of the Middle East. It depicts the most extreme forms of intolerance as the norm. It would be as if someone in the United States daily gathered the most outrageous proclamations of Pat Robertson, Louis Farrakhan, and Ann Coulter and then presented these quotes to intellectuals worldwide as representative of U.S. political thought.

Chalabi complimented Meyrav on MEMRI, lavishly. "He would keep telling me," Meyrav smiled at the recollection as she told the story, "'I read this fabulous stuff in MEMRI! I read that in MEMRI!'"

Meyrav explained that she and her husband and their friends, as they spoke about the Middle East, were absorbing a new ideology, in part inspired by Ahmad Chalabi. "Ahmad came, and all of a sudden, we had an angel! This intellectual idea that we were believing in regardless of him, all of a sudden we are like, here is the Arab democrat. See, they exist. Not all Arabs have horns. You know! God sent us this real democrat. And he meant it! He wasn't lying about his belief in democracy. Here's proof: Arabs can be democrats."

Mey Wurmser says she and her intellectual comrades were beginning to believe that if Saddam Hussein were overthrown, democracy could be brought to Iraq. It was a slight variation on a theme Ahmad Chalabi had been pushing for a long time. Through regime change, and by supporting Chalabi, the Middle East could be remade. The idea drew some of America's most powerful and influential thinkers together.

Perhaps these thinkers were looking for a man, and a message, that would give an indigenous, democratic reality to their dreams of overthrowing Arab dictatorships and installing regimes friendlier to Israel and the West. Chalabi's kind words about Israel, paired with his talk of democracy, played precisely to their desires. One man who was friendly with this group of intellectuals but says he was not part of it was Dov Zakheim (later the Pentagon comptroller under President Bush during the Iraq War). Zakheim was an ardent supporter of Israel and opponent of Iraq. But he says he could not understand his neoconservative friends' attraction to Chalabi. "I believe they were seriously misled. Although you know, when someone gets misled they may get misled because they were wishfully thinking something. It's like they want to be led in a certain direction. I mean, he was the answer to their prayers!"

It appeared that Ahmad Chalabi genuinely liked his new companions, though he was never an insider in their small group. He would eat with the Wurmsers and their neoconservative comrades in an informal dining club. Richard Perle was an extraordinary chef with a special stove. Chalabi was as always a splendid host and guest. He would show up in a van, often bringing a dozen other Iraqis, some of whom barely spoke English. By all accounts, these evenings were enjoyed immensely by their participants, who where thrilled to exchange their ideas about how to change the Middle East.

Still, Ahmad Chalabi needed more than ideological comrades at arms: he needed cold, hard cash. After the effort to raise funds from Taiwan had been unsuccessful, now there was a bold play to raise money with the help of the Israeli government, newly run by the Likud Party Prime Minister Benjamin Netanyahu.

Chalabi made a valuable ally over lunch one day during that period at Clyde's restaurant, a dark-lit burger place on Wisconsin Avenue in Washington. He sat down to lunch with two men there, at the solid oak table. One of the men was his friend and admirer Harold Rhode, the Pentagon analyst and scholar who had studied under Princeton professor Bernard Lewis. Rhode, though a U.S. government employee, thought the other man at the table might be able to help Chalabi. It was Max Singer, an intellectual warrior for Israel and ardent conservative thinker with considerable influence.

Rhode told Singer that Bernard Lewis had vouched for Chalabi. And according to the story that Singer tells, Rhode wanted Singer to meet Chalabi so Singer could help him curry favor with the Israeli government. It attests to the impressive breadth of Chalabi's allure that an American employee of the U.S. Defense Department would go to the trouble of introducing him, an Iraqi Arab, to a supporter of Israel to try to drum up the support his own government would not give.

Singer, in an interview, freely admitted that he knew little about Iraq before he met Chalabi at that lunch and that most of what he knows about it came from Chalabi. He was immediately impressed, and said his understanding of Chalabi's argument was that "the best situation was when the Turks ran Iraq." Singer had the impression that Chalabi was harkening back to the days of the Ottoman Empire.

Singer tried to explain his understanding of Chalabi's vision. Singer's voice is so deep it seems to come from some volcano in his chest. "What they came up with was the idea of a weak central government . . . democracy . . . meritocracy . . . which would have the mandate to keep the peace among the different elements of the community and leave each community to run itself. Not interfere. That's what he meant by democracy."

Chalabi won the old man over with ease. Just as Dewey Clarridge and Wayne Downing were veteran cold warriors, Max Singer was an elderly father of the conservative causes. "I worked with Herman Kahn," Max Singer now says, "who is widely recognized as a genius, and Chalabi is at the same intellectual level." Herman Kahn is an interesting comparison. Kahn is considered the model for Dr. Strangelove in the famous Stanley Kubrick movie with Peter Sellers. The intellectual father of the cold war theory of "Mutually Assured Destruction" or MAD, Kahn wrote *On Thermonuclear War* and was one of the most influential strategists to argue that nuclear wars can indeed be survived and "won." Together, Singer and Kahn co-founded the influential Hudson Institute, the conservative think tank where Meyrav Wurmser would find work.

Max Singer was so impressed by what he heard from Chalabi that he went and wrote up his interpretation of Chalabi's theories of democratic government in the Middle East. Chalabi would flatter him at how quickly he had come to grips with it. "Max got this in one lunchtime," Chalabi would say so that the old man would hear it. "It took us five years to figure it out." Singer smiled as he recalled the story.

Singer pursued friends in high places in Israel. On November 23, 1997, he wrote to two powerful men in the Israeli government on Ahmad Chalabi's behalf. One of the men was Uzi Arad, the former head of Israel's Mossad, who was currently working as a top adviser to Prime Minister Netanyahu. The other man was David Bar Ilan, Netanyahu's top spokesman.

Singer's note was an appeal. "The INC," he wrote, "would like Israel to help it" by recommending "the INC to individuals in the U.S. or elsewhere who might provide funds." In other words, if the government of Israel were to vouch for the INC, maybe they could raise some money. Singer did acknowledge in his note that "the idea of Saddam being replaced by a democratic regime sounds so crazy," but he attached an unpublished article he wrote to explain how Chalabi would do it. Chalabi, he said, "has a strong reputation for telling the truth." The article Singer attached concluded that, "If the INC comes to power in Iraq the implementation of this vision can begin a major change in the Middle East in a direction that offers great hope for the world."

Singer's pitch on behalf of Chalabi did not mention his conviction in Jordan, or his failed bank, or his family's banking troubles. Nor did it mention his years of support by the Central Intelligence Agency, the failed coup and invasion in 1995, or his subsequent expulsion from Kurdistan.

In other words, Max Singer, after meeting Ahmad Chalabi for an informal lunch, was so convinced by him that he was willing to pressure the Israeli government to help him financially, no questions asked.

Singer's plea to the Israelis got a response, although it was not the response Singer hoped for. Singer flew to Tel Aviv and was introduced by Netanyahu's office to some Mossad officials. In a restaurant, over dinner, he made his pitch to Israeli intelligence about his new friend Ahmad Chalabi. The Mossad agents were not impressed, he found.

In fact, it was a refusal. They bluntly told Singer they had dealt with Chalabi before. It was an intriguing tidbit. Things had gone sour and they had no interest in ever doing it again, they said. They would not elaborate. (It is quite clear that the Israeli government had good ties with the Chalabi family during its operations in Lebanon.) Meanwhile, the Mossad operatives told Singer they were well aware of Chalabi's criminal conviction in Jordan and the low regard in which he was held in the United States by the CIA and the State Department.

Singer was surprised to hear that the Israeli intelligence service had no interest in working with his new friend. "Military intelligence and the Mossad thought he was a bad man," Singer said, explaining his astonishment. So there in the restaurant in Tel Aviv Singer got upset at the Israeli spies and their intransigence. "I was saying that you got the wrong judgment about him. 'I'm telling you, you got the guy wrong! Look into it further!'"

But Singer says the Israeli officials would not budge. And neither would he. By this time Singer, a lifelong supporter of Israel and its security services, was so invested in his new relationship with Ahmad Chalabi that he was willing to ignore the judgment of the Mossad and Israeli military intelligence. He tried to argue with them; he told them they should reinvestigate the entire Jordanian criminal case against Chalabi and weigh the evidence themselves. They shrugged and said they didn't really care if Chalabi was a crook, but they didn't want to work with him.

In an interview, a former Mossad official and Netanyahu government adviser confirmed Max Singer's account in its entirety, and also confirmed the Mossad's take on Ahmad Chalabi. The Mossad simply wouldn't deal with him.

There is one other thing to point out about Max Singer. The elderly man and conservative activist has never taken a penny for all the work he has done for Chalabi: like so many other people, he volunteered his own time to help the wealthy Iraqi's cause.[5]

In June 1997, Chalabi gave a presentation to the Jewish Institute of National Security Affairs, a pro-Israeli think tank. Playing to his audience, he told them the first target of the Baath Party had been the Jewish community, but he didn't point out that the Iraqi Jewish community had virtually been extinguished in 1951 under the old monarchical regime of which his family had been a part. He fudged history a bit, telling his audience that "in March 1995, I led an attack on Saddam's forces in northern Iraq," although in fact he had not been near the front. He also claimed the small incident had almost led to the conquest of several cities. But Chalabi's key message was that overthrowing Saddam would be easy and require no U.S. troops. "We are prepared to fight for our country and are convinced that only an Iraqi Army can remove Saddam." He even said Saddam might have been involved in the Khobar Towers attack the year before, in Saudi Arabia, and in the 1993 World Trade Center bombing. And to emphasize how little effort it would take to overthrow Saddam, he joked that "the principal difficulty we will face is the care and feeding of the deserting Iraqi Army."

20

Frozen Assets and the Iraq Trust

"Best of all, the INC can do all this for free."

—Ahmad Chalabi's testimony to the U.S. Senate, March 1998

ONE OF CHALABI'S most interesting schemes was to try to persuade U.S. authorities to hand frozen Iraqi assets over to the INC. The notion apparently first occurred to him in 1992, which was a difficult time for him financially. Back then, exiled from Jordan and Iraq, with an Interpol warrant on his head, there were also arrest warrants out for his brother in Lebanon and an investigation in Switzerland. Friends and family members who had lost their life savings hounded him, trying to recover what they'd lost in the Chalabi Socofi investment scheme in Switzerland. But with all that, Chalabi was increasingly focusing his extraordinary mind on overthrowing Saddam Hussein and the government of Iraq. After Saddam invaded Kuwait in 1990, Western governments had frozen Iraqi assets, and in the United States and Britain, authorities sat on a treasure trove of $1.6 billion in Iraqi funds. The maddening thing was that the money was serving no useful purpose. Chalabi believed if the money were handed over to a "provisional government," they could put it toward a greater good. The concept seemed not only effective but just: using Saddam's own assets against him.[6] When would this happen, he was asked.[6] "Quite soon," he replied.[7] For a time, as his alliance with the CIA brought the cash he needed, Chalabi seemed to drop his efforts to access the frozen Iraqi funds. With the river of black U.S. money, untraceable to anyone, flowing through his account, perhaps his desire to lay his hands on the frozen assets of Saddam lost its urgency.

Even so, as time went on, Chalabi returned his attention to that cash sitting in a Federal Reserve account. His idea was this: once a provisional government, or "government in exile," was recognized internationally, there should be no legal barrier to giving that government the right to spend frozen Iraqi government funds. And with that kind of cash, a provisional government could, he argued, move quickly to overthrow Saddam Hussein.

One of the steps Chalabi took toward freeing up the money was to approach his friend Chibli Mallat. Mallat is a Lebanese human rights lawyer who met Chalabi when conducting research into one of the ayatollahs in Iraq. Mallat, too, had become consumed with the struggle to free Iraq from Saddam's rule. Mallat had worked to set up the predecessor to Chalabi's Iraqi National Congress, a group called International Committee for a Free Iraq, in 1991.

So when Chalabi approached Mallat about the frozen assets, Mallat says he thought the idea made sense. The Americans, Chalabi told him, were interested in finding a legal way to unfreeze Saddam's assets to use them for the opposition, for charity and to alleviate the suffering of Saddam's victims. Maybe, he suggested, there was a legal framework by which this could be achieved. In an interview, Mallat said he did not recall ever speaking directly with Americans about the frozen funds scheme. "What is true," he said, however, "is that in my dealing with Ahmad I don't recall having been lied to."

Mallat diligently set off to sniff out the possibilities. He consulted with British lawyers, learning the intricacies of British nonprofit law. The end result of his efforts, the creation he offered to Chalabi, was the Iraq Trust, a company incorporated on March 16, 1994. Chalabi would be the company secretary, while two other Iraqis were also brought on board: Latif Rashid, a representative of Jalal Talabani, and Muhammad Bahr al-Ulum, one of the founding figureheads of the

Iraqi National Congress and a major Shiite figure. Other directors in-cluded Chibli Mallat himself and journalist Edward Mortimer, an old-time Chalabi supporter who would later work for the United Nations.

Certainly the incorporation papers of the Iraq Trust say nothing about frozen assets. Instead they say that the purpose of the Iraq Trust is the "rehabilitation and resettlement" of Iraqi refugees.[8] Mallat, as one of the founders, and the brains behind it, says the understanding was that this charity work was to be achieved with the freed frozen Iraqi funds.[9]

It never happened. In reality, the Iraq Trust just sat there as an un-used shell, awaiting an infusion of money. Chalabi did his best to keep it alive, though. In the fall of 1995, actually at the very same time that the CIA was inspecting his operations in northern Iraq and determin-ing that he was not spending its money wisely, Chalabi was inking the documents on an Iraq Trust report.

Even after the Iraq Trust sputtered out, Chalabi did not give up on his plan to use the frozen Iraqi funds for his efforts against Saddam. Instead, as time went on, he adapted and refined it. In 1997 and 1998, thanks to his lobbying efforts in Washington, his idea for the frozen assets picked up steam among his American supporters and was one of nine recommendations appearing in an "Open Letter" to President Clinton on the subject of Iraq on February 19, 1998. The letter, which was signed by Richard Perle, Doug Feith, Paul Wolfowitz, Zalmay Khalilzad, Elliott Abrams, Peter Rodman, and others, said that Clinton should "recognize a provisional government of Iraq based on the principles and leaders of the Iraqi National Congress (INC)" and then "release frozen Iraqi assets—which amount to $1.6 billion in the United States and Britain alone—to the control of the provisional government." Their aims were transparent: what Perle and the others wanted to do was put Ahmad Chalabi in charge of a provisional gov-ernment with a budget of $1.6 billion of Iraq's money.[10]

Chalabi himself put up a spirited advocacy of the idea in testimony to the Senate in March 1998. His whole agenda could be achieved "for free," if his terms were accepted: "The funds for humanitarian, logisti-cal, and military assistance requested by the INC for the provisional government can be secured by Iraq's frozen assets, which are the property of the Iraqi people." And he provided a sophisticated adaptation of the original idea. Specifically, he said, the United States could "lend" money to the provisional government of the INC with Iraq's frozen assets as the collateral. In this way, the Iraqi government's assets would be monetized to the Iraqi opposition's benefit, without costing the U.S. taxpayer anything.

In the Senate hearing, Senator Chuck Robb was a bit incredulous. The funds were off limits, he told Chalabi. So Chalabi suggested a corollary scheme, which he seemed to have kept on hand: the United States could fund the INC operation by recognizing his "provisional government" and lending the INC money directly. After that the United States would seize Saddam Hussein's oil revenue directly to pay itself back and recover the cost of the loan. It was just the kind of creative financing Chalabi had engaged in at Petra Bank a decade earlier. This idea also went nowhere.

Chalabi's friends, such as Richard Perle and others, supported the scheme, but even other Iraqi opponents of Saddam were befuddled. "Under international law, how would you go about doing that, whether it was Saddam or anyone else? You are talking about a sovereign government!" said Faisal Istrabadi in an interview. He is a U.S.-educated lawyer and a secular opponent of Saddam who was a supporter of Adnan al-Pachachi. "It's screwy. It's bold. Whenever I put on a tie I ask my wife, 'Does this tie go with this shirt?' And if she says it's 'bold,' I need to find another tie. That was 'bold.'"

In the end the idea never worked, and there was no provisional government in any case. But as it turned out, the frozen assets weren't needed. Chalabi's lobbying on Capitol Hill was beginning to pay off in other ways.

21

Forming INDICT

"I cannot give you a guarantee of the future.
What I can tell you, measure me, judge me
as I go along. Judge us as we go along."
—Ahmad Chalabi, 1998

DURING THE DRY YEARS when no U.S. funding was coming in, Chalabi helped found INDICT, a group dedicated to exposing the war crimes committed by Saddam Hussein and his men. In January 1997, right in the British House of Commons, a Labour member of Parliament, Ann Clwyd, announced the launch of INDICT.[11] Clwyd had long been passionate about exposing Saddam's atrocities against the Kurds. Over the years, INDICT became a flower of success. The Clinton administration viewed it as a noncontroversial way to spend money on the opposition without putting it under Chalabi's control. The Democrats saw it as a legitimate way to build worldwide opposition to Saddam Hussein.

It got extraordinary traction. In the summer of 1998 Congress earmarked "not less than $3,000,000 as a grant to the Iraqi Campaign to Indict Iraqi War Criminals to be used to compile information to support the indictment of Iraqi officials for war crimes."[12]

INDICT's registered office in London was none other than Ahmad Chalabi's residence in London in Mayfair, the very same luxurious apartment where he had been recruited by the CIA, before his disastrous breakup with that agency.

Chalabi himself signed the corporate annual report for INDICT for 1999, listing himself as the corporate secretary and one of two directors. The registered address was 51 South Street. Clearly, Chalabi wasn't putting much of his own money into the endeavor: the report's balance sheet explained that INDICT had cash of only sixty-five pounds at the time.[13]

Chalabi's inner circle, formerly composed of INC members, quickly became INDICT officials. Zaab Sethna, the Zoroastrian Pakistani British public affairs specialist, told a reporter he was the organization's media liaison. Nabeel Musawi, another long-term Chalabi operative, told the reporter he was INDICT's "director of international operations." He said Saddam Hussein could be toppled soon. "With clear commitment and support from the Western alliance, Saddam will be history in seven months," Musawi insisted.

But Sethna complained that the flow of money from America's taxpayers to INDICT was too slow for the group. "It's frustrating," Sethna pointed out, "when you don't have the resources."[14] He said that the State Department wasn't getting INDICT the money they needed or even refunding airline tickets he claimed he purchased. "They told us, 'You'll definitely see a check in the month of October,'" he said, apparently aggrieved by the slow manner in which America disbursed its funds to him. "We came back and never heard from them again."

The State Department, for its part, wanted to fund INDICT. It seemed like a legitimate international group that could have an impact. But with its cumbersome bureaucratic methods demanding accountability, the State Department was trying to do things by the book. That was too slow for five Republican senators, who demanded Clinton come through with the money. "We urge the immediate provision of funding to the INDICT campaign against Saddam Hussein," they wrote. Soon, INDICT's board expanded and actually tried to fulfill its mission.

The address eventually moved from Chalabi's apartment in Mayfair, according to official records filed in the summer of 1999, and the board expanded to include the Kurdish Latif Rashid and Hamid al-Bayati, a member of the Shiite resistance group the Supreme Council for Islamic Revolution in Iraq (SCIRI). Peter Galbraith, the passionate former Democratic staffer and ambassador to Croatia under Bill Clinton, signed up as well. He was a longtime friend of Ahmad Chalabi's. And the U.S. State Department demanded that INDICT hire a professional to oversee what it did, and how.

In later years, the group earned some derision in England after it asked prosecutors there to consider charges against Saddam for hostages held before the first Gulf War. The head of the British police union was outraged at the way INDICT was using up resources. Metropolitan Police Federation chairman Glen Smyth was quoted as saying, "It's window dressing, posture politics of the worst kind, and certainly going to cost the taxpayers of London hundreds of thousands of pounds, which could be used for policing May Day riots and making sure children are safe from pedophiles."

In the end, Chalabi's interest in INDICT, which he had founded, subsided: he had gradually ceded control of it anyway, and the amount of money involved paled next to other funds the U.S. Congress was promising.

22

Ahmad Chalabi's Law

1998

"I am here as an elected representative of the Iraqi people."

—Ahmad Chalabi, May 2, 1998, testimony to
the Senate Foreign Relations Committee

WHEN HE VISITS ENGLAND, according to a family member, Ahmad Chalabi occasionally broods, sometimes eating in complete silence, staring and thinking and ignoring everyone else at the table, before he suddenly rises and leaves the room with no warning. One theory is that, as open and garrulous as he may be among his business and political associates, his extroversion can't be sustained at all points. He cannot always exude intelligence, charm, and humility. "It's a performance, very controlled, and I think it's fair to say it's not as effortless as it seems," said one man who has known him for fifteen years. "None of this is spontaneous. Like any actor, he needs his downtime."

Ahmad Chalabi must have had little downtime during his 1997 and 1998 lobbying blitz in Washington. The real targets of his efforts were the lawmakers on Capitol Hill, and by the end of his campaign the results ranked among his greatest achievements. In 1998, Congress passed a law that was quite literally written to help Chalabi: the Iraq Liberation Act. As he later boasted, it is no exaggeration to say that

Congress made Chalabi's interests the law of the land and adopted his strategy in the Middle East as America's own.[15]

Chalabi was not the only influence on Capitol Hill pushing to do something about Saddam Hussein, but he was the strongest. Some politicians had already championed his cause: John McCain, for example, had signed up as early as 1991. But Chalabi quickly recruited many others who took on his cause with the zeal of converts. A good salesman makes his customers think it is their idea to buy his product, and you could say that is what Chalabi achieved. Conservatives like Kansas Republican Senator Sam Brownback, Arizona's McCain, New York Congressman Benjamin Gillman, and California's Chris Cox gave him tremendous support. On the Democratic side he had supporters too, like Senators Joe Lieberman and Bob Kerrey, the decorated Vietnam-era navy SEAL.

Chalabi at that time operated in a context of an ongoing crisis with Iraq, in the eyes of Washington at least. The UN weapons inspectors (UNSCOM) were conducting inspections and encountering denial and confrontation. In January 1998 Saddam Hussein banned weapons inspectors of U.S. nationality, and by February 1998, once again there was talk of bombing. The headlines in the papers were ominous: "In Kuwait, U.S. Air Units Prime for War," "Clinton Struggles to Make Case for Bombing," "Iraqis Wait for Return of War."

It would be easy, in later years, to forget how aggressively the Clinton administration clapped for airstrikes against Iraq, and how controversial those bombing campaigns were at the time. Clinton's foreign policy team—Secretary of State Madeleine Albright, Defense Secretary William Cohen, and National Security Adviser Sandy Berger—tried to make the public case for intense airstrikes against Iraq in a town hall debate sponsored by CNN and were shouted down by audience members outraged by the prospects of war.[16]

And yet there was the daily drumbeat of WMD disclosures, as UNSCOM inspectors saw that, whether or not Saddam had weapons of mass destruction, he was at least obstructing their access. Chalabi played a small role in giving UNSCOM some of its leads, all of which turned out to be false. In January 1998, UN weapons inspector Scott Ritter visited Chalabi in his Mayfair apartment. Sitting in on the meeting was "Ahmed Allawi," whom Chalabi introduced as his "chief of intelligence." (Although Ritter didn't know it, Ahmed Allawi in fact was the alias used by Aras Habib Kareem, the Shiite Kurd and Chalabi loyalist who functioned as his top spy and enforcer. Aras was suspected by the CIA of being an Iranian agent.)

Chalabi made clear that one of the key tips Ritter recently had received—about underground hiding places near a presidential palace in Iraq—came from a defector allied to him. The tip would help ratchet up tensions for inspectors: it was the type of thing that was intriguing, hard to prove or disprove. Secret weapons materials, according to the information, were buried deep underground at a presidential palace at Jabal Mokhul, in the mountains. After a lot of inspection, the information later turned out to be false. There was indeed an underground drainage pipe, but it tended to fill up with water, making it unusable for secret storage.[17]

Chalabi also probed Ritter about what kind of information he was looking for. "This should have sent alarm bells sounding in my head," Ritter wrote, because knowing where the information gaps are can help an untrustworthy source manipulate the intelligence. Soon, using coded communications, Chalabi started e-mailing more tips and information, which, Ritter said, "simply didn't match reality."

By March 1998, Chalabi was the star witness at a Senate hearing called "Iraq: Can Saddam Be Overthrown?" It was one of the few public arenas where he faced any questioning about his plans, and it is well worth considering. "I am here as an elected representative of the Iraqi people," he announced. Possibly he was referring to a vote at the CIA-funded Iraqi opposition conference six years earlier. Chalabi, then a bit heavy, sat at the oak table in a Senate subcommittee as the only witness in the first part of the hearing. He laid out a stinging critique of the "racist" State Department officials responsible for Iraq's policy, who "view the Iraqi people as incapable of self-government, as a people who require a brutal dictatorship to live and work together." As for the Central Intelligence Agency, he criticized their efforts to recruit former Baathist security officials. "It is not up to the CIA to determine Iraq's leadership. It is up to the Iraqi people," he said.

Then he touched on the fears so prevalent at that time, WMD: "Saddam's chemical and biological warfare industry," he said, "enslaves tens of thousands of Iraqis who are virtually unprotected from the poisonous production." The sentence conveyed an image of a vast network of WMD factories where Iraqi workers inhaled the deadly viruses and poisons as they manufactured them.

He did warn, again, about an occupation: "I want to emphasize that the INC does not request any U.S. occupying force. . . . What is needed is not a U.S. army of occupation, but an Iraqi army of liberation." The solution he offered instead sounded like a simple and bold alternative. If the U.S. government would support him, ensuring a safe haven for the INC within Iraq, Iraqi units disgusted with Saddam Hussein would defect to him and move against their central command. Once again, he would be the catalyst for the defecting Iraqi army.

He wanted enclaves, he said, which the United States would protect with air power. Given such zones, he said, the regime would collapse "within a matter of months."

And he made sure to refer to UNSCOM and Scott Ritter. "I know from my own sources in Baghdad that Scott Ritter is an American hero," he testified. Chalabi also took the opportunity to attack the United Nations and its secretary general, Kofi Annan, accusing him of "craven behavior."

Zalmay Khalilzad and James Woolsey testified as well, and seemed completely supportive of Chalabi's schemes. Only one witness at the hearing was skeptical and tried to dampen the enthusiasm: it was Richard Haass, a former State Department official who had met Chalabi before the INC was even formed. By 1998 Haass was at the Brookings Institution, where he was warning people to be cautious about the rush to back Chalabi's plans. "Simply getting rid of Saddam is not a panacea," he said in his opening statement. As for Chalabi's scheme, it wouldn't work, he said. Chalabi's group wasn't really the functioning inclusive organization it claimed to be. He was right about this. Not only was Chalabi by no stretch an "elected representative of the Iraqi people," but by the time Haass gave that testimony, there was no functioning Iraqi National Congress. The organization consisted of just a few followers of Chalabi, some Iraqi and some not: Francis

Brooke, Zaab Sethna, Aras Kareem Habib, Nabeel Musawi, Mohamad al-Zobaidy.

While it was an effective tactic for Chalabi to continue discussing the Iraqi National Congress as if it still existed as a viable force in Iraq, the truth was, of course, that in 1998 the Kurds, the Shiite groups like SCIRI and Dawa, the Iraqi National Accord, and others had no part in it at all.

Haass, at the Senate hearing, was a wet noodle, a doomsayer. He warned that if the United States backed Chalabi's plan for "enclaves," Iraqis within the "enclaves" would be encircled and trapped, in a Bay of Pigs–type scenario. To rescue them, U.S. forces would end up "essentially invading and occupying Iraq." Haass's concern was that Chalabi's plan was chiefly a way for the United States to stampede to war. And he was skeptical of this too: "What began as a liberation would very quickly look like an occupation, and I just think we would get bogged down in Iraq."

=====

The inspection crisis ground on, and over the summer Iraq once again dug in its heels. Eventually Scott Ritter quit the UN monitoring team, charging that the United States and the UN failed to force Iraq to allow his WMD hunters enough access.

Ritter's involvement with Chalabi ended badly. One day in 1998, he says, Francis Brooke called him from New York City and then showed up at his house in upstate New York, to try to persuade him to work on Chalabi's behalf. Brooke, normally a beer drinker, drank up all Ritter's single-malt whiskey and crashed at his house. Later, in June 1998, before his resignation from UNSCOM, Ritter says Chalabi had him over to his Georgetown home and tried to recruit him along with some think-tank types. Chalabi hinted he'd help with oil contracts once the Saddam regime was overthrown, Ritter claims. "He said 'oil contracts.' He said he would have the ability to make oil contracts in a way to take care of people." Ritter says he turned him down flat. (Chalabi's people have denied this and called Ritter a liar.)

=====

But for Chalabi, 1998 was a good year. Chalabi's goal of "regime change" in Iraq became U.S. law that year. One reason for his success was that, as he wooed Congress in the second half of the 1990s, he paid special attention to the staffers. It is the aides on Capitol Hill who write bills, determine agendas, and determine their bosses' schedules. "A lot of guys think you have to just go meet senators," says Peter Galbraith, who was an aide to the late senator Claiborne Pell. "Chalabi understood that getting the right staff on board might be more important."

One staff member Chalabi got on board was Danielle Pletka, a formidable ally. Pletka, chief of staff at the Senate Committee on Near Eastern and South Asian Affairs, remembers receiving a cold call from Francis Brooke, after which Brooke and Chalabi met her in her office. Pletka was impressed by Chalabi's pitch. A tall woman with a direct and brusque manner, she does not suffer fools. Chalabi's argument in the meeting, she recalls, was not that he could overthrow Saddam but that he could rebuild the INC if he got funding. "He talked about the Iraqi National Congress," she explained in an interview, "the idea, why it was important to come back to it, why it was important to revitalize it. Why it was an important answer to Saddam Hussein, why it was good for American foreign policy as well as for Iraqi national policy, and it made a lot of sense to me. It made a lot of sense to a lot of people."

Pletka already despised the State Department and the CIA. Her analysis is fairly simple and incorporates what she believes to be the ingrained biases of the agencies: "They like working with Middle Eastern dictators, because they were comfortable with Saddam Hussein." She believed Clinton's policy on Iraq was driven by the ongoing Monica Lewinsky scandal. "His interest in changing policy and quote-unquote regime change was entirely coincident with his sex life, or the revelations about the sex life."

So Chalabi's complaints about the CIA, the State Department, and the administration struck a chord politically, not just strategically. But aside from politics, Chalabi's vision made a lot of sense to her. "I think he wanted to ensure that the INC was revitalized with a view to getting rid of Saddam Hussein, and that was something we all thought was a really good idea. And we backed it." (In later years Pletka would become the chief spokesperson for the American Enterprise Institute.)

Pletka was also a key ally because she was part of a husband-and-wife tag team in the foreign policy establishment. While she worked in the Senate Foreign Relations Committee, her husband, Steven Rade-maker, was a high-level aide at the House International Relations Committee.

Rademaker recalls being mightily impressed by Chalabi, whom he met at a Republican Policy Committee meeting. Rademaker had worked out of law school in the State Department during Ronald Reagan's era, under the leadership and tutelage of Elliott Abrams. Like Dewey Clarridge, another Chalabi supporter, Rademaker worked with the Nicaraguan Contras, although he did it as a lawyer, not a covert operative. "When I approached the issue of Iraq," he said, "and first started talking to Chalabi, it seemed that he had a vision of what he wanted to do in Iraq that was very similar to the vision behind the Reagan administration's policy in Latin America: a combined political strategy with a military component. The term we used back then was the 'Reagan Doctrine': helping freedom fighters."

Chalabi fit the profile of a freedom fighter, so Rademaker says he sensed an opportunity for Republicans to take control of Iraq as an issue. He took it upon himself to draft a bill. "That was sort of my job, to write bills." Rademaker says he did not actually discuss the legislation ahead of time with Chalabi, who "was pretty excited about it when he heard about it." This was no surprise. The bill Rademaker drafted called for aid worth $99 million to go to the Iraqi opposition. "In the back of my mind, in working on the Iraq Liberation Act, the animating vision was essentially drawn from the Reagan Doctrine," said Rademaker. The original draft did not use the names INC or Chalabi, but that was Rademaker's intent as he sat in front of his computer. "When I originally wrote this bill," he says, "I really just had Chalabi—well, not Chalabi—the Iraqi National Congress, the INC, in mind. That was the organization, it seemed to me, that seemed entitled to this. They were broad-based; they professed to have representatives from all different sectors of Iraqi society, and that's who I thought we should be helping."

Pletka, one of the champions of the law, now sternly downplays Chalabi's position vis-à-vis the legislation. "To suggest that somehow he was the architect of what ended up happening from a congressional standpoint is wrong," she insisted in an interview. And it is true that not all of the legislators who would vote on the issue were aware of Chalabi's central role.

A key part of the law concerned money: $97 million in aid was targeted as military aid—called "military drawdown"—for the Iraqi opposition. The United States would forward the equivalent in military equipment to the Iraqi opposition: bullets, rifles, uniforms, cots, and tents. Rademaker had seen what must have been a version of Chalabi's military plan, the one that was drawn up by former Special Forces Gen. Wayne Downing. In fact, Downing pitched in with some private briefings on Capitol Hill, spelling out the specifics of his war plan: "I was probably helpful," Downing recalled in an interview. "Well, it wasn't *probably*. I *was* helpful to him in getting support to get the Iraq Liberation Act passed. I went over on several occasions and, you know, talked to small groups of committees or in some cases individual Congressmen."

On top of all that military aid, the bill set aside $2 million in cash to fund broadcasting efforts. The total was less than $100 million, and that was key. Keeping it under that threshold was a bureaucratic maneuver only insiders would know to make the bill easier to slide through. At the time, Rademaker says, Congress could introduce bills and suspend certain debating rules if the amount of federal expenditures came under $100 million. The Iraq Liberation Act could now get on the fast track.

The money, though, was not the most important part of the Iraq Liberation Act. The real kicker was this: "It should be the policy of the United States to seek to remove the regime headed by Saddam Hussein from power in Iraq and to promote the emergence of a democratic government to replace that regime." The act made the policy of "regime change" in Iraq into U.S. law. As a policy matter, that went far beyond the "sense of Congress" resolutions that periodically passed to make politicians feel like they were doing something. This now meant that the government of the United States would be bound by law to seek the overthrow of Saddam Hussein.

On the Democratic side, Senator Bob Kerrey, vice chairman of the Senate Intelligence Committee, pushed hard for the bill. He said that's because he saw a stark divide in U.S. policy. "I was strongly of the view that if your covert policy is to overthrow somebody, that should be your overt policy."

In an interview Kerrey said it was clear that Chalabi wanted to run the provisional government. But, he adds, he personally never saw it as plausible. "In my wildest dreams I never believed the Iraqi National Congress had the capacity to *be* the provisional government. Never! In my wildest dreams." Kerrey found Chalabi implacable. "The most impressive thing about Ahmad Chalabi is he is relentless, he just doesn't give up, and he's remained a believer and he's tried to figure how to make it work."

Opponents of the bill, like Gen. Anthony Zinni, head of Central Command, who had authority over U.S. military operations in the Middle East, found it ludicrous and said so. The Downing Plan, he famously said, was a recipe for a "Bay of Goats," a plan doomed to failure that would suck the United States into a vortex of embarrassment and failure. For this Zinni earned the hatred of Chalabi's supporters.

Zinni claimed the opposition groups did not have "viability," a crack that cost Chalabi his facade of self-control. "If they were viable," Chalabi once howled, "they wouldn't need you, Mr. General Zinni."[18]

The *New York Times* editorial page called the act "throwing money and weapons at Iraq's feeble and fractious opposition," and pointed out that Chalabi's Iraqi National Congress "represents almost no one."[19]

For Steven Rademaker, the key to getting the bill turned into law was getting the approval of Senate majority leader Trent Lott. He lobbied a Senate aide named Randy Scheunemann, he says, who eventually came on board. Scheunemann would one day become an INC stalwart, a key figure it its victories. On September 29, 1998, Scheunemann's boss, Senator Lott, introduced the act in the Senate, the same day that Rademaker's boss introduced it in the House. Rademaker can't think of another bill that passed both houses so quickly: it sped through the House on October 5, steamrolling any opposition with a vote of 360–30. Then it raced through the Senate, passing unanimously two days later. By the end of the month it was signed by President Clinton—on Halloween, the day after Ahmad Chalabi's fifty-fourth birthday. Rademaker remembers there was a celebration.

23

The Money Returns

"*Akareet!*" ("You bastards!")
—Ahmad Chalabi, 1999

AHMAD CHALABI WAS IN A FURY—an anger that brought him near tears, some say—in the early hours one morning in 1999. After marathon negotiations in New York City, he slapped a rolled-up magazine into the palm of his hand with a crack and "strutted like a peacock," as one witness described it, out of the crowded hotel banquet reeking of cigarette smoke. A few followers rushed behind him trying to keep up. His anger was easy to understand: it seemed he had been politically outmaneuvered, and kicked out of the leadership of the very Iraqi National Congress he had founded.

The setting was a smoke-filled conference room at the Sheraton Hotel, near Fifty-second Street and Seventh Avenue in Manhattan. The State Department was finally trying to spend some of the money Congress had earmarked for the Iraqi opposition, and the gathering was abuzz with excitement. One thing on the agenda was to set up a structure for American support of the Iraqi opposition.

The conference started on Halloween a year after Clinton signed the Iraq Liberation Act, and the streets of New York were full of children preparing to trick-or-treat. They were dressed in costumes as Harry Potter, assorted witches, cowboys, and superheroes. Some of the Iraqi visitors at the conference were mullahs and ayatollahs, and when they walked down the street before the conference, they turned to watch the children in their costumes. The children stared wide-eyed at the grown-ups too, in what looked to them to be equally strange costumes—turbans, robes, and beards.

Three dozen members of Jalal Talabani's PUK showed up at the Sheraton front desk to check in. When the rival KDB faction arrived, the bitter enemies glowered at one another and called up associates to make sure to ratchet their side's numbers up.

The man who claimed to be the king, Sherif Ali, came as well, apparently invited by the State Department. Ayad Allawi showed up, too, with his band of former Baathists. And, of course, Ahmad Chalabi and some of his inner circle were there.

Various U.S. officials gave their blessings to the project. Democratic Senator Bob Kerrey delivered a speech, as did Republican Senator Sam Brownback. Under Secretary of State Thomas Pickering made an appearance.

Ahmad Chalabi and his core supporters were cynical about the effort but decided grudgingly to support it. Most journalists didn't even bother with the event, although the *Washington Post's* UN correspondent swung by and saw Chalabi, who was at that point gaining weight, distributing "Free Iraq!" T-shirts. It was small-time stuff for the banker and the opposition figure he had been, but he did it with enthusiasm—a politician doing what he had to. If a few New Yorkers and Iraqi expatriates would stroll around with "Free Iraq!" T-shirts in the early fall weather, it was better than nothing.

Chalabi's people used the occasion of the conference to allege the State Department mismanagement. What should have been INC money was being tinkered with by the State Department. The conference cost $2.1 million, or $7,000 per Iraqi, INC officials found out, and the State Department had hired a company called Quality Support Inc. to organize it. "Quality Support's mandate was to pile up money on the street and burn it," Francis Brooke, Chalabi's *consigliere*, complained to reporters later.[20] "It's all just nonsense," Brooke said of the State Department's efforts to *Time* magazine that month.[21]

And as amicable as Chalabi may have been at the "Free Iraq!" T-shirt table, what enraged him—the thing that set him off during that conference—occurred the second-to-last day. The conference had broken up into smaller caucuses, and each group voted on representatives to sit on a committee composed of six leaders. They were late-night sessions, involving yelling, wheedling, smoking, and cigarette butts squashed into the hotel carpet under heel. A deadline was approaching the next morning, and they had to settle their differences and find a credible group of leaders to present to the Americans.

By the early morning the stunning fact was that Chalabi had not even been appointed to the leadership committee. He was spurned completely, and then, to compound the insult, a man he and his followers considered an enemy was appointed. Laith Kubba wound up winning a caucus and a seat on the committee. Kubba and Chalabi, who are distant relatives, each from prominent Shiite families, had cracked heads way back in 1992, when Kubba, a driving force behind the INC, had been upset by Chalabi's refusal to reveal where his funding was coming from. Since then, they had not been on speaking terms.

It was not only an insult to Chalabi; it could have been economically devastating to him as well. The leadership of the INC—the committee he was being stripped from—was the group that would decide what to do with the U.S. funds that were supposed to pour in after the Iraq Liberation Act was implemented. That was his law—it was virtually written for him. It was as if the exile Iraqi community was conspiring to take over a revenue stream of U.S. tax dollars that was his by right.

And so his anger and his sadness are understandable. He was infused with energy that morning, slapping a rolled-up magazine into his hand like it was a policeman's billy club and storming out. According to one attendee, Chalabi said to the congregation as he marched out, "*Akareet!*" (Arabic for "You bastards!") and then swore that the assembled Iraqis would never see a penny of the American money. (One of Chalabi's supporters disputes this precise language and says that in fact Chalabi did not curse but rather told the assembly something more subdued like, "You are making a mistake," before marching out.)

The Iraqis left behind looked at one another in confusion and conferred among themselves like abandoned dinner dates. Sources say an American official went to talk to Kubba to ask him to back down, and then a group ran after Chalabi to reassure him and bring him back.

Apparently, the group belatedly realized that, without Chalabi's support on Capitol Hill, the fate of the money would be uncertain. The crisis was averted, and later that morning a proud Ahmad Chalabi walked back into the conference room.

One of the difficulties for Ahmad Chalabi was that, while he wanted to lead an umbrella organization to represent exiles, he disliked some of the other leaders in the community. One morning at breakfast at the Monarch Hotel in Washington over at Twenty-fourth and M, Chalabi was complaining about Adnan Pachachi, the distinguished and elderly Sunni statesman the State Department was trying to bring into the coalition it supported. Pachachi was an "old fart," he said, in his likable and informal way. "Too rigid. Not there. Doesn't understand the Americans."

Chalabi and his followers were even more wary of another exile: former Baathist Ayad Allawi. Their antagonism was legendary, even in the early 1990s. In 1995 and 1996, the CIA had ditched Chalabi's INC in favor of Allawi's Iraqi National Accord (INA). Chalabi and his followers resented Allawi's role in diverting the covert funding stream of the CIA that had kept Chalabi's operations alive. Operating out of Amman and London, Allawi was actually a relative of Chalabi through his wife, and the two men had once even attended the same school. But like many Iraqis back in the pre-1958 days, Allawi had been sympathetic to the revolution against the monarchy. Allawi was a Baathist, of the old pre-Saddam school, and fundamentally presented a different picture of what Iraq was really like. Democracy, he argued, would not be easy in Iraq, and the country needed a strong leader because of the fiercely competitive interests at work.

Americans who supported Chalabi often saw him as a counterpoint to Allawi, who was portrayed to them as a dark, brooding force. (Most, once they met Allawi, found him likable and warm. Ironically, he had been trained in the same school of hospitality and charm as Chalabi.)

═══

One of Chalabi's main themes was that he was not an Arab nationalist but an Iraqi nationalist. Unlike many Iraqis, according to his closest associates Chalabi never cared at all about the results of the 1967 war

of the Arabs against Israel, which had been so demoralizing and humiliating for the Arab consciousness. Even members of his own family, his nephews, had sought meaning in Arab nationalism as young
men. But Ahmad Chalabi had been steadfast in rejecting it ever since
the Arab nationalist revolution of 1958 had cost his family its position
in Iraqi society. The Arab cause was not his cause at all. Friends recall
him railing against the Sunnis and against Arab nationalism during
the Iran–Iraq War and earlier. The old Nasserite passion was a hostile
force to him as well. But it was the Baath, a completely different variant of Arab nationalism, that had destroyed Iraq's cultural fabric completely, in Chalabi's mind. The Baath, led by Saddam Hussein, was his
true enemy, and that is what those who followed him in America absorbed from their conversations. The Baath Party, it seemed to them,
was akin to the Nazi Party. Kanan Makiya, Chalabi's intellectual ally
and a man who carried a certain moral standing in the West, rein-
forced all this. With his almost disheveled intellectual air, Makiya
seemed like an anti-Chalabi, an impassioned thinker who never wore
a tie, seemed to pay no attention to money, and whose sincerity
seemed obvious. In his 1993 book, *Cruelty and Silence,* coming years
after his *Republic of Fear,* Makiya skewered what he saw as hypocrisy
in the Arab world.

"Millions upon millions of words have been written about the destruction of hundreds of Palestinian villages," he had written, "in order to bring about the creation of the Israeli state. And rightly so. Yet
many of the very intellectuals who wrote those words chose silence
when it came to the elimination of thousands of Kurdish villages by
an Arab state." It was an honest and insightful critique of Arab
hypocrisy, which could be exploited in American public opinion.

But Chalabi's opposition to Arab nationalism went further than
that. It was also a double-edged sword. It was a reason some Americans supported him, but it was also a hindrance, preventing him from
garnering any real support among the Arabs he wanted to lead.

Chalabi was of course not a neoconservative himself. But the
American neoconservatives molded what he told them of his goals
and ambitions and past to suit their own purposes. No written work
so well embodies the neoconservative adaptation of Ahmad Chalabi
as an unusual 1999 book by David Wurmser called *Tyranny's Ally:*

America's Failure to Defeat Saddam Hussein. Wurmser was one of the chief authors of the well-known "Clean Break" letter of 1996, in which a group of neoconservatives recommended that Israeli Prime Minister Benjamin Netanyahu take a series of steps that would undercut Arab dictatorships.

In *Tyranny's Ally,* Wurmser created a new history for Chalabi. Everything about him now seamlessly sprouted from his opposition to Arab nationalism and his aristocratic background. Wurmser touched on the Petra Bank case of Jordan but was so convinced of Chalabi's purity that he no longer saw profit as a motive for his banking enterprises. Instead, Chalabi's bank was an effort to combat pan-Arab nationalism: "To erode the potential for blackmail by these pan-Arabic nationalist movements, Chalabi established the Petra Bank of Jordan. The idea was to create an independent financial base to give the royal family independence from the PLO-run monopoly." This was untrue, and it ignores the fact that some of the main Petra Bank investors were the very Palestinian financiers Wurmser held in such low regard. As for Petra's collapse and takeover and the various audits, Wurmser ignored those too. He doesn't even mention the family businesses that crumbled in Lebanon and Switzerland. Instead, according to this version, "because the Petra Bank had prospered and threatened the PLO's monopoly over Jordan's finances, Chalabi was driven from Jordan." The book hints that Jordan's politics had now been righted, and is supportive of King Hussein and his legitimacy.

Another interesting part of the book is Wurmser's contention that Shiites of Iraq are moderates, unassertive politically, and friendly to the West. One subchapter is titled "Shi'ism's Western Affinity" and says of the Shiites that "the sort of spiritual faith characteristic of these Muslims is seldom compatible with zealotry." He seems to have in mind a particular slice of Iraqi Shiite society, encompassing Chalabi and other rich Shiite families. In Wurmser's adaptation of the Chalabi vision, empowering the Shiites of Iraq would simply bring good things with it: peace, a pro-Western tilt, and even a rollback of Iran's hard-line Shiite government. "Unleashing Shiism in Iraq would threaten Iran's Islamic revolution," he claimed. This conclusion is a marked development. Previously, others had been convinced that Saddam, the enemy of Iran's Islamic Revolution, would threaten it.

But now Wurmser and his fellows were inverting that: the explanation was that the peaceful, more moderate Iraqi Shiites, if empowered, would be a threat to the aggressive and radical Iranian Shiites. The "good" Shiites of Iraq, so to speak, would be a barrier to the "bad" Shiites of Iran.

The book beats the drum again of Chalabi and his Washington followers: that coup efforts against Saddam would never work. Even if it worked, a coup was undesirable because it would simply replace Saddam with someone like him rather than bringing about democracy and empowering the Shiites. This strained debate over "coups" or "uprisings" to topple Saddam was at the heart of much of Chalabi's efforts in the late 1990s. He was still determined to win the old argument about whether the United States should encourage a popular insurgency or what his champions derogatively called a "silver-bullet coup." Those who pushed for a coup were seen as "pan-Arabists," while those who pushed for an "insurgency"—led by Chalabi—were not only more realistic in their aims but more benign. The Downing Plan was still referred to as an "insurrection" rather than a coup, because of its underlying assumption that the Iraqi army would not initiate a coup but would simply defect and join the 2,000-man liberation force.

Significantly, despite Chalabi's purported appeals for democracy, the word doesn't even appear in the index. Instead, Chalabi is celebrated for his family's history as part of Baghdad's elite, unfairly dislodged from power. "He, his family and the organization he created represent an older Iraq and a traditional elite that have been battered, oppressed, and enslaved by pan-Arabic nationalist governments for forty years." His allure in this context had flipped like a pancake: no longer were his democratic qualifications important; instead, it was the opposite—his membership in a "traditional elite."

═══

During this period Chalabi and Francis Brooke in Washington were being nickel-and-dimed by the State Department, which was proving reluctant to hand out funds Congress had promised. To get things moving, they tried a maneuver of their own, launching their own lobbying organization whose purpose was to push Congress and the White House to implement the Iraq Liberation Act. In essence the

INC lobbied to implement the law it had already lobbied to enact two years earlier. In an effort to out-bureaucrat the bureaucrats, they set up The Iraq Liberation Act Committee. It was conceived as a lobbying group, or a political action committee, along the lines of the American Israel Public Affairs Committee (AIPAC).

Congress had approved $3 million as a grant for the INC in 1998 and another $3 million in 1999. But none of it was coming through. The State Department was holding it up. With all that congressionally approved funding, Chalabi must have been bursting with frustration, like a child staring at a locked-up candy store.

Francis Brooke incorporated the new organization, out of the Chalabi-owned home in Washington that he lived in. (Technically the home was listed as owned by Levantine Holdings, of the Cayman Islands.) He was supposed to file paperwork with the IRS to make it a tax-exempt organization as well. The board of directors of the Iraq Liberation Act Committee included Chalabi's cardiologist nephew from Texas, the gregarious and impassioned Mahdi al-Bassam, as well as Entifadh Qanbar, the INC Washington director, and some other Iraqi-American doctors and professionals, like Maha Yousif, a dentist from Connecticut.

Yousif, who never knew Chalabi well, said she got the impression that part of the money Iraqis were paying to the Iraq Liberation Action Committee was just to help Francis Brooke stay alive. Brooke lived in squalor at the Chalabi house on a beautiful and secluded lane in Washington's expensive Georgetown neighborhood, and he seemed to have no income to support himself or his family. "He didn't have enough to pay the electrical bills," said Yousif.

In fact Yousif had the impression that Chalabi himself was hurting for funds. Yousif couldn't have known it, but in a way the time was a bit like 1990 and 1991, after Chalabi had fled Jordan, leaving a collapsed bank behind. Chalabi seemed genuinely broke. Would she provide free dental services for his bodyguard, he asked her one time. She agreed, but Chalabi never followed through.

Yousif, the dentist, says one day she raised a delicate issue with Chalabi. Other Iraqi Americans were calling him a crook when she called to ask them to contribute to the Iraq Liberation Action Committee. Could he explain this? He sat her down, she said in an interview, and patiently explained to her that he had been framed—he had been set up by Saddam Hussein and the government of Jordan in the old Petra Bank case. It had haunted him ever since. She accepted his explanation.

Still, the committee never seemed to get off the ground. They did have some meetings with Congressmen, but Chalabi preferred his own private meetings on Capitol Hill.

Whatever the little committee did, in the end, the State Department had to start giving the Iraqi National Congress the funds it had been apportioned by Congress. The real holdup had been that the Iraqi National Congress was not actually incorporated anywhere. It was a problem Chalabi's organization had always lived with. Since it wasn't a legal entity, it couldn't own things in its own name, have bank accounts, or do any of the things organizations do. It couldn't hire people, pay taxes, sign contracts, or lease equipment. It wasn't even clear who could have cashed a check made out to the Iraqi National Congress. Back in the early '90s in London, there had been IBC Communications, Chalabi's company, through which CIA funding flowed. But that was London, and that was a for-profit operation.

So after repeated arguments, the INC set up an American subsidiary, the Iraqi National Congress Support Foundation (INCSF), through which American funds would be siphoned. Its papers say that the subsidiary was established "at the request of the U.S. Department of State to serve as a vehicle for the department to channel assistance to the Iraqi National Congress." The incorporated entity, that is, was formed to pass on money to the unincorporated entity.

One result of the incorporation was that not only Chalabi's friends but also his rivals in the Iraqi opposition were installed on the foundation's board at the insistence of the State Department. It included Ayad Allawi, Sharif Ali bin al-Hussein (who claimed to be the heir to the throne), Latif Rashid of Talabani's party, and Hoshyar Zibari from Barzani's.

But the important thing for Chalabi, Aras, Francis Brooke, and all the band was this: they had finally busted through. The dam was broken. They got their first check—a good federal government check—in March 2000, and Chalabi marched off to a Georgetown bank to deposit it, as Maha Yousif remembers it. The moment was treated with appropriate ceremony by the small group. The check would have been $267,000, if the auditor's records are correct, but it was a start. The INCSF reported a mere $1 million in 2000. That stretched to $11 million the next year, and then $13 million in 2002. In total, the INCSF would collect a total of $33 million from the U.S. State Department.

James Woolsey was by now quite friendly with Ahmad Chalabi, and his law firm, Shea and Gardner, helped file the papers. Shea and Gardner, in turn, would be paid by the taxpayer funds that would keep Chalabi's operations running. Woolsey himself stepped in as the corporate secretary for the Iraqi National Congress Support Foundation, according to its corporate records. It was an interesting thing: the former CIA director who had once overseen the anti-Saddam program, back in 1993, was later to work directly for an incarnation of the "opposition" group his agency had once funded. But just eight months after the INCSF was incorporated, Woolsey stepped away suddenly. He resigned in October 2000. With his firm collecting juicy legal fees, paid for with the American money funding the Iraqi group, Woolsey says he was concerned about the appearance of a conflict of interest for him personally. He says he sent a note to his law firm agreeing to forego any of the profits earned by the firm on the account.

Perhaps the best part of the deal went to the effervescent Francis Brooke, Chalabi's American loyalist, who had worked so hard for him and given so much for his Iraqi leader. He was still living for free at Chalabi's house, but soon any personal financial worries he may have had were over: eventually he was collecting a $100,000-a-year salary from the INCSF, getting paid directly with the U.S. taxpayer funds for which he had lobbied with such passion.[22]

24

BKSH: Representing Chalabi

WHEN AHMAD CHALABI stepped into the lobby at the modern granite building at 1801 K Street in Washington, D.C.—the heart of the lobbying corridor in America—he would then get into the elevator and ride it up to the ninth floor. Curiously, this elevator ride up was, in one sense, one small vertical leg of Chalabi's journey back to Iraq. The offices at the top floor belonged to Black Kelly Scruggs Healy (BKSH), one of the most powerful lobbying firms in the United States. The firm is owned by public relations powerhouse Burson-Marsteller. The PR and lobbying experts of BKSH would help pave the way for Chalabi's triumphant return home in the years to come, arranging, over years, the red carpet. The plot twist that few people could have foreseen was that the BKSH campaign on Chalabi's behalf was fully funded, once again, by U.S. taxpayers.

The firm was hired in the late 1990s, when Congress was earmarking funds for the INC that the State Department couldn't spend because of the incorporation hitch. By hiring a respected public relations firm, the State Department diplomats, under veteran Frank Ricciardone, figured they could funnel support to the INC while complying with both congressional intentions and normal accounting procedures. So, in retrospect, if one wants to cast blame on anyone for using federal funds to hire a publicity agent for Ahmad Chalabi, one would have to point to the State Department, and to officials who had decided to turn to the private sector.

Burson-Marsteller, a giant PR company, won the award and quickly handed the work over to its subsidiary BKSH. BKSH was the lobbying vehicle of the legendary Republican powerhouse Charles Black, one of "America's leading Republican political strategists," according to BKSH literature. "He served as senior advisor to Presidents Ronald Reagan and George H.W. Bush. He also served as a principal public spokesman for President Bush in the 1992 presidential campaign."

BKSH represented major defense contractors, governments, and international corporations, and the company was perfectly situated to leverage its expertise on behalf of the Iraqi National Congress. In an interview, Charles Black explained that his firm received $200,000 to $300,000 per year from the U.S. government. "It was to promote the INC," he says.

Black, in his pleasant Texas drawl, says the firm did "standard kinds of public relations and public affairs, setting up seminars, helping them get speeches covered by the press, press conferences." Black believes his company can take a lot of pride in a strong campaign. "The whole thing was very successful. The INC became not only well-known, but I think the message got out there strongly."

Most of BKSH's work for Chalabi was handled by Riva Levinson, a longtime Capitol Hill lobbyist. She had worked for Black when the firm had been called Black Manafort Stone and Kelly. More than a decade before working for Chalabi, she started handling the $600,000-a-year account of Jonas Savimbi, the leader of UNITA, a rebel group battling Angola's Communist government during the 1980s. That was what she was most well known for. The murderous Savimbi became quite popular in certain circles in Washington and had also received massive support from the CIA early in his career. Losing American support when he lost an election in 1992, he refused to accept the election results and funded his war through the sales of banned Angolan "blood diamonds." So the political disputes over Chalabi would have been like déjà vu for Levinson, who quickly became passionate about Chalabi's cause.

"Riva would spend her weekend thinking about 'How can I get press coverage for the INC next week?'" Black explained, "and then come in on Monday morning and schedule a speech or call reporters to get a speech covered or get Chalabi or the other leaders out to get the message out." Levinson even spoke out overtly as the INC's spokeswoman, giving interviews on its behalf. At the end of the day, the State Department's efforts to control Chalabi through Burson-Marsteller backfired, because in the battle over influence there, Chalabi won. Frequently, while criticizing the United States or one of his competitors in Iraq, Chalabi would conflict with the State Department's policy. "Basically the U.S. government couldn't make Chalabi do anything he didn't want to do," Black said. The government would complain to BKSH. "We'd tell him. . . . And he'd say, 'Fine' and go say the same thing over again."

So while U.S. taxpayers paid for BKSH's services, the company worked for Ahmad Chalabi. In addition to Riva Levinson, another BKSH lobbyist, Jeffrey Weiss, who was prominent in Washington social circles, took up his cause. Weiss and his wife, Juleanna Glover-Weiss, who later worked for Vice President Dick Cheney, would sometimes host parties for Chalabi during this period at their beautiful Washington, D.C., home.

Normally, before campaigning on behalf of a foreign interest (which, after all, was what Chalabi was), the agent would register under the Justice Department's Foreign Agents Registration Act. That's required whenever someone represents a foreign interest in a "political or quasi-political" way. Examples include groups that at times had been allied with Chalabi, like Talabani's Patriotic Union of Kurdistan and Barzani's Kurdish Democratic Party. But since BKSH was paid by U.S. taxpayer funds through the State Department, it never registered as a foreign agent. Since it was not technically a "lobbyist" for Chalabi, even though it was a lobbying firm, it never registered at Capitol Hill either, which would be the norm for a lobbyist. Although the transaction was not classified or secret, journalists, legislators, and the American public weren't told about it.

PART IV

25

The Uses of September 11

2001

ON THE EVENING OF SEPTEMBER 10, 2001, fifty-six-year-old Ahmad Chalabi raced through Dulles airport like his life depended on it, according to members of his inner circle. He checked in at the first-class ticket counter, as the story goes, but the attendant told him the gate was closing: he had missed his flight. He argued in his persuasive way: after all, he pointed out, he had a full-fare first-class ticket worth thousands of dollars. His pleasant manners convinced the attendant to call over to the gate and alert them, and then Chalabi made a run for it. He has a barrel chest and a bit of a gut but he could move. He plowed his way through the waiting passengers in the terminal and miraculously made the flight.

If Chalabi had not run so fast, as his followers tell it, he would have been forced to catch the morning flight: American Flight 77 on September 11. What might have happened is that he would have boarded at gate D26 at Dulles, and there in the first-class section he probably would have stepped past a young Arabic man with delicate facial features and a slight frame who was settled in an expansive and comfortable seat. Hani Hanjour was the leader of the Al Qaeda hijack team aboard that plane. Shortly after takeoff Hanjour's suicide team would have forced Chalabi and the rest of the passengers to the back of the plane. And then, at 9:38 a.m., Chalabi would have perished with sixty-four other people aboard the flight as it hurtled into the Pentagon in a ball of flames, just one of the thousands to die in the bin Laden attack against America.

If that had happened, what would the world have been like in the years to come? Without Chalabi to argue his case, to act as an inspiration to his followers, would U.S. foreign policy have followed the trail it did in the end? Friends of his, who worked in the very Pentagon where he would have died in the smoldering wreckage, might have forgotten him. Without his marvelous charm and his rich voice in the ear of the powerful, might subsequent events have unfolded differently? Certainly, there were many factors, and many players, in the United States's decision to go to war in Iraq, but Chalabi would go on to play his crucial and central role as purveyor of strategy and intelligence. Without Saddam Hussein, there would have been no war, but without Chalabi, too, what would have happened? If Chalabi had run a little slower that Monday night, September 10, if he had perished the next morning, America's path to Iraq would likely have been quite different.

═══

The rejuvenation of the Iraqi National Congress had actually started before the September 11 attacks, with the election of President George W. Bush. The INC, according to a former member, knew that its fate would be decided by the 2000 presidential elections in the United States. The issue was not war though; it was money. There were two sources of U.S. funding available at the time: $97 million in military aid, plus millions in cash pushed through in Congress, earmarked for the INC but locked up as if in a glass-walled vault by the Clinton administration's State Department.

John McCain, gamely pushing for the Republican presidential nomination, was Chalabi's favorite candidate, according to an INC member who was in the United States at the time. McCain had been a stalwart friend for a decade. In 1991 McCain had signed on as a patron of Chalabi's first organization: the International Committee for a Free Iraq, a group that now existed only as a handful of newsletters in some filing cabinets.

Once Bush trounced McCain in the Republican primaries, he became the default choice, but in fact Vice President Al Gore still seemed promising. Gore even acted sympathetic to the INC, meeting with Chalabi and a handful of other Iraqis as the campaign was under way. Saddam, Gore told them in June, "must be removed from power," and he told them that he would implement the Iraq Liberation Act if he was elected.[1] In October, just before the election, the Clinton administration finally released $4 million to the INC, and the INC credited Gore's pressure.[2]

Gore's campaign partner, Joe Lieberman, the Democratic vice presidential candidate, was one of the strongest friends Chalabi had on Capitol Hill. He signed an open letter from Trent Lott, Bob Kerrey, Benjamin Gilman, and Jesse Helms to Clinton just the year before, on Chalabi's behalf. Lieberman had pushed as hard as anyone for the Iraq Liberation Act, and he wasn't bashful about it.

That Chalabi's group could insert itself as an American campaign issue back then was an extraordinary feat. Certain components of the pro-Israel lobby came to believe that supporting the Iraqi National Congress was tantamount to supporting Israel. These pro-Israel advocates were either unaware or unconcerned that Israel's government and intelligence services distrusted Chalabi. Still, their views were best exemplified in a *Wall Street Journal* piece called "Is Gore Good for American Jews?" by Seth Lipsky. Lipsky wrote that "one of the questions a lot of American Jews will be asking as we go to the polls is what is really good for us." One answer he offered was transformation in the Middle East: "The most important test in recent years has been the free Iraq movement under the aegis of the Iraqi National Congress."[3]

The clincher, though, was that Richard Perle, Paul Wolfowitz, and other neoconservatives were snugly in the Republican camp. No matter what Gore and others said, the INC settled on George W. Bush.[4] And they chose right. After coming into office, Bush quickly jumpstarted things for the INC Support Foundation. The first step was a waiver of restrictions on what they could do inside Iraq. The Treasury Department's Office of Foreign Assets Control granted the waiver within weeks of the change in administration. It was a bittersweet win: they had the waiver, but the State Department wouldn't approve any funding inside Iraq anyway.

More good news came when Wolfowitz stepped into the administration. In London one day, David Hirst, the veteran British journalist who had known Chalabi for more than twenty-five years, was visiting him at his Knightsbridge INC office. Hirst recalls hearing a loud cheer go through the building. Wolfowitz had been nominated for the job of deputy secretary of state, he was told.

Things were moving fast for the INC: disclosures about Saddam continued. The venerable *Sunday Times* of London, on February 25, 2001, reported that Saddam Hussein "not only has nuclear weapons but has tested them." The reporter interviewed a supposed scientist who used a pseudonym, who sketched out Saddam's atomic designs. Corroboration came from a member of Ahmad Chalabi's inner circle: "'There was no doubt he was genuine,' said Arras Habib Kareem, who debriefed him in Kurdistan for the opposition Iraqi National Congress (INC). 'When other Iraqi nuclear scientists came north they recognised him within seconds. He knows a lot about the Iraqi nuclear programme.'"

Then in March, Chalabi got another waiver from the Treasury Department. Not only could he deal in Iraq legally; he was given extraordinary permission from the U.S. government. He could spend the American money in Tehran as well. Chalabi could rent a headquarters in Iran, appoint a permanent representative to deal with the Iraqi opposition based in Iran, and even deal with the Iranian intelligence agencies. It was an unheard-of license for a group spending U.S. federal funds.

But despite all the good news, Chalabi and Francis Brooke were distressed because once again they weren't getting the cash they wanted from the State Department. In 1999 Congress had approved $8 million for the opposition and earmarked $3 million in a bill directly for them, and then in 2000 Congress had budgeted even more. For 2001, Congress appropriated a whopping $25 million for the Iraqi opposition, with $18 million directed for the INC.

But the INC, through the INC Support Foundation it set up for the purpose, was just seeing a relative trickle of it. Millions were coming to them, but by right, Chalabi and Brooke felt, they should be getting more. So the INC made a bold pitch to the State Department: shell out $29 million for a five-month program. It was a package deal. That, they told the diplomats, would buy them a twenty-four-hour radio station inside Iraq broadcasting anti-Saddam propaganda. On top of that they would set up a twenty-four-hour satellite TV feed for the Iraqi audience.[5] Iraqis, of course, were not allowed to have satellite dishes under Saddam, and almost none did.

There is a well-documented trail of this financial tug-of-war as the INC tried to pry loose what it felt it was owed. The INC leaders held meetings at the Defense and State departments to press their case. But even their newly placed friends in the Defense Department could not help them.

State Department officials wanted to shell out the taxpayer funds slowly, and they insisted the funds be accounted for in the usual manner. Chalabi's followers blamed the delay on lingering influence from the departed Clinton administration. "In fact," the frustrated American Brooke complained to a sympathetic reporter, "what's happening is that three or four low-level Clinton holdovers have been blocking everything we're trying to do."[6] They made sure not to criticize President Bush, however.

Soon, Chalabi raised the pressure on the State Department, publishing an op-ed in the *Wall Street Journal* called "We Can Topple Saddam." The article didn't vary from his common refrain. "The INC has already proven it is up to the task," he wrote, implying the organization still existed as it had in the early 1990s. He warned that if Saddam were tolerated, "he will develop weapons of mass destruction and there is no doubt that he will use those weapons. If he is removed, Iraq can become the peaceful and prosperous country that its people, the region and the world deserve."[7]

The State Department was the faucet for the INC, so Chalabi could not lash out at it as he had at the CIA, but still, there was animosity. And then, in June of that year, in what struck the INC as a calculated ploy, the State Department sent a team of auditors into the INC's office on Pennsylvania Avenue. Auditors, just like the ones who had crawled all over the books of Petra Bank in Jordan more than ten years earlier and dug through the insider deals at Socofi, burrowed in and went to work.

Outwardly, it didn't seem to perturb Chalabi all that much, and anyway, that's when he was attending the annual American Enterprise Institute retreat in Beaver Creek, Colorado. The conservative group's gathering was hosted by the elegant Mrs. Lynne Cheney, and Chalabi managed to get an audience with the new vice president, Dick Cheney. Chalabi had known Cheney's point man on the Middle East for years. It was John Hannah, formerly of the Washington Institute for Near East Policy, a prominent neoconservative who was a full champion of his.[8]

But while the guests at the American Enterprise Institute conference were still enjoying their talks and watching the sunset in the mountains, auditors back in Washington were turning up rot in the INC's accounts. The auditors combing through the files learned that there was "a potential for fraud, waste, and abuse."[9] They discovered that $351,000 of the INC's Information Collection Program funds were spent without any explanation, let alone receipts.[10] And they found cost overruns of $1.1 million, which was equal to about a fifth of the INC's budget so far.[11]

There were other serious issues. It seemed that Chalabi held on to the purse strings tightly: none of the directors who weren't part of Chalabi's inner circle had any financial authority.[12] And to the auditors' surprise, the INC didn't withhold federal payroll taxes for its employees or even file as a nonprofit tax-exempt organization with the IRS, as it was supposed to.[13]

The cash flow that Chalabi and Brooke had worked so hard to secure was temporarily shut down. Even so, the INC was already applying for yet more funding. And soon taxpayer funds began flowing again, with $4 million in the tap. The State Department insisted that Chalabi hire an accountant to help him, and in fact the government, sources familiar with the transaction say, paid for the auditor at first. Instead of getting in Chalabi's way, as might have been expected, this new arrangement turned out to be a boon. Chalabi would make a potent new alliance with the accountant. Her name was Margaret "Peg" Bartel; she was a veteran of overseas projects and knew the intricacies of grant applications and reporting. And she would quickly become a close friend of Ahmad Chalabi's and one of the most useful Americans to him for a time. She would help him in his work with the State Department, and then she would help him with other funding.

One way the INC ended up tricking the State Department, according to former INC official Hamad Shoraidah, was through bogus con-

tracts. Shoraidah is a former Iraqi Republican Guard officer who im-
migrated to Norway and then spent time in the United States with the
INC. He even graduated from two U.S. government training classes
for Iraqi exiles. Years later, he became embittered at the INC, and he
kept what he says was a copy of a "Memorandum of Agreement" dated
March 1, 2002, between himself and the INC Support Foundation.
The document he has is signed by himself and by Aras Kareem, the
INC operations chief. Shoraidah's monthly "fee" was to be $2,500, and
his specific assignment was scrawled in a space in the printed document. It was to "analyze and collect information about Saddam's family and oil secure [*sic*]." Shoraidah claims, though, that this document
was just for the benefit of State Department accountants and that he
received nothing. It was a scheme to deceive the State Department, he
says, because officials balked at approving funds to spend on secret
operations inside Iraqi territory. "We made those phony contracts to
get money for the INC," Shoraidah says.[14]

Chalabi wanted to make sure not only that the U.S. funds kept flowing
but that he controlled them. Qubad Talabany, the younger son of the
charismatic Kurd Jalal Talabani, remembers one period when the State
Department settled on a $2 million grant for health-care projects in
Kurdistan "working with the faculty of medicines at universities. It
was the first time that the Kurds united to get something done—it was
a nonpolitical project, so the U.S. could easily deal with it without
thinking of the political sensitivities and worry about what the damn
Turks would think."

   But to the surprise and irritation of Talabani and Barzani, Chalabi
intervened through his friends on Capitol Hill. He insisted the money
flow through his INCSF rather than go to directly to the Kurds. Qubad
flew to London to meet Chalabi at the Knightsbridge office to tell
Chalabi to back down and let the money through. "I told him to just
let it happen and earn himself some brownie points. He could go to
our leaders and say that he was supporting this project. And this is
where he would make mistakes by not being strategic. He said, 'No,
but let it come through the INC and we'll spend it in the north.' That
is his goodwill."

In the end, the Kurds won that battle. But Qubad Talabany took the opportunity of that encounter to ask Chalabi about his relations with the CIA. "Ahmad," he said, "how do you think you're going to defeat the CIA?" The Kurds never understood why Chalabi continued using his friends to attack the agency. In their view, they had been betrayed by the CIA in 1974, and they still understood that they needed to work with the agency. Chalabi told Qubad, though, that he wasn't after the agency. "He said, 'I have nothing against them. They're the ones after me.'"

Young Qubad, as usual, found himself being persuaded by Ahmad. "He's the kind of guy," Qubad said, "that when you're meeting with him you have to constantly pinch yourself underneath the table so as to not get sucked into his charm."

Chalabi used his charm to protect his turf, but he could be harsh too. A group of potential rivals in the Iraqi opposition were getting State Department funding, and one Sunday afternoon they held a meeting at the Four Seasons Hotel in Georgetown. According to one account, Chalabi stormed in and confronted their American adviser. He called the American a "punk," right to his face in the hotel lounge, and then warned the group that he had friends at the top of the Defense Department.

26

September 11—A New Direction

DESPITE CHALABI'S FRIENDS and connections in the Bush administration, it was not until after the attacks of September 11 that the INC's snow really began to stick. Instead of dying in the crash at the Pentagon on September 11, Chalabi ended up making a visit to the undamaged part of the building just a week later. The debris of the plane he would have been on was not even removed yet, but much of the building was undamaged. So Chalabi was escorted, along with his American *consigliere* Francis Brooke, to the E-Ring on the third floor, the Pentagon's holy of holies.

There he gave a lecture to an august group of elderly men called the Defense Policy Board, about the threat Saddam Hussein posed to the world. Introducing him was the other invited guest, Professor Bernard Lewis of Princeton University, who told the gathering that democratic reformers in the Middle East needed help, "such as my friend here, Dr. Chalabi."[15] Then Chalabi stood up and went to the podium, as one attendee recalls. Speaking in his thick accent, he gave what was billed as a presentation about the Middle East. Ahmad Chalabi knows how to read a room, to feel the rhythms of his listeners. But that day, perhaps, he was a little off. Kenneth Adelman, one of the dignitaries on the board, remembers Chalabi's presentation, and wasn't impressed. "Within fifteen minutes he had made his point about how bad Saddam

Hussein was, and either I tuned out or he droned on," he said, irreverently. But Richard Perle, Chalabi's most vocal advocate, was chairman of the Defense Policy Board, and the other members were fans as well.

After the attacks of 9/11, the INC lost no time using the occasion to further its objectives. But Chalabi didn't take the lead; instead, the INC's campaign was conducted mostly through its allies. The first voice of authority to point to Iraq, after 9/11, was former CIA director James Woolsey, Chalabi's friend and a lawyer for INC officials. When the attacks of 9/11 took place, Woolsey had been in a morning meeting with colleagues. They all turned to watch the television in the conference room as the news broke. Driving home in a rush, Woolsey passed right by the smoking crater in the Pentagon.

The day of the attacks, as most of the nation watched the horrors unfold on television, Woolsey co-wrote an article with Mansoor Ijaz, a Pakistani American who was active in counterterrorist discussions. It was called "Revenge Is a Dish Best Served Cold." Woolsey argued that the resources "needed to conduct this war against the United States can only be offered by a regime whose track record against U.S. interests is proven, and Iraq comes immediately to mind." The piece appeared in the *Los Angeles Times* the next day.[16] In quick succession Woolsey appeared on a series of broadcasts.

As dawn rose on September 12, via live remote Woolsey told ABC News's *Good Morning America* anchor Charles Gibson that the United States should not solely look at bin Laden. "I think Iraq would have to be the principal candidate," he said. A few hours later Woolsey was on CNN's screen arguing that investigators "really need to look carefully at the possibility there may be state sponsorship here, and I think the most likely, certainly not the only, possibility is Iraq." And then on CBS News he suggested to Dan Rather that Saddam Hussein had been behind the 1993 attacks on the World Trade Center. "I hope," Woolsey told Rather, "if he was involved in this one, he's underestimated us again."

Another group of Chalabi's friends promoted similar views on September 14, at an American Enterprise Institute news conference. David Wurmser, who had written *Tyranny's Ally*, the tract touting Chalabi's ideas, announced that "Iraq is the key." Michael Ledeen stepped up to the podium. "Take off the restrictions, the outrageous, ridiculous, pedagoging, legalistic, self-defeating restrictions on the Iraqi National Congress," he demanded. Laurie Mylroie, billed as an academic and Iraq expert, was the first to speak, trotting out her theory that the 9/11 attacks were part of Saddam's war against the United States. (Mylroie's thesis, that Saddam was responsible for most anti-U.S. terror attacks, had been widely discredited by intelligence and law enforcement agents but was eagerly accepted by certain neo-conservatives and by the followers of Chalabi. Paul Wolfowitz was one believer.)

———

Suddenly that fall there was a fortuitous convergence of Chalabi's allies in government. Wolfowitz, Perle, Feith, Harold Rhode, and others already held official positions, but soon David Wurmser joined the Defense Department under Feith. Chalabi's old ally retired Gen. Wayne Downing was appointed to a new position as the National Director and Deputy National Security Adviser for Combating Terrorism. Linda Flohr, the retired CIA officer who had delivered the first funding to Chalabi, was brought into the NSC as well.

But despite the influence of Chalabi's friends, the United States went off to war in Afghanistan, not Iraq. It was, as well, a bureaucratic win for the CIA, which Chalabi despised so much, because the war against the Taliban was largely engineered by the agency. Case officers, not soldiers, were the first on the ground in Afghanistan, meeting with tribesmen and paying allies.

The Administration pursued Osama bin Laden and the Taliban. Impatient, Ahmad Chalabi and his inner circle determined to coax America back to the course they preferred.

27
Saddam's Airline Hijacking School

> "'Ever bought a fake picture?'
> 'I sold a couple once,' said Toby with a flashy nervous smile, but no one laughed.
> 'The more you pay for it, the less inclined you are to doubt it. Silly, but there we are.'"
>
> —George Smiley, in John le Carré's *Tinker, Tailor, Soldier, Spy*

ON NOVEMBER 4, 2001, almost two months after 9/11, Ahmad Chalabi called a telephone number in Lebanon, according to Mohamad al-Zobaidy, who took the phone call at his apartment in Beirut, greeted Chalabi and noted his instruction. Chalabi's code name in Zobaidy's records was Our Big Brother. Take care of the two men in your custody, Chalabi told Zobaidy on the phone. Don't let anyone see the men, he insisted. Don't let them talk to anyone.[17]

Zobaidy nodded and reassured Ahmad Chalabi before hanging up the phone. Zobaidy knew how to keep secrets and how to make sure people did what he told them to do. He's not a large man, but he carries himself as if he is. A veteran of the INC, he wears a rakish little goatee. And he lived the life of a secret agent, ranging across borders to serve the organization's needs. In fact, his own code name in the INC was Al Deeb, The Wolf. Zobaidy, who kept an immaculate diary, would later become bitter toward Chalabi and his

INC, but in 2001 and 2002 he was still a loyal and dedicated secret soldier in its cause.

Chalabi's phone call to Zobaidy puts Chalabi in the middle of one of the earliest and most significant propaganda operations run by the INC after 9/11: an elaborate series of claims that Saddam ran a school for training airline hijackers at a terrorist camp called Salman Pak.

═══

It was Francis Brooke who got the message out to Aras Kareem Habib and others right after 9/11: "Get me a terrorist and some WMDs, because that's what the Bush administration wants!"[18] He tells the story in various ways: "If you've got it, bring it on, because now's the time" is the phrase he used in another conversation.[19] Whatever Brooke's specific instructions were, the INC campaign had two themes: to find Iraqi defectors who were prepared to make allegations about Saddam's WMDs on the one hand and defectors who'd make allegations about Saddam's links to terror on the other. All in all Chalabi's people—defectors and sources—produced four major story lines about Saddam, all of them false, but all with worldwide media coverage.

The first of these stories centered on the purported Saddam Hussein hijacking school for Islamic terrorists at Salman Pak. The INC started pitching it within two weeks of the 9/11 attacks. Defectors had come forward, the INC claimed, who seemed to put Saddam smack in the middle of international Al Qaeda terror attacks. The first hint anyone in the U.S. government had about these stewing allegations was from James Woolsey, the former CIA director and ex-secretary of the INCSF.[20] Woolsey, well aware of the CIA's distrust of the INC, called the head of the Defense Intelligence Agency to relay the hair-raising intelligence.[21] Woolsey said he called DIA because there was a military component to the INC's warnings. With Woolsey cracking the door open, the INC stepped in.

The next day, September 28, in Washington, Chalabi joined an underling to brief DIA officers about one of the INC's "defectors"—a Col. Abu Zainab al-Querery—who claimed he had trained Arab terrorists and had seen them getting trained on how to hijack airliners. Abu Zainab, Chalabi and his aide explained, was in Turkey, seeking asylum. He had an assortment of interesting stories to tell, like how

Iraqi commandos destroy "mock-ups of U.S. Navy vessels." After Chalabi's talk with the DIA in Washington, things moved quickly.

For the next step of the INC's operation, Abu Zainab, the colonel himself, showed up at the U.S. Embassy in Ankara, Turkey, and was debriefed by CIA officers for several days. Classified reports soon found their way into the intelligence channels, like one titled "Terrorists Allegedly Trained in Iraqi Camps."[22] The September 30 report was hot stuff indeed coming just three weeks after the September 11 attacks—except that, even in those panicked times, few people within the government believed a word of it. The colonel turned out to be a short, plump Iraqi, a heavy smoker with a serious affinity for Johnny Walker Red. Finding him not credible in the least, the CIA showed him the door and left him on the Ankara sidewalk.

With its portly and heavy-drinking defector rejected by the U.S. government, the INC moved to the next phase of the operation: a massive press campaign. The man was smuggled to Damascus, where the INC could control him better. And the colonel suddenly had a partner who escorted him everywhere. His name was Amar, and he said he worked in the kitchen at a training facility at Salman Pak.

Even the phrase Salman Pak, for people who knew Iraq, was ominous. It first showed up in the international press in 1989 as a biological weapons research facility back when Saddam Hussein really had WMDs and was an ally of the United States.[23] In 1991, during the Gulf War, F-111s and F-117s bombed it to smithereens, and shortly afterward Iraq's government confirmed it had been researching biological weapons there.[24] Salman Pak remained a magnet of attention. In 1998 the *Sunday Times* in London even reported that Iraq had tested anthrax on prisoners of war held at the site.[25] For years UN inspectors had known of a derelict fuselage of an airliner at the site and considered it unremarkable.

Zobaidy, the INC's man on the ground, interviewed Abu Zainab and Amar and sent a report back, he says, to Aras and "Abu Hashem" (Chalabi). One thing he wrote in the report was that Abu Zainab had "poetic interests" and a good mind for making up stories. That didn't matter. Zobaidy had new instructions. Get Abu Zainab and his sidekick, Amar, to Beirut and wait for the reporters to show up. So he set them up in an apartment in Beirut.

And because he wanted to get reimbursed by the INC, he tallied up his expenses so far, which he says ran $3,622 for Abu Zainab. It was all to come from the U.S. government, after all, which was paying for this program even if it didn't want the information.

Abu Zainab referred Chalabi's people to another "defector" who, he said, could corroborate his tale, and who was living in the United States on a refugee visa. The INC quickly chased him down in Texas. Sabah Khodada claimed to have been a captain in the Fedayeen Saddam and said he had been at Salman Pak for six months in the 1990s. He is a short man of forty-seven with a military bearing, a bit of a swagger, and a smile that shows off his teeth. He seemed appreciative of the exile group's attention, and he was willing to tell his extraordinary story to anyone who would listen. The INC wanted him to talk to a few select journalists sympathetic to their group.

On October 12, one month after the 9/11 attacks, the American public—the taxpayers who paid the bills for the INC's programs, after all—first heard allegations of a hijacking school for Islamic terrorists. The news was delivered in a column written by Chalabi's friend Jim Hoagland at the *Washington Post*. Sabah Khodada, Hoagland wrote, "outlined to me here Wednesday details of the training given for airliner hijacking and assassinations in the Salman Pak area of Baghdad while he was there."

Hoagland hinted there was corroboration: "An Iraqi ex-intelligence officer . . . has told the Iraqi National Congress of specific sightings of 'Islamicists' training on a Boeing 707 parked in Salman Pak as recently as September 2000, [and] says he was treated dismissively by CIA officers in Ankara this week." The CIA, Hoagland mocked, "reportedly showed no interest in pursuing a possible Iraq connection to Sept. 11."

Once that piece came out, the story of terrorists training at Salman Pak picked up steam. William Safire repeated it in his *New York Times* column. The *Wall Street Journal* ran a column called "What the Iraqi Defectors Say." Khodada's story had matured and rounded out. In this version he "was responsible for training an elite commando team . . . in airline hijacking and sabotage in a high-security facility run by Iraqi intelligence in the Salman Pak neighborhood of Baghdad." The team was given "a daily regimen of exercises on kidnapping, assassination, and—using a Boeing 707 parked inside the complex—how to hijack a plane or bus without weapons." The *Wall Street Journal* column said the "the two defectors' accounts provide the missing link between the 19 hijackers, the mountains of the Hindu Kush, and the regime in Baghdad." The article quoted Khodada: "Everything about the operations, the style, the details tell me it was Iraqi intelligence. Whether the world accepts it or not, I am very, very sure."

The allegations were becoming bolder: Saddam Hussein was quite possibly behind the 9/11 attacks.

But while Khodada was publicly speaking in America in interviews arranged through the INC, Abu Zainab, still in the Middle East, had not yet given press interviews. Now the INC began to get him ready. Chalabi offered access first to Lowell Bergman, the former CBS producer who had produced a story about Chalabi in 1991. Now he worked for both *Frontline* and the *New York Times*. Bergman, a journalistic legend, couldn't travel to Beirut for the story, so the *Times* foreign desk assigned Chris Hedges of the Paris bureau, who had dealt with Chalabi in Kurdistan in the early 1990s and didn't trust him. "I stayed away from him because he had a terrible reputation," Hedges said in an interview. Still, Hedges accepted the assignment. He and Bergman chatted with Chalabi at his Mayfair apartment and at his office in London, and then Hedges flew to Beirut. He'd do the story for the *Times* and would conduct the TV interview as well for *Frontline*.

Back in Beirut, Zobaidy wrote in his diary that Abu Zainab—the colonel—went through a whole bottle of Scotch the night before he met the reporter. He got so drunk he vomited. Over the next day or two, the interview was conducted at the Vendome Hotel. It would be a doubleheader, a two-for-one deal that would hit both print and broadcast: the *New York Times* was a grand slam for the INC, and the widely respected *Frontline*, on PBS, was nearly as good.

Chris Hedges's print story in the *Times* broke on November 8, 2001—the headline was gripping, coming in those months after 9/11: "Defectors Cite Iraqi Training for Terrorists"—and it linked Khodada's and Abu Zainab's yarns together for the first time. "Two defectors from Iraqi intelligence," wrote Hedges, "said yesterday that they had worked for several years at a secret Iraqi government camp that had trained Islamic terrorists in rotations of five or six months since 1995." The story cited both Khodada and Abu Zainab, whom it called a "former lieutenant general." Abu Zainab was evocative in his descriptions, calling the Islamists at the camp "a scruffy lot" who had trained in Iraq how to take over airplanes. "We were training these people to attack installations important to the United States," Abu Zainab said in the article. "The gulf war never ended for Saddam Hussein. He is at war with the United States. We were repeatedly told this."

The *New York Times* article pointed out that the allegations were "likely to fuel one side of an intense debate in Washington over whether to extend the war against Osama bin Laden and the Taliban government of Afghanistan to include Iraq."

Chalabi lost no time in capitalizing on the publicity. Working over the weekend at the Pennsylvania Avenue address of the INC, just blocks from the White House, the INC was anxious to prove that the hundreds of thousands of dollars per month in information-collection program funds were being spent well. The INC dashed out a report to the State Department, boasting that it continued to "collect sensitive information that reveals Iraq's link with September 11th aftermath."[26] That's an intriguing part of the story, because it indicates that the State Department, while not believing Chalabi's information, should have been aware of the propaganda operation.

The *New York Times* story, meanwhile, intensified in the retelling. Newspaper reporters around the world were crawling over one another to interview Abu Zainab, the general or colonel, depending on who was telling the story.

The London *Observer* went even farther than the *Times*. In the *Observer*'s version, written by journalist David Rose, the "defectors" claimed that as soon as 9/11 happened, they figured it must have been people trained at Salman Pak. All in all, the media sensation was a remarkable success for the Iraqi National Congress and Ahmad Chalabi.

Soon *Vanity Fair* followed in its December issue with another story by David Rose, a compelling profile of Abu Zainab, who was now identified as a "brigadier general." Abu Zainab now revealed that he ran the training camp for a previously unknown strike force and that he had sent thirty men off from Iraq as "sleeper agents," with fake UAE passports. They were terrorists-in-waiting to be activated by Baghdad, according to his characterization. He described the sinking of a mock U.S. Navy destroyer, in which Iraqi frogmen proved their worth in a practice mission. And he said that when he saw the planes striking the World Trade Center, he immediately turned to a friend and said, "That's ours!" Like the *Times* article, the *Vanity Fair* story got tremendous pickup in other publications. "Dirty Thirty," screamed a *New York Post* headline, referring to the thirty alleged Iraqi secret commandos loosed on the world.

＝＝＝

Chalabi's chief secret agent, Mohamad al-Zobaidy, who received that phone call from Chalabi, now claims that the real story about Abu Zainab is not what it seemed at all. He said Abu Zainab had been a high-ranking Baath official, but he had never run a unit at Salman Pak. In fact, according to Zobaidy, Abu Zainab actually admitted that to him at the beginning. And those who met Abu Zainab's sidekick, Amar, say it was quite clear that he never went through the alleged training, since he actually admitted he had only worked in the kitchen at Salman Pak.

Zobaidy said the decision was made (he says he doesn't know who made it) to let Abu Zainab present the other man's information as if it was his own. Zobaidy said he believes the colonel did participate in human rights atrocities in Iraq, but he does not believe Abu Zainab's terror stories. The colonel was lying, Zobaidy said, and there was no doubt about it.

Nabeel Musawi, the INC official who escorted journalists to interview Abu Zainab, now says he didn't believe the colonel either. "The whole story did not ring true," he said in an interview. Musawi was also skeptical of the friendship between the colonel and Amar, his alleged friend from Salman Pak, a mere cook. How could the two men have been the friends they claimed to be? Still, Musawi was convinced that some of the colonel's tales of atrocities were true. The colonel's hands were bloody, even if he was lying about the terrorism link. "I didn't want to press him," Musawi now says, "but Abu Zainab was the bastard in the whole equation."

Musawi never told the journalists who scribbled down the colonel's story about his doubts, though. And Musawi insists, all the same, that he believes terrorists were trained at the Salman Pak camp.

So who coached the colonel, if anyone? How did he come up with the goods the INC wanted? No one has a convincing explanation. Also, there is the question of motivation. Why did the colonel lie? What sort of incentive was he given? And what role, if any, did the INC play in creating that incentive? Those questions have not been answered.

———

As dramatic as all the information was, the Central Intelligence Agency never bought it. "It was tainted," said one member of the Iraqi Operations Group. "We knew that Salman Pak was used to train Palestinians in the 1990s but not Al Qaeda." The agency's Iraqi Operations Group wrote up an analysis stating that "we have determined that much of his [Abu Zainab's] information is inaccurate and appears aimed at influencing U.S. (and probably Western) policy on Iraq."

And a year after 9/11, on September 29, 2002, well before any invasion of Iraq, the CIA produced a secret report to explain its views about Salman Pak. "At least one of these defectors," the CIA analysts wrote, referring to Abu Zainab,* "had embellished and exaggerated his access. . . . No al Qaeda associated detainee since 11 September have said they trained at Salman Pak."[27]

This might have put it all to bed, except it came far too late. At a bare minimum it was fifteen days too late. On September 12, 2002, President George Bush stood before the General Assembly of the United Nations and gave a speech that largely foreshadowed the case for war, as troops were already heading toward the Gulf.

That same day, the White House released a fact sheet to go along with the presidential speech, which was supposed to assist reporters in their coverage of the story. It repeated the now well-worn allegations about Salman Pak. "Former Iraqi military officers," it said, clearly

---

*One writer later claimed that Abu Zainab was actually an imposter, and that he'd stolen the identity of a real Iraqi general who lived in Fallujah. That makes the story even more confusing, but it seems unlikely. Even CIA and DIA officials who briefly interviewed him seemed to believe he was a former Iraqi official. Also, those who met him say he did have identity cards and proof of his Baath affiliation.

referring to Abu Zainab and Sabah Khodada, "have described a highly secret terrorist training facility in Iraq known as Salman Pak, where both Iraqis and non-Iraqi Arabs receive training on hijacking planes and trains, planting explosives in cities, sabotage, and assassinations."

It had been nearly a full year since Ahmad Chalabi met with the DIA to tell them the tale. It had been fully investigated and essentially discarded. Even Chalabi's own people didn't believe the chief source. But still, Chalabi's allegations about Saddam's role in training hijackers had found their way into the White House press office as it made the case for war.

The whole story cost the INC no money at all. Not a dime. After all, the group's budget was entirely paid for by the State Department, which grudgingly and unwittingly paid for all expenses. Abu Zainab's expenses, Amar's expenses, and everything the INC spent on their efforts was paid for by American taxpayers. Zobaidy says he was reimbursed for $5,000 by the INC for what he'd spent on Abu Zainab.

Well after the war, Sabah Khodada, the INC "defector" who claimed he was a captain in the Fedayeen training hijackers and that he had even been trained how to hijack airplanes himself, made a living as a shuttle-bus driver at the Dallas-Fort Worth Airport for Avis Rent a Car. He also took classes to become a car mechanic. But for a while during Chalabi's great Salman Pak publicity drive, Khodada had worked with the INC in its Washington office. The truth was, he wasn't a big fan of Chalabi or his staff. His impression, he said in an interview, was that Aras Habib Kareem, Chalabi's top aide, was really running the show. "Aras—he led Chalabi by the nose. This is what I've seen," Khodada said. That comports with the way other Iraqis saw the relationship between the two men, but it is unclear what the truth really is. Khodada also said the INC talked incessantly about Donald Rumsfeld before the invasion of Iraq. "They believed in Rumsfeld," he said, "that Rumsfeld was giving them full support, that Rumsfeld is behind the INC, that Rumsfeld is going to hand them the seat of power in Iraq."

28

The Case of the Underground Wells

"An Iraqi defector who described himself as a civil
engineer said he personally worked on renovations of
secret facilities for biological, chemical and nuclear
weapons in underground wells, private villas and under
the Saddam Hussein Hospital in Baghdad as recently as
a year ago."

—Judith Miller, *New York Times*, December 20, 2001

IN NOVEMBER 2001 a cheerful and potbellied thirty-eight-year-old Iraqi
civil engineer showed up in Kurdistan with two wives, five children,
and a dream of making a new life for himself. His name was Adnan
Ihsan Saeed al-Haideri. One of Haideri's two wives (four are permit-
ted under Islamic law) nagged him incessantly, which made life unpleasant. Haideri had brought not just his large family but also a pile
of documents he said he'd filched from his company in Iraq. Haideri
had a marked advantage over the other refugees clamoring for a way
out of Saddam's clutches: he knew a high-ranking official in the INC
from the old days. The man he knew had moved to America, and just
happened to run Chalabi's INC office on Pennsylvania Avenue: it was
the U.S.-educated, highly energetic Entifadh Qanbar. Haideri managed to reach him by satellite phone. After that, things moved quickly
for Haideri. He and his large family and his documents were scooped

up by the INC and shuffled along with great urgency and great care to safety in Damascus, as if he were a delicacy that could spoil if it were left to sit around too long.[28]

Haideri was the protagonist of the INC's second propaganda coup, which pivoted around his stories of underground hiding places for dangerous weapons. Once again, the INC official who handled his case was Mohamad al-Zobaidy—Chalabi's chief man on the ground in the Middle East. Haideri's goal, Zobaidy wrote diligently in his journal on November 21, 2001, was "to emigrate to Australia and get asylum." The next day, Zobaidy debriefed Haideri at length. Haideri said he worked on underground construction, using sealants to prevent water damage. He said he was a civil engineer who performed subcontract work for military projects in Iraq and talked of underground sites, like wells, where missiles were stored.

Zobaidy was wary, he claims, of some of the allegations: he says Haideri hinted there were large missile sites underground in a neighborhood called Waziria. But Waziria was a residential neighborhood where the type of construction he was describing would stand out, drawing unwanted attention, which would have been a problem in a tyrannical society like Saddam's Iraq.

But still, Haideri seemed to have valid documents, even if his WMD information was dubious. Zobaidy made the drive to Beirut to bring the documents triumphantly back. Zaab Sethna and Nabeel Musawi happened to be in town helping to interview another defector, and Zobaidy told them and another journalist of his latest find. He got a message to Ahmad Chalabi and Aras Kareem with a report, and the next day he received an e-mail back from Chalabi stating that Haideri was exactly what they were looking for. The e-mail implored him to "Take very good care of [Haideri] and use the utmost precautions." Sometime after that Zobaidy received some panicked instructions: we need him urgently in Bangkok.[29]

The INC viewed Bangkok as a safe destination when it wanted to get someone out of the Middle East. "It was easy to get a visa," explained Musawi. Zobaidy promptly dispatched a man he trusted to escort Haideri and his large family to Bangkok on Syrian Airways. There the Haideri clan settled in to an apartment hotel called the Five Star Hotel

Apartments. Each of Haideri's wives had her own room, and there was one for his children too. And there they waited.

Chalabi wanted to get Haideri's story into the press, as with those of most of the defectors, but he also wanted to get it into the U.S. government intelligence system. There were several reasons: the INC wanted to prove that the Information Collection Program, which was being funded by U.S. taxpayers, was achieving something. And of course, some sources say, they always wanted, jealously, to make the CIA look bad.

The journalistic part was easy: journalists were tripping over one another for WMD stories, and this one proved no exception. But if a reporter cared to look closely, there was not necessarily much to this story at all. Haideri had no firsthand knowledge of WMDs. The documents he had, if authentic, proved only that Iraq's military was concerned about water damage to underground sites; but the documents made no reference to chemical, biological, or nuclear materials. He had never seen a weapon; he had never seen containers that carried any biological, chemical, or nuclear material.

Some reporters were a bit skeptical. Even Chalabi's old friend Chris Isham, the chief of investigative projects at ABC News, wouldn't bite. In an interview, Isham recalled his concerns. "The problem with him was he was an engineer. He wasn't in the WMD program. He never pretended he was. It didn't rise to the level, for me. The rest was all speculation as to what it was for."

One journalist angling for the Haideri scoop was the English writer David Rose of *Vanity Fair* and the *Observer*. The INC had given Rose some hot exclusives already, but this time he was disappointed. Coming home from a long weekend, he hit the playback button on his voice mail and got a message from Zaab Sethna, Chalabi's PR man. "David, this story about this WMD," said the voice mail. "Dr. Chalabi has decided it's very important to get it into a big American paper, so Judith Miller is going to do it for the *New York Times*." Rose was furious that he'd lost out because his competitor was American. "Chalabi needed a big propaganda coup in an American paper. He didn't say propaganda. He said 'coup' in an American paper so the INC could justify its existence, show the Congress that it wasn't wasting money that it had been allocated."

So there in a Bangkok hotel, INC officials went over the information with Haideri. Haideri later told U.S. intelligence agents that he exaggerated and embellished his story "because that was what the INC told him to do," although they have denied it.[30] Musawi insisted that it wasn't him. (Sethna, the Pakistani British PR wizard and socialite who had been with Chalabi since 1991, refused to respond to any queries at all but has denied it in the past.)

By the time Haideri did an interview with Judith Miller in a Bangkok hotel, his story had been ramped up a notch and a bit more flesh was jiggling on the bones. Miller was a natural for the story. Not only was she a long-standing friend of Ahmad Chalabi's but she had written about WMDs for years, and co-written the book *Germs: Biological Weapons and America's Secret War.* She interviewed Haideri on December 17 and published an article on December 20, 2001, describing how Haideri had visited twenty biological and chemical sites. His account, she wrote, provided evidence that Saddam was still engaged in illegal WMD activity.

> The interview with Mr. Saeed [Haideri] was arranged by the Iraqi National Congress, the main Iraqi opposition group, which seeks the overthrow of Mr. Hussein. If verified, Mr. Saeed's allegations would provide ammunition to officials within the Bush administration who have been arguing that Mr. Hussein should be driven from power partly because of his unwillingness to stop making weapons of mass destruction, despite his pledges to do so. . . .
>
> Mr. Saeed's account gives new clues about the types and possible locations of illegal laboratories, facilities and storage sites that American officials and international inspectors have long suspected Iraq of trying to hide. It also suggests that Baghdad continued renovating and repairing such illegal facilities after barring international inspectors from the country three years ago.

The story splashed across the newspapers of the world like a can of paint. Reuters, the AP, and other wire services picked it up. Newspapers from Australia to Austin, Texas, ran the story. Network news anchors read terse accounts of it.

But Chalabi wanted to make sure the INC got its information directly into the U.S. government wash of intelligence in those months after 9/11, when it was clear that America's spy agencies were off balance and paranoid.

James Woolsey stepped in once again. The former CIA director called up a contact at the Defense Department to alert him to the defector and the allegations. Wheels turned. By late December, a DIA official working out of the embassy in Thailand took up the case. The Iraqis called him Mr. Nick, and he looked the part of an American secret agent: polite, soft-spoken, and muscular like an athlete. He seemed to be an experienced man, although Nabeel Musawi said the initial DIA agents who interviewed Haideri knew nothing at all about Iraq or WMDs.

But as the case moved forward, there developed an interagency rivalry. The DIA, sometimes the unsung and poorly funded member of America's fractious spy agencies, initially took hold of the Haideri case file. As Musawi recalls, there was initial confusion among the DIA officials in Bangkok, who were naturally specialists in Chinese affairs with no expertise at all in the Middle East or Iraq. The DIA did a polygraph in a hotel room there, which Haideri passed. At this point, though, the CIA still had no involvement whatsoever. Then there came a classic case of spy versus spy. An intelligence source explained with a chuckle that the Thai security service spotted the DIA operation and alerted contacts at the Central Intelligence Agency. Curious about the DIA dealings in what it considered its stomping ground in Bangkok, the CIA bigfooted the small DIA component. The CIA cabled home with a jaunty tone of bureaucratic victory that "We are now considering this a joint case."[31] Haideri secretly boarded a jet headed to the United States shortly thereafter, and despite whatever U.S. law may say about bigamy, his two wives accompanied him on the plane.

The two women, Haideri, and the children were soon ensconced in a Fairfax, Virginia, home at U.S. government expense. "He was scooped up in the furor of the moment. There was no adult supervision," a former CIA official said. The decision to bring both wives caused some stir at the agency, and an intelligence source says trouble arose quickly. "The wives didn't get along." The CIA officer laughed as he told the story. "They were fighting in their house. People were calling in disturbances. The cops were called."

Still, while the women were at each other's throats in this strange new suburban environment, Haideri must have been relieved to get away to brief U.S. government officials. CIA and DIA experts, eagerly trying to pinpoint Saddam's weapons, apparently listened to Haideri as if he were a scientist or military official rather than the simple subcontractor he was. An analyst wrote that Haideri had "exceptional access to information of interest to the U.S. Intelligence Community."

Miraculously, Haideri's knowledge about the tactical menace posed by Iraq seemed to increase the more time he spent in the United States. Simple questions prompted a deluge of information from this civil engineer: illicit trade, Iraqi prisons, communications security, "conventional weapons facilities." And the kicker was that he now knew of a nuclear site. It was a site underneath Haditha Tubtum—the "Medical City," as he put it. He wasn't quite sure what it was for or what they were doing, but he was convinced it was a prized part of the Iraqi efforts to build an atomic bomb.

To be sure, there were some words of caution along the way. A State Department analyst cleared for Haideri's material e-mailed dryly in March 2002 that "the source indeed has a remarkable memory, and has clearly been to many sites." The analyst was skeptical, though, and did not share the general enthusiasm: Haideri seemed to think everything was a nuclear site, he noticed. "Beware," the analyst cautioned. But there is no indication that his advice had any braking effect on the flow of information.[32]

The civil engineer with his two unhappy wives was one of Ahmad Chalabi's greatest PR successes. Haideri's information found its way into the National Intelligence Estimate on nuclear weapons in October 2002 as the Bush administration prepared its case for war. "New Nuclear Facility?" asked the title of a block of text describing Haideri's alleged observations underneath the medical complex.

And it is only fair to point out that, while the New York Times's Judith Miller may have written a flawed story about Haideri's information, she did not do much worse than the officials at the CIA's clumsily named "Weapons Intelligence, Non Proliferation, and Arms Control Center," or WINPAC. If she was taken in, then so was the U.S. government itself. And in fact Haideri's story made it to the highest levels. It spilled easily up into the White House press office. Along with the alarming tales of training hijackers at Salman Pak, Haideri's fables were part of the press package released when President Bush gave his speech at the United Nations on September 12.

29

David Rose

2001–2003

OF ALL THE JOURNALISTS who joined the energetic and loyal circle around Ahmad Chalabi after the September 11 attacks, none was drawn in more quickly and more closely than David Rose. A tall man with unruly hair, Rose has always written with thoughtful passion, gravitating toward stories exposing racism, prison abuse, injustice. He also has a flair for adventure and travel and risk. He dives into his reporting with remarkable sincerity. "I was used," he says now of his relationship with Chalabi. "Of course I was used. I was also charmed. By Chalabi, I mean. Chalabi is brilliant at manipulating people."

In 2001, in the weeks after the World Trade Center attacks, Rose was looking for a smart way to cover Mideast terrorism. When he first approached Chalabi's INC, he said in an interview, "I thought I was being clever." Years later, recounting the thought, he shook his head. Terrorism reporting was a crowded field in those days, and the mob of reporters jostling in on the Al Qaeda sources was tough competition. Casting about for a strategy to stay ahead of the pack, Rose had asked Jim Woolsey for advice. The former CIA director spoke highly of his friend Ahmad Chalabi and the Iraqi National Congress. "He said, 'Well, you should call the INC, they know all about links between Iraq and al Qaeda,'" Rose recalls. Rose was astonished at this possible rich new vein of reporting. "I thought, 'Wow, you're kidding me!'"

The first time he went to INC headquarters in Knightsbridge, in an elegant limestone building where Iraqis often gathered outside smoking, Rose met several members of Chalabi's inner circle. He chatted with the sleek Zaab Sethna, who seemed to travel in the best circles of London, and the dashing Nabeel Musawi. The men were pleasant, relaxed professionals, who seemed candid and sincere.

In his next visit just days later, Rose was ushered into Chalabi's office, and he immediately liked being there. Chalabi, with his informal grace, focused intently on him. Chalabi was clearly familiar with Rose's reporting and could even cite from some of his more memorable pieces. "Chalabi had *read* my articles, he *knew* where my interests lay." Rose was flattered. "He knew I had an interest in history. He just started talking about, you know, the second Punjab War." Rose is convinced that the INC carefully examined and mined his background for information so Chalabi would know how to elicit his sympathy. "If there is a leitmotif that runs through my twenty-five years of journalism," he says now, "It's writing about miscarriages of justice, human rights . . . oppressed people getting abused through a legal system, and that's what Chalabi saw. He researched me. He would always emphasize his implacable opposition to the death penalty." Chalabi's apparent reliability as a source was driven home to Rose early on, in an exclusive story that was only proved to be nonsense much later. During those frantic days of terror, the now-discredited allegation that Mohamed Atta, one of the nineteen hijackers, had met an Iraqi intelligence officer in Prague before the attacks was all over the airways for weeks. One day at the INC offices, Chalabi told Rose, "We have a fantastic story for you." Not just Atta but two *other* terrorists involved in 9/11 had met with Iraqi intelligence, Chalabi confided. "I went, 'Well, *that's* a good story!'" Rose remembers.

Rose went to a respected source of his, who ended up "confirming" that U.S. intelligence had heard the same thing. Excited at the possible scoop, he went back to the INC, where Aras Kareem, Chalabi's operations man, gave him more details. The gruff Aras wove a tale in which these other two hijackers had been spotted at a suspicious mosque in the United Arab Emirates, and the mosque, Aras confided, was a front for Iraqi intelligence.

It was explosive information, which, if true, meant that three of the nineteen hijackers had met with Iraqi intelligence officials. Rose again, somehow, got confirmation from his source in Washington. "And I was, like, 'Wow! These guys really know what they are talking about.'" He was hooked on Chalabi as a source. "That was the moment that my disbelief was suspended. Up to that point I had a healthy skepticism for anything the INC told me."

And then Rose became strongly sympathetic to the INC. He fully admits his enthusiasm, which became advocacy. Indeed, he could have been confused for a mouthpiece for the INC, quoting people they said were Iraqi defectors, laying out their agenda and adopting their cause as his own.

He enjoyed being around Chalabi, almost as if the man were a cult guru. "He has the regal manner, but if you're with him, you're part of the entourage, it's gone!" Rose snapped his fingers to explain. "And he's, like, so approachable, and that's part of it. It's like, 'You're one of my crowd.' And you immediately are part of it, and it's so effective."

Chalabi was an aesthete and a gourmand but also a regular at the Lahore Kebab House in London's East End, a remarkable, inexpensive kebab place where the waiters knew him. He had charming contradictions.

On December 2, 2001, Rose, who had virtually no exposure to Iraq issues until two months before, wrote an editorial for the *Observer* calling for military action against Iraq. "There are occasions in history when the use of force is both right and sensible," he wrote. "This is one of them." Rose considers himself a political liberal and didn't even know what the neocons were at the time.

One day he complained to Chalabi in bewilderment that other progressive intellectuals didn't understand the reason for war against Iraq. What could explain their obstinacy, he wondered. What kind of blinders were these antiwar liberals wearing? What kind of shortsighted, amoral positions were they taking? Chalabi, he said, responded reassuringly and kindly: they don't get it because they don't have the moral sense, David, that you do. At the time, Rose took comfort in that, but remained disturbed at the shortsightedness of his former colleagues.

Later Rose flew to Beirut with Sethna and Musawi to interview Abu Zainab, the alleged defector who knew so much about Saddam's links to terror. Rose wove a vivid and terrifying profile of Abu Zainab for *Vanity Fair* in December 2001, called "Inside Saddam's Terror Regime," which got extraordinary worldwide publicity. He wrote that Abu Zainab's trained commandos in Iraq had blown up a "specially constructed mock-up of a U.S. Navy Fifth Fleet destroyer, moored in central Iraq's Habaniya lake." Rose repeated the Salman Pak allegations and even expanded on them. Not only did they teach Islamists to take over planes without weapons; they also taught them to hijack passenger trains. Terrorist trainees who flunked Saddam's course were themselves used as targets in "live ammunition training." Abu Zainab even started talking about his own "brutal history of rape, torture, and mass murder."

Soon Rose flew off to Amman to interview yet another of Chalabi's defectors for another exclusive. He had become one of the journalists with an inside track at the INC.

He also flew to Washington, D.C., and was astonished at how Chalabi opened doors for him. When he was with his charismatic Iraqi escort, Rose could meet anyone among this powerful new neoconservative crowd. They virtually ate from his hand. Neoconservative sources close to Chalabi gave Rose the analysis they had assembled at Douglas Feith's Counter Terrorism Evaluation Group, presenting it as proof that Chalabi was right and the CIA was wrong. He met a variety of government officials—senators and congressmen and intelligence analysts—as he was carried along in Chalabi's wake.

The British reporter was even introduced to the deputy secretary of Defense, Paul Wolfowitz. Wolfowitz was certainly a fan of Chalabi, as Rose recalls it. But among the powerful neoconservatives who seemed so friendly, Wolfowitz was also the only source from whom he recalls hearing the smallest of doubts about Chalabi. Sure, he was supportive of Chalabi, and it was not exactly criticism, but "I'm not one of the people who thinks Ahmad Chalabi is the best thing since sliced bread," Wolfowitz confessed to him.

Chalabi, who was trying to lose weight, seemed to walk everywhere, and he moved quickly; Rose, though much taller, had difficulty keeping up. The journalist grew more and more fond of Chalabi. The man struck him as having extraordinary charisma, intelligence, and bravery, and yet he had a simple, and human, side. Chalabi was on a high-protein, low-carb diet, then called the Atkins diet after its inventor, an American doctor, who claimed avoiding carbohydrates was the key to weight loss.

Rose wrote an adoring profile of him for *Vanity Fair* called "An Inconvenient Iraqi," wherein he described many of his myths. He evoked the golden era of Chalabi's youth before the 1958 revolution, when Iraq was a peaceful country ripe for democracy, as Chalabi described it. Iraq in the 1950s was a promising and diverse place, Rose wrote. "Shots from the Chalabi family album depict a sumptuous party for Sir Edward Spears, the British Middle East envoy, held at their Baghdad home, a sprawling palace with 27 acres of garden. Clearly visible are a Catholic monsignor, Shia and Sunni Muslim clerics, and several Jews. (All these groups were also represented on the board of the Chalabi export firm.) Among the guests are scientists, bankers, writers, and physicians—an entire elite, most of whose members either were murdered or fled Iraq long ago."

Rose's article was also the first to report Chalabi's boasts to have worked while at university on a type of secret code related to prime numbers—of "public key code." That was the claim that had mathematicians around the world scratching their heads, because it is not often that complex mathematical concepts find their way to *Vanity Fair* and popular culture. The article quoted Chalabi's disclosure that the "authorities" had warned him away from his pursuit of the secret code. Rose was just one of many Chalabi confidants who believed it. Even Chalabi's CIA contacts had been convinced that he'd designed this "prime number" code. They were not aware that Chalabi's college classmate at MIT, Whitfield Diffie, had been one of the real inventors.

Rose described how effective the INC was in gathering intelligence, and even referred to Mohamad al-Zobaidy, Chalabi's Middle East agent, by his code name, Al Deeb: "In Jordan, Lebanon, and Turkey, I have witnessed one of its full-time case officers in action, a man known within the I.N.C. as 'al-Dheeb,' 'the Wolf,' and seen how he exploits his own local connections to conjure documents, photographs, and people across supposedly impermeable frontiers."

Rose acquitted Chalabi of wrongdoing in the Petra Bank matter and mentioned nothing about Socofi or MEBCO. "Chalabi maintains that Petra was always solvent," Rose wrote, "and that the embezzlement claims were a shabby pretext. The real reason the bank was closed, he says, was the manipulation of Jordan's institutions by Iraq." Rose quoted Chalabi's codefendant in the Petra Bank case: Ali Sarraf, the man who ran its foreign currency exchange division. "'Why would Chalabi steal from the bank when he owned three-quarters of its shares?' Sarraf says. 'He would have been stealing from himself.'" In reality of course, Chalabi would have been stealing from his depositors, not himself. And in any case he actually owned less than 1 percent of the bank shares, not three-quarters. Rose presumably was unaware that Sarraf had been convicted of embezzlement in the same case. Sarraf also had been an officer of Chalabi's IBC Communications, the front company through which much of the CIA funding to the INC had been funneled.

But the most striking part of the article was its portrayal of Chalabi's character, his brilliance and courage. In one anecdote, Rose describes how, "at the end of a strenuous hike in Great Falls Park, west of Washington, D.C., Chalabi sits on a vertiginous crag, his ankles dangling over the surging Potomac." Rose felt that he exuded an air of calm. "'You don't fear death, do you?'" Rose reported asking Chalabi. "He shrugs. 'I don't think about it.'"

Later, after the war started, Rose's journalistic skepticism, which had succumbed to Chalabi's charm, seemed to rise again. It was like a love affair was on the wane, and he began to see the blemishes.

30

The Man Who Invented the Mobile Labs

March 2002

"You two green-horns! Money, you think, is the sole motive
to pains and hazard, deception and devilry, in this world."

—One-legged man in *The Confidence-Man* by Herman Melville

OF ALL THE STORIES HE PENNED while he was under Ahmad Chalabi's sway
in the run-up to the Iraq War, the one David Rose came to regret the
most is a 2002 *Vanity Fair* piece titled "Iraq's Arsenal of Terror." It was
a riveting tale, well told, of a man with the innermost secrets of Saddam Hussein's efforts to acquire weapons, who surfaced to tell those
tales to Chalabi's Iraqi National Congress. "I trust my friends in the
INC," the man said. Rose evoked the man's fear and loneliness as a
whistle-blower reporting on Saddam's weapons. "I'm walking a way I
don't know where," the man said poignantly in the article. He talked of
radioactive weapons, of long-range missiles. And most shocking of all,
the man claimed he himself invented Saddam's fleet of mobile biological weapons that drove around the country churning out anthrax.

In the years to come, Rose would wince when he thought of the
story and shake his head at the strange things he believed back then. It
was the most egregious and transparent of the INC cases: the major
who bragged he thought up the mobile WMD labs.

The story of the defector who told Rose this tale, Mohammad Harith al-Assef, starts, as so many of the Chalabi defectors' accounts do, with the U.S.-funded Information Collection Program and Mohamad al-Zobaidy (Al Deeb). Harith approached one of Zobaidy's INC agents in Amman, Jordan, in late December 2001. He did have contract documents and he had the names of "front companies" that seemed to be in existence. He claimed to have been a major in the Mukhabarat. Ironically, he claimed that his cover as a spy was as a journalist.

Zobaidy's men videotaped a statement from Harith, and Zobaidy says he forwarded a report to the INC—Aras and Chalabi—in London. He soon got word of their interest. Hold on to him, they said. The INC decided that as usual it wanted a double impact with Harith: not just maximum news coverage but also to get his story injected into the stream of intelligence that U.S. policy-makers were lapping up. Back in Washington in early February 2002, Jim Woolsey reached out to his connections for a third time to get the ball rolling and get Harith into the DIA system. He says he doesn't recollect doing this, but on February 8 he contacted a Defense Department official who then passed the information on to the DIA.[33] Once again, the DIA bypassed the CIA.

As for the State Department, which was unwittingly paying for Harith and the entire case through the INC's Information Collection Program, it was also bypassed. Instead the INC briefed the DIA directly about Harith and relayed some contact information to Zobaidy back in Amman. He was to get in touch with a man named Mr. Dan, a U.S. intelligence operator in the embassy. Zobaidy drove Harith to the embassy. Mr. Dan, like the DIA agent known as Mr. Nick in Bangkok, turned out to be a muscular and tall military type with a crew cut. Mr. Dan said he'd call when he was finished with this unusual new "defector," and then he took Harith back inside to grill him. When he was done, he told Harith something important: don't talk to journalists for the moment.

At the Amman Embassy, Mr. Dan suspected that Harith had been coached and had embellished what he knew. But somehow Harith passed a polygraph test. And then the DIA wrote up a report based on what he said: there was good intelligence that in mid-1996 Iraq set up a mobile biological research laboratory. They sent the report out in March. It seemed to corroborate a stream of intelligence coming from a source who later became notorious: the man code-named Curveball. Curveball was an Iraqi expatriate living in Germany who had told German intelligence that Saddam had a fleet of mobile laboratories crisscrossing the country that churned out biological agents. After the Germans passed the information on to the Americans, it became part of the case for war.

While all this was going on, the INC decided to share its new defector with two trusted news outlets, violating the requests of the DIA official. David Rose would be one. He could publish the material in *Vanity Fair* and in the *Observer* of London.

But now there was also a new team from the CBS news magazine *60 Minutes* who joined the list of journalists Chalabi could trust. They were producers Richard Bonin and Adam Ciralsky. They had been introduced to the Iraqi National Congress by an intermediary in the U.S. government, Nabeel Musawi explains. He says the government official had long-standing ties to the INC and vouched for the *60 Minutes* team completely.[34] The INC already knew *60 Minutes* was a great place to go with an exclusive. Chalabi himself had first appeared on *60 Minutes* in 1991, in the months when he was financially almost completely wiped out and when his alliance with the CIA was just beginning. Later he appeared on *60 Minutes* again, in a compelling story about the secret incarceration of several members of the Iraqi opposition, produced by journalist Leslie Cockburn.

===

So the *60 Minutes* team got first dibs on Harith. Musawi flew to Amman with them. He says he went there "at the insistence of Richard and Adam," and not as an INC official who would in any way control the interview. His role was to guide the *60 Minutes* team and act as a facilitator, he says, since they did not know Zobaidy. The men met Harith and decided he was credible, despite his unlikely claims that as a nonscientist, he had invented the concept of a mobile fleet of biological weapons labs. They listened to his story, had dinner, and then the correspondent, Lesley Stahl, flew in.

They did their interview in a suite at the Intercontinental Hotel in Amman. Not only did Harith tell his fanciful tale about inventing the mobile labs; he outlined a trip to Africa where he claimed to have purchased radioactive material. He said he personally had escorted an Iraqi official on a trip to meet with an Al Qaeda figure. He went on and on. In the middle of the interview there was a clash: Zobaidy had one of his famous temper tantrums, he says. Zobaidy, who says he was skeptical of Harith from the start, says that during the *60 Minutes* interview he was angered that, on top of the wild tales Harith was already telling, he suddenly started inventing a new one once the camera crew was there. Harith suddenly claimed he had witnessed meetings between Iraqi officials and Al Qaeda.

Musawi confirmed Zobaidy's outburst, although he remembers it differently. Musawi says that Zobaidy was arguing that he wanted some information kept secret, rather than contesting Haideri's credibility. (*60 Minutes* declined to comment on the argument at all.)

Three days after the interview, Zobaidy says he went up to Harith and cornered him. Why had he suddenly come up with that outrageous story to tell to the reporters, he asked. Zobaidy claims Harith acted coy: there was an agreement that Zobaidy wasn't aware of. It was agreed on, and it wasn't Zobaidy's business.

When *60 Minutes* aired, the results could not have been better for the INC.[35] Most of the piece was an admiring look at Ahmad Chalabi. The correspondent took the D.C. Metro with him and asked him why they would travel that way: "Because it is the easiest way to get there," he answered. The CIA, she told, him, didn't think he was credible. "The feeling is mutual," he quipped.

There was a rejoinder by an expert, Kenneth Pollack, who was skeptical of Chalabi and had written a critique of his "insurrection" plan. And then *60 Minutes* showed the defector, Harith, in silhouette, without revealing his name. Nabeel Musawi, says Leslie Stahl on the track, "told us that he has verified that this man was an officer in Iraq's ruthless intelligence service, the Mukhabarat."

STAHL: The defector is telling Musawi that in order to evade the UN inspectors, Saddam Hussein put his biological weapons laboratories in trucks that the defector told us he personally bought from Renault.

STAHL: Refrigerator trucks kind of things?

UNIDENTIFIED MALE: Yes, yes.

STAHL: And how many?

UNIDENTIFIED MALE: Seven.

STAHL: Seven Renault trucks.

UNIDENTIFIED MALE: Yes, seven.

Shortly after the *60 Minutes* piece, David Rose, still deeply a believer in the Chalabi cause, interviewed Harith over the course of three days in early March 2002. The most unusual thing about the story was the spin Rose gave the now notorious "mobile biological laboratories" allegation. Not only had Harith seen the trucks; he claimed to have come up with the idea in the first place. Even *60 Minutes* had not aired this. In hindsight, it was a staggering claim, truly incredible, and not just because the trucks never existed. At the time, Rose, the reporter, believed himself to be sitting in a room with a man who helped conceive a diabolical mobile weapons factory for Saddam. He had so come to believe the story, and was so sincere, that he grimly and sarcastically told the man it had been a good idea. In his story he reports how Harith beamed and said in English, "Thanks a lot!"

The story, when it ran in *Vanity Fair,* was billed as a "Special Report," and made such an impact that Rose got time on CNN to talk about it. It reported that Saddam had launched a secret crash program to build a long-range ballistic missile called the Tamooz, which would eventually be able to "reach targets across a swath of Southern Europe." He did not name Harith but simply described him as a high-level defector. By the time Rose's story came out, in 2002, the DIA and the CIA were already fully and thoroughly convinced that Harith was a liar. The DIA even put out a fabricator notice, warning that they believed nothing the man said anymore. It didn't seem to do much good.

Colin Powell, famously making his case for war to the UN General Assembly in February 2003, announced with confidence that there was yet another source for the allegations of mobile biological labs:

"An Iraqi major, who defected, confirmed that Iraq has mobile biological research laboratories."

In the end, Zobaidy looked over his books. He says the Iraqi National Congress shelled out only $4,000 out of the hundreds of thousands it was receiving from the State Department to pay for Harith and his expenses. It was relatively low-budget.

And journalist David Rose would come, in time, to realize he had been lied to. "I'm absolutely convinced the INC was mounting a sophisticated disinformation campaign," he later said. Harith "was being coached very, very carefully."

31

Saddam's Mistress

September 2002

"Iraqi President Saddam Hussein met Osama bin Laden
on two occasions and gave money to the al Qaeda leader
in 1996, a woman who claims to be a long-time mistress of
the Iraqi leader told ABC News."

—Reuters, September 8, 2002

ONE NIGHT IN EARLY 2002 in Jordan, a fifty-four-year-old woman targeted
by the INC was upset, practically in tears. She refused to budge, no
matter what. So the two INC agents assigned to her made a quick and
exasperated phone call to their boss, Mohamad al-Zobaidy. She won't
come along and join us unless we bring along her pet dog, they told
him. It was a little lap dog that was interfering with a snatch operation
by Ahmad Chalabi's operatives.

Chalabi's men rushed back to the apartment where the woman had
been hiding out, after fleeing from Iraq. The dog came scampering to
them; they wrapped it in a cloth of some sort and hustled back to the
relieved woman, a Greek with Iraqi citizenship, so she could hug it to
herself and they could finally debrief her.

That's the story the way Zobaidy tells it, and he should know. It was
another caper run by Chalabi's group under the U.S.-funded Informa-

tion Collection Program. And it was the least known of the major INC operations: Saddam's mistress.

The woman named Parisoula Maria Lampsos was a key trophy for Chalabi's men. She would later tell the world that she knew all of the sadist's secrets. It was just the kind of news that Chalabi and his supporters in Washington were looking to promote. With Parisoula Lampsos, the INC was offering the world a peek at the monstrosity of Saddam. But her story eventually blossomed into something far bigger than that: she was the source of the allegation that Saddam had hosted and then sponsored the Saudi outlaw terrorist Osama bin Laden. Her story would get massive pickup and cause an intense investigation by the CIA and the DIA. The problem was, even the INC officials involved in the case didn't believe it and were shocked at the outlandish charges.

She had been watched by Chalabi's organization, Zobaidy says, from her days in Baghdad all the way to her arrival in Amman. But her real involvement with the Iraqi National Congress started that fateful night when she and her tiny dog were pulled from the apartment. "Very nice dog!" remembers Zobaidy with a smile.

Parisoula Lampsos met Zobaidy when she was shepherded into a room with him for a grim debriefing session. He was using yet another code name at the time—Haji. He was no fan of the woman, and he made his feelings plain to her. Still, he needed to hear her story to relay it to Ahmad Chalabi and Aras Habeeb Kareem in London. The first thing he told her before anything else is, "If you lie, I'll cut your throat myself." Over the next few days, in several sessions, she told what he believes to be the truth in hours of videotaped interrogation with the Iraqi National Congress.

Her story was long, extraordinary, and depressing. She talked of how she had been married, and had met Saddam Hussein. She said she slept with him in the 1990s, had been forced to divorce her husband, had been assigned to work for Uday, Saddam's son, helping him procure women for sex. Many of her stories had the ring of truth, and she could elaborate on the sadistic perversions of Saddam and his son. Her own daughters, she explained, had been forced to sleep with Saddam's sons; they had been "turned out," so to speak.

One story she told concerned a leftover puzzle from the Gulf War. She claimed that there were female Kuwaiti prisoners who had been snatched by the Iraqi forces and were being held in Iraq. She said she would make up the women, and Uday would force huge amounts of alcohol down their throats. When the women got drunk, they would stumble and perform a traditional dance while Uday and his guests egged them on and mocked them. That sort of detail, if it got out, would outrage the Kuwaitis and perhaps the international community.

But she mentioned nothing about Osama bin Laden in that first meeting, according to Zobaidy. She never mentioned that bin Laden had been at the palace, or that Saddam had given money to him. If she had, he says, he wouldn't have believed her.[36]

On March 4, 2002, Zobaidy wrote up a report for Chalabi and Aras. He says the word came back from the INC's London office to take extremely good care of her. They were very interested in getting her story out. The problem was that, for now, Parisoula was refusing to go public. If she did her daughter, who was still in Iraq, would be killed. It wasn't a good time for Zobaidy either. He became absorbed with a different INC defector and put thoughts of Parisoula aside for some time.

It wasn't until May that the INC introduced Parisoula to the media, and it was a slow affair. Chalabi had decided to give the story to ABC News, where it could get substantial play. There may have been several reasons for this decision. Perhaps it was important to diversify their messengers. Also, the senior investigative producer at ABC News was Christopher Isham, one of Chalabi's old friends. In the field, the ABC News producer who handled the Parisoula story was Christopher Vlasto, an ABC veteran who had broken plenty of high-profile stories.

Vlasto met the INC's man in Amman and clearly was taken by him. It was Zobaidy, but Vlasto knew him only as Haji. "He was Mr. Cool Dude, you know," Vlasto said. "He, to me, was the true 'spook' in this. They did this whole cloak-and-dagger thing with me on this. I had to switch cars three times." Zobaidy laughed a lot, lived large, swapped cars to avoid surveillance, and seemed the essence of what a rebel intelligence agent should be.

Then Vlasto met Parisoula at a border town in Jordan, without a camera crew. The holdup was that she was concerned about the safety of her daughter, who was still in Baghdad. They negotiated, and she came to trust Vlasto.

Still, the INC operatives were always hounding him for money. "I was asked for money by all of them," Vlasto said. He refused—it violates fundamental precepts of journalistic codes in the United States. But they kept on asking. "They said they were broke."

They may have been telling the truth, because in fact the INC was hitting a brick wall with the State Department, which refused to pay for the Information Collection Program after the late spring of 2002. The State Department was shelling out funds for the INC's salaries and rent but was at the end of its rope with the Information Collection Program. Chalabi, just as when he was first contacted by the CIA ten years earlier, didn't want to provide receipts and didn't even want to let the State Department see where the money went.

Still, the State Department was under so much pressure from Capitol Hill that it had to pay the INC something. By May, the INC was on what the department had dubbed an Austerity Budget of $2.4 million for two months. It certainly was a good deal for the INC, but Chalabi wasn't satisfied with it.

And Vlasto refused to pay. The INC would have to wait for money to come in when it resolved its negotiations with the State Department.

———

Saddam's mistress was flown to Lebanon and housed in Zobaidy's summer mountain home. Zaab Sethna, the Pakistani British PR wizard who had dedicated his career to Chalabi, flew in from London.

The rest of the ABC News crew, including correspondent Claire Shipman, who would do the on-camera interview with "Saddam's Mistress," flew to Beirut in May. There, in Zobaidy's home, they set up the elaborate lights for the two-camera shoot and started rolling tape. Suddenly, in the middle of the interview, Parisoula Lampsos made a claim that was new. She had never mentioned anything about Osama bin Laden either to Zobaidy or Vlasto. The only things that had changed were that Sethna was in town and the cameras were rolling. But suddenly she made that incendiary claim: "Osama bin Laden," she said on camera in her thickly accented English, "he came to Baghdad before four years one time. I know that."

Shipman followed up on this line. "Did he give Osama bin Laden money?" she asked.

"Yeah," said Parisoula.

Zobaidy was sitting on the side, listening. He says when he heard Parisoula mention the name bin Laden in the middle of the interview, he wasn't just surprised; he was flabbergasted. He was so shocked that he interrupted the interview, raising his voice in Arabic and calling for it to stop. Where had that story come from, he wanted to know? She'd never mentioned bin Laden. Why was she saying such a thing?

The ABC News crew was surprised as well. Vlasto, the ABC News producer on site, confirms that Al Deeb, or Haji, began yelling, although since it was in Arabic he didn't know what it was about. He says there were a few incidents where Al Deeb interjected himself. Vlasto says it was the first time he'd heard of the bin Laden allegations too, although Parisoula had hinted earlier of something that she would reveal.

Her allegation ratcheted up her news value. It was one thing to talk about Saddam Hussein and his sexual perversion, his sadism, his gaudy taste, and his mental instability. To claim he was giving money to Osama bin Laden, putting him in partnership with the force behind 9/11, was something else entirely.

ABC News had her explosive story on videotape, but suddenly there was a crisis. Until her daughter was out of Baghdad, the story could not air. Vlasto worked the phone, badgering Aras Kareem constantly. ABC negotiated with Chalabi to remove the roadblock. With every week the network waited, of course, the exclusivity of the story was at risk. What if Saddam's mistress's story got out to another network?

Finally, in September, the INC was ready. Parisoula's daughter was out of Baghdad. Even before the story aired, the publicists for ABC News got the message out, and the news began appearing around the world with a splash. In Britain's *Sun*, the country's biggest paper, the headline was "Bin Laden 'Given Money by Tyrant,'" and the story went on to say, "Saddam met Osama bin Laden twice and gave the al-Qa'ida leader money, according to a woman claiming to be the Iraqi tyrant's mistress."

When the story finally ran on ABC News on Thursday, September 12, it was the same day the Bush administration unveiled its long-awaited public relations push for preemptive war against Iraq. Then

Prime Time Live anchor Charles Gibson led into it, pointing out that the president had just spoken at the UN General Assembly. Gibson said that "the stakes couldn't be higher." ABC cut to a presidential sound bite: "We cannot stand by and do nothing while dangers gather."

And then ABC News told the story of Parisoula Lampsos, "Saddam's Mistress." "We traveled to Beirut, Lebanon, once ravaged by civil war and still a haven for terrorists, spies, and people who need to disappear," said correspondent Claire Shipman. ABC tipped its hat to the Iraqi National Congress. "She fled Iraq last summer with the help of the Iraqi National Congress, the leading opposition group." It was a strange story indeed, as ABC News itself admitted, and a titillating one. "Did he force you to have sex with him?" asked Shipman. "Saddam," replied Parisoula in her Greek accent, "he don't need to force anybody. Because you are afraid. You are afraid to say no."

Saddam used Viagra to help him sexually, she said, and Shipman explained the value of such tidbits in helping U.S. intelligence craft a personality profile. Parisoula testified to Saddam's legendary cruelty. This part of his behavior was confirmed later on: the way he'd watch videotapes of his torture victims, for example. She also said that Saddam sobbed when the U.S. forces drove Iraq from Kuwait in 1991. "His eye was red, red, red," she said.

"And what about Osama bin Laden?" Shipman said in a voice-over. "Parisoula says she saw bin Laden in one of the palaces in the late 1980s. But more significantly, she says Saddam's son Uday told her that Saddam met with bin Laden in the mid-1990s and that Saddam gave bin Laden money."

For ABC News it was a blockbuster story and a riveting exclusive. For the INC the report was a public relations coup that came at just the right time.

But there is still the question of whether the story would ever crack through the filters and get into the intelligence stream. Would it get the official stamp of approval from intelligence officials? Vlasto now says that, before the story aired, when he was attempting to figure out Parisoula's credibility, he asked for government help. The CIA, he says, dismissed her out of hand when it learned of her connections to Chalabi's group.

But Douglas Feith, now notorious for his activities in the Office of Special Plans, a unique office set up in the Pentagon to prepare for the Iraq War and coordinate policy, still had people busily digging through what they thought were the connections between Saddam and bin Laden. In response to queries from Vlasto, two Pentagon officials arrived at West Sixty-sixth Street, ABC's headquarters, to dig into the issue. Both had been dispatched by Feith's Counter Terrorism Evaluation Group. "They flew up to ABC News, and I had them watch the tape," Vlasto said. "Then they sent the real agents to talk to her."

The Counter Terrorism Evaluation Group was the small office Feith invented to counter the official intelligence findings of the CIA, which was skeptical that Saddam had anything to do with Osama bin Laden. The group's two employees were to sift through the mountains of old intelligence, reanalyze, and come up with patterns. They were in essence playing a vast form of Scrabble with U.S. intelligence tidbits, trying to spell out something others did not see. For years, Jim Woolsey, Paul Wolfowitz, Douglas Feith, and others had been pushing the theory that Saddam was at the center of the terror network, and now they were trying to prove it.

The account of Saddam's mistress seemed like just the thing. The Defense Intelligence Agency assigned officers to investigate her story of a meeting between Saddam and bin Laden. Her story ended up costing more U.S. intelligence operatives a lot of time to run it down. For several months, in Bangkok, they interviewed her. One thing they noticed: she appeared to be backing down a bit from her original statements on ABC News about bin Laden.

When they strapped her to a polygraph machine, rigging one strap around her chest and putting a sensor on her finger, she passed, but the tester said she had "emotional and psychological issues which could effect the test reliability," indicating she might believe she remembered things that had not actually happened. By October 2002, the DIA had reported secretly that her story was "more or less cogent, but perhaps contaminated with pockets of coached fabrications."[37]

In essence, U.S. intelligence believed she had had an affair with Saddam Hussein but knew nothing about bin Laden. Wrapping it up, in the end, like so many other parts of this story, it came to money.

By now the INC was having trouble paying its bills, and landlords were commencing eviction notices. The INC had been so obstinate with the State Department that the department had almost cut off funds. Immediately after the ABC News report aired, Zaab Sethna arranged for another interview with Parisoula Lampsos, and this time there was money involved. A British newspaper chain called Associated Newspapers agreed to pay Lampsos $50,000 for the details of her life. "In return for your cooperation in the interview and all rights outlined in this agreement, we will pay you a total of Fifty Thousand U.S. Dollars ($50,000) . . . which shall be payable upon the publication of the interview."[38]

But whether the money was for Lampsos or for the INC is in question. Zobaidy says he had laid out $28,000 of his own money on Parisoula Lampsos and was constantly badgering Aras Kareem to pay him.[39] Zobaidy, examining his bills, says that he paid $9,560 for Lampsos's bills in Lebanon and Jordan and another $19,283 in Thailand. He says he was assured that some of the $50,000 from Associated Newspapers would help reimburse him.

In the end, that didn't happen, and there was no money for "Saddam's Mistress." Sian James, features editor for the *Mail on Sunday*, says the reporters for the British tabloid spent time in Bangkok with Parisoula but did not find her story believable. "It didn't really come together," James said in an interview.

And Vlasto, at ABC News, no longer believes that Saddam met bin Laden. "Do I think she was coached? Maybe. Probably," he said. He has tried to figure out what it could have been. "Was she told or did she do it on her own? I don't know. Could she have made it up to make herself more valuable? I don't know. Maybe. Or did someone lie to her about it?"

Chalabi and his entourage packaged the "Saddam's Mistress" case with a particular target in mind—public opinion. That is true for all his post–September 11 work on "terror" and WMD intelligence. The target was as much the press as the intelligence world. The State Department paid for it, but the users of the information, the consumers, were handpicked journalists. Public opinion, and all that meant on Capitol Hill and in American political calculations, mattered more than the opinions of policy-makers. And there's no doubt those four main story lines pitched by Chalabi had a resounding public effect. On terrorism, Salman Pak's hijacking school and Saddam's mistress built a link between Saddam and 9/11. On WMD Judith Miller's story and the fabricator who claimed to have invented the mobile biological labs created the impression of imminent danger.

Of course, Chalabi was acting in a competitive environment. His WMD disinformation was just part of the wash coming through the various Iraqi exiles, the CIA, and foreign intelligence services. The CIA didn't even believe most specifics that came through his efforts and was getting all the other fake information elsewhere. Agency foul-ups can hardly be blamed on Chalabi. Still, Chalabi was just the most effective in getting his message out to the public and to his followers embedded in U.S. government. He kept the pressure up.

One interesting fact is that, while the Information Collection Program funds may have paid for the "defector" accounts, there was a lot left over. The defector accounts were the most important part of the ICP—which fed about $300,000 a month in U.S. funds to the INC—but only a small portion of the money actually found its way to Mohamad al-Zobaidy, who was doing most of the work, and whom David Rose had praised so effusively. Zobaidy maintains that from 2000 to February 2003, when the war started, he received $90,000 from the INC, leaving millions unaccounted for.

The other clear pattern is that the INC officials were themselves skeptical if not completely incredulous about the information their "defectors" were giving to the public. Again, Zobaidy says he did not believe the Saddam's mistress story about bin Laden, Abu Zeinab's story about Salman Pak, or Harith's account of his role. Zobaidy was convinced Haideri never knew anything about any WMDs. And, again, there is substantiation from both Vlasto and Musawi for his claims that in at least two key interviews he raised his voice to complain about the assertions of the "defectors."

And as for Chalabi aide Nabeel Musawi, he too now admits he was skeptical in three of the four cases. He did not believe Abu Zeinab, the colonel, who claimed to have seen hijacking schools at Salman Pak. He was completely dismissive of the fabricator whom he introduced to *60 Minutes*, which reported on the seven Renault trucks used for mobile labs. And he says he always believed that, in the case of the civil engineer and the underground wells, there was no direct evidence of anything larger.

The point is this: Chalabi's INC, even where it did not directly plant false information about Saddam's links to terrorists and his WMDs, believed that, in many cases, it was false.

32

The Run-up to War

Summer 2002–Winter 2003

"It was Congress that changed the objective of U.S. policy from containment to regime change by the passage of the Iraqi Liberation Act in 1998. The president is now asking Congress to support that policy."

—Defense Secretary Donald Rumsfeld, September 2002

THERE IS A SCHOOL OF THOUGHT among those who know him best that Ahmad Chalabi made his most significant contribution to the upcoming war not through his "defector" operations, and not even in his lobbying efforts for the Iraq Liberation Act. Instead, in this analysis, he deserves credit for forging a seemingly impossible alliance: a marriage between the Bush administration and the hard-line Iranian-led Shiite Islamist Iraqis of the Supreme Council of Islamic Resistance in Iraq, or SCIRI. He parlayed his influence in the United States and his loyalties to Iran into an unlikely union.

Out of the public eye, the bond between the Americans and the hard-right Shiites was strengthened in an expansive conference room in the Old Executive Office Building in August 2002. On one side sat the Iraqis: Kurdish leaders and Ayad Allawi. With them was Ahmad Chalabi. And there as well was the odd man out, a bearded cleric dressed in a robe and turban. It was Ayatollah Abdul Aziz al-Hakim, the brother of SCIRI's leader. Across from the polite and ceremonious Iraqis sat Defense Secretary Donald Rumsfeld and the chairman of the Joint Chiefs of Staff, Air Force Gen. Richard Myers.

But the most dominant presence was a man who was not even in the room. On a giant wall monitor was the face of Vice President Dick Cheney, joining the meeting via videoconference from his home in Wyoming. He bid a warm welcome to his guests from the Middle East.[40]

The man Cheney greeted from SCIRI was completely loyal to the government of Iran and was there with Tehran's full approval. SCIRI was one of the oldest anti-Saddam groups, and definitely the most credible. It controlled the 5,000-member Badr Brigade, considered a potentially powerful anti-Saddam militia, which had been trained by the Iranian Revolutionary Guard.

Abdul Aziz al-Hakim is the brother of SCIRI's leader, Mohammad Bakr al-Hakim. Historian Said Aburish writes that the old Ayatollah Khomeini had been so impressed by Mohammad Bakr al-Hakim that during the Iran–Iraq War he planned to install the younger man as the head of the "Islamic Republic of Iraq" if Iran managed to topple Saddam. If anyone qualified as Saddam's "troublesome priest," it was Hakim, and by 1988, Saddam had one of the Hakim brothers assassinated in Sudan. But Hakim never fit the cartoonish image Americans had formed of the ayatollahs. He was an educated and savvy politician. He was known not to trust the Americans, who had been making overtures ever since Bush had stepped into power.

The Bush administration knew that to successfully wage war in Iraq it needed the southern Shiites on its side. At a minimum, the thinking was, the administration needed to make sure SCIRI would not oppose the invasion. "They could not invade without the support of SCIRI," said one SCIRI member, proudly.

The man who had invited SCIRI to Washington and to that crucial meeting with Cheney, Rumsfeld, and Myers was Ahmad Chalabi. In the summer of 2002 Chalabi flew to Tehran saying he had a sincere message from the U.S. government. First Chalabi met with Iranian government officials to get their blessing for the merger of interests, and then Chalabi talked to SCIRI. The message was simple: the Americans were very serious about their war. They were going to topple Saddam. This time it was for real. Bush the son, the president, would not do what his father had and abandon the Shiites.

Thus the long-term alliance—a shaky marriage of convenience—between the United States and the Islamist Shiite party of Iraq began.

═══

At that same time, Chalabi's ties to the radical Islamists were already worrying more moderate Iraqi allies. Shortly after that meeting inside the government, other Iraqis committed to Saddam's downfall assembled in a Washington hotel with Chalabi. These were secularists, idealists—Iraqi oppositionists who thought they could prevent their country from boiling into religious war once Saddam was overthrown.

Faisal Istrabadi is a U.S.-educated lawyer who organized the meeting. "I've never met a man who can read a room the way Ahmad can," said Istrabadi, recalling his impression. He said Chalabi picked up mood shifts, body language, and reactions, and then played off them. The two men had a connection through their families. Istrabadi's grandmother had been killed in 1958, in the revolution, trying to rescue the old man Nuri as-Said. Istrabadi had met Chalabi in 1982, and they had quickly forged a bond. Chalabi told Istrabadi that he had seen his grandmother on the final day of her life, shortly before she was killed with Nuri.

And over the years Istrabadi had found inspiration in Chalabi. Other Iraqis were cowed from speaking out about Saddam's cruelty, but Chalabi, as Istrabadi saw it, had conquered that fear.

But during the meeting he and other secular Iraqis tried to plead with Chalabi. "I thought he would kind of share our liberal agenda," he says. He means liberal in the loosest sense there is: a nonsectarian way. Even if SCIRI was needed to make this all go smoothly, wouldn't Chalabi commit to women's rights, democracy, and minority rights, and make a strong public stand for them all?

"I was a political neophyte," Istrabadi explained in an interview, "may still be now, but I certainly was at that time, and in the meeting, I thought, 'This is *great!* Ahmad will do this, he'll do that, and he'll support us, and this,' and it seemed he had." But after Istrabadi left the meeting, he suddenly realized he had been manipulated.

"When I got back home—I mean, I'm a lawyer, it's not like I just fell off a turnip truck, I think I'm reasonably bright—when I got back home I realized, Ahmad Chalabi had not committed himself to one goddamn thing! And I sort of thought we'd been had. And he had come in, we sort of sat there for six hours or whatever it was, and he had not committed himself to one thing. All that had happened is that *we* had committed ourselves and he sort of nodded. He never actually said, 'I will do this'—but he had given us the impression that he had. It was a very curious thing."

Istrabadi, furious at himself more than anything after that meeting, called up the man he admired most in Iraqi exile politics. It was Adnan Pachachi, an elderly Sunni despised by Chalabi but well liked by most Iraqis. Pachachi had recently bowed out of opposition politics. Get back involved, Istrabadi pleaded. He had been so angered by what he saw as Chalabi's manipulation that he intended to fight back. And after that, whether it was prompted by Istrabadi's call or not, Pachachi did indeed get involved again—and became a potent force and counterweight to Chalabi. "I had become totally disillusioned with Ahmad after that meeting," recalled Istrabadi.

━━━━━

At that time, Chalabi still was on a high-intensity regime to lose weight. He was on the Atkins diet, avoiding carbs, eating just protein and fat. People noticed he drank tiny cups of coffee barely visible under vast clouds of whipped cream on top. Those who know him say he would enthusiastically explain how the diet worked at its molecular level, regaling his acquaintances with accounts of the effects of high-protein diets on insulin levels, for example. He spoke of the Atkins diet the way some people talk of their religion. He refused even to eat rice. It worried some of his friends, who insisted that he take in some starch and vegetables. His dedication to the diet was contagious. He apparently convinced the Kurdish leader Jalal Talabani that eating ice cream would help him lose weight and was good for him. Qubad, Jalal's son, says he had an argument with his father over this bizarre contention.

"Ahmad is a doctor," his father insisted happily, digging into a pint of Häagen Dazs. Qubad protested: Ahmad Chalabi is a PhD in mathematics, he said, not a *medical* doctor. Ahmad's lie, in that case, was innocuous. He had a knack for telling people what they wanted to hear: about ice cream, democracy, and Iraq.

═══════

As the U.S. government readied for war, and the troops shipped out on planes and vessels toward the Gulf, the pieces seemed to arrange themselves. All the Iraqi exiles tried to position themselves for a role to play, but none with more energy than Ahmad Chalabi. One mixed success he had in the fall of 2002 was getting his intelligence program—the Information Collection Program—shifted from the State Department to the Defense Department's Defense Intelligence Agency, where the INC considered the program to be in friendlier hands. The $340,000 intelligence-gathering effort, headed by Aras Kareem, was the pride of the Iraqi National Congress. It was the unit that had produced all those "defectors." No one knows where the money went, least of all Mohamad al-Zobaidy, who did most of the work for the program in the Middle East and couldn't get his bills paid. The State Department had become increasingly irritated with the quality of the program and frustrated by its own inability to monitor the INC's activities. State Department officials rolled their eyes when they talked about the ICP, and considered it "pure crap."[41]

Even worse, when diplomats paid a visit to the INC office at Tenth and Pennsylvania, they got a cold surprise. They walked into the office and were barred from examining the books. Chalabi's people told the State Department officials they weren't authorized to look at the product of the program their agency was funding.[42] The State Department was not necessarily aware of the role its funding had played in the case of the "hijacking school" publicity, the "Haideri" underground wells, or the fabricator who claimed to have invented the mobile laboratory program. But barring the State Department officials was a move of astonishing arrogance by the INC, and the standoff could not last. In the summer of 2002, the INC's Entifadh Qanbar laid out a lengthy defense of the program in a letter to the Senate Appropriations Committee. "The Iraqi National Congress (INC) Information Collection Program (ICP) is designed to collect, analyze and disseminate information from Iraq," he wrote. "U.S. Governmental recipients include the Department of Defense, Office of the Secretary of Defense . . . and the Office of the Vice President." He had the numbers of Bill Luti at the Office of Special Plans and John Hannah in Vice President Cheney's office. Both were prominent neoconservatives. He told the Senate that Aras Kareem Habib ran the program and distributed the information to Hogar Dizayee, a Kurdish INC member who had five "analysts" working for him. And then he listed as proof of the program's value: 108 stories written by Western reporters in the eight months since October 2001. Almost all the stories concerned the defectors handled by Zobaidy–Al Deeb. They were the stories about Salman Pak and the training for hijackers, about Haideri and his underground cement sealants, about Harith. *60 Minutes* was cited, as was *Vanity Fair* and the *New York Times*. All of those stories, of course, were false. His memo must have backfired. The State Department eventually dropped Chalabi's intelligence program, but it continued to fund Chalabi's other operation, and his friends in government made sure that the intelligence program was revived and funded through another federal agency.

Chalabi's intelligence operations, having been funded by the CIA in the 1990s and then the State Department in 2000 and 2001, were shifting once again, to the Defense Department. The decision came down from the National Security Council (NSC). It was as if a different account within the U.S. government, a different branch, would pay for it, even if in the end the money came from the same place.

The Defense Intelligence Agency entered the relationship unwillingly. It was simply ordered to, like an employer forced to hire an in-law even though he knows he has a drinking problem. The CIA warned the DIA early that the INC was penetrated by Iranian and "possible other intelligence services." One senior INC official might be working for both Iranian and Iraqi intelligence, the DIA was told.

It was probably one of the most unusual intelligence alliances ever made, and it was undertaken in a spirit of complete mistrust. As the DIA prepared a briefing on its plans, the agents were quite clear: "INC will use the relationship to promote its agenda." And the "INC is penetrated by hostile intelligence services."[43] It turned out to be a mixed blessing for Chalabi and the INC. On the one hand, the money was consistently coming in for the INC, and the program had an income of $340,000 a month. That meant the old uncertainty of dealing with the State Department was gone, and the nickel-and-diming was over. On the other hand, the DIA firmly forbade the INC from planting its WMD propaganda in the press. The "defectors" could no longer parade before reporters.

━━━

The path to war at that time looked pretty smooth. The president made his speech to the United Nations General Assembly in September. The next month Congress voted on a resolution over Iraq. There was no overt mention of Ahmad Chalabi when Congress voted in the fall of 2002 to support the war in Iraq. But in the Joint Resolution to Authorize the Use of United States Armed Forces Against Iraq there is a reference to the old 1998 law that had been Chalabi's greatest legislative victory. The "Iraq Liberation Act (Public Law 105–338) expressed the sense of Congress that it should be the policy of the United States to support efforts to remove from power the current Iraqi regime and promote the emergence of a democratic government to replace that regime."

Later that month, Chalabi climbed out of a long black limousine for a speech he would give at Hofstra University in Long Island. Policemen surrounded him to protect him from any threat as if he was a celebrity. In a speech, he let his smugness shine through just a bit too much. The "vision of the Iraqi National Congress," he said, "has come to be the vision of the United States in dealing with Iraq. I think this is called success."

33

The Committee for the Liberation of Iraq

Autumn 2002

ANOTHER BIT OF SUCCESS in the fall of 2002 was the founding of yet one more committee: The Committee for the Liberation of Iraq. Journalist David Rose flew in to Washington on a late flight from London, he says, and caught the party at Chalabi's Georgetown home, where Francis Brooke and his family lived. By all accounts Brooke normally kept the house in a slovenly state, but on this night he outdid himself. Rose believes the party was catered, and he says most of the key neoconservatives were there, all to celebrate the founding of this new organization that would lobby for war.

The truth about the Committee for the Liberation of Iraq is that it wasn't set up, strictly speaking, as another group linked to the Iraqi National Congress, although it did eventually morph into that. In reality, the Committee for the Liberation of Iraq started in the White House, in the office of Stephen Hadley, then the deputy National Security Adviser. It was a remarkable move by the Bush administration to invent a nongovernmental organization to push its policy.

The man the White House turned to for this sensitive task was lobbyist Bruce Jackson, a long-term interventionist, expert in transitional democracies, and former lobbyist for Lockheed Martin. He'd set up a committee to expand NATO in the past, and so he seemed like the perfect person to establish the new Iraq committee.

Jackson says that in the meeting in Hadley's office, at first he told Hadley he was the wrong man for the job. "I don't know anything about the greater Middle East or Iraq," he said. Jackson had spent his life working on former Soviet Union issues and Eastern Europe. "I didn't know what a Sunni triangle was, and still don't," he says.

Hadley told him he could bring aboard the people who would be the specialists but said Jackson could do the job because he had proven organizational abilities. Jackson accepted the proposal. He would do it. But what was the reason for the upcoming war, he asked. According to Jackson, "Hadley said the president hasn't decided on the *reasons* yet."

Jackson was puzzled. "He strongly implied the decision had been taken, but the exact *case* had not been fully agreed to and assembled by the Cabinet yet, which kind of worried me," he says. "He gave me to understand that war was inevitable but that the president had not fully composed the briefs to support that decision."

Recruited to sell a war he wasn't quite sure about, Jackson gamely signed up. Periodically he tried to sharpen his focus, he says. "I did go in a couple of times to see people like Elliott Abrams, Frank Miller, Dan Fried, to figure out what their reasons for war were. Because it's hard to explain to the American people what the stakes are if the American government hasn't figured out what the stakes are."

In the end, Jackson figured the human rights atrocities committed by Saddam were the best argument to make. With that premise, he figured he'd assemble a huge number of supporters. His committee, he decided, would work not just toward the war but toward democratization afterward, using the lessons learned after the fall of oppressive regimes in Eastern Europe.

The stated mission of the Committee for the Liberation of Iraq was "to promote regional peace, political freedom and international security by replacing the Saddam Hussein regime with a democratic government." Bruce Jackson did indeed assemble a vast group of international and bipartisan thinkers, diplomats, statesmen, and politicians to rally around this cause. Current and former politicians like Newt Gingrich, Steven Solarz, Bob Kerrey, Joe Lieberman, and John McCain joined in. Writers including Christopher Hitchens and Robert Kagan pinned their names on it. Of course, neoconservatives like Richard Perle and James Woolsey stepped up as well.

One key to the success of the "committee" was the man Jackson recruited to run the day-to-day affairs: Randy Scheunemann, a former staffer in the office of Senator Trent Lott and one of the INC's top supporters on Capitol Hill. From the Iraqi National Congress perspective, he was the perfect choice. The committee was situated in a building very close to the Iraqi National Congress, at 918 Pennsylvania Avenue. This was all good news for the INC. Their friends and supporters had a new platform to express themselves and push for war, a new venue that was identified with its cause.

And the committee was indeed successful in the mission Hadley had intended for it, even if the organizer didn't quite understand it. For example, in one operation, the committee coordinated a statement by ten Eastern European nations in support of the Bush administration's efforts. The statement from "The Vilnius Ten" lent apparent international legitimacy to the push for war. Albania, Bulgaria, Croatia, Estonia, Latvia, Lithuania, Macedonia, Romania, Slovakia, and Slovenia all banded together to call for action in February 2003. Their press release was sent out by the committee.

34

The Free Iraqi Forces and the End of the Iraq Liberation Act

Summer 2003–Winter 2003

"It's important to understand that the new Iraq will not be a country of warlords or competing military forces."

—Ahmad Chalabi, October 2002

BY 2002, CHALABI had come a long way. Three years earlier his Washington operation had been just an illusion: he and Francis Brooke making phone calls from the house up near Reservoir Road owned by Chalabi's Cayman Islands corporation. In 2000 they'd set up the office at 918 Pennsylvania Avenue, only blocks from the White House. They had the use of the BKSH offices over on K Street, close by too, and they leased a whole building in London. They had an office in Tehran, which American auditors were barred from visiting, and facilities in Jordan, Syria, and Egypt.

In total, the State Department funded Chalabi's operations from 2000 to 2003 to the tune of $33 million. The INC said it was engaged in "humanitarian activities" with the funds, but there is no evidence of that. It put out a little newspaper, but since it was banned from operating in Iraq, no Iraqis read it. The INC also received funding for TV

Liberty, which was said to broadcast an hour of programming per day on a satellite.

But Iraqis under Saddam Hussein were banned from owning satellite dishes.

=====

Despite all the millions the INC received from the U.S. government coffers, it wanted more. Ever since 1998, Chalabi and his supporters had coveted a resource that had been denied them. They wrote about it and talked frequently about it: it was the $97 million in "military drawdown" that was due them from the Iraq Liberation Act, for which they had fought so hard. Only a tiny portion had been spent. They lobbied and cajoled and threatened the U.S. government to shake it loose. The strange thing is that when Chalabi's wishes finally came true, when the Bush administration was about to implement the law and dish out that $97 million, the INC and Chalabi may have sabotaged the entire effort.[44]

In the summer of 2002, two Americans would end up assigned to the mission: one was a civilian at a Pentagon operation called the Office of Special Plans, and the other was a well-regarded army general.

When Chris Straub got the phone call in June, he was working temporarily at the Central Intelligence Agency, after a stint at a pro-life advocacy group. Straub, a former Army colonel, had worked for Democratic Senator Bob Kerrey and for the Senate Select Committee on Intelligence; in 1998 he had been one of the most aggressive supporters of Chalabi and the Iraq Liberation Act. But in June 2002, he was recruited to the Pentagon with an extraordinary offer. He was told the Bush administration was finally planning to fund the Iraq Liberation Act's key component: the training and equipment of Iraqi opposition forces, referred to as Free Iraqi Forces. He was getting an opportunity few could pass up: the chance to help implement the law he had helped to pass.

The Office of Special Plans, where Straub was assigned when it was formalized in September, was the Iraq policy office famously friendly to Chalabi. A navy captain named Bill Luti ran the Middle East section, while Col. Bill Bruner supervised Iraq issues. Luti was in close touch with Chalabi, Brooke, and various Iraqis.

Straub, now retired from uniformed service, would handle the civilian end of things, but on the military side, to implement the Iraq Liberation Act and actually train the Iraqis, the Pentagon picked Gen. David Barno, a twenty-six-year veteran of army infantry. At the time he was commander of the U.S. Army Training Center at Fort Jackson, South Carolina, but soon the Iraqi program took over all his time.

As grand and romantic as the Free Iraqi Forces sounded, conjuring images of dashing troops under Charles de Gaulle entering Paris when the Germans fled, no one knew what they would actually do. "There was talk, early on, whether this would be like the Free French," recalled General Barno. That theory was that the United States could stand up a mechanized unit of Iraqi soldiers. These Iraqi exiles would drive into Baghdad, waving from tanks, to put an Iraqi face on the U.S. invasion.

But General Barno and others threw up roadblocks. They pointed out that standing up any Iraqi fighting force as a unit in time for the invasion was impossible. And a mechanized unit would be even tougher. They had no recruits, no structure, no officers, no specialized training or military discipline. The most workable solution, and the only one the army wanted, was to train the Iraqis as sort of half-soldiers: men who would work as translators, cultural guides, explaining the terrain to the U.S. fighting forces.

So that's what General Barno started preparing for. His job would be to equip and train these forces, using what was left of the original $97 million from the Iraq Liberation Act. And Barno would set up a whole new system of training to accommodate an unusual and inno-vative way to go to war. Over the ensuing months, he built a training camp from scratch near a preexisting NATO base in Hungary. He brought in more than a thousand personnel to run the place. They worked in the snow, getting ready. And he ordered special badges with the insignia "F.I.F." But Barno, according to the agreement that was drawn up, was forbidden from recruiting to fill the ranks: the recruiting was all to be done by Chalabi's Iraqi National Congress.

Chris Straub's job, over at the Office of Special Plans, was to coordi-nate with the INC, which would provide the list of Iraqis who would enlist. The theory was that Chalabi could use his reputation as the head of an "umbrella" group to coax his fellow exile leaders into signing on. At first everything seemed fine. Early in the process, Chalabi seemed to be on board. He saw his vision finally coming together.

"The Pentagon will train Iraqi forces," he told a journalist. "It hasn't started yet. I expect it to start soon."[45] He made it clear that his view was that this would be a cohesive military force, and that he would be supplying the recruits: "The INC, as an umbrella organization, will provide the men and women. We have names of Iraqis ready to be trained. But the United States will not train political parties or militias. It will be an Iraqi military force."[46]

What is quite plain is that the Chalabi plan was to build an INC "military force" at that stage. That plan was radically different from what the Pentagon had really agreed on, which was that a group of Iraqi recruits would be sprinkled throughout the U.S. invasion force. And when the Pentagon insisted on doing things its way, Chalabi snipped the effort off.

General Barno got his first inkling that Chalabi wasn't keen on cooperating during a meeting they had in December 2002. The exiled Iraqi opposition had gathered under U.S. care in London for yet another conference. There was the usual elbowing and bickering that the Americans were used to whenever the exiles gathered. Chalabi and other exile leaders met near the U.S. Embassy, and the general spelled out his plans. He noticed a lack of interest from Chalabi. "He, just from body language, didn't seem to be too impressed with the effort at that point in time," Barno said. If the United States would not build Chalabi an army, it seemed, he was not interested in what they were doing with the Iraq Liberation Act funding.

Still, Barno moved ahead. His Hungarian camp was ready by January 2003. And then, like a restaurant in an empty city, he and his men waited for the customers. The trainers waited for Iraqi recruits to train; the logistics experts waited to equip Iraqis who would never come. The army cooks waited for Iraqi trainee mouths to feed. Army beds lay unslept-in, and weapons lay in their boxes unused. In the end, just seventy-four Iraqis were trained at a facility prepared to train 3,000.

Some estimates say $200 million was spent, and at a minimum, $60 million in U.S. military equipment was drawn down. Barno says he doesn't even know the total cost. It was an extraordinary waste of

American money though, since Chalabi sent none of the thousands of men who were on the INC's rosters. General Barno believes Chalabi pulled the plug on the operation because he quickly realized the men trained would not come under his command.

"My personal assessment was that they at some point in time realized that they would not have full control over these guys once we trained them, and so they weren't interested in recruiting people to fill those ranks if they didn't control them at the end of the day," Barno said. "So as a result, the numbers were teeny-tiny."

One Iraqi exile who was in the INC at the time was Hamad Shoraidah. He had signed a confidentiality agreement agreeing not to disclose information about the Iraqi National Congress. But he nonetheless was willing to corroborate General Barno's assessment. Shoraidah says the Iraqi National Congress had initially planned to send recruits to the U.S. camp but then decided against it. "We decided to go to the north of Iraq and start our own force there," he says.

So General Barno's 1,100-person force of American soldiers and trainers, all hoping to build up the Free Iraqi Forces, waited in Hungary in the snow, as the war started. Chalabi would send them no trainees. But it would not be the last time Barno heard of the Free Iraqi Forces. Before long Chalabi would use that same name for his very own little army.

35

The Birth of De-Baathification

Summer 2002

IN 2002, JUST AS AMERICAN TROOPS were shipping to the desert of Kuwait for the coming invasion, a new word came into usage in U.S. political discussions of Iraq: "de-Baathification." The noun would mean something quite important in the years to come, but it started out as simply a cleverly coined expression. It was invented, according to one account, by accident. Ahmad Chalabi brought his entourage to the editorial offices of a newspaper. One of the editors, according to a source who was present, asked him a question about his ideas for a postwar Iraq. In his distinctive way, Chalabi complimented the questioner, as if the query itself was insightful and new. He answered that Iraq would be a bit like postwar Germany, where the Americans had weeded out the Nazis. This was in line with the INC's practice of invoking the lessons of America's occupation of post–World War II Germany and Japan as models for Iraq. People at the meeting nodded when Chalabi discussed the old efforts against the Nazis. "De-Nazification," someone said, pinning down the word for it. Exactly, said someone else. And then someone said, "de-Baathification," and it was as if this encapsulated what everyone meant.

The word had resonance. It solved a public relations problem: "Baath" meant little to most Americans other than a dunk in the tub, and going to war to get rid of the Baath would not necessarily be that attractive. But this word, "de-Baathification," made it clear that Baathists, even if you didn't know what they were, must be similar to Nazis, since one does the same thing to both groups. Getting rid of Baathists sounded as morally acceptable as getting rid of Nazis.

Baathists could function as a metaphor for Nazis, and even as an effigy. The word "de-Baathification" appears in print for the first time, according to database research, in the *Times* of London in the summer of 2002, from the mouth of Ahmad Chalabi: "What we need is a de-Baathification programme like a de-Nazification programme." Then the *New York Times* on October 12, 2002, cited Chalabi's approval of U.S. war plans. "In an interview today, Ahmad Chalabi, the leader of the Iraqi National Congress, an umbrella group for the Iraqi opposition, who would presumably play a role in forming a new government, said: 'If the U.S. wants to do it, who are we to say no? We can't stop them. They are talking about demilitarization, and de-Baathification, which is very good, what we want."[47]

The scholar Kanan Makiya—who was treated as the "conscience" of the INC and had worked with Chalabi for years—used the word as well. On National Public Radio's *All Things Considered*, Makiya described the INC's postwar doctrine: "We have a whole section devoted to what we term de-Baathification of Iraq, which is modeled in some ways on the de-Nazification of Germany."[48]

And in fact, according to a confidential INC report, the Baathists would be purged ruthlessly. "High-ranking elements of the Ba'ath Party must never be allowed the privilege of socioeconomic and/or political rehabilitation."[49]

Just a month before the invasion of Iraq, Chalabi published an op-ed in the *Wall Street Journal* in which he chided the U.S. government for not planning to purge Baathists thoroughly enough. "Iraq," he wrote, "needs a comprehensive program of de-Baathification even more extensive than the de-Nazification effort in Germany after World War II."[50]

The Nazi analogy was historically flawed, but it proved an effective public relations gambit. It is important that World War II had none of the moral baggage, or the associations with quagmires, that plagued discussion of the war in the Philippines in 1898, the occupation of Panama in 1989, the Vietnam War, the invasions in the Dominican Republic, or elsewhere. Invoking the World War II parallel not only provided moral clarity but put to rest worries about what would happen after the invasion, which was one of the major concerns being raised at the time by those opposed to the war. And it worked brilliantly.

36

There Is Oil in Iraq

"We have a lot of oil; you need to buy oil. But while you may
think of us as your gas station, we may think of you as our
oil-storage depot."

—Ahmad Chalabi, London, 2002[51]

AMONG THE WASHINGTON THINK TANKS where Chalabi cemented so many
loyalties was the Institute for Advanced Strategic and Political Studies,
operating out of a cluttered set of offices on Sixteenth Street in Washington. The IASPS produced the notorious "Clean Break" paper in
which neoconservatives first lobbied Netanyahu about their plan to
remake the Middle East. It was a shop that was largely run by neoconservatives who had been heavily influenced by the political philosophy
of Leo Strauss. David Wurmser, the husband of Mey Wurmser and author of the Chalabi-inspired *Tyranny's Ally*, hung his hat at the IASPS
office for a while as well.

Among the less-known staffers was Paul Michael Wihbey, an American of Lebanese descent. He was an expert energy strategist who
spent much of his time analyzing oil trends and trying to figure out a
way to move America away from dependence on Saudi Arabian oil.
Wihbey, who never identified himself as a neoconservative, was
friendly with the Wurmsers and the others there. He was knowledge-
able about the Middle East, but he was not consulted about the Chal-

abi-driven plans to remake the region. Instead he talked to Chalabi about his own area of expertise, oil, and was impressed with Chalabi's knowledge.

While Chalabi rarely mentioned oil in public, in private it was very much on his mind. Wihbey says he discovered this one day when he was invited to an informal gathering at the Chalabi/Francis Brooke home in Georgetown. As usual, Chalabi first entertained the group with stories that demonstrated his encyclopedic breadth of knowledge. In this case, Wihbey said, Chalabi held court elaborating on the finer points of Japanese medieval history and the battles between feudal shogun rulers.

And then Chalabi told Wihbey, the oil expert, about Iraqi oil. "Ahmad claimed that Iraq had reserves which were greater than Saudi Arabia's. I was skeptical," he said. Chalabi argued that Iraq had massive reserves that had not yet been discovered. It was known to have the third-largest reserves, but Chalabi said it had even more potential. He believed Iraq had the greatest reserves in the world. He seemed to have a great grasp of geology and also of oil drilling technology and the latest tools to explore for petroleum deposits. Wihbey was awed by his detailed information and mastery of the subject matter.

"I think Ahmad was the one," said Wihbey, "who articulated the case for Iraq being the new Saudi Arabia on a geostrategic level, and that under *his* leadership, if he had the backing of the United States, he could play a role in re-establishing Iraq as a great oil-producing power and achieve American objectives on a macroeconomic level globally."

But although oil was a subtext of the war, it was never Chalabi's overt rationale. It didn't need saying, in a White House full of oilmen, that Iraq's rich oil wells would be better off in friendly hands. Wihbey thinks that central to Chalabi's allure was the promise that Iraq would break the Saudi monopoly hold on the OPEC cartel. OPEC, the Organization of Petroleum Exporting Countries, tried to control world oil prices and had always been a bête noire of some U.S. strategists.

Chalabi often hinted at undermining OPEC. Once the United States invaded, he promised in October 2002, "Iraq will need very large amounts of funds right away. Selling oil under current OPEC quotas will not be sufficient to meet Iraq's needs. So Iraq must look

for methods to generate cash to satisfy its debt-servicing require-
ments, its obligations and at the same time pay for its budget and development. . . . Iraqi oil is very cheap to extract."[52] His point was clear:
Iraq could break free of the OPEC stranglehold.

Overtly ogling Iraq's oil was a bad PR move, and Chalabi rarely did
it. One exception was in an interview with the *Washington Post*, when
he said that he favored a U.S.-led consortium to develop Iraq's oil-
fields. "American companies will have a big shot at Iraqi oil," Chalabi
told the *Post*.[53] And the INC's "monarchist" representative, Sharif Ali,
promised that the INC would not necessarily abide by Saddam's oil
deals. "We would have to review all contracts which have been signed
by this regime to make sure it is in the interest of the Iraqi people and
not just for Saddam Hussein,"[54] Chalabi said in interviews. "Any contract signed after 1991 is illegal, because of the United Nations sanctions. When sanctions are lifted, contracts will be re-negotiated." That
was a tantalizing promise, of course, to Western oilmen.

Former Marine Capt. Scott Ritter, who was only associated with
Chalabi for a short time, says that Chalabi promised him oil deals,
vaguely, in 1998, when he was trying to recruit him to support the INC.
"I know you will be making sacrifices in the short term," Chalabi told
him, but he said the financial rewards would come later, according to
Ritter. Once he ran the country, "he would have the ability to make oil
contracts in a way that would take care of people." Ritter insists that
Chalabi specifically mentioned oil contracts as a reward for his cooperation with the INC. He also insists he turned Chalabi down flat.

37

Getting Ready

Winter 2003

"We are using the Americans; 150,000 American soldiers are going to get rid of Saddam for us."

—Ahmad Chalabi, February 2003[55]

PUBLICLY, AHMAD CHALABI always opposed the idea of a U.S. occupation government in Iraq. Chalabi made the distinction, time and time again, between an invasion and an occupation. Liberation without occupation is the dream he sold. The concept was to invade and conquer but not occupy. And he kept up the mantra in 2002 and later, even after the war.

"We don't want Iraqis to lose sovereignty over their land, even for one day," Chalabi told reporters in November 2002. "We want to be prepared to come out with a strong body to take over authority in Iraq upon the beginning of the liberation operation."[56]

He wanted the United States simply to install him and a council of exiles to take over after the military ousted Saddam. "This occupation crap," he said to reporter Charles Glass, "the U.S. will be getting itself into serious trouble." Glass, who had seen far more of war than Chalabi ever had, pointed out that occupation is just a product of invasion.

You can't have an invasion without occupation, because the two go hand in hand, he said.

Yet whatever Chalabi was saying publicly, the INC was evidently arguing in private that postwar Iraq should be run as an occupation even if it wasn't quite called that. It wanted a provisional government installed, but that still meant an occupation: "The mode of a post conflict U.S. presence in Iraq must follow a framework somewhat similar to that of Japan, whereby a Japanese government was officially put in charge of the country."[57] That was the official view of the Iraqi National Congress as put forth by its "Research Branch." And there is no doubt in any historian's mind that the corncob pipe–smoking Gen. Douglas MacArthur wielded dictatorial power over Japan during the American occupation, no matter that he left Emperor Hirohito in place.

The confidential INC postwar plans suggested the Americans employ harsh methods on Saddam's family members, relatives, and friends, reminiscent of General MacArthur's efforts. They even compared Saddam's family and followers with the Zaibatsu of Japan: "Seizing their property and expropriating their lands must be a priority after the removal of the Saddam regime."[58]

So there is something out of joint in Chalabi's public posturing about "occupation" while his own organization was pushing for something along the lines of Douglas MacArthur's iron hand. The INC's analysis was that the United States could democratize Iraq by force, indeed, that Iraq could and should be molded as Japan was: "The study of the American Occupation of Japan, reveals the unlikely fact, that democracy can indeed be 'imposed' upon a people," according to the INC's confidential report, "and that it can profoundly permeate itself into the fabric of society."[59]

No matter what the INC, and Ahmad Chalabi, may have said about occupation or their goals in later days, it is quite clear that what they were pushing was an effort to "impose" democracy.

But then, few people ever actually called for an "occupation" in those days before the war. The "O" word was unmentioned. In the fall and winter of 2002, Iraqi exiles gathered and quarreled about what the future of Iraq should be and, even more important, who should control it. Chalabi and his "proxies," as some people refer to his followers in the exile community, lobbied endlessly for a "provisional" or "transitional" government they would run, ready to deploy behind the U.S. tanks.

That insistence on a provisional government was not so much philosophical as it was simply conniving, his critics argue. What he wanted, they say, was just a provisional government that he was part of. "He wanted to make sure that the U.S. government put him in a position to dominate the transition and take power in Baghdad," wrote David Phillips, a longtime expert on Iraq, who was an adviser to a State Department effort called the Future of Iraq Project.[60]

Certainly Chalabi's argument would have been more credible if he hadn't made it so obvious that he wanted to be part of the "provisional government." Chalabi bickered with the other exiles, with Ayad Allawi, his old nemesis, and with Adnan Pachachi. The hostile games they had been playing for years were now much more urgent. He had his allies working with him: Kanan Makiya, the idealist absent-minded "conscience" of the INC; Salem Chalabi, his nephew; along with his usual inner circle, the formidable Aras Kareem, Nabeel Musawi, and his old non-Iraqi public relations warriors, Francis Brooke and Zaab Sethna.

The issue and the infighting paralyzed the U.S. government, which ended up making no decisions at all. In Washington, at NSC meetings, officials gathered at conference tables to address the same question. Robert Grenier, who had worked at the Iraqi Operations Group in 1991 when Chalabi was first recruited, was back at the group after a twelve-year gap. He felt Chalabi's influence, as officials from Vice President Cheney's office and from the Office of Defense Secretary Rumsfeld lobbied for a provisional government to be put in place. "Provisional" was thought to be a code word for "Chalabi." "You knew they wanted to set up Ahmad, but they never said it. This would be the vehicle to put Chalabi in charge."

Grenier said he only saw Cheney argue the case once, and Cheney did not mention Chalabi specifically. Instead, he talked of the "provisional government" option. Cheney, as Grenier recalls it, said, "Look, what this comes down to is a choice between legitimacy and control. I think we should opt for control."

Then in November, with war still months away, Chalabi's cause seemed temporarily lost; officials who had held Chalabi's hand most tightly let go for a moment. Paul Wolfowitz and I. Lewis "Scooter" Libby, whom Chalabi considered relatively sympathetic, cosigned a letter with Richard Armitage, whom he considered an enemy, baldly opposing a "provisional government." It was a slap in the face.[61] According to Andrew Cockburn's biography of Donald Rumsfeld, President Bush flatly wrote off Chalabi before the war, telling Wolfowitz that Chalabi "is not my man."

But Chalabi still had his supporters, so he adapted. Burson-Marsteller's BKSH staged a preemptive press conference for him at an exile convention in London in December to announce that a "nucleus" government would take over once Baghdad fell, with Chalabi's Iraqi National Congress at its head. His grandstanding sparked an uproar in the Iraqi opposition community. Shortly after that, after a quick visit to the United States, Chalabi set off for Iran. That was going to be his way back to Baghdad, via Washington and then Tehran.

In Tehran in January 2003, Chalabi and his entourage received the welcome of an important ally: lavish meals, a guesthouse for him, and meetings with the top security officials of the county. Tamara, his eldest daughter, accompanied him, wearing the hijab in keeping with the country's strictures.

In Tehran Chalabi met with the Pasdaran, Iran's Revolutionary Guard, who oversee efforts to spread the Islamic Revolution through their ties to Hezbollah and other groups. The INC had an office in Iran and had dealt with the Ministry of Intelligence and Security as well as the Pasdaran. Both agencies had significant interest in the goings-on in America, and the INC officials regaled their Iranian hosts with anecdotes about their high contacts in Washington. The neoconservative movement was not unknown to the Iranians, who tracked every think tank paper churned out by the movement's strategists.

Some have argued that Chalabi's pro-Israel tilt as he dealt with the neoconservatives was opportunistic and expedient, and ultimately cynical. But the fact is that he never let down his pro-Israel patrons in the United States. He bluntly told the Iranians they should re-establish ties to Israel. Out of sincere conviction or perhaps naïveté, he argued that Israel needed to be accepted in the Middle East, which was an extraordinary thing to say in Tehran. Apparently, though, he could do no wrong in front of his Iranian hosts, who gave him support and an escort all the way.

Despite their mutual antagonism, Iran and the United States were always at the center of Chalabi's efforts to topple Saddam Hussein. But there is no evidence that Iran ever assisted Chalabi financially. The Iranian intelligence agency had given him right of passage over the years, back in the 1990s when he was really running an active INC; it gave him and his entourage quick visas. The agents listened to his tales about his U.S. supporters, about the neoconservatives and their ideas. But they did not, according to all available information, give Chalabi money. Only the United States poured millions of dollars into his efforts. America was far more generous to him than the rest of the world.

On January 30, 2003, Chalabi set off for northern Iraq again, the first time since he was expelled years before. Photographs of his 2003 crossing show him bundled up with a thick scarf wrapped around his head as if he had a toothache. He wore a long black topcoat and fine dress shoes as he trudged with bodyguards along a dirt mountain road in the snow at the Haj Omran crossing.

Money in Kurdistan was the hard part. Chalabi found that there was no effective way of carrying hundreds of thousands of dollars, let alone millions, all the way through Iran and then into Kurdistan. All of the INC's budget came from U.S. taxpayer funds, some left over from the State Department and some from the Defense Intelligence Agency, but Kurdistan had no functioning banking system. Nabeel Musawi, in an interview, explained with a pleasant laugh that the INC used informal wire transfers to get the U.S. funds into Kurdistan from London. It used a form of the ancient unregulated money transfer system known as Hawalla. The irony is that U.S. funds were effectively being laundered and transferred via a system the U.S. government itself was trying to end, in an attempt to cut off terrorists' financial networks. The Treasury Department, since 2001, had been demanding an end to Hawalla and insisting that countries around the world license and register all money transfer operations.

That task would prove to be largely impossible, though. For anyone with a little banking knowledge, such as Chalabi had, it was easy: the

INC set up bank accounts for the Kurdish smugglers in London. Then it deposited INC funds into the Kurdish smuggler accounts. When the INC got to Kurdistan, the Kurdish smugglers delivered to them the same amount in cash. At the end of the day, the Kurdish smugglers had clean, laundered funds in London, and the INC had suitcases full of cold, hard cash in Kurdistan.

The issue of money also arose on February 5, 2003, as Chalabi and his entourage huddled in the Kurdish chill awaiting action. Back in America two important things came out of the State Department on that important day. The first was Colin Powell's remarkable speech to the UN General Assembly about Iraq—a virtual call to war. George Tenet sat with the U.S. delegation. Powell's speech was riddled with errors, although most of them were credited not to the INC but to other assorted intelligence sources. He used information from the widely discredited agent code-named Curveball, who was not a Chalabi plant. He cited electronics intercepts that proved little. He even cited terrorism allegations, although not Salman Pak. He used the discredited information from a tortured Al Qaeda member that Iraq had offered "chemical or biological weapons training for two Al Qaeda associates beginning in December 2000."

Powell did use some false information that derived from Chalabi, such as the claims of the known fabricator Mohammad Harith, who had claimed to have invented the mobile biological laboratories. Powell said, "An Iraqi major, who defected, confirmed that Iraq has mobile biological research laboratories, in addition to the production facilities I mentioned earlier." Somehow this information had slipped into his speech despite repeated DIA warnings.

But the key thing for Chalabi, for all the other exiles, and for Chalabi's friends was Powell's powerful conclusion: "Leaving Saddam Hussein in possession of weapons of mass destruction for a few more months or years is not an option, not in a post-September 11th world."

The same day that Powell gave his speech to the United Nations, records show, Powell's State Department finally signed an agreement to release to the INC even more taxpayer financing. It was an odd coincidence, that is all, and not a conspiracy. Or at least it would be wrong to infer cause and effect. It was a confusing period, financially, because the Defense Department was handling the $340,000-a-month Information Collection Program, but State was still carrying the load for Chalabi's other expenses. And Congress had earmarked millions for the INC. This time, it was a $7 million installment, even though only a bare-bones INC staff remained in Washington and London. The State Department inked the deal despite the misgivings of officials like Armitage, Sherri Kraham, and Yael Lampert. And so, while Chalabi was broadcasting nothing, as far as anyone knows, the United States was paying for his TV Liberty and Radio Liberty operations. The $7 million was to last him until July 2003.[62]

That $7 million would be the last of the $33 million in State Department funding for Ahmad Chalabi. A comment Chalabi made at this time provides insight into his thinking about the United States. Charles Glass, the former ABC News correspondent who had first met Chalabi in the mountains before the Lebanese civil war, was skeptical about the war and its motives. He asked Chalabi bluntly: weren't the Americans just using him? "Who's using whom?" Chalabi replied rhetorically.

Just before the war started, Chalabi made a last-ditch effort to organize a provisional government with the Kurds at yet one more conference. Zalmay Khalilzad, the American envoy, put a spike in it. And anyway, Gen. Jay Garner was going to run things once the war started. Strangely, Chalabi seemed to think he'd won the argument: "The talk of a military government has stopped, and instead we have an Iraqi interim authority, which will take over immediately after liberation."[63]

Most of Chalabi's team gathered in northern Iraq, building up their tiny force in anticipation of the war. Francis Brooke was there, drinking beer in the mornings. The American ranted that Saddam was a "human satan." "I believe in good and evil. That man is absolute evil and must be destroyed," he said. Brooke told Glass that he would support the elimination of Saddam even if every single Iraqi were killed in the process. In surprise, Glass asked him to repeat it, which he did. Brooke bunked in a room with another non-Iraqi INC colleague, Zaab Sethna, where they kept two AK-47s. Another American who joined the band was Col. Ted Seel, a Defense Department attaché assigned as the Centcom liaison to the INC. Seel had fought in Vietnam and had served for more than thirty years in the U.S. military.

Harold Rhode, who revered Chalabi and worked at the Pentagon's Office of Net Assessment, did not get up north but volunteered to join Garner's occupation team, which was waiting at the Hilton in Kuwait. Rhode deployed to the Kuwait Hilton and awaited war. Tamara Daghistani, the old supporter of Chalabi who had protected him as far back as Petra Bank, got a phone call from Nabeel Musawi that said: "The Doc wants you to go to Kuwait." She agreed to join in the effort and trundled off to the Kuwaiti Hilton too.

By late March the war had started. Americans were slicing through Saddam's forces but facing a tougher time than they expected. Intelligence was poor and they didn't receive the welcome they had been promised. There were few, if any, flowers tossed at their feet.

Chalabi wanted his own little militia for his move into Iraq. Later on his force would be called the Free Iraqi Forces. Aras Kareem and Talal al-Obeidi, an INC stalwart with reputed close ties to Iranian intelligence, began recruiting. It was a crash assignment, standing up a militia in a month, but they worked fast. The source of recruits was chiefly Iraqi refugee camps inside Iran, according to Hamad Shoraidah and Nabeel Musawi. They offered the recruits cash, food, and a chance to be part of the team going back into Iraq. Some Kurds on the outskirts of their camp joined up as well.

Uniforms and guns were easy to obtain at the bazaar, with a bit of bargaining, and Shoraidah said Aras paid for it all. Shoraidah, who had experience in the Iraqi Revolutionary Guard, was one of the INC members who had received U.S. military training through some earlier programs. He says that when he arrived in the north of Iraq, the INC's force was in complete chaos, without military order or discipline. He tried to instill some order in it, unsuccessfully. Just as Bob Baer had found a "Potemkin village" in Kurdistan in 1995, so it was in 2003 when Chalabi rose again.

Soon, Col. Ted Seel wrote up an "Authorization for Foreign National to Travel on U.S. Military Aircraft.[64] Shoraidah flew off to Qatar to be the INC liaison to Centcom. For the INC, it was a major coup to get one of its own embedded in the U.S. command structure. Francis Brooke was exultant.[65]

Michael Gordon and Gen. Bernard Trainor have reported how Seel spoke to Gen. John Abizaid at Centcom, offering Chalabi's troops, and how the White House wanted an Iraqi face on the ongoing operation.

Chalabi put on a black Hugo Boss T-shirt. It was snug, but it wasn't laughable for a man his age. His race-walking in the morning and his Atkins diet had done him good. The layer of fat that once folded over his belt had melted away. Surrounded by the mountains and breathing in the crisp spring air, he stepped outside. There at the INC headquarters, near Dokun, the FIF troops took a flag that had been designed for Chalabi and danced around him. The flag was blue, green, and orange, with diagonal stripes and two five-pointed stars. ABC News videotaped the event, as the Iraqis whooped and Chalabi smiled mysteriously. The flag would fly as a symbol of his little, hastily thrown-together militia, a group that was, as usual, funded by America.

On that April day the hundreds of men and boys in their various uniforms pushed and shoved their way toward the U.S. military planes that would take them to southern Iraq, as Chalabi's men tried in vain to impose order.

Suddenly there was a holdup. Chalabi was about to head out from the protected north of Kurdistan to southern Iraq for the first time. But just when it was approved, once again there was a problem. Centcom said it didn't want an Iraqi politician; it just wanted U.S.-friendly Iraqi troops. Even with Chalabi's political backing in Washington, D.C., the generals in the field had been told they were not to appoint any particular leader. They took that command at face value. They were not flying other Iraq leaders in, and so they would not fly him in. The word came down through the chain of command. Chalabi didn't care. He would later claim that "I just went to the plane and nobody stopped me."[66]

As the Air Force C-17 transport plane roared up into the darkness, Ahmad Chalabi seemed to sink into himself, donning some earphones to listen to music. The Americans flew him and his men south, toward the early morning light of Nasiriya.

38

Entering Iraq

April 2003

"De Gaulle Reported Leading Smash into Paris."

—*New York Times* headline, August 25, 1944

ON THE NIGHT OF APRIL 7, 2003, Ahmad Chalabi lay down on a U.S. Army cot set in the sand in southern Iraq and went to sleep under the southern desert sky for the first time in forty-five years. He slept outside just as he had as a boy in the summer nights of Baghdad. American soldiers and Marines had already been fighting on the ground in Iraq for sixteen days.[67]

Chalabi stayed at Tallil Air Base, in southern Iraq near Nasiriya. Inside a derelict warehouse nearby, on the air base set up by the U.S. forces, slept hundreds of new arrivals, Chalabi's men, snoring: his militia, his Free Iraqi Forces.[68] He had brought them deep into the heart of the American military operation.

The thing was, it was impossible for him to know who these men in the warehouse really were. They seemed worse than desperadoes. They dug no latrines like normal soldiers would, and defecated wherever they wanted, creating an overpowering stench around them. Who were these hundreds of undisciplined soldiers with the Free Iraqi Forces? Tamara Daghistani, Chalabi's old friend, asked him one day after she arrived in Iraq. Chalabi replied that he didn't know. "I remember Ahmad himself saying they didn't belong to us," she said in an interview. Indeed, there is no way he could have known who they were.

"Of course he didn't know," said Hamad Shoraidah, the INC man who tried to instill order in the FIF at Tullil Air Base. Shoraidah, the liaison to Centcom, was one of the highest-ranking officials in the FIF. If anyone knew who these forces were, it would be him. "Nobody knew," Shoraidah said in an interview. "Some of them, as we discovered later, were thieves. Some of them were murderers; some of them were rapists. We didn't know who was fighting with us."

But even if Chalabi didn't know who made up his own militia, he and his champions in Washington still touted them as the nucleus of a new Iraqi army and a liberation force under his command. Chalabi and his FIF had landed at Tallil Air Base on Sunday, April 6, at 6:30 a.m., flown in by a U.S. military that didn't want him there. Journalist Charles Glass covered his ignominious arrival. Chalabi's FIF had no water, and young members of the group wandered around begging for it, he saw. The FIF, housed in large warehouses, was at first without support, direction, transport, or supplies.

The U.S. military didn't know who Chalabi's men were, either. The generals also were unaware that Chalabi's original plan had been to march first into Baghdad, in a repeat of de Gaulle's entrance into Paris. The U.S. military thought the FIF was there to assist U.S. forces, but the whole idea, Chalabi told Glass, was to get to Baghdad before the American troops could, so he could make sure the Americans did not impose an occupation government. Reality preempted Chalabi's Gaullist ambitions. His small and untrained force would have been crushed by the Saddamist troops and Fedayeen that remained in Baghdad, and in any case, the Americans were already there.

Over in Hungary, where his efforts were winding down with only seventy-four Iraqis trained, Gen. David Barno had been preparing what he thought was the Free Iraqi Forces for battle, in an effort to supply American forces with an embedded force of Iraqis who could help them navigate Iraqi society. Chalabi, Barno suspected, had sabotaged his effort by turning off the tap on the recruiting efforts. But on television, he was "disconcerted" to see Chalabi's force in the desert, and to watch the "FIF's" strange circular war dance around Chalabi.

"We thought they were thugs," he recalls. His FIF was nothing like this FIF, he thought. Chalabi had not only sabotaged Barno's program, he believed, but now he was appropriating its very name.

From Hungary, Barno made it clear to his chain of command that he'd had nothing to do with this new FIF, and that they were not U.S.-trained. Barno didn't know it, but Chalabi's mysterious force was also appropriating his gear. Americans issued them old FIF equipment, the holsters and badges, the webbing, and anything else they could use. It was U.S. military "drawn-down" equipment, the long-delayed product of Chalabi's 1998 law. The Iraq Liberation Act was finally bearing fruit. It had arrived in slow motion, but it had arrived after all.

In Washington, Chalabi's friends in the neoconservative movement were exhilarated. The news of Chalabi's arrival in Iraq spread around town quickly. His admirers called up reporters to bring their attention to the development. Iraqis, led by Chalabi, were fighting with the Americans, they explained.

Sandy-haired, bespectacled Francis Brooke, the American who spoke no Arabic, had flown down on the military transport with Chalabi. Chalabi's *consigliere* donned fatigues and called himself a "colonel" in the force of mismatched men and boys. "It's absolutely obvious," he quipped later, "that no Virginian can serve as less than a colonel in a foreign army."[69] Hamad Shoraidah confirms that Brooke was listed as a lieutenant colonel in the Free Iraqi Force on a roster given to U.S. Central Command. The absurdity of it was lost in the desert of absurdities: an American Christian loyalist to Chalabi was joining a U.S.-sponsored militia. Brooke's endless lobbying in the halls of power in Washington had brought him there, slinging an AK-47 over his shoulder just as if he were a real soldier, on this tragicomic adventure.

Chalabi had his little army now. But still, he looked like he had lost control of his destiny: a biker mama on the back of the American military's huge roaring Harley. So Chalabi began in earnest to do what he did best, through calls and meetings and endless committees and conferences, using his satellite phone and his friends as his implements of war. Was he making a desperate dash for power, to stave away irrelevance now that Saddam was toppled? Or was he simply eager to return to the Baghdad he dreamed of, where he had grown up in a jasmine-scented mansion, where the parrots screeched playfully, and he played ping-pong with his nephews? Or did he just want what was best for his country? It may have been all three, but in any case, with whatever complex set of motives, he was determined to inject himself back into the war.

One of his early tactics was to nag. The nagging of the United States often produced results. On April 9, he did an interview on CNN, deriding Gen. Jay Garner, the civil administrator waiting in Kuwait. Chalabi regarded Garner as a potential obstacle, since the general had already said he was not going to hire INC people.

Where is General Garner now? The people need assistance here in Nasiriyah. Why are they not here? Why don't they work to rehabilitate the electricity and water? Why don't they start working on the curriculum? Why are they in Kuwait? This area is in great need of assistance now. People are hungry. Their supplies are going to run out. Basic services have to be restored. This is true all over the town. Where are they?

In another interview, this time on NBC News, he pushed to get to Baghdad, demanding that his small and riotous group be brought closer to the action. "Free Iraqi Forces must be deployed in Baghdad and other parts of the country so that the looting will be stopped in complete coordination with the U.S."[70]

Col. Ted Seel, Centcom's liaison to the Iraqi National Congress, worked for the U.S. Army but seems to have been drawn close into the INC's heart, perhaps enchanted as so many others had been by Chalabi's magnetism. "They," the American colonel said, referring to the Pentagon, "are getting colder and colder and colder towards us." A career American military officer, he had come to identify so deeply with the INC as to refer to them as "us" and to the Pentagon as "they."[71]

When Jay Garner finally did host a conference near Nasiriya, Chalabi stayed away, but he did meet with Garner that night. "He and I immediately didn't get along," Garner said. "I thought he was a thug. I thought he was greasy."

(Garner's tenure in Iraq would turn out to be a short one, and that may have had a lot to do with Ahmad Chalabi, he believes. He'd crossed swords with the neoconservatives just weeks earlier. Before

Garner deployed, Douglas Feith, a Chalabi loyalist at the Defense Department, had called him at his home and chewed him out over a passing remark he'd made. "You undercut the INC!" Feith yelled. Garner yelled back: "I don't give a shit. Fire me or shut the hell up!"[72])

But in early April neither Garner nor Chalabi was yet in Baghdad, the heart of the mess. The United States had torn up the regime that smothered the country, and now havoc had been let loose. While Chalabi had been flown to Nasiriya with his followers, his old supporter and top Middle East agent, Mohamad al-Zobaidy (Al Deeb), had driven into Baghdad with his men. He had communicated with Chalabi via Thuraya on the way, and he had spoken with U.S. forces as well. Shortly after the Americans arrived in Baghdad, so did Zobaidy, in effect doing what Chalabi had wanted to do: put an Iraqi face on things. Flirting with absurdity, the INC's man called himself the mayor, or vizier, of Baghdad. In a sense, it made things a little easier for the American soldiers who were there first: at least they had an Iraqi they could deal with. This is how the *New York Times* reported it on April 14:

> Dr. Muhammad Zobaidy, appointed by American forces to manage Baghdad, began interviewing people to fill major positions in a new government. Dr. Zobaidy is a representative of the Iraqi National Congress, a coalition of political exiles headed by Dr. Ahmad Chalabi, the man some American officials want to take a leadership role in Iraq.
>
> Dr. Zobaidy will act as a kind of mayor of Baghdad to oversee, with the help of the American military, the restoration of order and the resumption of basic municipal services.[73]

Chalabi had known Zobaidy for fourteen years, but to see him there in Baghdad, while he was being held down in Nasiriya, must have been hard to bear. On Wednesday, April 16, Chalabi and his INC followers made the drive from Nasiriya to Baghdad, an apprehensive but merry band—driving up in a military-escorted convoy on the heels of the U.S. toppling of Saddam.

Part of the allure of the INC was something devastatingly simple: they were great characters, fun and even downright nutty, their eccentricity always guaranteed to make for colorful copy. On the INC's drive to Baghdad, almost the entire crew was there: Ahmad Chalabi with his beautiful and brilliant daughter Tamara, and Aras Kareem, the cool-headed enforcer. Zaab Sethna, the Pakistani British press adviser, dressed in camouflage gear, came along to handle journalists. He had served Chalabi for twelve years. Francis Brooke, styling himself a "colonel" in the Free Iraqi Forces, would be the American troubleshooter. Longtime loyalist Tamara Daghistani went along as well. She said she was so happy to be back on Iraqi soil that she surprised herself by hugging a tree.

They drove straight to the Baghdad Hunting Club in Monsour, a tony suburb of Baghdad where all the exile leaders were setting up shop. There, the INC settled in like conquering heroes with their Free Iraqi Forces militia encamped nearby, in another club. The raucous FIF quickly wrecked the place, defecating in the showers area and scrawling graffiti everywhere. The Hunting Club was a temporary headquarters for the INC. In those early days of the war, Chalabi and his men expropriated buildings they had an eye on, mostly in Monsour, and mostly ones that belonged to ousted regime members. Some they kept, and some slipped out of their hands. Sometimes even the U.S. soldiers who accompanied them had to restrain the acquisitions. One American first lieutenant said he and his men simply told the INC at one point, "That's enough."

By coincidence, John Kifner, one of the first of the *New York Times* reporters to meet Chalabi, back in the 1980s in Amman, was in Baghdad covering the war. Kifner, one of the most respected journalists at the *Times*, had never been impressed by Chalabi, but he was assigned to cover Chalabi's first press conference in Baghdad, which took place on April 19 at his new digs in the Hunting Club. Kifner watched Chalabi mysteriously smile as he looked out over the assembled journalists and gunmen. "He was like a cat at a canary buffet," Kifner recalled later in an interview.

As Kifner and a colleague reported in the *Times*, "Mr. Chalabi repeatedly declared today, in the well-worn tradition of political power brokers, that he was not a candidate for president. 'I am not a candidate for any position in the interim government,' he said. 'My role is to rebuild Iraq.'"

Suddenly after the speech, reporters heard the whip-crack of gunfire. One of the SUVs plastered with Chalabi's posters hurtled back toward the compound, riddled with bullet holes. The INC people hurried to attend to the driver, an INC employee with blood pouring down his neck, and to tear the Chalabi posters off the vehicle.[74]

39

The Dossiers

2003

"You flock of fools, under this captain of fools, in this ship of fools."

—Herman Melville, *The Confidence-Man*

THERE WAS A SECRET FILE on Ahmad Chalabi, a dossier in a cardboard binding compiled by the Iraqi Intelligence Service under Saddam Hussein, which was nearly destroyed by a fire, according to the INC official who salvaged it from destruction. Totalitarian regimes often keep meticulous records, and true to form, amid all the data collected by Saddam's feared agents, Chalabi's name was written in red on the front of a bound folder.

Chalabi recognized right away that the Saddam regime's old files meant power, money, and influence. The captured files meant power because he would have evidence against old Saddam loyalists. And the files meant money and influence because they offered leverage: information with which to trade with various forces and intelligence to offer to work with the Defense Intelligence Agency, which had been forced into a relationship with the INC and was now paying $350,000 a month to Chalabi's group.

And so Chalabi's men, led by Hamad Shoraidah, swept up the files. The "Ahmad Chalabi" folder, according to Shoraidah, cropped up by accident. Some Baathist files were kept, by strange coincidence, at a house that once belonged to a relative of Chalabi's. Tamara Daghistani was the first to find the place. It was crammed full of files stowed away as if in an effort to keep them out of the various government buildings. But other files, from the Mukhabarat, filled an old building near Fourteenth of Ramadan Street.[75] Thugs were just about to burn the documents when Shoraidah got there with a team of armed men; they collected all the records and trucked them to Monsour. Some of the files mentioned Saddam's intelligence operations. One mentioned Al Jazeera. A friendly reporter at the *Sunday Times* of London, Marie Colvin, wrote of Shoraidah's role in the intelligence coup, and then said that some of the recovered files "apparently reveal how Iraqi agents infiltrated the Al-Jazeera television station," dubbed "the CNN of the Arab world," in an attempt to sanitize its coverage of Saddam's regime.

But the *Times* of London mentioned nothing about the "Chalabi" file that Shoraidah says he found. Shoraidah says he didn't even open the Iraqi Intelligence Service file on Chalabi but hurriedly walked over and brought it to him. "He put his hand on it and he refused to let anyone else see it," Shoraidah says now. (Shoraidah is a good witness but an angry one. He has come to despise Chalabi, the INC, and the American occupation.)

And despite what Shoraidah says, the INC's Nabeel Musawi says he in fact did see the Chalabi file, and that there was not much of significance in it.

————

There were strange things going on in Baghdad in those early days of war, but of all the intelligence operations run by Chalabi's people, the least harmful and yet the strangest was the untombing and salvaging of the religious Jewish texts in April 2003.

The fact that it happened at all was thanks to *New York Times* reporter Judith Miller. Miller was embedded with a group of U.S. soldiers forming Mobile Exploitation Team (MET) Alpha. The team's job was to hunt down unconventional weapons, to leapfrog from one

WMD site to another, triumphantly uncovering Saddam's programs. The team had originally scoured southern Iraq looking for WMDs.

They soon realized their sites were dry: the warehouses of toxins and poisons and gas and germs just weren't there.

The American unit of about sixteen soldiers had never planned in the beginning to have anything to do with Chalabi. The soldiers ended up with him because of Miller. They had been in Karbala, on another fruitless search. In their frustration, one day, they gathered to take a breath, to brainstorm, according to Chief Warrant Officer Richard "Monty" Gonzales, who headed the team. They were in an old gray industrial control room full of disused knobs and levers and buttons, and they sat around discussing what to do next. After a frenzy of activity, it was a moment to rethink things.

Gonzales says he doesn't remember how exactly Chalabi's name came up, but he says that Miller mentioned she could introduce the group to him if they went to Baghdad. Perhaps he could help them, she said.

"I honestly cannot remember if I asked about Chalabi or if she suggested him to me," said Gonzales. "But she said she knew him and he was in the country." Gonzales thought they might as well try, since nothing else was working. Perhaps Chalabi could introduce them to WMD scientists who were only just then coming forward. "I drove to his compound at the Hunting Club," Gonzales said, "and she introduced me, since she had a long-standing relationship."

Miller had relied on Chalabi for years. And she trusted him. He had given her several stories about defectors and his goals for postwar Iraq, and she had a proprietary attitude about him as a source at the paper; he was hers. He "provided most of the front page exclusives on WMD to our paper," she noted in an e-mail to her colleague John Burns on May 1, when she thought someone was encroaching on her turf.[76]

By the time Miller introduced the army team to Chalabi, he was playing the role of fixer, or godfather, granting favors and hearing pleas from a long line of Iraqi supplicants who saw him as a liaison to the American forces. Chalabi offered Gonzales unlimited support. Aras Kareem and Francis Brooke were at his elbow offering their assistance and helpful tips. The MET team spent a lot of time with the INC and grew quite familiar with the Hunting Club, right in the shadow of the giant unfinished mosque in Baghdad. But none of the scientists Chalabi introduced them to led anywhere, Gonzales said. "We would talk to these people and make a report and then follow up. But most of what they gave us didn't really yield much. We went down every hole, and I was constantly reined in because there was just nothing there."

One problem they encountered, according to Gonzales, was that it was tough to distinguish INC bodyguards, as well as the boisterous FIF, from insurgents.

On a few occasions his troops almost mowed down INC or FIF forces. "There were a couple of times where I had to tell my guys not to shoot. Because there were these armed, unmarked men who were—on one occasion—guarding the Hunting Club. My guys reacted to Iraqis standing on a wall with AK-47s."

Judith Miller turned one of Chalabi's tips to the U.S. Army team into yet another exclusive for her newspaper on weapons of mass destruction. Chalabi provided an introduction to Dr. Nissar Hindawi, whom she interviewed for a story in the *New York Times* titled "Leading Iraqi Scientist Says He Lied to U.N. Inspectors." It was couched in dramatic terms, but it was fairly weak stuff. The U.S. military WMD hunters found Hindawi useless, Gonzales says, since he knew nothing about any biological weapons after 1989.

The only tip from Chalabi that finally paid off had nothing to do with WMDs. It was about the mystical Jewish texts buried nearby at the old Mukhabarat building. There was an ancient Talmud—or Jewish commentary on the holy book—they were told, dating from the seventh century, making it one of the oldest known commentaries.

So the army team went on a search in the filthy, flooded basement of the Mukhabarat. Beams of light from the soldiers' flashlights illuminated the fetid sewage as they pushed through the sludge, like walking through an underground swamp. The corners of submerged books peeked out from the black and stinking water.

As it turned out, there was no ancient Talmud, but there was box after box of Jewish texts mixed with Jewish trivia. There was an ancient Bible, rosters of long-defunct synagogues, bar mitzvah pamphlets. The find brought a rush of excitement. At least they were finding something, if not WMDs. "I asked my commander for permission to safeguard these documents, which were of some historic value," recalled Gonzales. "I went to Chalabi and asked him how many people he could give me to help pull this stuff out of there, because my team just couldn't do it."

Chalabi sent over about a dozen Iraqis to walk into the muck with them and do the heavy lifting. One of the Americans who came, wide-eyed, to the site was Pentagon official Harold Rhode, an ardent Chalabi advocate. An Orthodox Jew who spoke multiple languages, Rhode was the Defense Department analyst who'd studied under Bernard Lewis. He had originally been brought to Iraq as part of Jay Garner's team but quickly went to the Hunting Club to be with Chalabi. He helped supervise the examination of the material, like some daredevil archeologist at a scene of a new discovery. Chalabi sent pumps to help remove the muck from the site, and the men carted box after box of the books into the sunlight and shipped them off to the Hunting Club.

The oldest book they recovered was published in Venice in 1568; it was the third section of the Hebrew Bible. Another book was published in 1696. But the most significant was a Torah, the scroll containing the five books of Moses, written by hand on parchment, and the holiest artifact in the Jewish faith. They had to roll it out in the sun to let it dry.

Dov Zakheim, the Pentagon comptroller, who was no fan of Ahmad Chalabi, happened to be in Baghdad when the discovery was made. "I was there, and I saw them, I actually looked at them, because I read Hebrew," he said. "I picked up one book and it looked like something from the late eighteenth century, and someone had written marginalia on the side. And there were booklets that you give out after bar mitzvahs for grace with meals as well. The person who organized the salvaging of the documents was Chalabi, so you have to give him credit for that."

A journalist followed Harold Rhode and asked him, "So, isn't this like looting, if it's removed from Iraq?" Rhode got upset, the journalist said, and told him, "This has been approved at the highest level."[77]

The Jewish Iraqi materials were held at the Hunting Club for a time. But eventually, the collection was packed up in twenty-seven large airtight metal crates and flown out of Iraq to the United States by the US Air Force. The problem was this: with all the mold and dis-integration, archivists estimated it would cost up to $3 million to re-store the collection. For years, the collection has sat in a secure vault at the U.S. National Archives and Records Administration. It was not un-like the final scene in the movie *Raiders of the Lost Ark*.

Meanwhile, the DIA continued to fund Chalabi's intelligence oper-ation. Nothing about Chalabi's operations were simple, including the way the INC got its cash from the DIA. The cash flow to the INC's in-telligence operation worked like this: Francis Brooke, Chalabi's *con-sigliere*; Aras Kareem Habib, his chief executive and enforcer; and Margeret Bartel, his financial wizard, founded a company on paper in January 2003 called Boxwood Inc. Just as Chalabi had used IBC Com-munications in the 1990s to pass CIA funding to the INC, now he would use Boxwood Inc. The sole purpose of it was to collect the DIA cash and pass it on to the INC. Bartel came to handle the cash pay-ments, and the program just grew and grew. Eventually it seemed to morph into a security service operation in Baghdad, but at first it con-sisted of the file collection, with the INC operating as a giant vacuum cleaner sucking in what it could.

―――

Ahmad Chalabi seems to have always been drawn to the world of espi-onage. For years, he continued to brag to his friends that he had played a role in the invention of a new form of cryptography, and he would only have risked this apparent lie if he felt it was important. Se-cret codes, tradecraft, the CIA, the Mossad, double dealings: perhaps all of this appealed to his playful intellect—his knack for solving puz-zles. Or perhaps it played to his paranoia—his recurring sense that he was being persecuted. Either way, it was a lasting fascination.

After the war, Chalabi's old friend and loyalist Warren Marik, the CIA officer who had become so close to him in 1993, went to Iraq to stay with him. He says he stopped off first in Washington at the Spy Museum to buy various espionage movies and TV programs on DVD as presents for his host. And then, in Baghdad, according to Marik, the two men watched the classic BBC production of John le Carré's *Tin-ker, Tailor, Soldier, Spy* and *Smiley's People,* with Alec Guinness—set in the dreary gray London of the 1970s. Guinness's character is a retired master spy, Smiley, who hides his ingenuity behind a dull façade. "Topicality," Smiley says as he analyzes suspicious intelligence, "is always suspect." He roots out a traitor who has fed false intelligence to the British Secret Service while giving the Soviets the British crown jewels. "Everyone has a loyalty somewhere," Guinness's character says at one point. Marik and Chalabi watched the episodes hour after hour, late into the night in Chalabi's lavish villa in Baghdad, which Chalabi was already filling with old family furniture.

Marik was just one of Chalabi's Washington friends who visited him in these tours of the Iraq they were hoping for. Max Singer, the elderly conservative who had been converted to the cause over lunch six years earlier, flew over to stay with him for a while. Dewey Clarridge, the old CIA spymaster, went there too. Retired Gen. Wayne Downing, who had written up his war plan so many years ago, visited as well and was frustrated. Downing increasingly saw an "arrogant" side to Chalabi he didn't like. More than that, he didn't at all like the way Chalabi was criticizing American soldiers who were bleeding for Iraq. The general spoke to him sharply: "I told him, 'Ahmad, stick with what you know. This is not your field. Don't make judgments like that. You're unqualified.'"

—————

Chalabi's Free Iraqi Forces, billed as the "nucleus of a new Iraqi Army," came to an abrupt end. Within months of the FIF's formation, the U.S. military told the INC it had to disband its little army and gave all the men some cash to go home with. Some went to work for a security company affiliated with Chalabi, but most were superfluous, with few skills and no proven abilities as fighters.

But the story of the FIF's end must be finished in Washington, D.C., where it started. Francis Brooke met up with Steve Rademaker, the congressional staffer at the House International Affairs Committee who had written up the text of the Iraq Liberation Act. It must have been a somber if proud moment. In all seriousness, Brooke handed him the folded-up flag of the Free Iraqi Forces—the raucous crew whose identities the INC didn't even know—and told him it flew over them when they landed in Iraq and then went back to Baghdad. Dr. Chalabi, Brooke said, wanted Rademaker to have it, as thanks for the law he had written. It was a cloth flag, and the colors were painted on, not woven into it. Rademaker became a lobbyist at a powerful firm, and his office is not far from the White House. Today the flag of the Free Iraqi Forces lies folded on a small circular table in Rademaker's office. On top of it is a small model of the F-22.

40

An Armored Truck and $250 Million

April 2003

THE TREASURE INSIDE the Iraqi armored truck must have weighed it down so that it sank heavily on its axles. It was parked in the midst of the American military encampment that had been built up overnight at the Sheraton and Palestine hotel complexes by the river. The truck stayed there like a Spanish prize galleon hiding in a cove from pirates. Around it the rattle of gunfire and the grating of tanks resounded. Locked inside were some seventy stainless-steel containers built to hold $4 million each, and it had been backed up against the wall of the Sheraton Hotel, where the Americans were based, to make it tougher to tear open. Then Chalabi's men showed up with guns.

What happened next depends on whom you believe. Chalabi's people say he rescued the cash for the future of Iraq. Others say he planned to take it and was confronted and blocked by exposure before that was possible.

Part of the puzzle has to do with the power struggle that started before Chalabi got back to Baghdad. There was a group of Iraqis trying to keep the bare-bones mechanisms of government going. They were self-proclaimed administrators including Mohamad al-Zobaidy, the INC loyalist who announced himself "mayor" of the city. Another was a former Ministry of Finance official who oversaw one of the few municipal operations still standing.

Then there was Rafidain Bank, the government-owned bank. Chalabi may have reserved a particular place in his heart for it—a hard place, born of a grievance against its management—since it was founded in the 1940s by his family and later nationalized.

In the thick of the postinvasion confusion, some Rafidain Bank officials were trying to figure out whom to report to. There's a bit of Iraqi heroism here, amid the looters eating away at Baghdad from the inside. Bank officials tried to rescue Iraq's money from the robbers. They witnessed horrifying events. At the Qusam Abyat branch of the Rafidain Bank, looters had stolen almost everything and were battling with U.S. soldiers. Dollars floated in sewage in the basement.[78]

The Rafidain Bank officials begged and pleaded, and finally they got hold of a massive armored truck that belonged to the Ministry of Finance. They drove it to some government-owned banks and, with the help of American soldiers, piled the stainless-steel cases full of freshly wrapped $100 bills into the truck. Each case carried $4 million in crisp new U.S. currency.

They turned it into a rescue mission, hightailing it through the debris-strewn streets past looters and burning buildings to yet another bank, where they pulled out another $200 million and stacked it in their truck. The officials drove toward the banks of the Tigris with their precious cargo, to the place where the American soldiers had made their headquarters, at the Palestine and Sheraton hotels. That is where they parked the truck and wondered what to do with hundreds of millions in cash in the middle of a war zone.

Here is where the story gets complicated. Zobaidy and a former official at the Ministry of Finance told the men to deliver the cash to the tax-free zone, which was the only part of the Ministry of Finance still operating. It was Iraqi money, they said, and it should go to the Ministry of Finance. Instead, the bank officials turned to Ahmad Chalabi at the Hunting Club. Motive is unclear here, as always: one bank official says they saw him as a conduit to the Americans. They also say they suspected Zobaidy wanted to steal the funds in the armored car. "You have saved Zobaidy from himself!" Chalabi said to the bank officials, according to one of them. Chalabi dispatched his own men to the armored truck. Francis Brooke showed up, as did some Iraqi INC officials. And so did Col. Ted Seel, Chalabi's ally in the U.S. Army.

Zobaidy had worked with the INC for more than a decade, but he was now speaking out against it. He suspected Chalabi's people of wanting to steal the funds from the armored truck, he claims. One of Zobaidy's men showed up with a video camera to document the Chalabi loyalists climbing into the truck and driving it away. It was bound for the Hunting Club, according to Zobaidy. Chalabi's forces have denied this.

Zobaidy claims he rushed to see Chalabi at the Hunting Club and bullied his way in to confront him. He claims Chalabi said to him: "To rule Iraq, you need money." The only thing that kept Chalabi from keeping the funds, according to Zobaidy, was the threat of exposure. The truck did end up at the main Rafidain Bank vault, and soldiers carried crate after crate inside, piling more than $250 million inside the vault. Those present huddled to scribble a memorandum in Arabic. And four men signed it, including "Ted Seel, Col USA, LNO to INC" (Liaison Officer to Iraqi National Congress).

But Zobaidy claims that $51 million went missing. That is the difference between what was left in the truck and what arrived in the vault, he claims. There were originally seventy-six crates of cash in the truck—$304 million, according to Zobaidy. The bank manager who counted the crates said, "there were about seventy crates."

Zobaidy made his allegations public and shortly afterward was arrested by American forces. They demanded that he cease his posturing as mayor. Zobaidy is convinced, though, that Chalabi engineered his arrest.

Zobaidy's accusation about intended theft is not corroborated by other accounts, and is colored by his bitterness at Chalabi. Neither are the allegations by the Chalabi camp in any way corroborated. Perhaps no one had bad intentions. Still, the truck stuffed with Iraqi cash did make its way around Baghdad in those chaotic hours, and there are unanswered questions about what happened to its contents. Also, the INC had long regarded Zobaidy highly enough to place its trust in him, so it can hardly dismiss his allegations so easily now.

And as a former CIA official with the Iraqi Operations Group said, "Chalabi is not known for putting money back in banks."

41

De-Baathification, Part II

2003–2004

UP UNTIL JUST BEFORE THE WAR, there was no word for "de-Baathification" in Arabic. Since there was no Arabic term for de-Nazification, a literal translation didn't make sense. Sources say it was Ahmad Chalabi himself who invented a word for it in Arabic: "Ijtithath al Baath." It translates to "uprooting"—as in eradicating weeds. "He took great pleasure in that word. He was so proud of it," said one ally. He started using it just before the Americans invaded, recalled his friends.

Even close supporters of Chalabi, such as his childhood friend Tamara Daghistani, felt that the whole idea of de-Baathification was cruel, insulting, and counterproductive. "If you go back to the history of the Baath Party," she said, "Saddam's people weren't really Baathists, they were Saddamists! So why are we saying de-Baathification? I'm totally against de-Baathification. It's madness!" But Ahmad Chalabi had defined members of the Baath Party, not just Saddam Hussein, as the enemy. One day in the Hunting Club, when the euphoria of Saddam's collapse was still fresh in the air, Daghistani tried to argue it out with Chalabi. "How can you blame them all?" she asked. "Many of them were forced into this." Chalabi just wouldn't agree, she said, and brushed her off. The conversation ended quickly.

As much as L. Paul Bremer and Ahmad Chalabi would come to hate and despise each other, Bremer, who replaced Jay Garner as America's overseer in Iraq, danced unwittingly to Chalabi's tune when he issued the de-Baathification order on May 16, 2003. He carried out Chalabi's policy, although, he explained later, it was merely adapted from a law handed to him directly by Doug Feith.

And then Bremer quickly installed Ahmad Chalabi as the head of the commission to "de-Baathify" Iraq. On the top floor of the Iraqi government building, in the Green Zone, Chalabi entrenched his De-Baathification Commission, which assumed the aura and reputation of an Inquisition. "They had tons of money," explained one Iraqi involved with the commission. "Their fortunes have risen and fallen many times, but when they were first created, they were a much-feared organization that occupied one of the floors of the building the government used. And I know people quaked even going there. If your file entered there, God knows what they would do to you."

Chalabi had the extraordinary power now to end anyone's employment, strip away his pension even, leave him destitute. If Chalabi chose to paint someone as a leading Baathist, that would mean his prospects of government employment were over. And of course it left him open to arrest by the Americans, who barely monitored the committee's methods.

It was immediately clear to anyone who cared to know that not all Baathists had blood on their hands and that patriotic Iraqis were being pushed out of their jobs and turned into beggars because of the process led by Chalabi. "It was like 'de-Sunnification,'" said one diplomat. The most competent administrators, who had been forced to be Baath Party members, were banned from working in government jobs. "De-Baathification appears to have gone some way toward dismantling a state that had been left largely intact by the unexpectedly swift war," as *The Economist* put it.

In September 2003, Chalabi tried to initiate the next phase of his de-Baathification efforts. Businessmen and merchants who had profited under Saddam were warned they were targets. Their properties, if obtained through Baathist wrongdoing, would be confiscated. They would be banned from new contracts. "All those who benefited from the previous regime have to be prevented from gaining any more business," said a Chalabi ally.[79]

It was dubbed "economic de-Baathification," and Chalabi's commission began "to collect information about businessmen and merchants to prevent them from dealing with Iraq in the future." Rend Rahim Francke, an old ally of Chalabi's, pushed hard on this theme: "There was such a thing as Baathist capitalism in Iraq during the Saddam era," she said, "and very little attention has been paid to economic de-Baathification." Something needed to be done about businessmen who had done trade with the old regime, she argued. "The continuing dominance of Baathist businessmen is contrary to the economic democratization."

It may very well have been sincerely meant, or it may have come from hearts full of zeal, but the problem with "economic de-Baathification" quickly became apparent. It could easily be used for shaking down those who had kept their wealth under Saddam. And according to several sources, that is exactly what took place. Merchants were threatened by Chalabi's committee that they would be targeted. There were allegations that they were asked for money to settle cases, but that was never proven. What is true is that one of the families that Chalabi had in his sights, according to sources, was the Bunnia clan. They were merchants involved in everything from growing dates to building bridges to banking, and they quickly became the target of a whisper campaign. Journalists were steered to look into the source of their wealth, and they were accused of profiting from Saddam's regime. Mustafa Bunnia, one of the brothers, merely winced when asked about this at the time. In the end, nothing really happened to their wealth, and economic de-Baathification seems to have drifted away, undone like so many good and bad schemes by the violence that shook apart Iraq.

42

Chalabi vs. Bremer

May 2003–April 2004

"I am fighting to keep Americans in Iraq."

—Ahmad Chalabi, quoted in the *New York Times*,
September 23, 2003[80]

CHALABI WAS ONE OF THE FIRST to spot the arrogance and incompetence of Ambassador L. Paul Bremer, the U.S. viceroy hurriedly appointed to run Iraq after Gen. Jay Garner. Bremer, he said, suffered from "the sin of pride." Still, tension between Bremer and Chalabi took a while to develop because at the beginning Bremer's ineffectual rule seemed to smile on Chalabi. Bremer's de-Baathification order, for example, fully met Chalabi's specifications. Chalabi was flattering initially: "Mr. Bremer was decisive, and he gets full credit for declaring a policy of de-Baathification," he said.[81]

But Bremer was immune to Chalabi's charm, which tended to work best with people of philosophical or adventurous bent, people with a tinge of dissatisfaction looking for a leader, people to whom flattery matters. Bremer did not qualify. He was too stolid, too much of a bureaucrat to impress in that way.

Bremer also stood like a wall between Chalabi and the sovereign "provisional government" that he had dreamed of for so long. As *New*

York Times reporter James Risen wrote about the neoconservatives' plans for postwar Iraq, "After Chalabi, there was no Plan B."[82] Bremer was a loyal Republican and a plodding bureaucrat; he was no neoconservative. And despite the strict neoconservative insistence on Chalabi on the part of people like Feith and Wolfowitz, Rumsfeld had deliberately said he would not take sides. Bremer took Rumsfeld at his word.

Chalabi's champions in Washington were floundering, unable to position him properly.

Bremer stomped awkwardly and pompously in Iraq. First, to try to put an Iraqi face on his rule while making sure everyone knew it was still his rule, Bremer appointed a "Group of Seven" Iraqi leaders made up of the returned exiles: Chalabi, Pachachi, Allawi, the Islamist parties, as well as the Kurds. Then Bremer expanded that group to a twenty-five-member "Governing Council." He had decided that he wanted to water down even the influence the exiles had. The Governing Council was a government in the same sense as a student council at a high school: it had structure with no authority. Chalabi and twenty-four other Iraqis were forced into a role of humiliating irrelevance.

At every step, Chalabi pushed for ending the "occupation" and installing an Iraqi government made up of himself and some others. But he never wanted the U.S. troops to leave. It was a fine line but an important one: he wanted to be the head of a sovereign country that was still occupied by U.S. troops. It might resemble a puppet regime, but at least it would be technically "sovereign."

His newspaper, *Al Mu'tamar*, the same name he had used in the 1990s, sang his praises and called for his installation as leader. "Iraqi political circles and public opinion," the paper wrote, "strongly believe that Dr Ahmad Chalabi, leader of the Iraqi National Congress [INC], is the strongest candidate to head the next government."[83]

By the summer of 2003, the United States had decided on a prolonged, thorough occupation and to rebuild Iraqi society by force. They would "uproot" not just the Baath but the nationalized economy, the politics, the culture, and police. In essence, the United States was doing what Chalabi's Iraqi National Congress had called for earlier in secret when it suggested an occupation based on the Japanese model and argued that democracy could be "imposed."

And in a parallel effort, privatization of the Stalinesque economy of Iraq was the idea. The factories and the industries would be turned over to private hands so that market forces could get things moving. On the economy, Chalabi and Bremer seemed to share visions. "It has to be privatized immediately," Chalabi told a *Wall Street Journal* editorial page writer before Bremer even arrived in Baghdad. "We will sell to foreigners," he said.[84]

But now Chalabi, unwilling to wait and see if he could maneuver into the position of power that he desired, tried to play the role of a spoiler at every turn. He chose to sabotage what he could of Bremer's plans. He was smarter then Bremer, and more cunning. He was Iraqi, but he had unbelievably loyal friends in Washington who would ally themselves with him over Bremer in an instant. But Bremer had something going for him too: he had the U.S. Army behind him.

43

The UN Gets a Warning

Summer 2003

"I believe there were fears about the spread of Iranian influence and Islamic fundamentalism, which I think are basically unfounded."

—Ahmad Chalabi at the Council on Foreign Relations, June 2003[85]

IN JUNE 2003, to celebrate his daughter's graduation from Harvard, Ahmad Chalabi visited the United States. Just as her father was engrossed in Shiite culture and politics, so was Tamara: her PhD thesis examined the Shiites of Lebanon. The Chalabis had been the bankers for the Shiite community of Lebanon and a stalwart bastion of Shiite support. Tamara, groomed by Chalabi as his intellectual heir because of his son Hashem's disability, was now becoming a Shiite historian as well.

In America and Europe, his history had come under renewed scrutiny. *Newsweek*'s Mark Hosenball and his colleagues had recovered old files concerning the collapse of the family businesses: Socofi, MEBCO, and Petra Bank. The magazine reported on the "financial legerdemain" that brought the companies crumbling down so long ago, in 1989 and 1990, revisiting the Petra Bank case and mentioning that two of Chalabi's brothers had pleaded no contest to charges in Switzerland.

But still Chalabi was welcomed like a star by his old fans. In Washington, lobbyist Jeffrey Weiss and his wife, Juleanna Glover Weiss, hosted a fine party at their stately home for Chalabi and his daughter, a celebration of her graduation. Weiss was a key staffer at BKSH and had worked closely with Chalabi. Juleanna worked in the office of Vice President Dick Cheney and was a socialite in Washington. At the event, partygoers reported, Chalabi stood erect in the salon, nodding, and silently accepting the praise and congratulations of his old champions.

The House Republican Policy Committee, led by Congressman Christopher Cox, invited Chalabi for a visit and applauded him. In New York, Chalabi addressed the Council on Foreign Relations, which had been a gracious venue for him going all the way back to 1991.

He sat on the dais next to Tom Brokaw, the NBC news anchor who moderated the event. Brokaw complimented him on his daughter's graduation and suggested the motto "Tuition-free in '03!" to the Iraqi. Chalabi, dressed in his gray suit, laughed quickly and uproariously, throwing his head back. His adherence to the Atkins diet rules seemed to have worked: he was leaner than he had been in years.

Chalabi bemoaned the U.S. flip-flop on an Iraqi political structure. He once again called on Bremer to install a provisional government, a temporary government that could at least have an Iraqi face. "It seems that the powers, the occupation powers, are reluctant to have an Iraqi process immediately," he said. "There are certain concerns and fears, and those are being expressed and those are delaying the full Iraqi political process to get going." At this point, Chalabi was not yet fully personalizing his attacks on the ineffectual and stilted Bremer, who was still seen as an obstacle but not an enemy.

But Chalabi did put his finger on one of the key issues confounding the U.S. government in the chaotic new Iraq it had unleashed. "I believe there were fears about the spread of Iranian influence and Islamic fundamentalism, which I think are basically unfounded," he said. In fact, Iranian influence was glaringly obvious, almost impossible to ignore in Iraq, and concerns were well founded. Yet Chalabi was acting here perhaps as half diplomat and half advocate, trying to assuage America over the "unfounded" fear.

At that Council on Foreign Relations symposium, he also faced some persistent questions about weapons of mass destruction. This was the intermediate period when many people in America were beginning to realize there may have been no weapons of mass destruction after all. Nothing was turning up. Judith Miller of the *New York Times* was being skewered in the press for her reporting on his "defectors."

Chalabi, at the Council on Foreign Relations, began what would be a long process of distancing himself from the defectors he and his INC had produced. "We did not give information," he told the audience, "that we said came from defectors. We never did that. What we did was take the people, introduce them to them, and let them decide through their own methods and resources whether these people are credible or not."[86]

During that June visit, with the Iraqi crisis building inexorably, Chalabi made a point of taking the time to declare war on an institution that was trying to do something to solve it—the United Nations. Chalabi has always been haunted by vendettas he believes others have against him, and his followers tend to demonize those they believe to be his enemies: General Zinni of Centcom, Ayad Allawi of the Iraqi National Accord, Dr. Mohammed Said Nabulsi of the Jordanian Central Bank.

Among the institutions that Chalabi holds to be his enemies are the Central Intelligence Agency and the State Department. He and his followers blame these agencies for vilifying him and blocking his funding over the years. But in June 2003, he heralded that he was on the warpath as well against the United Nations.

He took the time to make a special phone call to his old friend Edward Mortimer, chief spokesman for UN Secretary General Kofi Annan. Mortimer, who had known Chalabi since 1991, had been steadfast in his condemnation of Saddam Hussein. Time and time again Mortimer had stood by Chalabi. By most people's standards, Chalabi would have owed him loyalty. But Chalabi viewed Mortimer's boss, Kofi Annan, less favorably. He saw Annan as a lesser enemy: someone to be dealt with but cautious of.

The old friends met at a secluded table at the dimly lit Ambassador Lounge at the Millennium Hotel bar near the UN. It's a quiet meeting ground for diplomats. Chalabi had brought his daughter as well, and he got down to business. The meeting was a warning. He was about to launch a "campaign" against the UN. Mortimer says he was confused by the threat from his old friend. Chalabi emphasized his campaign would be a public attack—he was going to accuse the UN of permitting Saddam to profit under the oil-for-food program. And he believed the UN was in the pocket of the Sunni governments, not sympathetic to Shiites. "He was obsessed with the Sunni–Shiite divide," Mortimer recalled later, which surprised him.

There was another subtext, Mortimer believes, although it was not what Chalabi and his daughter brought up at the meeting. It was the UN resolution of the month before, which wiped out the sanctions against Iraq. The text of Resolution 1483 referred to the United States and Britain as "occupying powers." That small phrase, in the minds of Iraqis, gave the "occupation" legitimacy in the form of UN recognition, undercutting everything Chalabi had been trying to accomplish.

Even more of an issue, the UN put all of the Iraqi government's funds under the jurisdiction of the U.S. and Britain, into a new account called the Development Fund for Iraq. The Iraqis on the Governing Council had no power over the money; they were simply figureheads.

And so Chalabi gave his friend Mortimer a sound warning. "I was surprised," Mortimer says now. "I don't know why he said it to me." For the moment, though, Chalabi's threats were empty. He needed the United Nations. In time, the probe into oil-for-food would accelerate, but that could wait. He had a role in the investigations, spurring them on wildly, but the UN's corruption caught the eye of plenty of journalists and policy-makers who were independent, too.

And although he was planning to launch a campaign against the UN, Chalabi knew how he could use the organization. It provided a forum to strike back against the occupation and push for Iraqi sovereignty. One of Chalabi's early moves against Bremer came in September 2003, as the leaders of the world gathered at the UN General Assembly. A year earlier they had heard Bush's condemnation of Iraq, and this year they would hear his defense of his war. Ahmad Chalabi, by chance, was the "president" of the Governing Council that month, a rotating position, and claimed the Iraq seat at the United Nations.

Temporarily setting aside his campaign against the United Nations, he decided there was a better gambit. Mortimer watched a press conference the Iraqis gave in amusement: "It was rather amazing to me how he skillfully plonked himself in the middle and grabbed the microphone."

The French, a thorn in the side of the Bush administration, had recently suggested that the Coalition Provisional Authority hand over power to the Iraqi Governing Council, proposing that Iraq be free, at least, of the U.S. occupation, and then let the political process totter on from there. It was exactly Chalabi's position, and he looked for allies wherever he could find them. So he paired himself with the French, angering Bremer even more.

"The Bush administration is locked in a deepening dispute with the leader of Iraq's American-installed interim government, Ahmad Chalabi," reported the Associated Press, "over a timetable for self-rule."[87]

The neocons did not denounce Chalabi's new alliance, but President Bush himself was dismayed at Chalabi's betrayal. Bremer wrote in his book, *My Year in Iraq*, that he had brought up Chalabi's antics in a private conversation with the president. According to Bremer, Bush said, "Really pisses me off. I had planned to lay into him when he came through the receiving line at the reception I hosted in New York yesterday. But he had his daughter with him, and I didn't think it was appropriate to chew him out in front of her. But he's being a real pain in the you-know-what!"

It seems Chalabi got the message and backed off, just a bit. There are indications that Chalabi knew he had gone too far: "We have no disagreement with the U.S. government. We are not at odds with the United States," he protested at a press conference at the UN after the deluge of news reports.[88] And then, with characteristic persistence, he quickly headed to Washington, where he met with Wolfowitz and various congressmen.

━━━

Chalabi had a point: the occupation model that Bremer was trying to implement simply wasn't working, especially since Bremer didn't even

pretend to understand Iraq. At least MacArthur in Japan had compre-
hended the reverence the Japanese had for their emperor and used it
to his advantage. Bremer ignored what he wanted in Iraq. It was a disaster. Chalabi wasn't the only one who was making the argument: he
was just the loudest. Adnan Pachachi, also appointed to the Governing
Council, worked with him on the effort to roll back Bremer's program
in one of the few things the two men did together.

But by undercutting Bremer in complex political maneuvers, Chalabi held back his own political future at the same time. Chalabi was
more adept and nimble in both American and Iraqi politics than Bremer, but his sabotage of Bremer also made an enemy of him, which
was dangerous. In the same way, Chalabi's neoconservative followers
at home were sabotaging their own president. Unless and until Chalabi was at the helm in Iraq, his neoconservative friends would never
support the president's policy in Iraq. No matter how much the president supported Bremer, the viceroy's bitter relationship with Chalabi
turned the neoconservatives against him. No matter that Bush wanted
the UN's help; Chalabi's assault on the UN meant the neoconservatives could undercut Bush's initiatives. Even when Bremer wanted one
accounting firm to deal with oil-for-food and Chalabi wanted another, the neoconservatives sided with Chalabi.

In the end, Chalabi partly won his battles with Bremer. Bremer was
forced to acknowledge reality: the CPA, the occupation government,
would not work. That became clear even to him by the fall of 2003. An
Iraqi interim government, exactly what the Iraqis had been calling for,
would have to be installed. They announced the plan in November:
Bremer and the CPA would be out by July, they said.

It should have been what Chalabi wanted: a victory. Instead it became the start of yet another battle for him.

44

The State of the Union

January 2004

"The killers will fail, and the Iraqi people will live
in freedom."

—President George W. Bush

THE MOST POWERFUL MEN AND WOMEN in the United States assembled in
the House of Representatives for the President's 2004 State of the
Union address. There was a standing ovation throughout the magnifi-
cent domed chamber when the president came in. In a prominent position in the gallery, Ahmad Chalabi, in a gray pinstripe suit, sat to the
right of Hoshyar Zebari, the Kurdish foreign minister of Iraq. Directly
below him was First Lady Laura Bush, next to her guest of honor: Adnan Pachachi, that month's "president" of Iraq, under Paul Bremer.

Chalabi had not been invited at first, according to an Iraqi diplomat. But when he learned Pachachi was attending, he made sure his
friends pushed for him to be there as well. Surely he had more to do
with the Iraqi venture than any other Iraqi. And notwithstanding their
occasional collaboration, Chalabi held Pachachi in contempt, while
Chalabi's followers, like Zaab Sethna, openly ridiculed Zebari.

Suddenly, the eyes of the world were on the three Iraqis. "And
tonight we are honored to welcome one of Iraq's most respected lead-

ers," said President Bush, "the current president of the Iraqi Governing Council, Adnan Pachachi."

But there the "cuts" cameraman, the staffer who shot the reaction shots, got confused. As usual there were several cameras covering the event: one locked down on the president as he spoke, one getting crowd reaction shots, and one shooting the faces of the listeners. This cameraman sought to locate Pachachi, but he made a mistake and focused on Ahmad Chalabi instead: perhaps the Iraqi he recognized. Chalabi smiled as the crowd applauded for Pachachi. The senators and the members of Congress all turned to look at Pachachi. But still, the pool camera stayed on Chalabi.

Chalabi, not Pachachi, was being videotaped by one camera, and he was one of the first to stand as the applause continued, and he clapped for Pachachi. "Sir," the president of the United States continued, "America stands with you and the Iraqi people as you build a free and peaceful nation."

Eventually the camera moved off Chalabi.

Chalabi's tilt away from the United States came at the same time as the State of the Union address, ironically. It was not simply political gamesmanship but an expression of his true political commitment: Shiism. "He will never take an anticlerical position," explained a close associate of his. "He will never veer from the position of the *marjiya* [the Najaf-based Shiite clerical leadership]. Not out of religious observance but because he thinks they are a principal prop to the existence of the Shiite community."

Chalabi is a master of political ploys, forming alliances to create power, and his creation of the "Shia House," or Beit al Shiite, was an example. This became a political bloc within the otherwise weak Governing Council. Creating such a bloc suddenly gave him relevance and gave the Council, by dividing it, a sharp set of teeth. Paul Bremer had tried to dilute the Shiite influence, but by forming a bloc, they reasserted themselves.

Chalabi did not ally himself with Muqtada al-Sadr—a firebrand cleric and the son of an ayatollah assassinated by Saddam—until a bit later, but he did embrace a strident sectarian brand of Shiite politics almost from the beginning.

The Shia House was the first step in this direction, according to some Iraqi politicians. Faisal Istrabadi says he saw this happening back then. He was acting as a deputy for Pachachi, he says, when a dispute came up. Salem Chalabi, Ahmad's nephew and deputy in his dealings at the Governing Council, joined the religious Shiites in a walkout after a contentious meeting. The issue concerned women's rights and the insistence by Shiite religious parties on certain regional prerogatives. The Chalabis apparently believed that Shiite cohesion and flexing the Shia House muscles were more important than women's rights. That's when Istrabadi first warned about consequences, and even talked of the possibility of civil war. "I said to Salem," Istrabadi recalls, "'If we end up in a civil war,' I said, 'in the chain of causation, one of the causes, if there is a sectarian civil war in Iraq, would be the foundation of the Shia House.'"

But the Shia House fractured and dissolved within months. The Shiite bloc could not hang together with so many competing leaders, once it seemed to be dominating politics.

In December 2003, troops from the 101st Airborne captured Saddam Hussein. Chalabi was one of the four Iraqi leaders Paul Bremer invited to visit the dictator. From Bremer, that was a gesture of respect at least. Deep in the U.S. base, in Saddam's cell, Chalabi pulled his chair the closest to him of all the Iraqis, as if he was inspecting him. Chalabi's face is in all the photographs of the meeting. And he was the first to rush out, inexplicably cutting the meeting short. "He's learned nothing," Chalabi said to himself, repeatedly. "He's learned nothing."

He was asked later if that was a defining moment for him, this opportunity to confront his captured and humiliated enemy. He responded cryptically, "I don't gloat." It can only be the case that his little confrontation with Saddam Hussein did not provide the satisfaction that he craved. He had spent his life trying to overthrow him, and once he did, the moment he met him face-to-face must have been disappointing.

Yet still, Chalabi's newspaper used the moment, splashing a photograph of Chalabi and Saddam on the front page on December 18, under the headline: "After Saddam Begged His Jailers to Meet Al-Chalabi,

Al-Mu'tamar Publishes Historic photo of Dr Al-Chalabi With the Detained Tyrant."

And then it came: a new plan by the U.S., a plan for sovereignty at least in name. Once Bremer announced an interim government, it should have been exactly what Chalabi wanted. It was the result he had demanded in all his public calls. One could see triumph approaching, an interim government and a free Iraq: protected by American troops but not dominated by them. He was finally coming to his own.

Yet the tragedy for him was that he had undermined his own position. By the early winter of 2004, the United Nations was entering the game again: the UN stepped in to work in partnership with Bremer and the Americans to pick the interim government that Chalabi himself had pushed for. The U.S. had turned to the UN as a last-ditch effort—President Bush himself confirmed it. As for the interim government, "That's going to be decided by Mr. Brahimi," President Bush said, referring to UN envoy Lakhdar Brahimi.

Chalabi closed the door to his own future in that interim government because he wanted nothing decided by Lakhdar Brahimi. He had made Brahimi and the UN the enemy. His campaigning against the UN was negative to the point of being comical: Chalabi struck out wildly. He tried to end its role completely, after it was already there. Ali Allawi, his nephew and fellow Iraqi official, mentioned Chalabi's campaign in his book *The Occupation of Iraq.* He said Chalabi became a "nuisance," pointing out that Chalabi even tried to turn the *marjiya* against Brahimi.

As usual Chalabi used his supporters in the U.S. to make his point as well. The *Wall Street Journal* editorial page joined his call, turning against President Bush on the matter. "What Iraq needs isn't a White House abdication to Mr. Brahimi," one column said.

Chalabi claimed Brahimi was anti-Shiite. "The UN envoy is acting as if he were a crown prince who will form a government," Chalabi complained.[89] He turned up the heat on the oil-for-food scandal, trying to involve himself and the Governing Council. Though the Council had virtually no power, he wanted to take over all the oil-for-food files, which documented Saddam-era trade with the world. He wanted to run the investigation, so he could control it.

The oil-for-food investigations into UN corruption were just one phase in Chalabi's campaign against the United Nations, about which he had warned his friend Mortimer. The campaign against Brahimi was survival, in a sense, for Chalabi, while the campaign on oil-for-food issues was about staying on the offensive. In reality Chalabi was affiliated with the investigations but did not really drive them. Probes churned on various committees in the U.S. House and Senate, in Iraq, and in the United Nations itself. In reality, he was a voice of outrage, but there were many others. Not only had the UN's apparent lack of support for the Iraq venture angered many Republicans but the garish nature of the corruption under Saddam was becoming more and more clear. Judith Miller, at the *New York Times*, began to cover the oil-for-food beat now, sharing a byline on a story called "U.S. and Iraq Spar Over Who Should Run Corruption Inquiry Into Oil-for-Food Program,"[90] which reported that "Mr. Chalabi, a former exile who returned with the strong backing of many senior Pentagon officials, has strongly objected to Mr. Bremer's decision to bypass the council on the oil-for-food inquiry."

In the battle to undercut the UN's Brahimi, Chalabi showed a somewhat spiteful side to his personality. He and his followers always sought to punish their enemies by publicly shaming them. They had tried it with General Zinni, with Tenet, with Said Nabulsi, and with the old king of Jordan. Now their target was Brahimi and Adnan Pachachi, the gracious old man of Iraqi diplomacy. Brahimi was leaning toward recommending Pachachi as the first postoccupation prime minister. Under Chalabi's constant heat, he backed down.

Adnan Pachachi finally lost the candidacy due to Chalabi's work.

45

BKSH at War

2003–2004

THE LAST WEEK OF OCTOBER 2003 had been particularly gory in Baghdad. Rockets tore into the al-Rashid Hotel, where Paul Wolfowitz lay sleeping on a rare visit. Terrorists destroyed the International Red Cross Compound, and then on Wednesday, October 29, a land mine gutted a U.S. Army M1 Abrams tank in Baghdad and killed two soldiers.

That was the day Burson-Marsteller (BKSH) and the Iraqi National Congress were honored for their work on Chalabi's behalf in the run-up to the war. The award ceremony took place far from the violence in Iraq. It was in London, where more than 1,000 of the public relations industry elite assembled in black tie in a ballroom at the luxurious Grosvenor Park Hotel. *PR Week*, the most prestigious journal in public relations, hosted the event, its annual awards dinner for public relations companies. Burson-Marsteller, whose subsidiary BKSH carried out the work, was named the winner in the annual public affairs category.

The "Awards Supplement" of *PR Week* called BKSH's work a "solid, disciplined campaign that is totally deserving of this award." "Of particular importance," said the citation, "was positioning INC founder Dr. Ahmad Chalabi and other Iraqi opposition spokespeople as authoritative political leaders." BKSH "compiled intelligence reports, defector briefings, conference and seminars. . . . The PR team also ran a contact building program, focusing on the European Union, Downing Street, the Foreign Office and MPs in the UK, matched to a U.S. program aimed at the White House, the Senate, Congress and the Pentagon."[91] The awards description does not mention that the funding entirely came from the U.S. government.

But by the time BKSH won the award, the State Department's funding for the program had stopped, with the American troops surging through the desert. That did not mean that BKSH's Iraq work would end. Instead, having contributed to returning Chalabi to Baghdad, BKSH would now use its ties to Chalabi to get into the business of what was then being called "Iraqi reconstruction."

The business elite were eager for a seat at the table: investing in Iraq would be both profitable and patriotic for Americans. Corporate executives flocked to conferences on Iraqi reconstruction, corporations set up divisions to work on developing business there, consultancies thrived, and newsletters proliferated to detail legal niceties and dispense advice.

BKSH was going to get in on the ground floor of the industry. Charles Black, the key partner in BKSH, said that it was a busy time. "After the overthrow of Saddam Hussein a lot of U.S. companies, some of our long-term clients as well as some people who weren't our clients, came to us and were looking to do business in Iraq," he explained.

The problem, he said, was that BKSH was not "going to be over there. We didn't have an office over there or have full-time personnel." While BKSH had no one on the ground in Iraq, Peg Bartel and the Chalabi operation were firmly ensconced there. Bartel was taking in Defense Intelligence Agency funds and delivering them to Chalabi's intelligence operation. Zaab Sethna, the Pakistani British press aide to Chalabi, was also in Iraq.

As Black explains it, "Peg was there and Zaab was there, so we just referred business to them." Bartel and BKSH reached an agreement: in exchange for a referral fee, BKSH would refer clients to Bartel's company, which would set them up with contacts, influence, housing, security, and everything else they would need to get themselves started on Iraqi reconstruction. In the gold rush of 1849, they say, it was not the miners who got rich but the operators who sold the picks and the shovels and the wagons and the denim. So it was in Iraq, with the likes of Peg Bartel, the INC, and BKSH. The American businessmen would be the miners taking their chances, and the PR operatives and INC loyalists were selling the picks and shovels.

In essence, all it required was a small adjustment in their previous efforts. BKSH and Chalabi simply pivoted their operation. They realized that with Chalabi on the ground they could sell access to him using the same sophisticated lobbying regime they already had in place. He had the sort of influence that corporate executives could use in their search for contracts.

One of the businessmen who signed up for the Iraq package was Albert Huddleston, an old BKSH customer. "Albert is a longtime client," Charles Black explained. Those who know him say Huddleston, a tall Texan with a taste for adventure, seems like a model Dallas oilman. Oil was his career. In one sense, it could be said that he married into it. That is, he had married into a branch of the Texas Hunt family, a fractious and competitive clan of billionaires. His father-in-law was Nelson Bunker Hunt, one of the brothers who tried to corner the world's silver market in the 1980s in a spectacular business failure.

Huddleston is a staunch supporter of President George Bush. He was a "Bush Pioneer" in the 2000 election, raising over $100,000. Then, in the 2004 election he did just as well, contributing a hefty $100,000 to the Swift Boat Veterans for Truth, the group that targeted Senator John Kerry's campaign by publicizing discredited allegations about his military service. Huddleston's daughter even worked in the White House for First Lady Laura Bush.

Huddleston's interest in Iraq was logical and straightforward: he wanted oil deals, and his company, Hyperion Resources, wanted a seat at the table when the oil valves finally opened. So it was only natural that BKSH would refer him to the Chalabi allies who were offering to help American businessmen. "He was definitely interested in Iraq," Charles Black of BKSH recalled, "and we definitely hooked him up with that organization."

The veterans of the PR and lobbying efforts of the INC went to work for Huddleston. They had focused for years on claims of human rights, democracy, and freedom, and now they were dedicating more and more time to oil and business. Over time, Zaab Sethna became indispensable in the efforts. "Whatever Albert wanted," recalled one associate, "it was Zaab's mission to go get it done."

In the years after the Iraqi invasion, Huddleston did his best to forge ties in Iraq. What he found at first, as did most oilmen, was that there was no legitimate government to deal with under the occupation. Early on the problem was that Paul Bremer had no authority to negotiate oil deals. It is a simple precept of international law that occupying powers can't legally make decisions about a country's natural resources. By occupying Iraq, the United States had undercut its own oil ambitions. Of course later on, after Bremer left Iraq, the Iraqi government couldn't pass an oil law to regulate the industry.

Nabeel Musawi, by then in the temporary Assembly, remembers Chalabi, Sethna, Bartel, and their guest Albert Huddleston coming to dinner to petition for help. They wanted to see if he could set up a meeting between Huddleston and the oil minister. Clearly their own efforts were coming up short. Musawi says he wanted to help but had to shrug them off because the oil minister was out of town.

Huddleston is a huge man, standing well over six feet tall, and he is quite heavy; he would tower over Chalabi when they met. Chalabi was well aware of Huddleston's connections to the Bush White House, and he fawned over the Texan, taking him out and offering him gifts. Chalabi presented him with a lavish crystal sculpture of an Iraqi reed house, which had to be shipped back to Texas.

The underlying obstacle for Huddleston was that the prewar promise of rosy prospects for American oilmen like him was turning out to be an illusion. Certainly Ahmad Chalabi and others had talked about Iraq's oil and the gushers to come, but despite all the oil under Iraq's desert, it was unobtainable. Deals made during the occupation would be shredded later. Huddleston never did make his huge oil strike in Iraq, despite the money he paid to Chalabi's people there.

Another early client in the BKSH/Peg Bartel effort to leverage Chalabi's connections was U.S. businessman and defense contractor Dale Stoffel. Stoffel was forty-three years old, with a goatee that gave his grin a mischievous appearance. He was an enthusiastic supporter of the war as well as a bit of an adventurer. Stoffel's business niche had long been a narrow one: the procurement, in legal if unusual ways, of exotic Eastern European weapons systems for clients in the U.S. government who wanted to take them apart and examine them.

But he picked up on the Iraq reconstruction bug too. In April 2003, he'd signed up as a client with BKSH, and then in January 2004, Riva Levinson, the lobbyist on the INC account, made a pitch to him. By then Stoffel was working with a Pennsylvania-based construction company called CLI. "We can get you in [into Iraq] using the connections we have on the ground," Levinson told him, according to someone familiar with the meeting.

Stoffel and his associates took a quick trip to Baghdad in January 2004 and returned to Iraq a month later. Bartel helped him and his associates hunt for business and set them up in quarters in the Chalabi compound. Chalabi's team by then had its own virtual neighborhood in Monsour under its armed guard.

Stoffel, who had recently remarried and had a newborn child back in Pennsylvania, had not intended to stay in Iraq but was sucked into the whirl of opportunities. It was an exciting time for a businessman in Iraq. "I love this shit," Stoffel would say. "This is what I was born for." He traveled around the country initially with security provided by Bartel, obviously with ties to the Iraqi National Congress. He imagined deals, contracts, billions of dollars to be made.

When Stoffel got to Iraq, his arms-dealing contacts came in handy. He managed to parlay them into some influence at the Ukrainian Embassy in Baghdad's "Green Zone," and he even brought Chalabi and Aras along for a visit. The Ukrainians, who were technically part of the coalition involved in the occupation, were a useful group to know. They had massive stores of arms back in their country and were willing to sell them to the highest bidder.

Stoffel never grew close to Chalabi and it is unclear if he really talked to him, but he bragged across Baghdad that he was living at the Chalabi-controlled compound. He tried going into business with Faisal Chalabi, one of the Chalabi clan, but the relationship collapsed, with each side accusing the other of fraud. (Faisal had invested in construction and later, sources in the Iraqi reconstruction industry say, ran a "vetting" service for American companies, checking out the backgrounds of their Iraqi employees, for a fee, to make sure they weren't former Baathists.)[92]

Whether Stoffel was buying arms from the Chalabi operation or selling is not at all clear. He told his friends both things happened, so he may have been a buyer and a seller, for in that industry there are always complications. Certainly there are strong indications of a relationship in the arms business: one e-mail hints that the weapons business was looking lucrative. Peg Bartel, the onetime auditor brought in by the State Department to tidy up Chalabi's books in 2000, was now on a gun-buying spree.

She sent him an email in April 2004 titled "Ammunition." She was apparently looking to get the prices for some weaponry for what she called "our security company." A source says this may have been in preparation for a bid of some kind to get a bit of reconstruction security work. And Dale Stoffel was always a good fellow to go to if one was in the market for armaments. Bartel listed the lethal items she was pricing out:

> 9mm ball—27,000
> 7.62 mm ball—57,600
> 12.7 ball with every fourth round a tracer—381,000 (bands
>   of 1,000 and should fit rifle below
> 12.7 mm midrange machine gun—128
> 9mm pistol with 3 mags each—512
> 7.62mm rifle auto—512. Prefer AK or 5.56 Galiel, but also
>   would like price for MP5.

There is no indication whatsoever that this ambitious purchase of hundreds of weapons was ever completed.

Stoffel enjoyed living well. He had brought with him a snappy cigar case he'd bought at Georgetown Tobacco: each metal cylinder had its own cap, like a row of torpedo tubes. He used to smoke cigars in Baghdad with one of Chalabi's nephews, Ghazi Allawi, whose brother, Ali Allawi, was defense minister for a brief period. Acquaintances say Ghazi and Stoffel were like-minded souls who abstained from idealist dreams and instead enjoyed living well. Sources say the two men were quite friendly with each other. While Stoffel never actually got any "Iraq reconstruction" business through Ahmad Chalabi, meeting with Ghazi Allawi did help. One day, according to a source, Ghazi introduced Stoffel to a man named Mashal Sarraf, a well-heeled civil servant who worked at the Ministry of Defense in the new Iraqi government, a key contact for any arms deals he wanted to make in Iraq.

Stoffel eventually fled the Chalabi compound in early May 2004, after an armed confrontation. As Stoffel told it, one day, the security guards supplied by Peg Bartel and the Chalabi group suddenly turned against him.

The guards the INC and Bartel supplied complained they weren't getting paid and demanded money from Stoffel and his crew.[93] And then the guns had come out, he said—a kind of Mexican standoff in Baghdad. Stoffel loved telling the story. "I stood there, right like this," he recalled, pretending to hold a rifle to his chest and with his feet planted apart, "and I didn't draw down at them, I just stood there. And they said, 'No, Mr. Dale, you can't go, you can't go!' And I said, 'Boys, we're leaving. That's the end of it.' And they could tell I was this close. This close!"

═══

By the summer of 2004, Stoffel had cut his overt ties to Chalabi's people, and he was locked in a bitter dispute with Peg Bartel over her fees. But he still had that contact he had made in the Ministry of Defense, who had survived the handover to a new regime; a new minister of defense ran things, and Chalabi was not a welcome name. Stoffel finally seemed to hit pure reconstruction gold. The gold he found was actually military scrap iron. Stoffel and his colleagues saw opportunity in the relics of Saddam's army, the thousands of tanks and armored vehicles stowed away in desert depots. They could be worth hundreds of millions on the international scrap-metal market. (One of Stoffel's associates estimated the value of the scrap to be at least $1.5 billion.) In a collapsing country, he figured, he could at least sell the junk.

Some of Saddam's tanks and personnel carriers had barely a scratch; they could be refurbished for use by the new Iraqi military. Many of the other vehicles in the depot were beyond repair, but their heavy plates could be removed and used to armor the trucks that Iraq's new soldiers used on patrol. Such was the chaos of reconstruction planning that apparently no one within the American or Iraqi hierarchies had, in the year and a half since occupation, thought to make use of this material.

Iraq's new minister of defense gave Stoffel the first part of a contract: an award to Wye Oak of $24.7 million to refurbish three battalions' worth of armored vehicles.

It must have felt to Stoffel like a fantasy come true. He was now an integrated part of the U.S. "victory strategy" in Iraq, with tens of millions in profits to boot. Faced with one of their most important projects in Iraq, the U.S. military had turned to him.

The Ministry of Defense "paid" Stoffel $24 million through a middleman, in what it called a bank guarantee. But just when everything seemed to be going perfectly, the deal collapsed for Stoffel, the roguish American entrepreneur with a patriotic streak. The middleman never handed over the money; Stoffel and his team were left empty-handed. Stoffel went on a crusade, on a lobbying rampage, flying back to the States, visiting Capitol Hill and the Pentagon. "Heads will roll," he warned in one e-mail, if the corruption in the deal was exposed. He threatened to blow the whistle on it all.

In December 2004, in Taji in Iraq, Stoffel climbed into his car holding his Heckler and Koch MP-5 close to him. His laptop computer was in the back. Two days later, Stoffel's car was discovered in a grim neighborhood along the Tigris. The hood was crumpled like a paper bag, the windshield a maze of cracks. The dashboard was covered with blood. Stoffel had been shot repeatedly in the head and upper back. His friend and employee Joe Wemple had been shot once through the head.

Just weeks after the bodies of Stoffel and Wemple were found, an unknown group calling itself Jihad Brigades claimed credit for the killings. A few months later, another group calling itself Rafidan, the

Political Council of the Mujahedeen, celebrated the killing of "the devil Stoffel," a "CIA shadow manager" who had conspired with Chalabi and others to siphon off Iraq's riches. In a video, a man with his face concealed announced in Arabic that "it is the biggest crime that has ever been committed through the ages and wars." Stoffel, according to the message, "was killed on the 8th of December 2004 after close monitoring of our moles on [sic] the hands of the Islamic Jihad Brigades."

In a series of web postings, the material about Stoffel continued emerging. Documents and photographs that had apparently been on Stoffel's laptop were all strung together in a fairly well-assembled production. It was a wealth of material, a mishmash of scintillating tidbits. There was a picture of Stoffel with President Bush at a fundraiser. There was a photograph of Ahmad Chalabi at the Ukrainian Embassy in Baghdad, and another of Stoffel there as well. Also posted on the Internet by the insurgents was a picture of Peg Bartel, Chalabi's financial adviser, who worked with Stoffel, jauntily smoking a cigar.

For all that, among Stoffel's friends and associates, few believe that he was killed at random. Other theories circulate instead: Stoffel could have been killed over the tank contract, they claim, because he was threatening to blow the whistle on corruption. In the blizzard of violence in Iraq, his death was just a small incident, and the truth was never known. Whatever the case, by the time of his death Stoffel no longer had any significant business ties to anyone in Chalabi's circle.

═══════

There is a strange addendum to the BKSH story, and it ties into Ahmad Chalabi, even if just through sheer serendipity. Wayne Drizin, the disbarred Florida lawyer and failed brothel owner who had done business with the Chalabis in the late 1980s, reappeared on the scene. He had been busy in small-cap ventures. In 2003, a federal jury convicted Drizin in a wire-fraud case in Arizona. The charges involved shares in a biotech company that claimed it had a cure for AIDS.[94]

But by that time, Drizin had found his way to another publicly traded start-up company, which was trying to pitch a new security technology. By this time, the disbarred lawyer was claiming he was the inventor of homeland security technology. The company was called e-Smart, and it had ties to BKSH, the same powerhouse K Street company that had spread Chalabi's message so effectively. Drizin told people at e-Smart about his old ties to Chalabi, and one day he even told a company executive he would reestablish ties to Chalabi to help drum up business. Drizin's background with the Chalabis was also summarized in e-Smart's securities filings: "In 1988, Mr. Drizin orchestrated the sale of Welfin SA to Swiss-based multi-national banking group indirectly wholly owned by the Chalabi Family including Mr. Ahmed Chalabi (a prominent member of the Iraqi National Congress)."

But Drizin had that federal criminal conviction hanging over his head and was sentenced to five years' probation. That's when Charles Black, the Republican power broker who was the chairman of BKSH, stepped in. Black was on the board of e-Smart, and he tried to intervene on Drizin's behalf in 2005 to make sure the fraudster could keep traveling. He wrote a letter to the federal judge presiding over Drizin's case. Black wrote that he considered Drizin's technology important to U.S. national interests and had "come to understand the unique role and contributions of Wayne Drizin." Black told the judge that Drizin's technology "could prevent entry into this country of known terrorists."[95]

Just as Ahmad Chalabi had always insisted that he had been framed by the government of Jordan, Wayne Drizin had insisted that his own federal case was due to a frame-up of U.S. prosecutors and investigators who had it in for him and the company. Charles Black appeared to buy into this and sent a brief to the U.S. Justice Department calling for a "criminal investigation" into the federal prosecutor and postal inspector who had pursued Drizin.

But in 2006 Drizin's history showed itself. He and e-Smart began countersuing each other. E-Smart's lawyers learned more about Drizin's background. Charles Black and e-Smart tried frantically to back off from their ties to him. They sent a letter to the federal judge to "retract" their support.

Black, in an interview, said he hadn't even realized that Drizin had ever had any connection to Ahmad Chalabi. It was just coincidence: Drizin and Chalabi, both of whom are persuasive businessmen who claim to have been framed, ended up in the same circle, dealing with the same political lobbyist.

46

Banking in Iraq

Summer–Fall 2003

ONE OF AHMAD CHALABI'S political triumphs in postinvasion Iraq was installing his grandnephew Hussein al-Uzri as head of a new multibillion-dollar banking institution in Iraq, although Uzri had uncertain qualifications. It was called the Trade Bank of Iraq, or TBI, and it would become immensely important to Iraq's economy, virtually monopolizing international purchases by the government.

The occupation government was already freckled with Chalabi family members and friends: Haydar al-Uzri, one nephew close to Chalabi, was anointed for a time to run Rafidain Bank, which had control over all the money in the armored car incident. Another nephew, Salem Chalabi, worked closely with Ahmad Chalabi on the political front and initially organized the prosecution of Saddam Hussein. Ali Allawi, yet another nephew, was at the Trade Ministry and then Defense Ministry, although it is unclear if he was close to Chalabi.

And Chalabi was not the only Iraqi accused of nepotism: many members of the Governing Council were engaged in the same practice in this new Iraq. It was the rule, rather than the exception, and for good reason. These Iraqi politicians were understandably tempted to rely only on those they could trust, their relatives. One cleric had his son installed as oil minister.

Still, the Trade Bank of Iraq was significant. It was an innovative scheme announced with great fanfare in the financial press in the summer of 2003. The idea was that it would take over from the dissolved and corrupt old oil-for-food program, which had operated under the United Nations and handled the international financial transactions of Iraq's largely socialized state. For the international banking community, the TBI concept meant billions in business. The financial press, struggling to decipher Iraqi reconstruction, was intrigued. "Banks from New York to Sydney are scrambling to form alliances to compete to run the trade bank," reported the *Wall Street Journal*, estimating it meant business of "$100 million a month to start."[96] JP Morgan and a consortium of other powerhouses won the bidding, and then the jostling started in Baghdad over who would actually get to run it on the Iraqi side.

Chalabi, as a member of the Governing Council, had the right to submit names, and he suggested Hussein al-Uzri. Uzri was forty-three, hearty and stocky, with thick unruly black hair and a broad smile. He had been educated in the United States. He was the grandson of Chalabi's sister Thamina, the woman who had tried bravely to help Nuri as-Said flee from his pursuers in 1958.

But the Coalition Provisional Authority was leaning toward the other candidate, a technocrat and finance expert at the Oil Ministry named Radwan Saadi. After all, Saadi had obvious qualifications. "He was a senior bureaucrat, well seasoned," said a member of the Iraqi government. Saadi was considered someone who knew a lot about Iraq's trade and finance issues and was politically acceptable to everyone.

As for Chalabi's grand-nephew Hussein al-Uzri, that was most certainly not the case. "Under normal conditions," explained the Iraqi official, "if you put his CV out for a job in the banking sector, he would not get a job at a bank because he has no banking experience. Simple. His background was in computer software."

Uzri had experience in software because he had worked for five years at the Chalabi company Card Tech, which was doing better and better every year. Technically, Uzri did have a link to the banking industry, since Card Tech handled the software for ATM machines and credit cards, but Card Tech was no bank, let alone a trade bank. Still, Uzri had been tapped by the family to open up the Eastern European and Russian markets, and he had done quite well. In the late 1980s he had worked closely with Ahmad Chalabi's Petra Bank, when he was assigned to run a meat processing company called Pinar in Amman.

But whatever Uzri's qualifications or lack thereof, Chalabi's lobbying was insistent and implacable. When the cards were down at the end of the play, Uzri, his grand-nephew, stepped in enthusiastically to head the trade bank. "We are back internationally," Uzri announced about the TBI in November 2003.[97]

Two weeks later the United States and fifteen other countries offered $2 billion in financing to the new bank, and Hussein al-Uzri signed the deal.

═════

Meanwhile, Chalabi cronies were feeding at the vast trough of Iraqi reconstruction. Chalabi's old friend Huda Farouki, whose old firm had borrowed heavily from Petra Bank, won prized and heavily contested awards from the Coalition Provisional Authority. Chalabi had loaned Farouki's company millions when it was already in bankruptcy proceedings in a series of mysterious decisions in the 1980s.

Now, Farouki had set up a fresh young company called Nour USA. The Americans wanted to equip the new Iraqi army forces; they were standing up after so disastrously dissolving the last Iraqi army at the beginning of Bremer's term. Nour USA, with a low bid of $337 million, was tapped to supply everything from uniforms to rifles for the new army. The award was quickly thrown out and rebid, and then Nour won again.

Eventually Farouki wore out his welcome at the INC compound. His firm continued to do business, but INC insiders say they told him they didn't want cars and traffic at the compound for security reasons. They warned him. Nabeel Musawi became angry at him. He says he'd ordered Farouki to stop doing business at the INC compound. He would allow Farouki to live there but not to run his business operations. Finally, Musawi's guards shot up Farouki's office one day when Farouki wasn't there, like an American gangland assault. Farouki got the message, and after complaining to everyone, including Chalabi, he moved away: he was not going to get any more protection from Chalabi.

Another Chalabi associate who profited from the reconstruction was his fellow INC deputy Mudhar Shawkat, who operated out of the INC compound. Shawkat won a valuable Iraqi government license to offer a monopoly of cell phone service throughout southern Iraq.

There was also Chalabi's nephew Faisal and his construction company, as well as the security firm he later founded, called Baghdad Fire and Security. U.S. government sources say the company specialized in "vetting" potential Iraqi employees, for a fee, whom American firms wanted to hire. The company promised it could screen out Baathists, and the Americans suspected it was using files gathered by Chalabi's people early on to help it in its research. Faisal insisted in at least one conversation with an American that his uncle Ahmad had nothing to do with the company.

Peg Bartel and Zaab Sethna, neither of whom are Iraqi, ran their "referral business"—trying to help American businessmen get situated in Iraq—using the resources they'd acquired at the INC. But if Ahmad Chalabi and his friends cashed in on Iraq, so did so many others—Iraqis and Americans. He was, in this regard, not unusual.

47

Chalabi Under Siege

May 2003

"Let my people go."
—Ahmad Chalabi, May 2004

IN MARCH 2004 Iraqi police investigators from a division called the Major Crimes Unit received a report of an apparent kidnapping and a robbery in Monsour. It was an occurrence so common in Baghdad that it would barely arouse police interest. But this case was different: sources said the victim, a prominent doctor, escaped. He leveled charges that he had been abducted by members of the Iraqi National Congress. They had beaten him, he said, questioned him about weapons of mass destruction, and then stolen his money.

The Major Crimes Unit, based in Adhamiya—the neighborhood where Ahmad Chalabi had been raised, which is now dominated by Sunnis—earned praise as a rare success story among the Americans' efforts to train a police force. The Americans had fostered the effort in the disintegrating country, vetting the investigators carefully, training them, and encouraging them to pursue investigations of terrorism, organized crime, public corruption, and kidnapping. FBI special agents on assignment in Iraq worked with the unit full-time providing assistance.

At that time, the Major Crimes Unit was increasingly clashing with Chalabi's freelance espionage operation. That espionage operation, funded by the Defense Intelligence Agency and led by Aras Kareem, was leaving a wider and wider footprint in Baghdad.

Chalabi would claim the investigation into his operations was a conspiracy. Was the Major Crimes Unit politically motivated in targeting Chalabi? There's no way of knowing. But even if it were true, there were actual flesh-and-blood victims making real complaints that needed to be investigated, and there was an extrajudicial intelligence operation run out of his compound.

═══

Chalabi at this time was coming under increasing scrutiny, and the ground under his feet was a bit shaky. He was increasingly shoring up his ties with the hard-right wing of Shiite politics in Iraq, the forces of Muqtada al-Sadr, somehow surfing on its anti-American bias. Now, thirteen years after the financial mess, Chalabi was again in the middle of a police investigation, this time in his own war-riddled country. The Chalabi intelligence unit—paid for by U.S. taxpayers through the DIA—had matured in the ten months since its launch. Peg Bartel, the American accountant originally hired by the State Department years before, cheerfully continued to handle the financial end of the intelligence operation, accepting the American cash payments from the DIA through the Virginia company Boxwood Inc. and then doling the money out to Aras Kareem.

The DIA went so far as to actually station officers on-site, to work with Aras and his team, at the INC intelligence headquarters. The operation was situated at a facility that used to belong to Saddam's old Mukhabarat—not the headquarters but a minor directorate. The American officers—about a dozen at some points—worked right inside the building, next to the Iraqis. Once again, the DIA and the CIA were at loggerheads. CIA officials, critical of the DIA operation and always skeptical of Chalabi, insist that it was run poorly. They say the very idea of embedding officers into a group like that is simply bad tradecraft. "It led to information bleeding out," said one CIA official who was in Iraq at the time.

Another problem for the CIA was that Chalabi's group was hoarding records looted from Baathists and intelligence organizations. One officer laughed as he explained, "They just kept it! They thought because they found it, it was theirs!" Eventually the agency and the U.S. military demanded that Chalabi's group hand over the records, and they believe they got the lot. "The operation tightened up."

Still, Chalabi had support, and it was not just the neoconservatives who blindly sided with him. Air Force Gen. Richard Myers, chairman of the Joint Chiefs of Staff, testified at one point that the intelligence from Chalabi's group had "saved soldiers' lives." Critics flatly say he was misinformed.

Effective or not, the heavy-handedness of the INC's extrajudicial intelligence arm got attention. Iraqis couldn't tell what was espionage and what was simply crime. "They started commandeering vehicles," said a well-known Iraqi diplomat. "They literally were stealing people's cars, stopping them at gunpoint. What do they call that? Carjacking. This is why he became so disliked. He earned this reputation. Going down the street, there's forty cars. They are shooting in the air and making all this kerfuffle."

At one point INC forces and the Iraqi police engaged in a gun battle. At another point there were reports of clashes between the INC forces and corporate security for a giant cell phone company.

When the Major Crimes Unit of the Iraqi police first began investigating, the officers weren't aware there was an "intelligence" operation at the INC. To them, it sounded quite simply like organized crime, involving abduction and robbery. The case expanded quickly as more and more allegations surfaced of illegal activity. Sources say in late April 2004 an Iraqi judge signed a secret arrest warrant for Aras Kareem. Three quick searches of the INC were conducted. Elements of the 89th Military Police secured the perimeter, the gunners scanning for threats in their Humvees. They were protecting the teams of Iraqi police raiding the INC offices. The Iraqi police found Iraqi government vehicles belonging to the Ministry of Finance that were being kept at the INC compound and carted them off to the Major Crimes Unit's parking lot in Adhamiya to figure out what they were doing there. *NBC Nightly News with Tom Brokaw* was the first to report on the investigation.

But the big raid on Chalabi's house by the Iraqi police came much later. On May 19, 2004, Iraqi police and U.S. Army MPs sketched out the final touches on their raid plans for the next day. They planned to arrest the six INC officials who they believed had been committing crimes. They had arrest warrants in hand, signed by a judge. They had plans to grab what evidence they could: computers, papers, and forged currency they had heard about. Paul Bremer had been notified of the raid weeks before, and it had been delayed repeatedly. They finally had the go-ahead.

———

Coincidentally, that very night, as the raid on his house was being planned, Ahmad Chalabi was hosting one of the top American investigators in Baghdad. His guest was Stuart Bowen, the man newly assigned to investigate waste, fraud, and abuse in the multibillion-dollar Iraqi reconstruction industry. Back then, Bowen was new at his job and knew little about Chalabi. Francis Brooke, Chalabi's American aide, had called Bowen and invited him over. "He said, 'Yeah, my boss knows some stuff about CPA corruption. Why don't you come over for dinner tonight,'" Bowen recounts.

Bowen didn't realize who the "boss" was until he arrived at the "China House." "I walked in, and it was this nice house, and I go, 'Who's your boss?' And he says, 'Ahmad Chalabi.' And I said, 'What?' And I turned to my chief investigator and said, 'Should we stay?'"

They stayed. When Chalabi walked into the room, he bathed Bowen in his intense charm. "I was struck right away by his smile, and his articulateness and his intelligence and his wit. And it was clear this guy knew how to operate!" Chalabi brought him to the dining room. "We had the best dinner I've had in Iraq," Bowen recalls. Chalabi then began to regale him with stories: "We talked about everything: the history of Islam, the history of Iraq, Shia culture, CPA, and his views of Jerry Bremer, which were negative. And then we finished dinner and he said, 'Let's have dessert,' and I realized the table behind us had been set with dessert. And so we stood up and we walked over to the next table and we had fruit, some of which I never tasted before." Chalabi, as usual, flattered his guest, who had once worked directly for President Bush. "He knew I was a friend of the president, and he said—I think he was just playing to me—'I love your boss, he's a great man.' Just sort of gratuitous comments."

And then Chalabi launched into a litany of allegations about the CPA. Americans were demanding kickbacks, he said. The contracting process was corrupt. Interestingly, he hit the mark square on, because corruption indeed infested the Green Zone. But everyone already knew that. Chalabi had no specific allegations. Bowen said none of his tips ever led to a single criminal case. "I always listened to him with a little bit of irony when I'd hear him say he was determined to fight corruption. I realized I was looking at a man who might be a crook himself."

Stuart Bowen didn't tell Chalabi this, but he had already recruited other, more accurate informants. One was that adventurous American arms dealer named Dale Stoffel, who had been living at the Chalabi compound. Stoffel was paying BKSH, Chalabi's old lobbying firm, as well as Chalabi's accountant Peg Bartel, while he looked for reconstruction deals. Stoffel was also entangled in a business dispute with Chalabi's nephew Faisal Chalabi. Bowen, very soon, offered Stoffel complete immunity from prosecution if he helped in his investigations. And Stoffel may easily have known much of what was going on at the Chalabi compound.

━━━

Chalabi keeps unusual hours in the Middle East, and the next morning, he was still asleep in bed at 11 a.m. Perhaps it is because he had been doing so much lobbying by phone with the United States and had been working on East Coast time. In any case, that was the hour when the Iraqi police finally executed their raid on his house. They raided INC intelligence headquarters and the political office too, leaving the normal wreckage of a raid and carting off computers. They found none of the suspects they were looking for.

Chalabi's American *consigliere*, Francis Brooke, watched as it happened. And Peg Bartel, who had helped Chalabi collect U.S. government funds for four years, stood outside trying to talk to the Americans who were on-site and making phone calls to try to figure out what was happening.

Aras Kareem immediately fled to Iran, his safe haven, to wait out the crisis.

━━━━━

Chalabi plotted a public relations and political counterattack. Under assault he was at his most adept. Interviews with his neoconservative supporters at the time showed a certain sanguinity mixed with outrage. The apparent consensus among Chalabi and his American supporters was that this would, in the long run, be a beneficial thing: it would establish his street cred in Iraq and symbolize a break with the Americans.

So later that day, Chalabi called a press conference. He appeared blazing mad, his aides say. Journalists flocked to his Monsour neighborhood, to another one of the buildings the INC had claimed as its political headquarters. The American networks came, as well as the big American newspapers. CNN and MSNBC sent live trucks to beam the conference around the world. Arabic journalists joined in too, many apparently pleased by this development.

Gruff Kurdish pesh merga guards frisked the journalists and ushered them into a luxurious hall. Chalabi's entourage and his attendants gathered at the side. The American Francis Brooke insisted to a reporter, "I am an Iraqi!" When they had waited just long enough, Chalabi himself strolled in.

He didn't say a word at first. Instead, dressed in his elegant suit and tie, he stood silently and looked out at the assembled journalists, in their photographers' vests and their cargo pants, disheveled. The journalists, once again, would be the medium he would use to save himself from the authorities. He picked up a panoramic photograph of his family, one he had always showed to those he wanted to impress in the old days before the war. During the police raid, the glass had been broken. He let a smile play upon his lips and he held the photograph in both hands, turning to the right, and then the left, looking out at the reporters, scribbling in their notebooks. He held it there as if he were displaying proof of an atrocity, evidence of a wrong done to him. He turned slowly, so that all could see, and gave a dramatic presentation:

We avoided by a hair's breadth a clash with my guards. I was asleep, I
opened the door and the police went into my room . . . carrying pistols.
They had been through other rooms of the house. I told them to get
out. They said we are slaves under orders. Nevertheless I told them to
get out. Then I learned later that they had attacked this headquarters
and other headquarters of INC.

His central message was that the police officers who had raided the
compound were Baathists. "The Baathists are coming here to attack us
under American supervision," he told the puzzled reporters.

When Ahmad Chalabi is accused of corruption, he often attacks his
accuser. It has happened in Jordan, Iraq, and the United States. This
time, Chalabi pointed his finger at his new nemesis—Paul Bremer,
whom he accused of abetting and overseeing corruption in the Green
Zone. Bremer had joined the rogues' gallery of Chalabi enemies:
Zinni, Nabulsi, Richard Armitage, and Lakhdar Brahimi. He took the
opportunity to attack Bremer, the American administrator who
seemed to have stepped so rudely between him and the U.S. president.
"I am America's best friend in Iraq. If the CPA finds it necessary to direct an armed attack against my home, you can see the state of relations between the CPA and Iraqi people."

At moments he sounded downright biblical. "My message to the
CPA is let my people go. Let my people *be free.* We are *grateful* to President Bush for liberating Iraq, but it is time for the Iraqi people to run
their affairs." The strangest part of all was his spirited defense of Aras
Kareem Habib, the suspected Iranian agent. Aras was like Chalabi's
partner in his efforts: his operations officer, his enforcer. Yet he was
believed by Americans to have varied loyalties. It was a downright
weird thing that Aras was taking U.S. intelligence money for running
his extrajudicial spy shop out of Chalabi's headquarters, even while
the CIA believed him to be an Iranian spy.

Chalabi: My security chief Arras Habib is *the* most important Iraqi in
the counterterrorism effort against the Baathists and the foreign terrorists in Iraq. He is a brave, tireless, competent, and very smart patriot
who has been working very hard with Iraqis and Americans the entire
past year. And he is responsible more than anybody else for the meager

successes that were achieved by everyone against the terrorists. His name was on the warrant.

Reporter: Why was it?

Chalabi: Because Arras is against the Baathists. He has fought the Mukhabarat. And he has . . . the CIA has a very big grudge against Arras for the past decade. They don't like him. He is successful and they are not.

So, according to Chalabi, CIA bitterness had led to this raid, not the organized-crime investigation. Just as he once blamed the Jordanians for the Petra Bank case, he blamed the CIA and Bremer for this crisis. Chalabi also theorized in the press conference that the reason for the raid was his oil-for-food investigation, part of his campaign against the United Nations. He alleged that the only copy of an investigative report on the program was taken.

The press jumped on the story. *Newsweek* ran a blistering story by Mark Hosenball and Christopher Dickey, and the cover encapsulated the way Chalabi's fortunes had shifted. "Our Con Man in Iraq," it said, over his photograph.

But his American supporters quickly rallied around the interpretation that had been agreed on: the raid had showed his independence from America. Some said it was part of his own political effort to establish himself as an independent figure. "You don't get it," one said, shaking his head and smiling at a reporter. "It's all part of his plan." Paul Bremer, they said, was merely playing into Chalabi's hands.

"This crude and outrageous assault on him will only improve his prospects," Richard Perle said, in his erudite, almost British accent. Perle led an aggressive effort to defend Chalabi in the inner circles of power. Perle, with Jim Woolsey and Newt Gingrich, even marched into the White House office of Condoleezza Rice, then National Security Adviser. Perle was at his most defensive of Chalabi, the man he revered so much. "There is a smear campaign under way," Perle then told the *New York Times*, "and it is being perpetrated by the C.I.A. and the D.I.A. and a gaggle of former intelligence officers who have succeeded in planting these stories, which are accepted with hardly any scrutiny."[98]

Peg Bartel wrote an angry dispatch to Laurie Mylroie, who ran an online newsletter dedicated to the INC and its view of Iraq. "Paul Bremer's imperious manner," Bartel e-mailed angrily, "has resulted in a tremendous loss of American and Iraqi lives."[99] Bartel, who was still the financial link between the DIA and Chalabi's INC, passing money from the Americans to Aras Kareem, was soon to have even more frustration at the U.S. government: the money stream finally stopped.

In the middle of May, Paul Wolfowitz agreed to cut off funding for the INC's intelligence operations. The State Department, over Chalabi's protests, had already cut off the subsidies for "humanitarian affairs" and publishing newspapers. But the DIA intelligence subsidy of $4 million per year was ongoing. According to George Tenet, President George Bush himself mandated the end of it. "I don't think he ought to be working for us," Bush said at one meeting. Later, Tenet recounted, Wolfowitz claimed to the president that Chalabi's information was saving American lives. The CIA said it wasn't aware of any examples. Finally, according to Tenet, at a meeting, the president told Condoleezza Rice, "I want Chalabi off the payroll."[100]

For the first time in years, the INC would have to pay for itself. The tap of U.S. taxpayer funds had finally been turned off. This had happened before, of course, when the CIA had slashed its ties to Chalabi and left him without U.S. cash. But the State Department had picked up the slack after a few years, and then the Pentagon did too. Now, once again, the United States was cutting him off. Still, he was hardly suffering financially. He and his INC had built a massive war chest since the invasion.

Chalabi quickly turned to one of the few remaining allies who would accept him, the unpredictable and fiery Muqtada al-Sadr. Sadr, since Saddam's fall, had become the rallying point for the impoverished Shiites of Iraq. He wore the black turban of the Sayyid, the descendant of Muhammad, but he earned his popularity not through religious learning so much as through his brutal charisma, his message, and his unalloyed appeal for Shiite empowerment. Sadr's scowling and fleshy countenance, his tufted unkempt beard, was visible on posters throughout Sadr City. His soldiers called themselves the Mahdi Army and overtly promised suicide missions. They fought pitched battles against American troops. He is accused of masterminding the gory, public murder of a rival imam who had been flown into Iraq by the United States early in the war. According to one very well-informed Iraqi source, Sadr's Mahdi Army received a vast amount of money from Iran. Sadr may not have acted solely on Iran's orders, but he was under Iran's influence. Of that there is no doubt.

Chalabi embraced this thuggish and anti-American imam. He even brought his entourage to meet with Sadr, including his *consigliere*, Francis Brooke. Brooke, whose allegiance to Chalabi apparently never wavered, must have been one of the few Americans ever to meet Sadr.

It was an incomprehensible alliance to outsiders, but one that made sense from a purely political standpoint and given the loyalty both Sadr and Chalabi had to the Shiite platform. Sadr, the thuggish cleric, gained from Chalabi's ingenious machinations, and Chalabi could suddenly point to an actual political base. "He sided with Muqtada al-Sadr, coached him, became his principal adviser at one point. He provided him with strategic thought and information that he didn't have," explained Qubad, Jalal Talabani's son.

Sadr paid close attention to Chalabi's advice and plans. Even this did not disturb Chalabi's American friends. One writer who admired Chalabi went so far as to compare the pair to an ancient Greek emperor and classical philosopher. Sadr "has shown a willingness to play Alexander to Ahmad Chalabi's Aristotle, learning the game from the master."[101] Chalabi himself was now the *consigliere*, whispering in Sadr's ear, just as he had once whispered in the ears of the most powerful men and women in Washington.

=====

The cutoff of U.S. funding in the late spring of 2004 coincided with the supposed end of the occupation. Chalabi had fought a vicious, hearty fight against Bremer. He had used his allies in the United States and Iraq to undercut the man's efforts, and he had finally won.

Still, even after the legal occupation was declared over in July 2004, the more toxic parts of Chalabi's campaign against Bremer and the White House and the United Nations splashed back against him. When Ambassador Paul Bremer quietly left Iraq, a defeated viceroy, Chalabi's victory was far from complete. If there was one man Chalabi's aides reviled more than anyone, it was Ayad Allawi, his old rival in the Iraqi opposition. Chalabi's people had run a campaign against him since the early 1990s. And yet, Allawi was now ascendant in the new "sovereign" Iraq. He was even still collecting CIA funding, sources say. Allawi was appointed to run the new interim government that had been organized with the help of the United Nations, as prime minister. Iraq finally had what Chalabi wanted: an interim government. But he wasn't part of it. And he would do his utmost to fight against it.

Later a judge with the Iraqi Central Criminal Court filed an arrest warrant against Chalabi himself. The charges raised the eyebrows of everyone, even Chalabi's enemies. It was a bizarre set of allegations, involving counterfeiting charges stemming from an old program to trade dinars (which had pictures of Saddam Hussein on them) to more recent ones. The charges did not sound credible, but Chalabi had made a lot of enemies, and they could have come from anywhere.

Even weirder was the case brought by the same judge against Chalabi's nephew Salem, a set of charges that were widely derided as absurd. The judge suggested that Salem was implicated in murder, but Salem was known to be a harmless and affable lawyer. Salem, who had an uncanny resemblance to Ahmad Chalabi, was the younger son of Jawad Chalabi, Ahmad's brother, and he had been one of the few family members to join Ahmad in his political efforts in Iraq during the war.

Ahmad Chalabi struck back, but against an odd target. In August 2004, he lashed out at the Jordanian government, filing a suit in federal court in Washington, D.C., charging the Hashemite Kingdom of Jordan and its Central Bank with engaging in a massive conspiracy against him. He had fled Jordan in 1989 to evade their talons, and they had committed "kidnapping, attempted murder, mail fraud, wire fraud," and other crimes, he claimed.

He was going to right the wrongs done to him by the Jordanians so long ago. His enemies in Jordan, Chalabi now alleged with a new set of allegations, had "secretly removed" 106 million Jordanian dinars from Petra Bank, or about $150 million, causing the lack of liquidity in Petra Bank. Not only that. The Jordanians, he said, were also responsible for false allegations that he had passed secret U.S. information to Iranian intelligence. He signed and verified his complaint, under threat of perjury, on August 10, 2004, in Tehran.

48

The Iran Connection

"The permutations are infinite, once you've brought off
the basic lie."

—George Smiley in *Tinker, Tailor, Soldier, Spy*

THE IRANIAN REVOLUTIONARY GUARD'S Quds Force, which is tasked to prop-
agate Iran's Islamic Revolution, divided its operations in Iraq into
three directorates after the U.S. invasion. The southernmost is referred
to by the Quds Force as the "Ramadan," or "Ramazan" (in Farsi), command, and the complex Iranian operations there are overseen by Gen.
Ahmed Frouzanda (sometimes transliterated as "Frohazendah"). It is
the most important region of Iraq, from Iran's perspective, not just
because of the shared border but because the area is home to Iran's
Shiite constituency. Ayatollah Khomeini had sought to make it his second Islamic Republic.

Frouzanda is one of Iran's master operatives. U.S. military and
counterterrorism officials treated him as a "high-value" intelligence
target for years, even before the Iraqi invasion, and they try to track
his whereabouts. They believe he cut his teeth working in Lebanese
Hezbollah operations against the United States and Israel in the 1980s.

Chalabi had met him at least twice before the war, according to former INC offical Nabeel Musawi. Frouzanda is said to be distinctive in
appearance, getting portly in his fifties but with handsome features

and a salt-and-pepper beard. He is, as Musawi points out, a "handsome" man. Musawi says he was at a lunch meeting with Frouzanda and Chalabi, where they discussed how to ensure that INC operations in southern Iraq went smoothly.

There can be no doubt about Frouzanda, according to American intelligence experts. "He is a murderer of Americans," said a former CIA official familiar with Frouzanda's file and with the hunt for him. "He is an intelligence officer of a hostile service which is directly involved with operations that kill Americans. He is a paramilitary officer with the Revolutionary Guard and a skilled one. He is an enemy of the United States."

Once the United States invaded Iraq and Chalabi continued to accept DIA cash, according to U.S. intelligence sources, he did not cut himself off from Frouzanda or other members of Iranian intelligence. In the late winter and spring of 2004, the United States was battling Sunnis in the west of Iraq and Shiites in the south, and cracking down on Muqtada al-Sadr's Mahdi Army. Chalabi had positioned himself ever more closely to the Shiite bloc.

It was then, sources say, that the CIA believed there was another meeting between Ahmad Chalabi and Frouzanda. The meeting, they believed, took place in northern Iraq, near the small border town of Penjwin, and was set up by Aras Habib Kareem, Chalabi's enforcer and intelligence chief.

It was in this same time frame that the NSC intercepted communications indicating that Tehran had been warned its codes had been broken. It was a high-level breach of U.S. intelligence. Soon, the FBI began investigating. "It was an enormous investigation," said a CIA official on the ground at the time. FBI agents from their counterintelligence squads, as well as their national security division, began trying to uncover the source of the breach. They quickly pulled the DIA agents in from their assignments over at the Iraqi National Congress headquarters to interrogate them. DIA agents were sent home to the States in shame for questioning.

After the case went public, an FBI official involved in it said the agents quickly tried to set up an interview with Ahmad Chalabi. "We were not looking at him as a subject," the agent emphasized. "Chalabi was looked at as a witness." From an FBI perspective, even if Chalabi had revealed U.S. secrets, it is not at all clear that he would have been committing a criminal offense. More important to the bureau was how Chalabi would have learned of the information in the first place. That was the riddle, the FBI official said: could it have been espionage, or indiscretion, or even an accident—unintentionally disclosed by an American? Over the next few months, the FBI, according to the agent, hashed out an agreement with a member of Chalabi's U.S.-based legal team. He agreed to do an interview, the agent said, but it never happened.

Certainly Chalabi continued to deal with Iran. Middle East intelligence sources maintain that Chalabi's operation collecting Baathist files and documents after the U.S. invasion was useful for the Iranians. One intelligence source alleged in an interview that "He gave intelligence documents to the Iranian MOIS" (Ministry of Intelligence and Security). But if he did, there is no law against this, especially if they were not actually U.S. documents.

Officials began to reexamine the relationship Chalabi's INC had maintained with the Iranians all along. "The Defense Intelligence Agency has concluded that a U.S.-funded arm of Ahmed Chalabi's Iraqi National Congress has been used for years by Iranian intelligence," reported *Newsday*'s Knut Royce, "to pass disinformation to the United States and to collect highly sensitive American secrets, according to intelligence sources."[102]

After the war, some speculated that Chalabi may have been an Iranian intelligence "agent" throughout the 1990s and may have lured America into war on behalf of his real spymasters in Tehran. Both the CIA and the DIA suspected the INC was penetrated by the Iranians all along. But this new allegation ratcheted up the concerns several notches, in calling Chalabi an active agent. It is also almost certainly a myth, though. Iran, no doubt, had the same difficulty that the United States had in controlling him.

A more precise analysis is put forward by former CIA officers who believe that Chalabi was probably an "agent of influence" for Iran. They doubt he was paid anything but believe there was a convergence of interests and a loyalty to the Shiite regime there. Whitley Bruner, who first contacted him all those years ago on behalf of the CIA, came around to that view after seeing how influential Iran was in the new

Iraq. Bruner acknowledges that there are different ways to see it. "You can make a coherent case that he's been an Iranian agent since the beginning. If you look at it from that prism, it makes sense," he says. But Bruner actually discounts that "agent" theory in favor of the "agent of influence" interpretation. "It became a question to me: what were his long-term objectives, and where, other than himself, are there allegiances? I think when he thinks big, Iran plays a major role. I guess I come belatedly to the idea that there was a very close sense of identity with Chalabi in terms of Iran, and a very emotional tie. Whereas the Americans were always just a means to an end. We were much more of an instrument. The Iranian role was long-term."

Robert Grenier, who also was part of the CIA's Iraqi Operations Group in the early days and later during the U.S. invasion, says he doesn't think Chalabi is anyone's agent; he thinks Chalabi worked with Iranian intelligence only opportunistically. "Ahmad has always had the ability to manipulate people he needs to," Grenier argues.

No one will know unless a mob of outraged Iranians revolts against the mullahs in Iran and the crowd opens up the files of the Revolutionary Guards, just as they once opened the files of the cruel SAVAK. Then, perhaps, they will pull out the Chalabi folder. But he is no Manchurian candidate of the Iranians in Iraq. The real question is not whether he was an Iranian agent but whether he was more loyal to Iran or the United States. Certainly in pure intelligence terms, weighing his behavior over the years, he was indisputably more helpful to Iranian intelligence than he was to the CIA, with whom he had such a troubled relationship.

Key is this: there is no evidence that he ever told U.S. intelligence anything about his contacts in Iran, while there is significant evidence that he told Iranian intelligence about his dealings with the United States.

As for Chalabi's American neoconservative patrons, those scholars and journalists and thinkers who were so influential and who despised Iran's government, there was an eerie symmetry between his dealings with them and his dealings with Iranian intelligence. Each side knew something about Chalabi's contact with the other. A naïve comment by Chalabi's arch-admirer Richard Perle epitomized the blithe neoconservative view of Chalabi's Iranian connection. "I think Chalabi has been very shrewd in getting the things he has needed over the years out of the Iranians without giving anything in return," Perle told the *New York Times*'s Dexter Filkins. In Perle's view, his friend Chalabi had outwitted the Iranians.[103]

Perle's claim to the *Times* would probably be more accurate if just one word were changed: if one replaced the word "Iranian" with the word "American," or even "neoconservative." Perle's sentence could then read: "Chalabi has been very shrewd in getting the things he has needed over the years out of the *Americans* [or the neoconservatives] without giving anything in return." It is also fair to say that Iranian intelligence proved more perceptive than Chalabi's American backers, and got the better part of the deal. The Iranians knew more about the neocons than the neocons knew about them, and they devoured the various tracts coming from the Washington think tanks. And as time went on, with Iraq unraveling into a wasteland of chaos and endless war, Chalabi came to need the Iranian government far more than he needed the Americans.

49

Weapons of Mass Destruction

REPORTER: Do you still believe that Iraq has weapons of mass destruction?

AHMAD CHALABI: Yes.

REPORTER: Where are they?

AHMAD CHALABI: Hidden.

REPORTER: Where?

AHMAD CHALABI: We don't know. They must be found. They constitute a danger to the Iraqi people. The Americans have failed to find them. We will look for them after sovereignty.

—Press conference, May 2004

BY 2004 ONLY THE VERY OBSTINATE, to be polite, still believed that Saddam Hussein had a viable WMD program by the time of the war. Former weapons inspector David Kay announced in January of that year that "we were all wrong." Judith Miller's newspaper, the *New York Times*, disavowed her reporting. A colleague of Miller's at the *Times*, Jim Dwyer, earned her anger when he tracked down Mohamad al-Zobaidy, the embittered INC official who had shepherded Chalabi's defectors and who now revealed that the INC had embellished the defectors' tales.[104]

Adnan Haideri, the Iraqi civil engineer and "defector" about whom Miller had written, and who had been relocated to the United States with his two quarrelsome wives, was flown back to Iraq by the CIA. The Iraq Survey Group, hunting banned weapons, was coming up dry and wanted him to show the site where the suspected nuclear material was hidden. Case officers drove him to the "Medical City," where he claimed the nuclear site was buried, a claim that made it to the National Intelligence Estimate. He stood there on the street, unable to pinpoint it, and broke down in tears, to the irritation of the incredulous CIA officers.

The truth was beginning to dawn on David Rose, the *Vanity Fair* reporter who had been so inspired by Chalabi and who had written passionately about Saddam's WMDs and links to terror. "I started to investigate my own reporting," Rose said, as if in pain, "how I'd been suckered."

After the fall of Baghdad, Chalabi had continued pitching ideas and story tips to Rose, and the last pitch of Chalabi's was a complete and garish lie. "He told me that Ayman al-Zawahiri had been to Baghdad a year before 9/11, that Uday had given him $10 million. He personally told me that. He wanted me to investigate it," Rose said. Zawahiri was famously Al Qaeda's number two, the Egyptian doctor who had appeared in videotapes with Osama bin Laden. The idea that he had been in Baghdad was ludicrous. Just a few months earlier, Rose would have jumped at that extraordinary tidbit, but he now realized that something had gone terribly wrong. To his credit, he was one of the few to confront what he had done, and to face squarely the sheer quantity of nonsense he had written based on Chalabi's tips. "I had a tremendous crisis of conscience," he explained. "I thought I should just give up being a reporter. To get this story so badly wrong, with such devastating consequences."

Tracing back over his steps, he talked to Francis Brooke about the defectors the INC had introduced him to. "Their story now is, 'We never said this guy is telling the truth. We just said, "Listen to what he says."'" The INC was by now arguing that it never vouched for anyone's credibility; it simply made introductions. "Brooke says, 'This guy is just giving you a window into what it's like working for the Saddam regime,'" Rose confronted Brooke. "I said, 'Well, hold on a second, at the time you were telling me that you'd corroborated all this information through your amazing network of contacts in Iraq and that your analysts had gone through it all with a fine-tooth comb and it had all been triple-checked.'"

Brooke's response, says Rose, was so brash it makes him laugh to think of it. "He said, 'No, no, no! You must have misheard!' And of course that's now their line: 'We never claimed that these guys were telling the truth.'" If someone believed their defectors, it was hardly their fault, the INC loyalists said. The CIA and DIA should have been more careful.

But that, of course, is like a Nigerian e-mail scammer blaming his victim, or a stock fraudster who plays on his customer's greed. Perhaps Chalabi's listeners, too, wanted something for nothing. Chalabi himself famously told the *Daily Telegraph*, about the false defector reports, that "we are heroes in error," because their tales had brought about the U.S. invasion, although he later denied saying it.

But his position evolved. By 2005, he repeatedly called the idea that he deliberately misled the American government "an urban myth." With an intimate grasp of the subject, he frequently pointed to page 108 of a 2005 Presidential Commission headed by Charles Robb and Lawrence Silbermann. The commission investigated the disastrous flawed prewar intelligence on WMDs. Page 108 said: "CIA's post-war investigations revealed that INC-related sources had a minimal impact on pre-war assessments." And in fact the CIA's flawed information on WMDs largely had not come from Chalabi, because the agency tried, with partial success, to weed out anything with his fingerprints. The commission's report continued, discussing a notorious National Intelligence Estimate: "The October 2002 NIE relied on reporting from two INC sources, both of whom were later deemed to be fabricators." Of course, it was referring here to Haideri and the case of the underground wells, as well as the case of the INC's fabricator.[105]

But all this aside, the INC's slew of cases had a massive public impact before the war: the Salman Pak hijacking school, the underground wells, Saddam's mistress, and the fabricator, though, were all traceable to the INC. And in 2006 a Senate Intelligence Committee report concluded that "The Iraqi National Congress (INC) attempted to influence United States policy on Iraq by providing false information through defectors."

50

Almost at the Top

IN FEBRUARY 2005, AHMAD CHALABI, sixty years old, almost came to rule Iraq. Or put another way, it was as close as he would come in those years after the invasion, because at least he was a contender for fourteen days. It was rumored in the circles of his followers to be a done deal, and it was a remarkable return to credibility for him. His resurgence was duly noted in a wave of articles in the U.S. press: "Iraq's Chalabi Comes in From the Cold," reported Reuters. "Ahmad Chalabi Is on the Brink of a Comeback," blared the small, pro-neocon *New York Sun* on February 9, 2005. "Chalabi Rises From the Ashes" was the *Chicago Tribune*'s headline. Such headlines have appeared time and time again throughout his career.

The way Chalabi's ascendancy was supposed to work was this: the people of Iraq were given not just one democratic election but three, in quick succession, in the wake of Paul Bremer's departure from Baghdad. The first vote, January 2005, was to choose a very temporary—almost an ephemeral—government to replace the Ayad Allawi interim regime. Then there would be another vote in October to approve the new Iraqi Constitution. And finally one last vote would cap it off eleven months after the first one, in December 2005, to choose the country's actual leadership for a four-year administration.

Chalabi had started his comeback with style, in the fall of 2004, in preparation for the first of those democratic votes. Mentoring Muqtada al-Sadr gave him some political weight to throw around, and with the backing of the Mahdi Army he was now a figure to be feared, too. In preparation for those first elections, he had been busy. As Ali Allawi wrote in his book *The Occupation of Iraq,* the *marjiya* in Najaf, the very pinnacle of the Shiite religious authorities, had conceived of forming a united Shiite political bloc called the United Iraqi Alliance. All the Shiite parties were loyal, of course, to the *marjiya,* even if they fought among themselves. But now, with the blessing of Ayatollah Sistani, the Shiite parties like Dawa and SCIRI would not need to compete against each other for votes; they could steamroll over the Sunnis and the Kurds if need be. The bloc would be entirely sectarian. Ahmad Chalabi eagerly pitched in to help. Chalabi still periodically mentioned the ideal of inclusiveness, but he saw that sectarian politics was his only way in. He analyzed the political realities, as his old supporter Nabeel Musawi said, and made his choices. Musawi continued to watch as he thought Chalabi undercut the liberal, or secular, Iraqi politicians.

In later years Nabeel Musawi came to blame Chalabi and his political gamesmanship with the end of the secular and nonsectarian politics of Iraq. Chalabi's influence helped blast away the "liberal" trend in Iraqi politics, undercutting the possibility for secular politicians to lead. "Chalabi single-handedly managed to dilute, to suffocate, the liberal movement of Iraq that was coming to light," Musawi explained one day in a London restaurant. "He did not embrace them, he abandoned them." Musawi was upset that Chalabi shunned the non-Islamist politicians, pursuing narrow sectarian goals for his own political future. "It had to do with reading the political map," he said. Certainly there were antisectarian idealists early on in Iraq, even people like Chalabi's longtime booster Kanan Makiya, or pragmatist politicians like Adnan Pachachi, and others. Musawi himself, a Shiite, had never dreamed that Chalabi would become an advocate of hard-line Shiite clerical leaders. Musawi, who had worked so hard for Chalabi in the past, now saw him as the man who tore away any middle ground. In Musawi's opened eyes, Chalabi had betrayed his own followers and must take blame for blocking reconciliation and helping to stoke the sectarian divisions. That is a devastating allegation from a man who had supported Chalabi since the founding of the INC in 1992. "I don't approve of what he did, and you can quote me on that," Musawi, no longer just Chalabi's young aide, now said with a nod.

In December 2004, Chalabi published another op-ed in the *Wall Street Journal* called "The Future That Iraq Deserves." It was an effort to defend the new Shiite political bloc to American conservative readers. As he had in the past, he hailed the Iraq Liberation Act. The *Journal* op-ed is difficult to read because Chalabi's written English, for some reason, had become less flowing. "The Iraq Liberation Act," he wrote, "voted in Congress in November 1998 and hence set as part of U.S. law, clearly stated the pursuit of democracy as a primary motive for regime change in Iraq."[106] Then he launched into a defense of the Shiite United Iraqi Alliance, calling it "an important achievement. "Their Shiism has been the first call for persecution. That is the very identity that has cost them so much. To rally along that identity as a first expression of their political voice is but natural."

But for the moment, in an unusual phase, America was less the audience he cared about than Iraq was, because of the impending elections. In the January 30 elections, the United Iraqi Alliance became the biggest bloc in the country, but it did not win the two-thirds of the vote it expected. Instead, the Shiites emerged with just under 50 percent support. The Shiites had to accommodate the Kurds to appoint their prime minister, but at least they would be able to pick whoever it would be.

On February 9 Chalabi announced he was a candidate for prime minister. His own newspaper in Iraq, *Al Mu'tamar*, covered his nomination. "In an irreversible and unchangeable decision," the paper reported in Arabic, "the most powerful parties forcefully nominate Dr. Ahmad Chalabi to the post of prime minister." It was unabashed propaganda, but in the context of Iraqi politics, it was not unusual or even embarrassing. "The largest and most powerful political groups in Iraq believe that Dr. Ahmad al-Chalabi is a qualified leader most suitable to head the new government," *Al Mu'tamar* wrote. "They will insist on the decision and will not accept a substitute."[107]

At first Chalabi was one of six candidates, then three, and then just two. The other candidate who emerged was Ibrahim al-Jaafari, the head of the religious Dawa Party. For two weeks, Chalabi lobbied and jostled and made promises. He wanted the Shiite bloc to anoint him as its candidate. The nomination would have redeemed him, acquitted him, and brought the whole Iraq enterprise full circle.

In the end it didn't work. Chalabi's allies insist he would have won a secret ballot but that he selflessly stepped down to preserve Shiite peace. "Ahmad Chalabi had to withdraw his nomination for the prime minister to save the alliance's unity, in spite of the fact that he had the majority of votes," Entifadh Qanbar, still working for Chalabi after all those years, told a reporter.[108] The tiny *New York Sun*, whose editorial board was immensely supportive of Chalabi, reported that he had only stepped down after a meeting with Iran's ambassador to Iraq. The Dawa Party's Jaafari became the candidate for the job. And with that, it ended: Chalabi's bid to rule the country was over. It took two months to iron out the rest of the short-lived new government.

Vice President Dick Cheney put in a good word for Chalabi in the midst of the wrangling, in an interview with that very newspaper, the *New York Sun*. Chalabi's shaming—the WMDs, the Iranian connection, the missing funds—had apparently never shaken Cheney's confidence. "I know Mr. Chalabi myself," Cheney said. "I've met with him. I wouldn't have any problems meeting with him today. If there's any prohibition against meeting with him, I'm unaware of it."[109]

On April 28, 2005, the new Iraqi National Assembly confirmed the new, transitional Jaafari Cabinet. While Jaafari was the prime minister, Chalabi was deputy prime minister and an acting oil minister. It was, really, the first government elected in the country with even the patina of democratic backing. Ministries were divvied up among the various political parties, as the spoils.

Jaafari told the National Assembly that he had assembled his team because of their integrity. "The fundamental quality we stressed was honesty," he said. "You know well that corruption had become widespread due to an accumulation of problems from the old regime."[110]

51

Inside Deal

2005

THE DAY CHALABI WAS CONFIRMED as deputy prime minister was the day the Trade Bank of Iraq announced its agreement with Card Tech, the Chalabi family company. Even though Ahmad Chalabi had been out of power since the dissolution of the Governing Council, his grand-nephew Hussein al-Uzri had continued to run the government-owned TBI. It gradually grew in power and influence, monopolizing Iraqi international trade finance through its ties to JP Morgan and its official status.

The April 28, 2005, announcement was crystal clear:

Card Tech Ltd. (CTL), the United Kingdom-based card management systems' provider and processor has signed a strategic agreement with the Trade Bank of Iraq (TBI), to provide card issuing and acquiring processing services for the bank's planned range of Visa card products.

TBI's suite of products will include a Visa Classic Card targeted for travel and entertainment usage and a Visa Electron salary card.

Following the launch of its card portfolio, the bank will immediately deploy 10 Automatic Teller Machines (ATMs) in Baghdad. This constitutes the initial stages of the bank's long-term strategy to introduce modern, mass financial delivery systems into Iraq.

"CTL was selected as the ideal processing partner by TBI. It assisted TBI in coordinating with various parties to launch our card product in record time, utilizing its good offices with the payment systems," Badawi Al Naqeeb, TBI Deputy General Manager, said.

In a brief phone interview in 2007, Uzri said the award to Card Tech was not made because it was a Chalabi family business where he used to work. He claimed that Visa, the credit card company, actually recommended his old company. "We became members of Visa and they recommended a few companies, and one of them was Card Tech," he said. In the end, he explained, even though the deal was billed as "strategic agreement," all that Card Tech did was help Visa process its Visa Card portfolio. "It was a board decision" in any case, he said, "not mine."

The TBI award to Card Tech must have indeed been important, since the "strategic agreement" is the only one that TBI has ever publicized. The agreement got little pickup except in the specialized press, and there was no mention of Ahmad Chalabi's connection. Nor was there any reference to the ownership of Card Tech. Even the name of Card Tech's general manager, Jaffar Agha-Jaffar, Chalabi's nephew, did not appear in the press release. (Agha-Jaffar had been convicted with Chalabi in the Petra Bank case in 1992 in Jordan and sentenced to two years in absentia.) Nor did anyone note Uzri's connections to Card Tech, for which he had worked for five years, nor to Petra Bank. To be precise, Uzri pointed out in an interview that he never really worked for Chalabi's Petra Bank but "for one of the companies." He ran a meat-processing plant that was controlled by Petra in the 1980s.

What is indisputable is that, at the time of the award, Ahmad Chalabi was a part-owner of a Card Tech affiliate, Corporate records in London confirm that there were 1,000 shares of the privately held "Card Tech Research," and Dr. Ahmad Chalabi was listed as one of five owners, with 200 shares in his own name.[111]

Rather quickly after that "strategic agreement" between the government of Iraq and his family company, Deputy Prime Minister Ahmad

Chalabi transferred his Card Tech Research shares to his wife's name. The date of the transfer was June 7, 2005, about five weeks after that important day of April 28. In official records in Britain, Chalabi listed his address as London rather than Baghdad. He transferred the shares to his wife, Leila Osseiran, at South Street in Mayfair, the same apartment where he had lived all these years since fleeing Jordan.[112]

The TBI–Card Tech deal is a useful marker, a milepost from which one can look back on what happened. Fourteen years had passed since Chalabi had sat in the somewhat shabby Card Tech office in London and first accepted CIA funding. It was in Card Tech that the roots of the Iraqi National Congress really lay. And Card Tech's initial funding, according to one family member and some documents, had come from Petra Bank. So in a certain sense, things had come full circle.

There is not a wisp of evidence that Chalabi pushed his nephew to award the deal to his company, but still it would stretch plausibility that Uzri or other family members never mentioned it to him. Would they have announced an award on such an important day without telling the most dominant member of their family? One family member says the timing of the deal was sheer coincidence. Would Uzri have given Chalabi's company a contract without notifying the uncle who had actually gotten him his job? There is also no way of knowing how profitable the deal was for the Chalabi company. Uzri himself said in an interview that it was a minor deal.

As for the Trade Bank of Iraq, while it was owned by the government of Iraq and was supposed to be financing Iraqi government purchases, it also sought to broaden itself. By 2004 TBI was already a mammoth institution. It had issued $3.4 billion in letters of credit in 2004, with assets of more than $400 million. And the growth was spectacular. Three years later, in 2007, Hussein al-Uzri would announce extraordinary things: "The Bank is already one of the success stories of the country. We have overseen $21 billion in trade finance, introduced Visa cards to Iraq and implemented the first banking system in the country." Twenty-one billion dollars is a massive sum for just one start-up bank, but to a certain degree, it was the gatekeeper, the funnel, for all international business by Iraqi government institutions. Ahmad Chalabi had engineered Uzri's role, and now that role was becoming key to the country's entire trade effort.

In May 2005, shortly after his confirmation in his new post as deputy prime minister, Ahmad Chalabi pushed to get his old Jordanian conviction dismissed, and he had the help of an old friend, British adviser Claude Hankes Drielsma. Hankes, a lanky, distinguished former executive with Price Waterhouse, was said to have connections to British royalty. He had also worked with Chalabi in 2004 on the oil-for-food probe during the Bremer days, and had testified before Congress about United Nations corruption. Hankes spoke publicly of his efforts to overturn the conviction. "I am confident that it can be done in the very near future," he told the *Sunday Telegraph*. "It will be most important for both Jordan and Iraq that a constructive new relationship can be developed, given that Mr. Chalabi is one of the most influential politicals in Jordan now."[113] But Jordan had no intentions of dropping the charges, and the effort died down.

In 2006, as it happens, Claude Hankes Drielsma was knighted by the Queen of England. He became Sir Claude Hankes, Knight Commander of the Victorian order.

In 2007, Uzri announced he was hiring an adviser. It was none other than Chalabi's friend and advocate Claude Hankes. As Uzri, TBI's chairman and president, said, "Sir Claude Hankes is a distinguished strategist and financial adviser and the Trade Bank of Iraq is delighted to gain his expertise." Uzri spelled out grand plans for the future: "Our development will require international backing and finance and so we are developing an international presence both in the region and of course in London, the world's financial centre."

52

The Vote

2005–2006

"Ahmad is an energy force—an energy field, if you want to call it that—and you have to be careful you are not drawn too close into his orbit. Very few Iraqis have been drawn into his orbit and stayed in his orbit. The only people who have been drawn into his orbit and stayed in his orbit are his Western cronies."

—An associate of Ahmad Chalabi

CHALABI IS A BIG PERSONALITY, and maybe there is a limit to how long he can sit in someone else's tent. As Iraq was preparing to vote for its permanent government, Chalabi abandoned the Shiite party he had helped found, the United Iraqi Alliance. The party's leaders tried old-fashioned political horse trading to keep him with them—offering a guarantee of five seats in the next Parliament. He petulantly demanded ten.

Then he struck out on his own, with a campaign slogan that had Iraqis gritting their teeth. "We liberated Iraq," his posters said.

"'We' liberated Iraq?" asked ABC's Terry Moran in an interview. "You and what army?" Chalabi's reply was an insight: "I'm saying that getting the American army, working with the United States, putting the case of the Iraqi people to the United States, had something to do with the liberation of Iraq."[114]

He was by now unabashed about the way he had steered America toward Baghdad. His campaign was as earnest and sophisticated as his message was naïve. His campaign seemed to ignore the Iraq he lived in. Just as he had seen a warm and friendly Iraq as a child, it seems he imagined that he saw one now. Iraq by 2005 was a place barren of real social services. There was no clean water or working electricity. A corrupt government run by Islamists presided over security forces who murdered and tortured at will. American forces plagued by ignorance of the country continued to occupy it with a deadly determination. Fewer and fewers Iraqis called the hell they were living in "liberation."

He had no bloc of voters who cared for him. And that's "the one thing he's never had," observes Qubad Talabany. "He's got brains, charisma, money—but the one thing Ahmad Chalabi doesn't have is street—a real constituency. All his life he's been trying to find this constituency." His real constituency, of course, was in Washington, and there's good reason to believe he was egged on in his quixotic campaign by his American supporters, who still were convinced that he would be the next prime minister. That was their dream, and they believed in it with the desperate certitude of a gambler shooting craps. "Just wait, he's going to be the prime minister and then he's going to stick it right up Colin Powell's ass!" said one longtime American supporter, with a chuckle. Their confidence was high and their faith was firm.

In fact, Chalabi took time off from campaigning in Iraq to make a lightning-quick trip to the United States in November 2005. As usual, he traveled through Iran (almost everyone who left Iraq in those days flew through Amman, but that was impossible for Chalabi because of his conviction in Jordan).

His trip to the United States came at a strange time. It was certainly awkward for the New York Times. "Chalabi, as Iraqi Deputy, Gets a Cautious Welcome in Washington" was the headline on November 9. That very day, the New York Times announced that Judith Miller, the laughingstock of reporters now for her close relationship with Chalabi and her role in the Valerie Plame case, would leave the paper.

But Chalabi managed to turn the trip into a success. Working, once again, with his lobbyist Riva Levinson at BKSH, Chalabi toured Washington and New York. He met with Donald Rumsfeld at the Pentagon and with Secretary of State Condoleezza Rice. He had come to the State Department fourteen years earlier, when he first started taking American money. Back then, as a disgraced banker, he had been a humble and graceful supplicant. He had toted around a tray in the State Department cafeteria. Now he sat comfortably with the secretary of state as a deputy prime minister. It represented an epic shift in his fortunes.

On his trip in November he also visited his old stomping grounds at the American Enterprise Institute, where the stern Danielle Pletka, now AEI's spokeswoman and still his friend, introduced him. "We are sorry for every American life that is lost in Iraq," he told his listeners. "As for the fact that I deliberately misled the U.S. government, this is an urban myth."

By now he had earned a mythical stature in certain quarters with his ever-present half smile, for his feats of persuasion, his pervasive influence in the U.S. government, his apparently hypnotic hold over the neoconservatives. His reputation for false promises had reached legendary proportions.

His old friends didn't care. The negative press, they were convinced, came from his enemies at the CIA. So they gathered to slap him on the back at another celebration in his honor at the townhouse of Jeffrey Weiss of BKSH and his wife, Juleanna Glover Weiss. Reportedly, the well-wishers included Jim Woolsey, Chalabi stalwart Richard Perle, and journalist Christopher Hitchens, who had joined the flock of Chalabi supporters in 1998.

One bit of unpleasantness that marred his trip to the United States was caused by the Federal Bureau of Investigation. The FBI case into the potential leak of information to Iran was still active. The FBI, according to an agent involved in the case, was now ready to interview Chalabi, and they had prepared their questions. FBI special agents reached an agreement with Chalabi's attorneys to do the interview while he was in Washington. They were convinced it was just a matter of arranging the time and place. But it fell through. FBI agents say he never carried out the agreement.

One of Chalabi's lawyers, in a brief conversation, confirmed that Chalabi had agreed to meet the FBI during his trip but explained that the press of time made it impossible for him to follow through: "He was over here at the time visiting with Condoleezza Rice and Dick Cheney, and he didn't have time." Instead, Chalabi now suggested, the FBI representatives were welcome to meet with him in Baghdad. "He said, 'Contact me in Baghdad,'" his lawyer said. "'You've got FBI agents all over the place. I'll sit down and talk to you and tell you everything I know, which is nothing.'" But whether he was serious or not, the FBI agents hoping for a breakthrough in their Iran case were left hanging while Chalabi bustled from meeting to meeting.[115]

And these FBI negotiations were private and concealed from the world anyway. Publicly Chalabi disavowed any such thing. "I have no knowledge of any investigation concerning me, except what I read in the paper," he said at AEI in response to a question. "So if you say so, I'll take your word on it." The crowd laughed.

Upon his return to Iraq, he was joined again by his daughter Tamara, "covering" his campaign as a journalist now, for an online news service, in a deal arranged by BKSH, his lobbyist. He campaigned at his normally manic level. His charms were on full display, his enthusiasm still boundless. One of the things he advocated was a fund in Iraq to distribute oil revenue, much in the way that Alaska spreads a portion of its pipeline wealth. It sounded great, but there was not enough revenue even to fund the government by then.

He launched into an attack on the corruption that infested the Iraqi government under the short-lived Ayad Allawi administration. His critique was on the mark. Allawi's Defense Ministry, he pointed out, had presided over a case of alleged embezzlement of $1.3 billion.

Chalabi smiled his mysterious smile wider than usual. He put forth proposals and ideas and platforms just like a candidate anywhere would. Remarkably, he even backed off on de-Baathification to spread his appeal. "The De-Ba'athification Act was sometimes used as a tool to persecute people, which we reject," he told *Al Arabiya*, boldly. "The Central De-Ba'athification Commission is not authorized to confiscate or seize people's properties."[116] This was a radical shift from what he had argued just two years earlier.

The strangest thing, through it all, even to his remaining Iraqi friends, was his continued embrace of Muqtada al-Sadr and the Mahdi Army and the offshoot party called Fadillah. Nabeel Musawi, one of the former members of his inner circle, says Chalabi was convinced that the Sadrists would vote for him and that he had their full support. Chalabi seemed to think that he had won over Sadr's constituency with some old-fashioned horse trading.

Ever since the beginning of the occupation he had pushed to unite the Shiites. He had moved against the secular, pro–human rights Shiites and bound himself to the religious extreme, which had received so much support from Iran. And he did not now cut his ties to them.

Nabeel Musawi, from his own party, claims he had a heart-to-heart with Chalabi. Musawi is secular, although he comes from a family with a rich and solid Shiite religious tradition. He told Chalabi that Sadr's followers would never vote for him. He says Chalabi was convinced the Mahdi Army was on his side but was obviously fooling himself.

The vote on December 15, 2005, took place in remarkable calm after a bloody period. For all Chalabi's high hopes, the voting returns were a humiliation: the voters of Iraq rejected the man who had fought so hard for their democracy. He got less than 1 percent of the ballots. Just 8,000 people in Baghdad voted for him, statistically insignificant. Instead, the United Iraqi Alliance, which he had abandoned, swept the day.

The scale of his loss is what would have hurt the most. Voters treated him like he didn't even exist. At first he and his supporters in Washington wouldn't accept it. They considered complaining about the voter fraud that was so common in Iraq's polling. But that might have spoiled the soup for everyone, at the exact time the Bush administration was hailing the vote as a victory for democracy.

Once again, Chalabi's American neoconservative followers had to figure out which way to turn. "They like the American administration, but they support Ahmad Chalabi," said a neoconservative at the time. "They don't want to turn against the administration," but when it turns on Chalabi, "they believe it is making a mistake."

53

The Rescue of the Journalist

2005

WHATEVER AHMAD CHALABI HAS DONE, and despite the friends he's lost, there are things he does periodically to redeem himself. There's a mother in Ireland who won't hear a bad word said about him. She's never met him and she may not know much about him, but she believes he saved the life of her son Rory Carroll, a thirty-three-year-old journalist on assignment in Baghdad for London's *Guardian* newspaper.

On October 19, 2005, Carroll had just finished off some interviews in Sadr City and was about to head back to his hotel when he was grabbed suddenly by members of Muqtada al-Sadr's Mahdi Army. The assault was a well-practiced burst of efficient violence. When a kidnapping is done right, it comes with no warning, like a sudden and inevitable car wreck: the victim realizes that ten seconds of activity has changed his life forever. Carroll was bundled up and locked in a pitch-black space built under a staircase. He huddled there in the darkness.

In the outside world there was a frenzy of activity to free him. Diplomats around the world pulled out all the stops. The *Guardian* editors reached out to anyone in Iran who might be able to influence the captors. The British and Irish governments started negotiating with their contacts around Iraq. David Hirst, the longtime *Guardian* reporter who has been a friend to Chalabi for thirty years, reached out to him and pleaded for his help to get Carroll out.

Everyone's working assumption was the correct one—that Carroll been grabbed by the Sadrists. The counterintuitive hope was that the Iranian Revolutionary Guards had operating control, and therefore that they would have leverage over the kidnappers too. Late the second day of Carroll's capture, his door was unlocked, and he was let out into the light. His captor got a call on his cell phone. You're going home, the captor told him. Carroll was shoved into the trunk of a car. Folded there uncomfortably, in the oppressive black space, he still had no idea what his fate would be. He was driven around for twenty minutes before his captors transferred him to an Iraqi police 4x4. There, he was allowed to sit in the back seat.

He was barefoot and ragged when the car pulled over. His captors told him to get out and walk, at the gate of an estate. He was in Khadimiya. "I walked into this compound in the dark and then this dark figure approaches, and he gets closer and it's Chalabi," said Carroll. With typical mastery of the moment, "he shook my hand, then said, 'You need to change those clothes.'"

Carroll changed into some clothes he was offered by Chalabi's aides, and in a state of walking shock, grinned. He was elated. He could barely stop smiling, as he describes it. Chalabi had him sit next to him at the well-lit swimming pool under the open night air. Francis Brooke walked up with a can of beer at the ready. "You look like you need this," Brooke joked. For the next hour, Carroll sat and ate and drank in the elegant setting, taking in the surreal quality of his release from captivity, while Chalabi accepted phone calls from around the world and bathed in the attention. The premier of Ireland, Carroll's country of nationality, called Chalabi to thank him, as did the foreign minister. Chalabi was at his ancestral home, receiving the appreciation of the world under the polluted Baghdad sky.

Chalabi listened to the young reporter's story and told him he was very lucky, emphasizing his own role several times. Carroll was to understand that he was in Chalabi's debt. "He said thanks to him I was freed. Had he not interceded I would have been sold on quite quickly." A Westerner kidnapped in Baghdad can often get sold up the chain to Al Qaeda groups, where prospects for release are grim. Even Shiite groups can make the sale. Chalabi was smug, and deserved to be, in Carroll's view. "He was reveling in his role as the guy who pulled it off. He made it quite clear that I owed him quite a lot."

There was a strange quality to their meeting like this. Carroll had never met Chalabi before, but for months he had been pursuing an interview with him. He had even pleaded with Brooke for a chance at a Chalabi profile. The Chalabi people were wary of Carroll's newspaper, though, since one of Carroll's colleagues had done a stinging critique of Chalabi a year earlier. Brooke had made it clear to Carroll, during the reporter's pleadings, that the INC held a grudge over the story. Even in his shock, Carroll saw the irony in the evening.

Carroll says he has nothing but feelings of gratitude toward Ahmad Chalabi and thinks he deserves any credit for the incident that he can get. "I was and am immensely grateful. I owe him one."

Epilogue

"You can't separate people from their backgrounds."
—Ahmad Chalabi, 2007[1]

FOR A WHILE, STARTING IN MID-2006 AHMAD CHALABI had lost any prominent political role in Iraq, although he held on to his title at the de-Baathification commission. A new Iraqi government had finally stepped in, presumably a permanent one, and Chalabi seemed unsteady as he scrambled for new allies, trying one thing after the other.

He tottered a bit politically, but records indicate that he, or at least his family, thrived financially. On July 11, 2006, Ahmad Chalabi and his family cashed in on Card Tech, the firm that they had run for seventeen years. They sold Card Tech to an American company called Total System Services, headquartered in Columbus, Georgia. The price tag was $54 million, a windfall. Card Tech, founded while Petra Bank was still in business, had long been a thread in Chalabi's complicated life. The Card Tech office was where he first received American money as he launched the INC, and then it received a contract in the new Iraq, awarded by a family member who had been installed in his position thanks to Chalabi's own maneuvering.

But when Card Tech was sold, Ahmad Chalabi's name did not show up in the transaction at all. His name is glaringly absent. It takes a look at dull corporate records in London, and in U.S. Securities and Exchange Commission filings, to find the traces. Shares of Card Tech Research were sold by a woman named Leila Osseiran the day of the sale. That's the maiden name of Ahmad Chalabi's wife, who lives at their apartment in Mayfair in London. The records show that, the day of the sale, she transferred 200 shares of Card Tech Research.[2]

Those shares alone would have been worth at least $4 million. But if Chalabi or his wife did indeed receive a simple 20 percent share of the income from the $54 million sale, that would probably mean about $11 million that summer, just as he was trying to sort out his future with no strong position in Iraq's troubled government.

━━━

The family's old business ventures, the remnants of a scandal, would not rest either and continued to haunt the Chalabis. Justice in Lebanon moves slowly when it moves. The case of MEBCO, the Chalabi family banking operation whose collapse in 1990 threatened to wreck the lives of Shiite depositors of Lebanon and spurred street demonstrations, continued working its way through the courthouse.

In 2006, in a confidential thirty-page document, an investigative magistrate forwarded the MEBCO file to the prosecutor's office. Why this finally occurred sixteen years after the bank's failure is a mystery, and there are various theories about it. Whatever the reason, the document alleges that Chalabi's brother Jawad, who had run the bank, "embezzled and squandered the money of MEBCO Bank's depositors." Ahmad Chalabi's old bank, Petra, gets a mention too. The branch in Washington, the report says, would cover Jawad's accounts.

Jaafar Jalabi, a nephew of Ahmad's, was also charged for his role as a government regulator who failed to do his duty when it came to the family bank. Jaafar was the former Amal militia spokesman during the TWA 847 hijacking who was later appointed to Lebanon's Banking Control Commission. The Beirut criminal case, however, is unlikely to affect him. He had made a fortune of his own, creating one of the most lavish shopping and entertainment malls in Europe, in Madrid, Spain. He called it Xanadu. It even has an indoor ski slope and a snow machine. Jalabi, according to various family members, no longer gets along with his uncle Ahmad.

The Lebanese document also blasted Salem Chalabi, another nephew, who was accused of helping his father, Jawad, embezzle from the bank. It was a striking thing because of Salem's recent role in Ahmad Chalabi's Iraq escapades. Salem, a lawyer by training, had stepped into the public eye when the U.S. first invaded Iraq in 2003. Stirred by the invasion's possibility, and by his uncle's leadership, he was one of the few Chalabi family members ever to help Ahmad in his political efforts. A man described universally as likable and friendly, he had worked as Chalabi's deputy in Iraq during the 2003 and 2004 period, when Paul Bremer ruled Iraq. Ahmad had helped place him as the first head of the court established to prosecute Saddam Hussein in the early days of the American occupation. And Salem had worked in Baghdad drafting Iraq's Transitional Administrative Law in 2004, which established the way Iraq would be ruled after Bremer left.

In July 2007, Lebanese magistrates decided to pursue some of these charges. The magistrates also dropped some charges, like the ones against Ahmad Chalabi's other brothers, Hazem and Talal. The two had already been convicted, in 2000, by Swiss authorities in the Socofi case in Geneva.

Reached by phone for comment in London, Salem Chalabi did agree to talk about the most recent charges in Lebanon, his former home. "A judge decided to reopen the file," he said, "and we don't know why." He argues that the MEBCO liquidation was a success and that the bank was not bankrupt after all. Six million dollars in assets are left over, he says, in a surplus following the liquidation. There was no wrongdoing by the family, he insists. And he says the investigations don't bother him. The warrants against him and his father have been dropped, in any case, he maintains, so that even if a criminal case may be moving forward, he can travel to Lebanon freely if he wants.

═══

As for Petra Bank in Jordan, that never ended for Ahmad Chalabi. He continued to maintain that he and the shareholders, not the bank's depositors, were the victims of the takeover of 1989. He would continue to seek the real perpetrators behind his bank's failure. Chalabi had his American lawyers pursue his U.S. federal lawsuit against Jordan's government. It was his windmill, one could say. In August 2007, a federal judge in Washington, D.C., threw out Chalabi's lawsuit, because the statute of limitations had long passed. It was no surprise that Chalabi would not give up even then: Chalabi's lawyers filed an appeal.

And as that legal wrangling continues, the record of the damage wrought by Petra Bank and Chalabi's disastrous tenure there lingers on in the Kingdom of Jordan—carefully preserved still in the ledgers of the Jordanian Central Bank. In August 2006, Jordan's Central Bank published its annual report. On page 124, the accounts show that 217 million Jordanian dinars, or $300 million, is still owed to the Central Bank by Petra Bank.

═════

If one is reviewing old debts, there is another sum that must be added up: the total U.S. government funding for Chalabi and his Iraqi National Congress. One former member of the INC put it at about $90 million, but a safer and conservative estimate of the total American taxpayer subsidy to Chalabi and his party is $59 million over the course of eleven years. This includes an estimated $20 million from the Central Intelligence Agency secret budget in the early 1990s (although it may be far more); add to this $33 million from the State Department in the years leading up to the war and $6 million from the Defense Intelligence Agency starting in 2002. The tally is quite high, and in exchange for that $59 million America bought his organizing skills, his propaganda, and a handful of false intelligence tidbits.

There are few foreigners who have had as much impact as Ahmad Chalabi has had on U.S. government policy and perhaps even on U.S. history. And none except Chalabi have done it fully funded by the U.S. taxpayer. It may be tempting to see Chalabi, with his mysterious and satisfied smile, as malevolent, because of the impact he has had. Indeed, some people apparently possess an unseemly hatred of him, as virulent as his followers' devotion. But it's possible to see him more as a Puck character than an Iago to America's Othello. If he became influential, it is because others let him. An illuminating perspective on him comes from his old friend Peter Galbraith, a centrist Democrat who became a scathing critic of the Iraq War. "If it were not for him," Galbraith writes, "the United States military likely would not be in Iraq today." Ahmad Chalabi, he points out, "owed no duty to the United States. He was an Iraqi seeking the liberation of his country. He did not have an army, and so he needed to persuade the U.S. to lend him one."

As Galbraith puts it, "any fault lies not with Chalabi but with the U.S. government officials who uncritically accepted what he was saying."[3]

Indeed Chalabi, with all his charisma and conniving, coached and pushed the Americans. But they, not he, made the decision to go to war. Chalabi has claimed credit for the "liberation" of Iraq; he has boasted he "used" the Americans, but of course they allowed themselves to be used. Chalabi set himself in opposition to one of the world's worst dictators. It takes a peculiar type of individual to do that. Was he a "con man," as he has often been called? He certainly shares most of the con man's characteristics, there's no doubt of that. He is manipulative and he works hard at gaining confidence and trust, getting inside people's heads, becoming a mentor. He raises funds obsessively, while convincing his donors he doesn't care about money. But he is more than just that: there's no doubt that he's a leader who inspired disparate followers to do extraordinary, sometimes calamitous things. He literally changed history. And like so many leaders, he was perhaps delusional as well, possessed of a strange sense of his own grandeur and destiny. He's Don Quixote and Captain Ahab and Elmer Gantry all rolled into one contradictory and tragic bundle.

As time went on, Chalabi maintained the loyalty of many of his friends in the United States, but their influence was waning. Eventually acknowledging the devastation in postinvasion Iraq, they said it was not the invasion that was the problem, but the failure to stick with their original plan. Their prescription wasn't followed properly: Chalabi, they said, was scapegoated, and the real problem was that George Bush imposed occupation instead of an Iraqi regime with Chalabi at its head. This became their rote explanation of the problem. Interestingly, after it was all over, even Vice President Dick Cheney argued that a "provisional" Iraqi government should have been installed, along the lines of what Chalabi had called for.[4]

Chalabi himself said everything would have been just fine if it had been done his way. In an interview with Dexter Filkins of the New York Times in the summer of 2006, Chalabi painted a picture of his vision. "We would have revitalized the civil service immediately," he said. "We would have been able to put together a military force and an intelligence service." With Iraq out of control, he said everything could have worked if he had been heeded. "There would have been no insurgency. We would have had electricity. The Americans screwed it up."

The blame for fouling Iraq's happy possibilities, then, lay not with him but elsewhere; the peaceful Iraq that was so close at hand had been shattered by someone else. "The real culprit in all this is Wolfowitz," he declared, to everyone's surprise blaming Paul Wolfowitz, one of his old allies. "The real culprit in all this" was an interesting phrase, a bit childish and almost identical to the phrase he had used on another occasion when he wanted to blame someone else. "The bad guy in all this is General Zinni," he had said back when things were going against him in 1999. Chalabi's reflex was to point to a "culprit" or a "bad guy" when he failed.

Chalabi and his followers—the Chalabistas—are right about some things. There is a strong case that Ambassador L. Paul Bremer's arrogant and ineffectual rule of Iraq was a disaster. Perhaps things might have been different if a competent viceroy had been put in place, if an appropriate U.S. force had deployed in the first place, or if strong and well-organized Iraqis had been put forward to run the government. But that analysis is a fairly widely accepted one, and Chalabi's opponents argue the very same thing.

As for Chalabi's claim that "there would have been no insurgency" if he had been in charge, it is barely worth considering, any more than what would have occurred if Bremer had worn dark-colored boots instead of tan ones. This utopian Iraq of peace and plenty that would have blossomed if Chalabi was installed as leader may live on as nothing but his own rueful fantasy.

━━━

Chalabi seemed to make a public comeback in the fall of 2007. One day in late October, dressed in one of his dark suits, he climbed into a U.S. army Black Hawk helicopter in Baghdad. As the helicopter rotors thumped, Chalabi was surrounded once again by American military men. That day he joked amicably with top American army officials who treated him with deference. His host was General David Petraeus, the commander of the multinational force in Iraq.

It was only thirteen months since a majority of the members of the U.S. Senate Intelligence Committee back in Washington found that

Chalabi's INC had "attempted to influence United States policy on Iraq" before the war "by providing false information. . . ."

But Chalabi had survived, and he was soaring over the capital of Iraq in an American helicopter. The new Iraqi government had appointed him to a new committee to oversee Baghdad "services." The hope was that Chalabi with his organizational skills and his charm could cut his way through Iraq's rad tape and spur on the efforts of the Health, Electricity, Communications, and Transportation Ministries. And the Americans, once again, thought they found a man they could work with.

In Baghdad, Ahmad Chalabi lived in what was once his sister's house in Monsour. It was not far from the home of his nephew Hussein Al Uzri, who ran the Trade Bank of Iraq. Sometimes Chalabi stayed, too, in the splendid mansion of his forefathers, in the orchard, called the Seef, with the swimming pool, in Khadimiya. He even had it renovated in a pleasing and sophisticated way. Much of Khadimiya had been cleansed of Sunnis. And in a final and bloody drive in November of that year by Shiite militias, most of the Sunnis of Hurriya City, an adjacent enclave, were also chased away or killed. The area was protected by a mishmash of Shiite militias tied to the official security forces, some Badr Brigade and some Mahdi Army. Chalabi had a good relationship with commanders in both groups, by the accounts of those close to him.

Toward the beginning of the war, though, Chalabi paid a visit to the grounds of his old home in Adhamiya. The neighborhood of Adhamiya at that point in the war had not yet become a Sunni insurgent stronghold, although that's what it turned into as Baghdad's ethnic cleansing progressed. Chalabi made his visit while some journalists and members of his entourage were there, and he wandered the grounds he had left so long ago. There in the back was the basketball hoop he had put up as a child, where he used to play with the guard's son. One witness described an interesting scene: Chalabi, at the age of sixty, looked behind a wall and pulled out the ping-pong table from a hidden place where he had left it before fleeing after the revolution of 1958. It was still there, miraculously, like an archeological relic; no one had disturbed his game in all that time. Ahmad Chalabi propped the ancient folding ping-pong table on its edge, looking at it: the green slate of the tabletop was cracked with age, the particle board was rotting and crumbling, a thing he had hidden.

Acknowledgments

IN THE COURSE OF RESEARCHING THIS BOOK I met remarkable people. Some of those who helped me were great friends and supporters of Ahmad Chalabi. I would like to thank them first. Their loyalty and devotion to him is extraordinary. In addition, there are people in Chalabi's family I would like to thank but whose names I will not mention. I hope that this book, in telling the truth, has done none of them any harm. The Chalabi family is made up of accomplished and brilliant men and women.

Many veterans of the Iraqi National Congress and other opposition groups helped me as well. Several are now Iraqi politicians or activists of some sort; most insisted on anonymity. I enjoyed meeting them, and I owe them all a tremendous debt. Of those I can mention publicly. I want to thank Nabeel Musawi in particular for sharing his insights and recollections. It is part of the nature of investigative reporting that one relies on people who disagree with each other. I would also like to thank Mohamad al-Zobaidy for his time and help, and for granting me access to his meticulous diaries and various documents.

This book could not have been written without the assistance of the many American officials who worked with Ahmad Chalabi during his interaction with the U.S. government. I owe a tremendous debt of gratitude to many former intelligence officials and diplomats; some are named in the book, and others must remain anonymous. I am privileged that they agreed to talk to me. Some had spent years in secret wars. They opened my eyes to history and unraveled the oddities of intelligence operations, and I am immensely grateful for their insights.

Some current and former members of the U.S. armed forces were likewise invaluable. One former military official I must acknowledge is the late Army Gen. Wayne Downing. He was convinced this book was important. He passed away in the summer of 2007, and he was universally acknowledged as an extraordinary man.

Dale Stoffel, who was killed in December 2004, was also a valuable source on some of this material. I wrote about him for *Washington Monthly* and used some of the material in this book.

In Jordan, I thank Tamara Daghistani for all of her help. She is simply a wonderful person to spend time with, and I hope she likes the book. Thanks as well to Riad al-Khouri, who offered me his insights and understanding and made it all make sense, and to Moufak Khatib for all his help. Thanks in addition to the research department of the *Jordan Times*. Many Jordanian officials shared data, documents, and recollections, and I must thank them without disclosing their names.

In Lebanon, thanks to Mustafa Kassam for his help. There are several others whom I must not name who gave me extraordinary guidance and help; I would like to thank one individual in particular for his help in Beirut, but he must remain anonymous. Thanks to Professor Nabeel Dajani of American University of Beirut for helping me get my bearings. Thanks as well to the research department of *An Nahar* newspaper, whose help was invaluable.

And of course very special thanks to Leila Hatoum, who made so much possible with her guidance on legal research in Lebanon and in all sorts of other ways. Without her, much of this book would not be what it is.

Thanks to Swiss journalists Sylvain Besson and Sylvie Arsever for generously helping me understand the background of Socofi and MEBCO in Switzerland. Likewise, there are several others I would like to thank in Switzerland whose names, again, must not be mentioned.

Many thanks to Judith Kipper for sharing her time and thoughts and recollections with me; she is an encyclopedia of knowledge and understanding. I also want to add my thanks to network journalist Christopher Isham, a former boss of mine, who is a good friend of

Ahmad Chalabi's. I must thank Meyrav Wurmser as well for all her help over the years.

Rick Holzworth made this so much easier by transcribing tapes for me. Abdelaziz Bettayeb helped me translate and interpret and understand so many disparate bits of documents I gathered from various places.

NBC News gave me immense support. Thanks to my old friends and colleagues Richard Greenberg and Albert Oetgen, and to Joel Seidman for everything. Thanks too for support from Andrea Mitchell, Thomas Bonifield, John Zito, Cheryll Simpson, and many more for all their support—so many friends helped me from NBC that I can't name them all. Thanks as well to the NBC News Research Library and Marcie Rickun. And of course I owe, especially, Erika Angulo. Special thanks as well to Robert Windrem for very helpful documents and for all the guidance.

I must extend my heartfelt thanks to everyone at the investigative unit, Amna Nawaz, Richard Gardella, and especially E.J. Johnson, for everything. His help and friendship made this book so much easier.

I don't know how to express my thanks to NBC's Jim Popkin, chief of the investigative unit, who let me wander off to do this project, and then read and edited sections for me and made them infinitely better. My debt to NBC's Lisa Myers is beyond expressing, and I thank her with all my heart. Together over the years, we did several stories about Ahmad Chalabi for NBC News. Lisa guided me, taught me, encouraged me, and when it came to this book, she always made sure I felt confident to move ahead.

I also don't know how to thank NBC's Alexandra Wallace, who quite literally made it possible for me to write this book. In addition, her confidence, enthusiasm, and encouragement made it so much easier. I have known her for a long, long time. NBC News management helped make this happen and asked nothing in return. I am immensely grateful to everyone in NBC News management, including so many people in the Washington Bureau, like Wendy Wilkinson and Brady Daniels. In New York, I am so grateful to everyone as well.

I was always skeptical of the phrase "corporate culture" until I came to NBC, when I came to realize its culture was something quite special.

Heartfelt thanks to Carl Bromley at Nation Books, who launched and shaped this book and helped me give it the form and narrative it has. As for Betsy Reed at *The Nation*, without her it would not have been written at all. I owe her so much, not just for her extraordinary wisdom as an editor but also for bringing this project forward from the beginning.

Thanks to Ruth Baldwin too. Many thanks to Hamilton Fish at The Nation Institute for his insight and support; somehow he understood key aspects of the subject matter before I did. And many thanks to The Nation Institute's Joseph Conason, who agreed to provide funding that made much of the reporting and research possible.

A special thanks to Mark Sorkin, not just for copy-editing so carefully but for keeping it on track and pointing out all those things that needed examination. And of course many thanks to Kay Mariea of Perseus Books, the project editor who made it clear that there really was an end in sight and that the book was manageable after all. I am in awe of the professionalism of those at Basic Books and Perseus. Many thanks to John Sherer for his support and to Michele Jacob and Greg Houle.

I owe a huge debt to so many journalists and friends. Thanks to Mark Hosenball for his guidance on the financial matters of Petra and Socofi and MEBCO. Thanks to Andrew Cockburn for his insights, and to John Kifner of the *New York Times* for his recollections. Thanks to John Dwyer of the *New York Times*, as well, for helping to put me in touch with a key figure in the book. Thanks especially to David Hirst, who knew Chalabi so well over the years. David Rose opened up to me and confided in me, and I hope I wrote his story well; I owe him tremendously. I also want to thank T. Christian Miller, Peter Beaumont, Tracy McVeigh, James Bamford, Mohanad Hage Ali, Laura Rozen, David Rohde, Solly Granatstein, Sarah Abruzzese, and so many others. I am immensely grateful to Knut Royce for his enthusiasm and help and for the documents he shared with me.

And special thanks to my friend Charles Glass, who not only is in the book but helped introduce me to many others who are in it.

I want to thank to my friends Lailing Jew and Rob Clark for always being there and for their readings and advice. Rob's photographs were a remarkable gift. Special thanks as well to Elizabeth Rappaport, who always steered me right and heard my complaints and made sure I printed it out. Thanks to Rinat Akhmetshin for all the introductions and ideas. And thanks to so many people and good friends whose support and advice made this happen. Jeff Stein read and massaged sections. Ti-Hua Chang gave me ideas. Denise Moritz helped me not just with her knowledge of auditing but with her enthusiasm too. Ira Arlook helped me tremendously with introductions and encouragement. Ralph Hamrick, of course, read sections and made suggestions. Thanks to Brent Furer, Roberto Marques, Kathy Ellis, and so many others.

My father and mother, Michael and Chanit Roston, offered extraordinary encouragement and wisdom and a certain confident enthusiasm. Thanking them, with my love, feels so inadequate. My sister, Carmel, was the source of so many unexpected bits of wisdom and insights, and I thank her. My brother, Miles, read, analyzed, and cheered me on with his experience. He was a great editor and inspiration.

Most of all I need to thank, with my all love, Natalia Mironova. She was there with her tenderness, her love, her humor, her insights, and her beauty.

Notes

PROLOGUE

1. Videotaped interview with Ahmad Chalabi, April 28, 2005.

PART I

1. Hanna Batatu, *The Old Social Classes and the Revolutionary Movements of Iraq* (Saqi Books, 2004), 802.

2. "King Shot to Death by Army Captain," *Washington Post,* July 21, 1958.

3. David Rose, "An Inconvenient Iraqi," *Vanity Fair*, January 2003.

4. Batatu, *The Old Social Classes*, 315.

5. Ibid.

6. David Frum, "Can Iraq Recapture Its Golden Age?" *National Post*, July 19, 2005.

7. Rose, "An Inconvenient Iraqi."

8. Muriel Bowen, "Faisal's Young Bride, Pretty Iraq Princess to Be Wealthy Queen," *Washington Post*, May 4, 1958.

9. Ibid.

10. Geoff Simons, *Iraq: From Sumer to Saddam* (St. Martin's Press, 1996).

11. Waldemar J. Gallman, *Iraq Under General Nuri* (John Hopkins Press, 1964).

12. Ibid.

13. Batatu, *The Old Social Classes.*

14. Ibid.

15. Simons, *Iraq: From Sumer to Saddam.*

16. Dana Adams Schmidt, "U.S. and Britain Will Limit Intervention; West to Keep Out of Iraq Unless Oil Is Threatened," *New York Times*, July 18, 1958.

17. Dexter Filkins, "Where Plan A Left Ahmad Chalabi," *New York Times*, November 5, 2006.

18. This is drawn from the accounts of various family members.

19. This is drawn from the account of Ambrose's son, Adam Ambrose.

20. Said K. Aburish, *Saddam Hussein: The Politics of Revenge* (Bloomsbury, 2000), 73.

21. Rose, "An Inconvenient Iraqi."

22. Petra Bank application to the Board of Governors of the Federal Reserve System to form a corporation to do business under Section 25(a) of the Federal Reserve Act, April 7, 1983.

23. Batatu, *The Old Social Classes*, 315.

24. Petra Bank application to establish an EDGE corporation in United States, April 7, 1983.

25. Sally Quinn, "The Man Who Would Succeed Saddam," *Washington Post*, November 24, 2003.

26. The Berri deal with Jamil Zaid at the port of Zahrani has been described before, for example, in *Middle East Intelligence Bulletin*, December 2000. The source who described Berri's deposit was closely affiliated with MEBCO and was aware of the deposit. Berri's office would not comment, and a source close to the Amal would not address this particular issue.

27. Golonka spoke by phone in two conversations but said he would say no more unless Ahmad Chalabi approved it, and this did not happen.

28. This description of the closing of MEBCO is drawn from witness accounts.

29. Ian Brodie, "British Loan Sets Up Mustang Ranch Sale; $25 Million in Financing Backs Purchase of Reno Area Brothel," *LA Times*, September 7, 1980.

30. Patrick O'Driscoll, "Action on Second Storey Brothel Delayed," *Reno Journal*, July 18, 1981.

31. Clerk of the Court, Case No. 82003103CF10A, State Reporting No. 061982CF003103A88810, Broward County, Florida, March 22, 1982.

32. Debarment proceeding, *Florida Bar v. Wayne A. Drizin*, Supreme Court of Florida, October 7, 1982. No. 61411.

33. Deposition of Wayne A. Drizin, *Banque General Du Phenix et du Credit Chimique v. Wayne Alan Drizin*, November 19, 1991.

34. Ibid.

35. Affidavit of Anthony Colin Wakelin, *Arab Allied Bank v. Taj El Arefin Hajjar*, February 12, 1987.

36. Ibid.

37. *US v. Spyridon Aspiotis*, US District Court, Criminal Case No. 97-01317.

38. Chapter 11 filing, American Export Group and American Export Group International Services, United States Bankruptcy Court for the District of Columbia, Case No. 87-00368, Case No. 87-369.

39. Swiss Federal Supreme Court, Decision 2A.169 et 2A.170/1989, Le Cour de Droit Public, March 6, 1990.

40. Socofi liquidation report signed on April 10, 1990, by a three-person liquidation team. Many thanks to *Newsweek*'s Mark Hosenball. Also available in Mohammad Said Nabulsi, *The Double Banking Scandal* (Sinbad Publishing, 2006) Appendix 8.

41. BBC Monitoring Service, "Jordan Central Bank Issues New Monetary Measures," June 6, 1989.

42. Reuters, "Petra Bank's Chalabi Denies He Left Jordan Illegally," August 12, 1989.

43. Petra Bank and Jordan Gulf Bank Management Committee Report, March 11, 1990.

44. Arthur Andersen & Co., Petra Bank Balance Sheet, August 2, 1989; auditors' report, 8.

45. Petra Bank and Jordan Gulf Bank Management Committee Report, March 11, 1990, 8.

46. Ibid.

47. Ricardo Sandoval, "Keating Speaks Out: American Continental Corp. Chairman Fires Back at Critics of his Lincoln Savings Role," *Orange County Register*, July 15, 1990.

48. Asked for comment, the Amal would not comment directly regarding the issue. But a source in the Amal said in a statement that the "Amal Movement, like any other Lebanese individual or companies or NGOs, has the right . . . to have a bank account or more and this was the case with MEBCO no more no less." He maintained that the Amal lost a total of about $80,000 in MEBCO after it was all over.

PART II

1. Annual return of Card Tech Research and Checkrelay.

2. Flora Lewis, "Eliminate Saddam Hussein," *New York Times*, January 22, 1991.

3. Ahmad Chalabi, "A Democratic Future for Iraq," *Wall Street Journal*, February 27, 1991.

4. Newsletter, International Committee for a Free Iraq, May 1992.

5. Guy Gugliotta and Tom Kenworthy, "Congress Is Reluctant to Intervene in Iraq; U.S. Options Seen as Limited, Public Called Unenthusiastic on Further Military Action," *Washington Post*, April 3, 1991.

6. Leslie Phillips, "Congress May Put Pressure on Bush," *USA Today*, April 4, 1991.

7. Said K. Aburish, *Saddam Hussein: The Politics of Revenge* (Bloomsbury, 2000).

8. "Warrant in Absentia in the Case of Chalabi," *An Nahar*, January 25, 1991.

9. Deposition of Wayne A. Drizin, *Banque General Du Phenix et du Credit Chimique v. Wayne Alan Drizin*, November 19, 1991.

10. Declaration by Ahmad Chalabi, *A.I. Trade Finance Inc. v. Petra Bank*, May 3, 1991.

11. Deposition of Reem Khalil, *Petra International Banking Corporation v. Levantine Holdings*, S.A., Civil Action No. 93–1614.

12. The State Security Court, Case No. 17/92, Hashemite Kingdom of Jordan.

13. "Iraqi Opposition Gives Saddam Hussein Black 'Birthday Presents,'" Agence France-Presse, April 28, 1992.

14. Andrew and Patrick Cockburn, *Out of the Ashes: The Resurrection of Saddam Hussein* (HarperCollins, 1999), 56.

15. "Saddam Hussein Opponents Arrive Here for Treatment for Poisoning," Agence France-Presse, April 23, 1992.

16. "Anti-Saddam Iraqis Seek United Front," *Washington Post*, June 18, 1992.

17. The State Security Court, Case No. 17/92, Hashemite Kingdom of Jordan.

18. Ibid., count 23.

19. Ibid., count 21.

20. Ibid., count 18.

21. Ibid., count 29.

22. Ibid., count 7.

23. Ibid., count 30.

24. Ibid., count 16.

25. Sally Quinn, "The Man Who Would Succeed Saddam; Ahmed Chalabi's First Big Political Test? Surviving Washington," *Washington Post*, November 24, 2003.

26. Interview with former CIA official associated with the Iraq Working Group.

27. The radio designations were disclosed by former officials who want their names withheld.

28. Affidavit of Ahmad Chalabi, *Petra v. Levantine*, August 8, 1994.

29. Deposition of Rim Khalil, *Petra v. Levantine*.

30. Robert Baer, *See No Evil: The True Story of a Ground Soldier in the CIA's War on Terrorism* (Crown, 2002).

31. Andrew and Patrick Cockburn, *Out of the Ashes*, 184.

32. Ibid., 182.

33. Report of the Select Committee on Intelligence on the Use by the Intelligence Community of Information Provided by the Iraqi National Congress, September 8, 2006.

34. Baer, *See No Evil.*

35. Andrew and Patrick Cockburn, *Out of the Ashes*, 185.

36. Select Committee on Intelligence INC report, September 8, 2006.

37. Andrew and Patrick Cockburn, *Out of the Ashes*, 279.

PART III

1. Barry Yeoman, "Portrait of an 'American Patriot,'" *Duke Magazine*, March/April 2006.

2. Jane Mayer, "The Manipulator," *The New Yorker*, June 7, 2004.

3. Yeoman, "Portrait of an 'American Patriot.'"

4. ABC News, *Unfinished Business.*

5. Letter from Max Singer, November 23, 1997.

6. Sonali Paul, "Resistance Asks Unfreezing of Iraqi Assets for Relief," *Platt's Oilgram News*, August 10, 1992.

7. Ibid.

8. Memorandum of the Association of the Iraq Trust, Companies House, March 9, 1994.

9. Professor Mallat, who still admires Chalabi, said this in a phone interview on April 9, 2007, emphasizing that he was speaking on the record, and then elaborated in further conversations. However, he apparently changed his mind later. He asked that anything written be "cleared" with him before publication, which the author refused to agree to. Later he wrote in an e-mail: "I just do not want to regret my good faithed conversations with you, and the need to have to denounce or correct some of these statements."

10. Open Letter to the President, February 19, 1998.

11. "Movement to Indict Iraqi Regime for War Crimes Launched," Federal News Service, Mid-East Newswire, January 15, 1997.

12. Omnibus Consolidated and Emergency Supplemental Appropriations Act, Section 590, 1999.

13. INDICT Ltd. directors report and financial statements for the period ended September 30, 1998.

14. Susan Taylor Martin, "Hussein's Cash-Strapped Foes Plot From London Base," *St. Petersburg Times*, December 8, 1998.

15. "Iraqi Opposition Leader Speaks of a Post-Saddam Iraq," Associated Press, October 9, 2002.

16. Barton Gellman, "U.S. Officials Heckled at Iraq Seminar," *Washington Post*, February 19, 1998.

17. Scott Ritter, *Iraq Confidential: The Untold Story of the Intelligence Conspiracy to Undermine the UN and Overthrow Saddam Hussein* (Nation Books, 2005), 268.

18. Dana Priest and David B. Ottaway, "Congress's Candidate to Overthrow Saddam Hussein; Ahmed Chalabi Has Virtually No Other Backing," *Washington Post*, April 21, 1999.

19. "Expensive Fantasies on Iraq," *New York Times* editorial, October 19, 1998.

20. "State's Saddamists: State Department Blocks Financial Aid to Iraqi National Congress,"*Insight on the News*, March 19, 2001.

21. Mark Thompson and Douglas Waller, "Firing Blanks: The Plot to Oust Saddam and the Constant Pounding From U.S. Jets Are Going Nowhere," *Time*, November 8, 1999.

22. 2002 IRS Form 990 for the Iraqi National Congress Support Foundation.

PART IV

1. "Opposition Leader Al-Chalabi Comments on Meeting With U.S. Vice-President," Al Jazeera, June 29, 2000.

2. Marie Colvin, "U.S. Gives $4m to Iraqi Rebels," *Sunday Times*, October 1, 2000.

3. Seth Lipsky, "America Chooses: Is Gore Good for American Jews?" *Wall Street Journal* (Europe), November 7, 2000.

4. Interview with former INC member.

5. "State Department: Issues Affecting Funding of Iraqi National Congress Support Foundation," GAO report, April 2004.

6. "State's Saddamists: State Department Blocks Financial Aid to Iraq National Congress," *Insight on the News*, March 19, 2001.

7. Ahmad Chalabi, "We Can Topple Saddam," *Wall Street Journal*, May 21, 2001.

8. Jackie Calmes, "Top Rebel Presses His Cause Before GOP Powers," *Wall Street Journal*, June 22, 2001.

9. State Department Office of Inspector General audit, September 2001, 7.

10. Ibid., 8.

11. Ibid., 9.

12. Ibid., 11.

13. Ibid., 14.

14. Memorandum of Agreement between Iraqi National Congress Support Foundation and Consultant. Also interview with Hamad Shoraidah, May 20, 2007.

15. Bryan Burrough, Evgenia Peretz, David Rose, and David Wise, "The Path to War," *Vanity Fair*, May 2004.

16. James Woolsey said in a telephone interview that his coauthor on the op-ed did most of the writing.

17. Mohamad al-Zobaidy keeps meticulous diaries, and much of this is drawn from these and from interviews with him.

18. According to David Rose.

19. Barry Yeoman, "Portrait of an 'American Patriot,'" *Duke Magazine*, March/April 2006.

20. Report of the Select Committee of Intelligence on the Use by the Intelligence Committee of Information Provided by the Iraqi National Congress, September 6, 2006.

21. In an interview for this book, Woolsey said he believes he called the DIA because military issues were discussed, rather than simply to make an end run around the CIA.

22. Select Committee on Intelligence INC report, September 8, 2006, 68.

23. "Iraq Developing Biological Arms, U.S. Officials Say," *New York Times*, January 18, 1989.

24. Eric Schmitt, "A Search and Destroy Priority: Unconventional Iraqi Munitions," *New York Times*, January 30, 1991.

25. Marie Colvin and Uzi Mahnaimi, "Iraq Tested Anthrax on PoWs," *Sunday Times*, January 18, 1998.

26. Select Committee on Intelligence INC report, September 8, 2006.

27. Ibid.

28. Information concerning Haideri's family makeup comes from Mohamad al-Zobaidy, Nabeel Musawi, and an American intelligence official.

29. Zobaidy diary.

30. Select Committee on Intelligence INC report, September 8, 2006, 54.

31. Ibid., 41.

32. Ibid.

33. Ibid., 57.

34. Interview with Nabeel Musawi, March 18, 2007.

35. Interview by Lesley Stahl, *60 Minutes*, CBS, March 3, 2002.

36. Parisoula Lampsos was friendly in an e-mail exchange but did not answer specific questions.

37. Select Committee on Intelligence INC report, September 8, 2006, 43–44.

38. Agreement between Parisoula Lampsos, c/o International Creative Management, and Associated Newspapers, September 20, 2002.

39. Letter from Mohamad al-Zobaidy.

40. This description was provided by Qubad Talabany, who was there with his father.

41. "Pure crap" is the phrase used in separate interviews by two separate State Department sources, both of whom were familiar with the Information Collection Program.

42. Select Committee on Intelligence INC report, September 8, 2006, 29–30.

43. Ibid., 33.

44. Interview with Gen. David Barno, April 24, 2007.

45. "Iraq Opposition Says U.S. to Train 10,000 for Combat," Reuters, October 17, 2002.

46. Ibid.

47. David E. Sanger, "Bush Says U.S. Won't Force Its Ways on a Beaten Iraq," *New York Times*, October 12, 2002.

48. Interview with Kanan Makiya, *All Things Considered*, NPR, November 19, 2002.

49. "The American Occupation of Germany and Japan," INC Research Branch, January 13, 2003.

50. Ahmad Chalabi, "Iraqis Must Rule Iraq," *Wall Street Journal*, February 19, 2003.

51. Bob Drury, "After Saddam: A Democratic Iraq?" *GQ*, February 2003.

52. "U.S. to Train 10,0000," Reuters, October 17, 2002.

53. Dan Morgan and David B. Ottaway, "In Iraqi War Scenario, Oil Is Key Issue; U.S. Drillers Eye Huge Petroleum Pool," *Washington Post*, September 15, 2002.

54. "US to Train 10,0000," Reuters, October 17, 2002.

55. Charles Glass, *The Northern Front: A Wartime Diary* (Saqi Books, 2006), 113.

56. "Opposition Leader Wants 'Civilian Coalition' Government in Iraq," Agence France-Presse, December 15, 2002.

57. INC, "The American Occupation of Germany and Japan," 8.

58. Ibid., 88.

59. Ibid., 7.

60. David Phillips, *Losing Iraq: Inside the Postwar Reconstruction Fiasco* (Westview, 2005), 76.

61. Ibid., 93–94.

62. GAO State Department report, April 2004.

63. *60 Minutes,* CBS, April 6, 2003.

64. Col. Ted Seel, "Authorization for Foreign National to Travel on U.S. military Aircraft," March 29, 2003.

65. Glass, *Northern Front*, 223.

66. Conversation between Ahmad Chalabi and Tom Brokaw, Council on Foreign Relations, New York, June 10, 2003.

67. Glass, *Northern Front.*

68. Ibid., 243.

69. Yeoman, "Portrait of an 'American Patriot.'"

70. Interview by Tim Russert, *Meet the Press*, NBC News, April 13, 2003.

71. Mitch Potter, "Pentagon Favourite Drawing Iraqi Fire," *Toronto Star*, April 19, 2003.

72. Interview with Jay Garner.

73. John Kifner, "Hussein Foe Tries to Get Baghdad on Its Feet," *New York Times*, April 14, 2003.

74. Potter, "Pentagon Favourite."

75. According to Hamad Shoraidah.

76. Howard Kurtz, "Intra Times Battle Over Iraqi Weapons," *Washington Post*, May 26, 2003.

77. The journalist did not want his name used.

78. A Rafidain Bank official who was present during much of all this provided this account but did not want his name used. He was admittedly sympathetic to Chalabi and was introduced to the author by a friend of Chalabi's. Still, that doesn't mean he wasn't telling the truth.

79. "Dangers of the Inquisition," *The Economist*, November 29, 2003.

80. Patrick E. Tyler and Felicity Barringer, "Iraq Council Head Shifts to Position at Odds With U.S.," *New York Times*, September 23, 2003.

81. Council on Foreign Relations, June 10, 2003.

82. James Risen, *State of War: The Secret History of the CIA and the Bush Administration* (Free Press, 2006), 133.

83. "Does Presenting Chalabi With the List of Candidates for the Ruling Council Indicate He Will Be the Next Iraqi Prime Minister?" *Al-Mu'tamar*, July 8, 2003, cited in BBC Monitoring Service.

84. Robert Pollack, "Politics for Lunch in Iraq," *Wall Street Journal*, May 7, 2003.

85. Council on Foreign Relations, June 10, 2003.

86. Ibid.

87. Tom Raum, "U.S., Iraq Official Clash on Timetable," Associated Press, September 24, 2003.

88. Betsy Pisik, "Chalabi Minimizes Dispute Over Iraqi Self-Rule, *Washington Times*, September 25, 2003.

89. "Iraqi Council's Al-Chalabi Says Public Opinion 'Against' UN Envoy Brahimi," BBC Monitoring Service, April 26, 2004. Text of telephone interview with Chalabi in Baghdad by presenter Khadijah Bin-Qinnah, *Today's Harvest*, Qatari Al Jazeera, April 25, 2004.

90. Susan Sachs and Judith Miller, "U.S. and Iraq Spar Over Who Should Run Corruption Inquiry Into Oil-for-Food Program," *New York Times*, May 17, 2004.

91. Awards supplement, *PR Week* Awards, October 29, 2003.

92. One of the sources is an American government official who dealt with Faisal Chalabi, and another is an Iraqi businessman who worked with him.

93. This account comes from Dale Stoffel, whom the author knew before Stoffel's death, and from Stoffel's associates.

94. Dennis Wagner, "Man Convicted of Fraud in Biotech Scam; Investors Taken for $2.5 Million, Prosecutor Says," *Arizona Republic*, October 8, 2003.

95. Defendant Wayne Drizin's Sentencing Memorandum and Request for Probation, *United States of America v. Wayne Allan Drizin*.

96. Neil King Jr., Michael Schroeder, and Mitchell Pacelle, "Bank Consortium to Handle Iraq Trade: U.S. Officials Will Choose International Alliance to Issue Letters of Credit," *Wall Street Journal*, July 23, 2003.

97. Khaled Yacoub Oweis, "Iraqi Trade Bank to Start Operations Next Week," Reuters, November 18, 2003.

98. Elisabeth Bumiller, "Conservative Allies Take Chalabi Case to the White House," *New York Times*, May 29, 2004.

99. Laura Rozen, www.warandpiece.com/blogdirs/000708.html.

100. George Tenet, *At the Center of the Storm: My Years in the CIA* (HarperCollins, 2007), 447.

101. Bartle Breese Bull, "Iraq's New Power Couple," *New York Times*, October 15, 2004.

102. Knut Royce, "Iranians duped U.S., Officials Say," *Newsday*, May 22, 2004.

103. Dexter Filkins, "Where Plan A Left Ahmad Chalabi," *New York Times*, November 5, 2006.

104. Jim Dwyer, "Defectors' Reports on Iraq Arms Were Embellished," *New York Times*, July 9, 2004.

105. Commission on the Intelligence Capabilities of the United States Concerning Weapons of Mass Destruction, Report to the President, March 31, 2005.

106. Ahmad Chalabi, "The Future That Iraq Deserves," *Wall Street Journal* (Europe), December 22, 2004.

107. "Al-Chalabi Emerges as Favourite for Iraqi Premier," BBC Monitoring Service, February 10, 2005.

108. Eli Lake, "Jafari Is Pick for Premier of Free Iraq," *New York Sun*, February 23, 2005.

109. Ira Stoll, "Cheney Would Meet With Chalabi, Though He's Not Choosing Sides," *New York Sun*, April 4, 2005.

110. "Iraq's New Government," *The NewsHour With Jim Lehrer*, PBS, April 28, 2005.

111. Card Tech Research Ltd. 363s Annual Return, 2004.

112. Card Tech Research Ltd. 363s Annual Return, 2005.

113. Colin Freeman, "Chalabi: My Conviction for Fraud Will Be Quashed," *Sunday Telegraph*, May 8, 2005.

114. "The Power Broker: A Look at Ahmed Chalabi," *Nightline*, ABC News, November 30, 2005.

115. Interview with John Markham, September 2007. Markham did not return subsequent phone calls to discuss other issues concerning Chalabi.

116. Text of report by Dubai-based news channel Al-Arabiya TV, BBC Monitoring Service, December 13, 2005.

EPILOGUE

1. Sudarsan Raghavan, "Maliki's Impact Blunted Over Party's Fears," *Washington Post*, August 3, 2007.

2. Total System Services Inc. 8K filing with U.S. Securities and Exchange, July 11, 2006. Exhibit: "Agreement for the Sale and Purchase of Shares in Card Tech Research Limited between Jaffar Agha-Jaffar, Bashar Chalabi and TSYS Card Tech Holding Limited. Also, 363s annual report for Card Tech Research, 2006, UK Companies House, 6.

3. Peter Galbraith, *The End of Iraq: How American Incompetence Created a War Without End* (Simon & Shuster, 2006), 86–87.

4. Steven Hayes, *Cheney: The Untold Story of America's Most Powerful and Controversial Vice President* (HarperCollins, 2007).

Index